"This material changed my life. *BrainStyles* filled in the gaps that were missing for me in all the other systems I've studied—including the Myers-Briggs test and numerous other personality systems—with real validity. This is really breakthrough stuff because it explains how someone thinks *now* in such a simple way, you can use it immediately to improve and work much more effectively as teams."

—John P. Fullingim, Director,
The Addison Marketing Group, Dallas, Texas

"*BrainStyles* is a common denominator across all humankind regardless of gender, race, ethnic origin, etc. It is something that brings diverse people together on common ground."

—Henry Ho, Group Marketing Manager,
The Procter & Gamble Company, Fayetteville, Arkansas

"*BrainStyles* helped me change my life to one of self-contentment and renewed spirituality. I feel in control now so I can be much more empathetic of other people's shortfalls and focus instead on their strengths. The net result is that my relationships and career are much more successful than in the past."

—Beth Struckell, Vice President, General Manager
Frito-Lay Inc., Plano, Texas

"Best/most practical diversity training I've been involved in."

—Tom Muccio, Director, Customer Business Development,
The Procter & Gamble Company, Cincinnati, Ohio

"This is a whole system for living. I use it with my family, friends, and people at work. Knowing *BrainStyles* has made me more secure with people, especially new customers, who I have to get to know quickly in a pressure situation."

—Dan J. Carrithers, Product Manager,
The Dexter Corporation, Detroit, Michigan

"Over the last six years, *BrainStyles* and the principles associated with it have helped me develop higher performing teams: teams that possess a full range of skills to manage and lead all aspects of business. . . . I think *BrainStyles* helps us understand and value diversities like never before. The differences in race and gender have become second to how people think, as I deal with them. That's what my organization really needs."

—Gary Weihs, Division Distribution Manager,
Pepsi-Cola Company, New York

"Becoming aware of my strengths empowers me to do what I do well, and not to spend time trying to become something I'm not. This has been very powerful for me and my relationships with and expectations for other people."
—Steve Trozinski, North American Logistics Manager
Monsanto Corporation, St. Louis, Missouri

"*BrainStyles* is the most valuable training program in which I have ever personally participated or involved our sales staff! Personal achievement levels of our account executives have risen dramatically, and they now view themselves as part of a unit. They have become much more accepting of themselves and each other. The benefits have been obvious and consistent during the past nine months."
—Brian Brown, Vice President, General Sales Manager,
Radio Stations KDGE, Irving, Texas,
WBEB, Philadelphia, Pennsylvania

"I always respected my sister, but as we grew up I thought she was smarter than me—and a bit mean. Since reading *BrainStyles: Be Who You Really Are,* I have focused on my *own* strengths more—stayed in my job, solved problems I would have walked away from before. And I now know I'm smart in a different way than my sister."
—Marilyn Mixon, Department Manager,
Wal-Mart, Turner, Maine

"After reading *BrainStyles: Be Who You Really Are,* I reevaluated my whole career. I am greatly relieved to know why I never enjoyed being a counselor—it's not because I'm an uncaring person, it's because that wasn't my real strength. I enjoy what I do now, working as a personal investor, much more."
—Ann Logan-Lubben, M.A., **Counseling**,
Dallas, Texas

"Working with my group on the four *brainstyles* was invaluable. Understanding this enabled me to capitalize on their strengths and minimize their weaknesses. Projects and work teams could then be assigned to take advantage of these synergies and maximize results."
—Guy Marsala, General Manager, Southern California,
Pepsi-Cola Company, Irvine, California

"I wanted to tell you how fascinated I am with your *BrainStyles System.* In reading your book, I had no trouble recognizing myself as a Knower. It definitely turned on lightbulbs for me. What really fascinated me about my brainstyle is

how it is reflected in *every* aspect of my daily life—it affects my relationships with my family and even dictates my style as a professional artist."
—Fran Di Giacomo, **Portrait Artist**,
Dallas, Texas

"It's okay to be myself. People have always tried to change me. I will now look at some of my 'weaknesses' as *strengths*."
—Theresa Lewis, Customer Service,
The Procter & Gamble Company, Fayetteville, Arkansas

"Knowledge of my *brainstyle* has enabled me to produce stronger solutions."
—Ann Ross, President,
The Dallas Women's Foundation, Dallas, Texas

"Congratulations on your outstanding book! . . . You've provided the foundation for a lifetime of growth for all your readers, no matter what their *brainstyle*. . . . The *BrainStyles* concept is the best I've seen so far, and it's certainly not the first of the techniques I've used to try to understand myself and others!"
—Celesta K. Weise, Former IBM Executive,
Quality Consultant, Irving, Texas

"*BrainStyles* really works! I just landed a major account by telling *and* showing the client what I'm *naturally* good at. In starting my own software consulting business by knowing my strengths, I don't feel like I always have in the past —trying to climb the mountains of what I don't know. I'm much more self-confident and more convincing."
—Don Waudby, Principal,
Automated Business Concepts, Dallas, Texas

"This seminar should be *required* for all management. The *BrainStyles* seminar focused on reaching a *win-win*. I learned you must maximize your capabilities. Trying to improve your liabilities is like multiplying times zero."
—Jim Wells, Microwave Technical Service Engineer,
Alcatel Network Systems, Dallas, Texas

"As a current MBA student and full-time worker, I see great value in these concepts to complement my personal and professional development. I feel this approach will help me focus on my strengths in order to make future decisions in life which are more congruent with my 'real self.' "
—John Arnold Smith, Consultant,
Spectra Corporation, Dallas, Texas

"BrainStyles helped me better understand my management style. I find that I now do the work that I am better suited for and delegate the rest appropriately."

—Gary Miller, General Manager,
Credit Bureau of Alaska, Anchorage, Alaska

"My ability to see the big picture allows me to know what resources to tap on the team. I am also growing more aware of the various *brainstyles* in the group and use them not for a means to an end but as consultants who are part owners of the business."

—Tregg Brown, Marketing Logistics Manager,
The Procter & Gamble Company, Fayetteville, Arkansas

"When my wife chose to stay home to have a family, I feared we wouldn't grow together. The power of *BrainStyles* is it gives you a common language that transcends what you do—entrepreneur, housewife, corporate person. It relates you back to a central purpose; it makes you two partners who can rely on each other and grow together. I believe this can keep marriages together."

—Mark Breden, Marketing Manager,
The Procter & Gamble Company, Fayetteville, Arkansas

Change Your Life

Without

Changing

Who You Are

MARLANE MILLER

SIMON & SCHUSTER

SIMON & SCHUSTER
Rockefeller Center
1230 Avenue of the Americas
New York, NY 10020

SIMON & SCHUSTER and colophon are registered trademarks
of Simon & Schuster Inc.

Designed by Karolina Harris

Manufactured in the United States of America

2   3   4   5   6   7   8   9   10

Library of Congress Cataloging-in-Publication Data
Miller, Marlane.
BrainStyles : change your life *without* changing who you are /
Marlane Miller.
p.   cm.
Rev. ed. of: Brainstyles / by David J. Cherry and Marlane Miller.
© 1992.
Includes bibliographical references and index.
1. Typology (Psychology)   2. Cerebral dominance.   3. Cognitive
styles.   4. Self-actualization (Psychology)   I. Cherry, David J.
Brainstyles.   II. Title.
BF698.3.M55   1997
155.2′64—dc20   96-22182
CIP
ISBN 0-684-80757-2

Acknowledgments

Over the years of developing the concepts and writing of them, all I have worked with and met have had to listen, be interviewed, or in some way get involved. These are a few to whom I owe a great deal. THANK YOU to:

Jane Albritton, a wise and gentle writer and editor, who got us out of the starting gate on the first book, then helped me cross the finish line on this one.

The good professor, Dr. Larry Peters, has quantified the power of the concepts through *The BrainStyle Inventory*® with rigor, vigor, and real care. He has continually been a support for me personally and professionally.

Rusty Robertson, the Red Tornado, who put wind in my sails, Bob Asahina, who said yes and expanded the idea, and Melissa Roberts, who edited with style. My *other* editors, Kendra Madrid and Lana Latchford, thank you for your time.

Suzi Prokell, who rowed the boat, hoisted the anchor, and never lets me get far adrift.

Henry Ho, whose insights and applications, not to mention sponsorship, put these principles to work with so many; Mark Breden, Jeff, Brad, Carol Kapity, Daniel the Wise, and Leslie among them.

Pam Arnold, Carol Heil, Terri Firebaugh, and Renée LaCoy, thank you for *all* the revisions.

Lee Ballard, principal of *The Naming Center,* not only came up with the rationale but also the names of the four brainstyles, as well as the word *brainstyle.* A very intelligent and spiritual collaborator to work with.

Gary Weihs, a tireless winner, who gave openly of his cliffhangers and triumphs, as he has marched up the corporate ladder, balancing business and family brilliantly. Steve Trozinski, a natural supporter, you and your friend Mike have been invaluable.

Fran the *fantastic* and Marilyn; Edie Lycke, the best and most literate friend a person could have, who gave unstintingly of her time and concern, not to mention a marvelous book signing; my intelligent brothers, Greg, Mike, and Gary; John Fullingim, Joe Prokell, Bob DiLaura, and of course, my left brain, Frank Campbell.

Thank you for being yourselves and telling me about it or using your gifts on my behalf.

This book is dedicated
to my husband, David,
father of this work

Contents

Deep within, you know already

that you are perfect,

just as you are right now.

Introduction

Tony Bennett was being interviewed recently about his long and successful career as a ballad singer. He said times were pretty tough in the 1960s and 1970s. When taste in popular music changed, Tony didn't get many club dates. He went to his longtime friend Count Basie and asked him if he should change his style and his music to rock or disco. The Count told him, "You don't change an apple."

All your life people have told you to change, to improve something about yourself "for your own good," to fit in, to get ahead, to get along. They were wrong then and they are wrong now. They were telling you how to be like *them*. To use *their* answers.

This book is built on a single premise: you can't change people. For that matter, you do not need to change them or yourself. You cannot train yourself to be different from who you naturally are. This is the good news: to improve yourself, all you have to do is be *more* yourself.

You can change your life without changing who you already are right now.

The purpose of this book is to get you started in a new and honest relationship with yourself, a relationship that will set you on a path to personal satisfaction, ease, self-esteem, and ultimately, mastery of your natural gifts. Once you are more at home with yourself, relationships with others will improve easily, and you will see your life as a whole —not a series of roles and boxes—at home, at work, and at play. Using this material, you can sort through the self-help and personal-growth programs you've been considering to get to the ones that will work for you.

The stories in this book are of real people with real successes. But I am not telling you about them so that you can copy what they—or I

—have done. You don't need another *role model*. This book is intended to start you on your own special journey toward self-mastery.

WHERE BRAINSTYLES COMES FROM

BrainStyles is a concept forged out of a desperate need to rescue a struggling business, to financially survive, and launch a new partnership when the experts bet against all three.

My husband, David, and I married in 1980 and moved to Texas. He was a highly successful technical and marketing maverick in a high-tech field, and I a corporate consultant. We met because of a mutual interest in personal development. We both had jobs helping others grow and learn. Each of us had known the pain of failed marriages. He built businesses. I helped people learn how to get along better in them. He was a chemical engineer by training, I was a human resources professional with a background in education, organizational dynamics, and teamwork. Two weeks after we were married, he was promoted to run one, then three businesses out of state. We began a commuter marriage just when we should have been learning how to live together.

When we married, there was a big difference for me between being a professional woman at work and then changing into my grubbies and being a wife, stepmother, and homemaker. I lived in a number of boxes. I was trying to change, to improve, to achieve more by using goal-setting programs at home and work. I was very competitive at the office and continued to be at home. We argued a lot.

In 1981 David saw potential in the small, high-tech, industrial plastics manufacturing business he was managing in Texas. The home office did not share his opinion and so accepted his deal to buy it. David became an entrepreneur, leaving his sizable successes in the corporate setting behind. He also left behind a place where you earn and spend Other People's Money; he put everything we had on the line to start his own company. Since we'd already moved to Dallas, I continued to commute weekly to New York. Things were very tough right from the start, and then they got a whole lot tougher.

Sales in the new company were about $5 million with losses of about $400,000 a year. Interest rates were 24 percent (!) All the major equipment broke down in the first year, idling three shifts of workers. Product quality was inconsistent at best and the management team David led was struggling with everything, including one another.

As David and I talked about their teamwork, my specialty, it seemed that all the communications strategies and problem-solving techniques I could offer to solve their problems were having little, if any, effect. And so David set out to define what *would* work with his team while they built the company together. *BrainStyles* was invented at our kitchen table between the hours of one and four A.M. as David figured out how to get a team of people who didn't like each other very much to work together.

He began with the premise that people can't change. We fought over that one premise for about three years. All my background in education, psychology, human and organizational behavior was about one thing: change. Change the environment and you'll change the business and the people along with them. I trained people to make changes—to modify their behavior and learn new ways to lead and manage, to follow management models based on case studies of successful people. I followed the same idea in my personal life: Identify what you most "deeply desire." Next, take stock of your current "weaknesses," and then set up a self-improvement, goal-setting plan to correct them.

David saw that this program didn't work. He observed his team, and after futilely trying out all the traditional motivational, counseling, reward-and-punish strategies with them, he looked beyond what he could see, and with minimal information on how the brain works, created a whole new paradigm for identifying people's strengths. He applied the concepts as he worked with his team. We both tested them on ourselves, then applied them with our family and friends. My work with clients gained in clarity and power as I incorporated the ideas into my practice. My research and personal growth during the four years of writing the first book for businesses expanded the concepts David formed into a whole way of living, now called *The BrainStyles System*.

Our results have been powerful. Liberating, in fact.

People who have broken off engagements to be married have called to say how they've read our book and not only reunited, but were entering marriage with a whole new outlook—more real and more respectful. Men married for many years have found renewed appreciation for their wives. An artist has used her new insights about her strengths to grow personally and professionally with a new focus for her painting.

And David's company?

In five years, David and his team took their high-tech polymers business from substantial losses at $5 million in sales to over $40 million in sales and a strong bottom line, breaking into new markets and achieving patents in new product areas along the way.

How did this happen? For the employees, the thing that counted in their workplace was how the company was led. There was an absence of "politics." People were not engaged in figuring out what the boss wanted. *BrainStyles* discussions meant open agendas. Everyone was included. The environment was safe for all to express their own point of view. David's role as chief was to provide a unifying vision and keep the teams focused.

The result that still means the most to me came up when I interviewed employees for a goodbye videotape upon David's departure from the company (after it was acquired by a Fortune 200 firm in 1986). Among all the kudos, many cried and told me that he had "changed their lives."

He did it by insisting people be themselves, not who they thought they should be—*especially* if they thought they should be different or think differently to please their boss.

Taking the principles that helped a team work together to save a struggling business and applying them at home has worked for us in our marriage. We are still a dual-career family with high-stress jobs. And neither one of us is that easy to live with. Yet our partnership has become more loving, our fights rare, and our respect much stronger for each other as we practice what we preach. Our first book, *BrainStyles: Be Who You Really Are,* which was published in 1992 after four years of collaboration, did more for our marriage than anything else.

At the end of a talk we gave in Dallas in 1993 to executives of high-tech firms, the last question of the evening was a woman's. "How has this brainstyles material affected your marriage?" she asked. David's response summed up his feelings for the growth we've experienced as we've learned to live together: "I make a living, and she makes my living worthwhile."

The purpose of this book is to share with you how to have the same feeling about your marriage or any relationship, to take these principles and tools into your daily lives, at home, at work, and at play.

HOW THIS BOOK GOES

Chapter One asks you some personal questions to get you thinking about what you want to change. You'll be introduced to some new research about why your answers so far have been unsatisfactory. You'll meet some people for the first time whom you'll get to know much better as we explore their strengths and limitations later on.

Chapter Two introduces some research on why you try to be perfect, why you can stop trying (what a relief!), and what to do instead. There is a no-fault no-fail quiz at that point to help direct you to identify your natural brainstyle strengths, and where to go next.

Chapters Three through Six describe four core strengths called brainstyles. You'll learn how to define each genetically based, brain-defined set of strengths so you can start redefining how you see yourself. You can then read about other people's gifts so that you can redefine the way you see them and use their strengths *without changing either one of you.*

Chapter Eight will tell you how to apply brainstyles to create synergy in relationships with anyone anywhere. Here you will find out how to use timing to allow each of you to be natural, get in sync, and bring out the best of yourself and others. You might, as many have told me, fall in love or make your work a road to your dreams all over again.

Chapter Nine gives you some tools to transform your relationship with yourself, your "enemies," and your colleagues at work. You'll read success stories of real people who have succeeded in daily life to feel freer to be themselves and made a much larger contribution to everyone they know.

CHAPTER 1

Change Your Life Without Changing Yourself

WHY IT HURTS: YOU THINK YOU NEED TO CHANGE

Nearly everything I pick up to read or watch suggests the Quick Fix to the inadequacies, victimization, or powerlessness that we assume control us. Gurus keep telling us we need *their* solutions to fix our suffering, our lives, our careers. Bunk.

I want to introduce you to the most important person in your life. *You.* By the end of this book I want you to understand that *you are your own best teacher and role model.*

What you will read is not a prescription for how to act or speak. The principles you will explore in this book will teach you how to uncover your strengths and non-strengths, how to ask for and get what you need from others without feeling more or less than another, and, finally, how to start working with others without asking either side to adapt or *go along to get along* in unnatural ways. (You'll also find some surprising answers to the above items you may have agreed with.) When you know who you really are, then you'll know how to go to those other books or gurus to take what you need to move down your *own* path.

When I talk to myself, is this what I say?

- My job is too stressful. I'm unsure what to do about it.
- There are several areas of my personality that need to improve in order to get along better with others.
- I'm a perfectionist. Nothing seems to get done right unless I do it myself.
- I need to be more assertive. People tell me I need to speak up more.
- I'm too strong. I only get along with other strong people.
- I need to change my personality to fit the situation (depending on what's required to get what I want), but it's stressful moving from work to home to social life.
- I'm not a team player. I don't know how to take advantage of this fact.
- I have big dreams, yet people doubt me.
- I have always had role models who inspire me by doing things I could never do. How can I incorporate some of those things?
- I like being with people who are different. I'm bored by people like me.
- I'm afraid to have kids of my own. I don't want to repeat my parents' mistakes.

SOME BARRIERS

Why is it so difficult to accept ourselves as we are?

Defining your strengths may sound "old hat" at first. You may be thinking, "I *already know* what I'm good at. What I need to *fix* is all the other stuff."

Consider this. We make two basic errors in our lives:

1. We focus on our weaknesses.
2. We do not focus on our strengths.

Why do we overlook what comes easily? For the first time, brain technology available in the 1990s gives us an answer. Reports as recent as 1992 tell of PET brain scans given by UCLA researchers to people who had previously taken an IQ test. The brain scans reveal colored pictures of the brain at work, with red indicating high activity and blue indicating low activity. The researchers predicted that the smarter the person, the harder the brain would work. Their hypothesis was a reasonable one given a commonly quoted observation that "most of us use only 10 percent of our brains." Consequently, *we believe that the more of our brain we use, the harder we work, the smarter we are.*

Wrong. Just the reverse is true.

> Those who performed best on the IQ test tended, on average, to produce "cooler," more subdued PET scan patterns (blue and green colors), while their less intellectually gifted counterparts lit up like miniature Christmas trees ("hot" red and various orange hues). The brain of the less intelligent person seemed to have to work harder to achieve less.[1]

It appears that when we operate in our "element," we produce results effortlessly and quickly. But when our work is effortless, it is hard to measure: it is invisible to us. We pay attention to time-consuming effort and struggle because struggle captures our awareness and holds it hostage.

We *must* know more about our strengths or we will overlook them. In fact it is highly probable that we base our self-images on flawed thinking and distorted perceptions right from the beginning. We value what we *should* be—*not* who we are. By definition what we are *not* becomes better than what we *are*. To make it even worse, when you revisit your past, often you only remember the embarrassments. As you think back on how you handled a situation with your parents or children or ex-girlfriend, you will look with the critical eye of what you did *not* do or say or accomplish. Oh, the inadequacy. The guilt. The regrets.

When we settle for the way we've turned out, we must then resign ourselves to mediocrity and apologize all the time. What a drag.

We want to grow. Great. But we try to grow in the wrong areas— areas that we may need to be competent in, but not areas that we necessarily need to master. Not so great.

If you think that focusing on your strengths means that life should become a perpetual party or that you can suddenly do whatever you feel like doing and to heck with everyone else, ask yourself this question: Do people, doing what they love to do, ever want to take a break from it?

For over twenty years, psychologist Mihaly Csikszentmihalyi has studied states of "optimal experience," or peak states of enjoyment, concentration, and deep involvement that lead to growth. He calls it "flow," or what people report when feeling strong and alert, when they experience a state of "effortless control," where they are "unself-conscious" without a sense of time, when they forget emotional problems, where there is "exhilaration and transcendence," going beyond the boundaries of identity. He noted that the descriptions were the same "regardless of culture, stage of modernization, social class, age, or gender." [2]

The professor describes what it is like when you use your natural strengths to do something. You find things within your grasp: your concentration is keen, and your skills are stretched by the challenge. You can tell during the experience that you're gaining on the challenge —from rock climbing to socializing to competing in a game or sport, to writing, gardening, computing, or even reading. You have a sense of control and accomplishment.

How can you create your own "flow" at what you do? Clearly, one of the first steps is to have more information about what your natural strengths really are.

FINDING "FLOW" THROUGH YOUR BRAINSTYLE

In order to achieve "flow," you need the opportunity to apply your strengths to your activities at least 50 percent of the time according to Professor Csikszentmihalyi. When 60 to 70 percent of your daily efforts draw on your strengths, you experience a joyful life, full, rich, and satisfying. And, according to studies done in America, *flow occurs most frequently* for more people *at work.* Yet when asked, most people predicted that they would feel the best, and experience the most enjoyment, when they were *at leisure.*

"Oh, I can hardly *wait* until my vacation." How many times have you heard that? "I might just have a great life—if only I didn't have to have this lousy job." Research done around the world tells us that American workers, more than those in other countries, see their work as restrictive, less pleasurable than "true" enjoyments like TV, movies, sitting around having a brewski with friends, you know, *fun.*

However, when asked about situations where they experienced involvement so intense that they didn't want to think about anything else, so engaged that they forgot themselves and their emotional problems, so focused that they lost track of time and felt a real sense of accomplishment afterward, guess where they were?

Of course. More often than not, they were at *work*.

It appears, then, that whether at work or at play, people experience real satisfaction when they use their natural gifts to solve some problem.

Still, we manage to doubt ourselves when it comes too easily, and whatever doubt we don't bring, others will help us manufacture.

Are you one of those people who have a quick and simple solution to things? Can you get to the bottom of things in a complex situation rather quickly even when you're confronted with something brand-new? Do you get frustrated by people who continually get off the subject, jam up the works, and bog down the system with all their endless personal agendas and concerns? Do they then turn around and, instead of appreciating the fact that you want to get things moving, that you have a way to do what *they* want to do easier and faster, do they then blame you for being insensitive, pushy, arrogant, or dogmatic —bringing everything to a halt?

You may relate to Dick the consultant, trainer, and author who knows very well what to do but can't always get people to do it for the same unfathomable reasons. Or you may be interested in meeting Peg. Finding out what's inside the "family snob" just might be a surprise for some who find women like her a bit "aggressive" or "cold." And you may appreciate how their "flow" occurs most clearly when they work alone, and how it ebbs as the number of people they have to work with increases.

Dick and Peg both cut to the chase, talk bottom line easily, and have no problem getting the best deal, whether in their roles as parents or professionals. You'll meet several people in Chapter Three who think along the same lines they do. You'll go way beyond how they appear and sound, to learn how to describe the value they (and perhaps you) add to friendships, families, or teams by the way they make decisions, set goals, plan a picnic, or lead a business. By the time you get to Chapter Eight, you'll read about how to take advantage of what you learn with others in ways that will help you finish the job that you do so well.

Or perhaps you, like so many of us, are slogging away at shoring up your terminal weakness: taking things personally. (You may be dynamite when it comes to supporting everybody else—figuring out what others need—like Leslie. Leslie has questions about where all her dedication is leading. You may have the same type of worries.) You may say the wrong things, just blurt them out sometimes, and spend time being embarrassed and apologizing. You, like Brad, know so quickly, so surely what people are feeling—even thinking—that you react without thinking and then people react to *you*. You have such great ideas, so much potential; your major frustration is that you just can't put all that magic into words or on paper so that others will support it.

So many things inspire you, and you can do so many things well, it drives you nuts when people can't understand your type of professionalism and keep quoting the policy manual about what the rules are. People say you're "great with people" with the kind of smirk that says "if you can't be good at something that *counts*." When you meet Brad and May in Chapter Four and find out how they have overcome their own need to be perfect in order to breeze on by the naysayers, gossips, and taskmasters to succeed, you may think again about how you look at your own strengths. Even better, by the time you get to Chapter Nine, you will have some practical strategies for getting along with the most difficult people on earth without trying to adapt or pretend to be something you're not.

If you are still trying to change to fit in, Chapter Two will explain why you can't change who you are, even if people think you're the most adaptable, easygoing one in the bunch. It's time to focus on what you do well and what to make of it.

Perhaps you have always felt different from others. You get frustrated that people can't understand you, that they badger you with questions about how the heck you came up with that idea, that assumption. They want you to keep explaining yourself. It's boring. They will just not trust or respect your ideas, it seems, even when you have demonstrated that you can run rings around them with new possibilities, strategies, and answers for the future. Perhaps, like Carol or David, those in your family or workplace just can't quite seem to follow your thinking and, therefore, don't want to hear what you have to say. You spend a lot of time in your head, inventing and visualizing answers to things others can't even see as problems. Nothing is as much fun as whirling around those images on your mental screen and coming out with a brand-new way to swing the golf club, link up computer equipment, or design a new answer to an old problem. Your joy is in the new and untried. You, like John and Kay, whom you will also get to know in Chapter Five, enjoy, no, demand change. You are the one that pushes the edge of the envelope with analysis, reason, and wild-eyed, fantastic, and random intuition. Nothing is more frustrating to you than rule-mongering policy mavens who know all the reasons why: Why something cannot be done, Why something has already been tried, Why they cannot bend the rules to help you. By the end of the chapter, you should feel the comfort of knowing you are not weird. And you're not alone.

If you haven't recognized your strengths so far, but have thought: *I do all of those things,* you may be part of the vast majority of those gifted in doing lots of things well. You see yourself succeeding in a variety of situations, and are very aware of distinctions. You may prize how well you learn and so are continually exploring new ideas as you challenge those little gray cells. You see yourself and things in your world as complex, interesting, worth exploring as shades of color, but certainly not black or white. There *is* more to the stars of Chapter Seven—and you—than meets the eye. You'll meet three brothers who appear very different, have very different lifestyles and careers, and yet, looking past the superficial to their strengths, they have a common brainstyle.

BEING WHO YOU ARE

Consider this: you have always been mature and immature at the same time—wise and unwise, skillful and unskillful, right from the start. It is no joke that out of the mouths of babes regularly come insights that astound. Your job in life is not to learn how to be different; it's to spend more time realizing and living from the best that's already within. The difference between people who "realize their potential" and those who don't is not the amount of the potential, but the amount of permission they give themselves to use it.

GROWING UP: MASTERY, *NOT* CHANGE

Over a lifetime, we do not change our core strength, we mature it. We add a variety of skills in other, less natural, strength areas, by learning to function in different situations. It is a necessary discipline to learn things in our *non-strengths** in order to be competent and function with other humans in daily life. There is a fine line, of course,

---

* The term "non-strengths" is used to distinguish it from "weaknesses." This is explained fully in Chapter Nine.

between getting along and going along. Learning in order to please is the path we take when we are afraid of ourselves. When we go down that fearful road to the glittering city of Looking Good, we find empty storefronts and nothing worth buying; we've already spent our inner wealth.

Find your center first. This is the core of you that you know isn't going to change. Begin a quiet friendship with yourself, just as you are right now, *regardless* of the situation or expectations of others. Out of a peaceful center you will find ease, discover new abilities, and create *your* response to situations. You will know enough to call in other troops to supply what you cannot. You will be liberated from the tyranny of reaction, or the immobility of giving something outside of you the power of defining you and your gifts to the world.

Now is the time to value your natural gift *above* what you have learned. The very process of being better at your thing will make you better at all things. When you stop taking for granted the very qualities that are your gift to others, you may, as one client observed, start "feeling younger." You may discover why you are on this earth.

CHAPTER 2

Why You Don't Have to Change

"Our brains are built to process things in certain ways, and no amount of education or training can take us beyond these built-in characteristics."

MICHAEL GAZZANIGA, *Nature's Mind,*
neuroscientist, co-discoverer of split-brain theory

**YOU *CAN'T* CHANGE THE WAY YOUR BRAIN WORKS.
YOU *CAN* CHANGE THE WAY THAT YOU USE IT.**

Scientists have pondered the following extraordinary story for more than a century. Today, we can read in our local papers the answers to centuries of mysteries regarding how the brain works to affect our daily lives. Phineas Gage, a pleasant enough man before the accident, was a strong but fair supervisor. He was married and a kind and intelligent spouse. After he sustained this bizarre brain injury, he never knew why he became so short-tempered, changeable, and erratic. He was fired, divorced, and could barely sustain himself as a waiter for the years he lived after his accident. This story demonstrates how important knowing about the brain is in defining our personality and the way we live in the world.

Science Update

1848 Head Injury Patient Still Offers Lessons to Neurologists

Doctors are still learning about the brain from arguably the most famous head injury patient in history.

Phineas Gage, 25, was in charge of the detonations that prepared the New England terrain for the Rutland and Burlington Railroad. On Sept. 13, 1848, a premature explosion hurled a tamping iron up through the bottom of his chin and out the top of his skull. Mr. Gage was momentarily stunned but otherwise unaffected by the accident.

Or so it seemed. Although Mr. Gage was as intelligent and agile as ever, his personality was transformed. Once a reliable and popular man, he became rude and irresponsible.

By examining the man's skull—which with the tamping iron, is on display at a Harvard University museum—and reconstructing the brain with modern imaging techniques, researchers have zeroed in on the damaged areas that soured Mr. Gage's personality. They conclude that the iron damaged the ventromedial region of the brain's frontal lobes. Based on Mr. Gage's case and other brain-damaged patients, the scientists believe the ventromedial region is vital for emotional processing and social cognition.

—*The Dallas Morning News,* May 23, 1994

Scientific findings have so rapidly accelerated in the past decade with computer-assisted technology that the 1990s were rightfully declared the "Decade of the Brain" by Congress in 1989. New techniques take color photographs of what your brain actually looks like when you're thinking.* Just as amazingly, we are reading in our daily papers about just what specific part of the brain controls which action, emotion, and type of thinking.

For centuries everyone involved with studying human behavior has raised questions about why we act the way we do. Two very different answers have emerged from the modern sciences. They have been captured in the *nature versus nurture* debate.

---

* Positron emission tomography (PET) scans register heat generated by cell activity and glucose being oxidized. Fast magnetic resonance imaging (MRI) machines turn pictures of brain scan activity into movies by detecting blood flow and the faint magnetic signals carried by the blood as it moves to help us think.

Sociologists study the effect of the group on the person. Their position is firmly on the *nurture* side of the argument, which claims that how you turn out is largely dependent upon how your parents and friends treat you. Societal issues like gangs, peer pressure, crime, parenting, and business issues like management are explored regularly from the point of view that we are a product of our environment, and as such, attention and resources must be directed at changing the environment in order for humans to thrive within it. However, in recent years, more researchers in the "hard sciences" such as biology and neurology, which measure tangible things as opposed to the "soft sciences" like sociology, which measures the observed effects of human interactions, have been exploring the *nature* side of the debate. The most recent studies [1] of genetics and personal development show that from 30 to as much as 80 percent of human behavior can be directly attributed to the genetic material we are born with. [2]

This is how it works: genetics sets up our aptitudes and establishes how we react to our environment. Because of the way biology works, you may see a challenge, while another sees a crisis. This premise means watching for the impact of the individual's response and how it controls what is around them, rather than the other way around. For example, researchers observed babies in new and unfamiliar situations (where they couldn't have *learned* what to do) where the babies had to respond automatically, and found, for instance, that those who approached strangers or unfamiliar situations with a smile or with curiosity tended to get picked up, held, or were responded to positively by those around them. Those babies grew up viewing the world as an accepting place, where they were free to roam, as the following study explains.

In a rare, if not one-of-a-kind, look at the effect of the environment on children, Emmy Werner, of the University of California, Davis, studied a group of 698 "high-risk children" over a period of thirty-two years. [3] The children grew up on the island of Kauai, Hawaii, in "the most discordant and impoverished homes, beset by physical handicaps." Not unexpectedly, for most of us educated within the all-powerful influence of our parents and environment, two out of three children developed serious learning or behavioral problems by the age of ten. "Surprisingly, however, one out of every three of them . . . developed instead into competent, confident, and caring young adults." *Why?* A remarkable finding showed there were three similarities out of literally hundreds of variables found in the successful group.

1) The babies were born happy, regardless of the circumstances; positive affect (smiling, acting happy) was well established by the time the babies were one year old. They were in no way trained or nurtured to become happy. As toddlers and young adults, the positive babies developed to take charge of their own environment. "Though not especially gifted, these children used whatever skills they had effectively."

2) At least one adult, not necessarily the parent, was a continuous personal caregiver who believed in them when those in the group were infants. As the "resilient" group grew older, they continued to seek out emotional support outside the family, at school, with close friends, and in church. About one third said that faith and prayer were significant internal, personal supports for them, supplementing outside personal relationships.

3) Those in the "resilient" group each had a hobby of some sort that they pursued independently, outside of the view of anyone else.

Internally driven, private successes continued to reinforce positive results as those in the "resilient" group controlled their own reactions to their personal environment.

Recent studies substantiate that "adverse or depriving experiences in infancy do *not* fix personality development." When children are taken from difficult situations as late as six or seven years old, normal IQ and behavior can still occur by the teen years.[4]

Managing the present situation well *can* override bad memories.

Moreover, there is further research which substantiates that genetic influences become more dominant as we age.[5] Our strengths become more defined, our neural pathways larger and more easily accessed, as we get older. Think of how illnesses like Alzheimer's and Parkinson's diseases—both genetic, both diseases of the brain—show up in later life. Think of how you've always said that people get more set in their ways as they get older. Perhaps all we're seeing is more of what has always been there in the first place.

Extraordinary examples of genetically based strengths appear in those labeled "idiot savants," as dramatized in the movie *Rain Man*. Those who, like the character played by Dustin Hoffman, have heightened functioning in specific areas of the brain may show instant genius by a very early age. They can draw or play the piano or do extremely complex mathematical calculations *all at once,* with no training or instruction, using only their own heightened abilities of observation and memory to capture a piano concerto or draw complex architecture. Other parts of the brain are seemingly dormant and do not develop, so that the person cannot function as well in everyday problem-solving situations.[6]

One of the most famous geniuses of our century was Albert Einstein. One of his legacies was to tell us that we are only using 10 percent or less of our brain hardware. A humble man, he must have been trying to inspire others with the old idea *if I can do it, so can you.* Einstein is a classic example of a man with specific brain-based gifts, however. Gary Lynch, a psychobiologist at the University of California, Irvine, tells of the results of using new technology to study a slice of cells taken from Einstein's brain.[7] Although most of us know that this brilliant man was unable to do simple math and couldn't talk until he was nearly four years old, you've probably never heard about the source of his real strengths. Einstein had many times more of a particular kind of cell—glial cells—than average people have, in regions of the brain that make associations. His brain had more hardware to come up with global generalizations and abstract theories of the universe.

David Lykken, researcher at the University of Minnesota, studied identical twins who were separated at birth and reared apart in different environments. His work not only supports the Kauai study, but also breaks new ground in defining the source of a whole list of personality factors.[8] Lykken actually measured a genetic base to establish the positive personalities of the twins. On a more hopeful note for those of us who weren't born with the sunniest of dispositions, he notes that negativity seems to be learned in the family and, therefore, can be changed more readily.

This research and more contradicts one of the most commonly held assumptions in family life today: that we are brought into the world as blank slates upon whom the family writes, creating who we are. Dr. Michael Gazzaniga, co-discoverer of the functions of the left and right sides of the brain, takes it even further when he says, "Our brains are built to process things in certain ways and no amount of education or training can take us beyond these built-in characteristics."[9] Parental influence creates an interplay with the child's genetics, but certainly does not work in the way we have always hoped and feared. Mom doesn't deserve as much of the blame or the credit she's been given. Nor do our peers, bosses, friends, or enemies.

Two child psychologists at Pennsylvania State University use genetics in their studies of children and their families with a focus on siblings. Robert Plomin and Judy Dunn talk about the effect of the family on the young child:

> "It's startling at first," Plomin admits. "But all the evidence points to the same conclusion: What we've thought of all along as 'shared family environment' doesn't exist. That's because *we each carry around between our ears our own little customized version of our environment.* From our first days of life, and perhaps even before, we perceive everything that happens to us through a unique filter, every skewed event changing us in a way that affects how we'll experience the next event." [10]

> . . . the argument that we have outlined removes some of the blame (and credit) that parents have received in relation to the development of their children. For example, because societally important traits such as mental illness run in families, it used to be assumed that this was evidence for parental influence. *But we now know* [see Chapter Two] *that what runs in families making siblings similar is parental DNA, not parental treatment.* [11] (emphasis added)

Their prescription? "It is surely useful for parents to recognize [this] hypersensitivity of children to potential injustice, and to acknowledge that *differential appreciation* (to the extent it is humanly possible) is more likely to help their children than *preferential treatment.*" [12]

Lykken, questioning what we inherit from our parents, wondered how a European mathematical genius, Karl Friedrich Gauss, could be born to a bricklayer and a peasant woman, and have no offspring with any mathematical talent to speak of. He answers the question by explaining that an individual's genetic material *combines uniquely within each person,* on an individual basis, to create specific abilities. Gauss's unique genes for mathematical ability were not passed on to his children, nor were his own abilities inherited directly.

Lykken's work, not to mention Plomin and Dunn's applications in families, not only calls into question the amount of influence the environment created by the parents has upon the child, but may also lay to rest some of the guilt we've managed to feel about passing on defective genes to our children. It is a startling new look at our genetic strengths and limitations—or what we cannot change.

By learning about the children who succeeded in Kauai, and drawing from genetics research, it's obvious that to become our best, we must *now* take charge of the natural strengths we were born with by accepting ourselves and our parents just as we are. Only then can we master the old prejudices and expectations of our family and co-workers. Even better, past traumas can be healed *today* by applying our natural gifts to construct a positive environment for ourselves. Natural nourishment for our children will come from respecting *their* gifts, the "differential appreciation" that the psychologists Plomin and Dunn recommend, to create the next generations of healthy families. It starts with the respect we have for ourselves.

ACCEPTING OUR LIMITS MEANS WE CAN BE UNLIMITED

The purpose of this book is to give you enough information to open possibilities in the way you view yourself and others, male or female, of whatever race or background you are, not to be technical and teach you all about genetics or your brain. It is to give you some reasons to become more accepting and energized about who you are. And that starts by accepting—not judging, resenting, or excusing—the limitations of the hand you were dealt.

Talking to Karol, you are aware of a speech difference. She speaks breathily and through her nose, as if she has a cleft palate. She says she had a particularly painful nerve disease that effectively damaged her hearing when she was a little girl. People either made fun of her, or were sympathetic and pitied her for the painful tumors that appeared on her body as she grew up. "I didn't understand other people's reactions," she says, when asked how those judgments made her feel. "I just took it for granted that how *I* felt was normal, and went on about my business." She is now and has been a fund-raiser for a variety of nonprofit organizations. Her job involves frequent public speaking. I wonder if she works hard at giving speeches *because* of her speech impediment. She responds that her real problem is hearing what people say. Her goal is not to "fix" her non-strengths; instead, she concentrates on her message and getting the results she sets out to get. She tells me how she lip-reads to get around not being able to hear something said quietly or outside her range of vision. She talks about what she enjoys: selling and organizing—doing the things that she is best at. She talks of the fun she has in her job. She demonstrates how to focus on strengths in order to take care of non-strengths.

Charles Schwab, the now multimillionaire discount brokerage firm founder, discovered in midlife that he was dyslexic. Although he always had a deficiency in reading and dealing with specifics, he compensated by concentrating on his imaginative visual gifts to create breakthroughs in the brokerage business when no one in the entire industry had ever heard of "discounting" or "no fees." "I've always felt that I have more of an ability to envision, to be able to anticipate where things are going, to conceive a solution to a business problem than people who are more sequential thinkers," he said.[13]

Those who have physical limitations are our teachers, the best role models we could have. Observing them, rather than pitying them, brings answers. Those who are happy use their limitations as a boundary, and then focus on and master their strengths. The non-strengths are given enough attention that the strengths can be leveraged to move them forward in their lives. They don't spend a lot of time resenting, denying, or defending what can't be helped.

AND NOW A WORD ABOUT THE BRAIN,
OR CREATING YOUR OWN REALITY

In 1981, psychobiologist Roger Sperry won the Nobel Prize for Physiology and Medicine for his work at the California Institute of Technology on "split-brain" studies on the functions of the two hemispheres of the brain. Sperry, together with a student of his and a neurosurgeon, studied the effects of cutting the corpus callosum—the mass of nerve fibers that connects the two hemispheres of the brain—in people with epilepsy so severe that this surgery was the only available assistance for them. What Sperry discovered is now commonly known as left-brain/right-brain theory. He found that the corpus callosum is a communications network that sends information back and forth between the two hemispheres of the brain. Without the link, neither side knew what the other was doing. Moreover, with each hemisphere isolated, Sperry and his associates were able to determine that each hemisphere has distinctly different functions and processes information in its own distinct way. (See Exhibit A for a list of left- and right-hemisphere functions.)

Since this initial work done by Sperry and his colleagues, much more sophisticated work has been done to show that the "left-brain" functions Sperry originally defined as physically based in the left side of the brain are not, in fact, 100 percent exclusive to the left hemisphere. The same goes for the right side. And communication between these functions is dominated by, but not limited to, the corpus callo-

EXHIBIT A

HOW THE BRAIN FUNCTIONS

The LEFT Hemisphere	The RIGHT Hemisphere
The LOGICAL Side	The INTUITIVE Side

The LEFT Hemisphere — The LOGICAL Side	The RIGHT Hemisphere — The INTUITIVE Side
• SPEAKS	• CREATES IMAGES
• PROCESSES DATA	• PROCESSES SENSES
• EVALUATES	• SYMBOLIZES
• ANALYZES DIFFERENCES	• SEEKS SIMILARITIES
• IS FACTUAL	• IS SPIRITUAL
• IS STRUCTURED	• IS SPONTANEOUS
• HAS TIME AND MEASURES	• HAS *NO* TIME OR MEASURES

SPEAKS BUT CANNOT KNOW   KNOWS BUT CANNOT SPEAK

You use the LEFT side of the brain when you know what you're looking for	You use the RIGHT side of the brain when you "know it when you see it"
LEFT-SIDED ACTIVITIES:	RIGHT-SIDED ACTIVITIES:
• TALKING	• FEELING
• SETTING GOALS	• SPECULATING
• PLANNING	• VISUALIZING
• MEASURING	• EMPATHIZING
• SEEING DIFFERENCES	• SENSING SIMILARITIES

sum. Chemicals are released to activate different brain areas at varying speeds. Thus, while this book uses the terms "left-brain" and "right-brain," these terms are actually metaphors for the very complex interactions of the parts within the brain that perform the functions noted as "left" and "right."[14] Our senses produce sight and hearing by having different parts of the ear and eye deliver entirely different information to the left or right sides of the brain, *which then must be combined* for us to get a total image or understand a word.[15] What is important is that parts of our brain need to communicate with one another in order for us to perform. And that takes time.

Robert Ornstein explains it this way:

"We can never operate with a 'full deck' but with only a small selection of the total mental apparatus at any one time. This means that all our faculties of mind are never available at once. So, at any one time we are much more limited, much more changeable, than we might otherwise believe of ourselves."[16] We all have access to both sets of functions in both hemispheres, the genetic functions that we were born with. We *do not, however, access all functions of the brain equally, at the same time, or at the same speed.*

Dr. Terry Brandt, the director of the Center for Staff Development in Houston, works with neurophysiologists and other specialists to track how the brain works to solve problems. One of his findings is the measurement of the neural firings generated by the brain when we think. He reports that the number of "thoughts" (information bits) registered inside the human brain is about fifty thousand per minute. This exceeds by *hundreds of times* the number of sensory inputs we register. We can literally measure the fact that *we generate more "thoughts" inside our own brain than we get input from the environment.* As one of the neurophysiologists whom Dr. Brandt works with put it on measuring how the brain works, "you create your own reality." This is obvious every day: people hear what they want to hear, see what they want to see, and report different interpretations of the same event.

A NEW WAY TO DEFINE YOUR NATURAL STRENGTHS

Here is a simple way to organize how you define your thinking abilities. We call it a brainstyle. It's shorthand for the way your brain works to define your particular set of gifts.

The long definition:

A brainstyle describes how you take in information through your senses, how your brain communicates that information in the cerebral cortex (just under your skull), how you store the information in your memory, and how you then express it through your behavior. And, most importantly, at what speed you complete this process.

The short definition:

A brainstyle, then, is your set of brain-based, natural gifts. You at your best.

WHAT A BRAINSTYLE LOOKS LIKE

An individual brainstyle is a whole pattern of strengths. It is what you are naturally good at, can be counted on for, and what you love doing. Your brainstyle is your basic approach to work, family, and relationships. You can recognize this pattern when you make decisions. It is in new decision-making situations where you must take in information and think about it—process the information with the brain hardware that you have—as babies do in new situations. They cannot recall what to do, they have no memory. Over time, your decision-making approach shows a pattern of brain-processing strengths, like being right-handed, or being able to read music or learn computer code easily.

When we see people using their strengths, we say things like, "She doesn't even have to work at it." Or, "I thought *I* was good at numbers —until I saw Gary." Or, "He's always been good with people, but his brother has to make an effort just to say hello." Or even, "We *never* asked him to study science, he just sort of found it on his own. He was always interested in how things worked inside."

A COUPLE OF DEFINITIONS

A brainstyle is not the same as, nor does it have anything to do with, the fuzzy notions involved in being "smart."

- IQ, as in, "He has a high IQ." This really means he has specific verbal, math, and memory skills. Although the Intelligence Quotient is a universally accepted measure, noted psychologist Howard Gardner comments that the test was begun with the idea that all brains work alike. We know now that that is simply not true. Gardner, for one, defines "intelligence" as the ability to solve problems or create products.[17]
- Memory, as in, "He's so smart. He remembers everything." Memory is prized in traditional schools. Being able to listen and recall are continually applauded. Memory is an important component but

does not nearly describe the range of strengths available to be "smart." Memory is a storage and retrieval system now known to occur in at least three different forms (short-term, recent, and long-term) and is "filed" throughout the brain. As such, it can be considered a gift independent of brainstyle. Anyone can have it. As the psychobiologist Gary Lynch says, "Once a pattern is formed [for memory], the pathways are there forever."[18] So as we acquire memories, we lay down a nearly infinite number of neural pathways that help us organize what we see. We imprint our memories with information selected by our own unique way of processing information. What we know is shaped by our brainstyle.

DETERMINING A BRAINSTYLE: TIME AND THE BRAIN

THE BRAIN AND BRAINSTYLES. Different brain processing produces different types of abilities or strengths. What we recognize as "intelligence" is largely a product of brain *speed*—or how quickly one moves back and forth among the brain's functions and retrieves from memory.[19]

How do we determine our natural gifts? The unique concept defining how the brain responds in a new situation, called a Time Zero event, is the starting point.

Think of a time you didn't know what to do, a time when you couldn't rely on your memory to decide—you had to think about it. You were starting a new job, learning about something you knew nothing about, or even coming to an unfamiliar place while driving and you needed to decide what to do. As kids, we have millions of these events. In the chart below, that new time—where you could not remember similar, previous situations—is called a Time Zero event.

It is at these times, when we are in new, unfamiliar situations, that we use our brain most naturally. As we take in information, our brain "processes" it by sending it back and forth in nanoseconds across those billions of neural networks, from left side to right side and back again in a dazzling electrochemical surge. This is the time we refer to as Time Zero. Your response at this time is one in which you must think before acting. You must "process" incoming information from the scene around you, back and forth in your brain as you decide what to do. We experience a Time Zero event in our lives when we cannot remember what to do; we must think about it.

EXHIBIT B

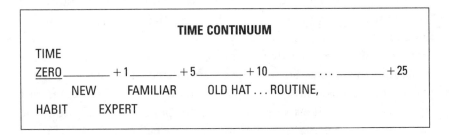

TIME CONTINUUM

TIME
ZERO————— +1————— +5————— +10————— ... ————— +25
    NEW   FAMILIAR   OLD HAT...ROUTINE,
HABIT   EXPERT

At Time Zero, or in what you perceive to be a NEW or UNFA-MILIAR EVENT, you are using your natural way of thinking, your *brainstyle,* to respond. This is how your "hardware" works: you call on different parts of the brain in a pattern of sorting or analyzing or reacting depending on the brain functions that are easiest and most natural for you to get access to. This becomes a pattern of strengths over a long period of time. And so, a *brainstyle* is determined in new events and it shows up over the long run as your natural way of doing things. This is you at your best.

HOW CAN YOU TELL THE DIFFERENCE BETWEEN WHAT IS NATURAL AND WHAT IS LEARNED?

After we confront these new decisions, we gain "experience"; we store how and what we decide in our memories. We are much more comfortable with memory. As the neurobiologists tell us, we've now laid down a neural path, and with repetition (practice, habit) we can go up and down that path like a slippery ski slope, to become the expert with the fast answers (as shown in the Time Continuum, Ex-hibit B). We are much more polished, much quicker after practice in *recalling* than in *thinking things through.* Ah, the magical state of that hand raised in the air, the teacher's recognition, and Yesss!—you know the answer. Smart. Quick. Bright. We learn to prize that time so highly when we've *learned* things, because it is more comfortable to use pathways in our brain that are already there in our memory than it is to construct new ones. And besides, the answer is known. Sure. Certain. But at Time Zero, when we are uncertain, we rush to get past those brain searchings that try to sort out the new and unfamiliar as quickly as we can.

And yet those new moments are *precious*. Those unsure times when you must engage your mental hardware are the very times when you are most yourself, most uniquely you. You are operating at a pace most comfortably yours, directly in line with your brainspeed.

What's the hurry? For the most part, society mandates that fast is smart and slow is dumb. Quick counts more and wins the game that has a scoreboard. This seems to come, in popular culture, from the way we view athletics, so often used as a metaphor for the Game of Life in which we must use endurance, skill, and persistence to overcome its hurdles. So far, so good. However, an athlete's speed and youth are not the metaphor for the entire experience. Those who cannot keep up are not less valuable than anyone else.

Breakthroughs, and the gifts that bring them, hatch from raw, unformed originality, outside of time, speed, or measures, build on stored experience, and use natural strengths as their source. Your personal breakthroughs cannot be conceived when the emphasis is to get past that initial, natural decision time, to recall someone *else's* smart answer. If you work hard solely to look good by remembering rather than by coming up with your own ideas, all you are left with is copied cleverness.

If you look at the Time Continuum, you might think of how much you respect expertise and try to get past those Time Zeroes as fast as you can. As you do this, your strengths become invisible.

Think about times when you're *stressed*. Aren't you racing past those Time Zeroes faster than your natural brainstyle allows? In hyperdrive, you are pushing to get answers and make decisions quicker than your best can deliver. You cannot draw on or develop all your gifts.

Beth, as recently as two years ago, was tense, focused, impatient, and spoke quickly. She often interrupted others in conversation; she was literally on the fast track of the corporate promotion list, and had the pace to match. "I'm paid to solve problems," she announced then, "not just *think* about them." She prized herself for her tough, get-it-done approach. She had just taken over a business area and had a list of problems to solve. Her boss wanted a quick turnaround and she was going to *get it done. ASAP.*

Today she says her life is different. "I was rushing into brick walls with people. I was trying to go so fast, I was only getting one answer

—mine—and trying to cram it down their throats." Several things happened to slow her down: "I finally had to admit I couldn't do it all, then I started to rely on someone else to help me work with my new team. I *had* to slow down, and when I did I used more of my abilities. Then I had a baby." She smiles broadly.

Beth looks different today, her face is more relaxed and confident, younger. "Now I include other people and their ideas, my results are better, my marriage is wonderful, I've discovered a spiritual side to my life, and I have *four* job offers." She doesn't interrupt, she listens. Her team says she is a very effective boss.

We do a lot with our timing. Unconsciously, we exert a lot of effort doing things to get the peace we need to think things over in our own time. Have you noticed people repeating themselves? Using long preambles before their point? Asking lots of questions? They need time. Relationships are dances in time, with leaders and followers continually seeking a rhythm together. We want our partners to have a similar pace to our own. We cut ourselves off from those with different brainspeeds who interrupt (too fast!) or drag us down (too slow!). We have a natural rapport, and often communicate easily without words with those like us. When two people have the same or complementary brainstyles and pace, you find male bonding, best friends, or "soul mates." Teacher's pet. Mom's favorite. Just being together is comfortable. More than likely, similarities mean being hired and admired at the job.

BrainStyle Clue:

We are not a combination of strengths. We have one basic way of taking in information at Time Zero. We learn, with practice, how to use other strengths, more or less, yet never with the same ease and speed of our natural gifts.

For the majority of us who think we have no outstanding talent, discovering a core *strength,* our brainstyle, to define how we think and go about our daily business, can be invaluable: it can bring clarity and focus, it can become a foundation for self-esteem, relationships, and career, it can be a way to manage our hardware, rather than be managed by it.

BRAINSTYLES BASICS: THE PUNCH LINES

How BrainStyles Work

- Your brain is your genetically determined "hardware" to process information and make decisions.
- You do not choose how your brain functions. You choose how to apply what your brain naturally provides.

It has become apparent that we can no more choose to process information differently at Time Zero than we can choose to do other physical functions differently. We can learn to compensate for or improve something—run faster, speak more distinctly, retrieve the use of a damaged limb—but we cannot change the basic functioning of the "equipment" we have, even if we choose to do so. Even when we learn to improve a mental function outside our natural area of strength, it will never really perform as well, as quickly, or produce the results and satisfaction afforded by our natural gifts.

- The left and right sides of the brain each perform different functions, are accessed at different speeds, and in different sequences in different people.
- The speed of information exchange between the brain hemispheres manifests itself in four general patterns of decision-making, expressed as a variety of behaviors. This pattern is called a *brainstyle.*

Separating *brainstyle* strengths from outward behavior is the same process you use when making a friend—you look behind actions for the good things they do. Using these principles means expanding the number of people you can be friends with. You can learn to strategize with rather than react to others. You can stop trying to get another to do what they don't want to—or can't do. You can start working with who they are *now.* You can begin reevaluating old relationships, sorting out what counts from what never has. Understanding how to time your own decisions and interactions is the foundation for win-win relationships—where you do not have to take things personally.

- A person's *brainstyle* can be determined by observing what happens in situations that are new to the person, where there are (or seem to the person to be) no prepared answers to the situation. These new situations we call Time Zero events. Responses to events *after*

Time Zero involve *learned behavior,* i.e., actions that have been tried out at least once. These learned behaviors are practiced ways of responding to situations. They can include behaviors natural to all four brainstyles.

- You cannot determine a person's behavior by observing learned behaviors.
- *Brainstyles* cannot be learned.

Your *brainstyle* is your natural response to new situations in which you use the most personal and comfortable way for you to think. There is nothing to "become." You're already there. The main thing you need to do is stop trying to be who you're *not.*

The Principles for Applying BrainStyles

- People in the same *brainstyle* can appear very different from one another.

Using the criteria of a Time Zero response, all the following people are in the same *brainstyle:* the comedienne Lucille Ball, former Secretary of State Henry Kissinger, Mother Teresa, Britain's Prince Charles, American Airlines chief Robert Crandall, the talk-show host David Letterman, the artist Andy Warhol, and nearly half the population we've studied (see Chapter Six).

- There are no bad *brainstyles,* just bad "fits."

There is no *brainstyle* that is smarter, stronger, or worthier than any other. Each strength has its blessings and its pain, its good news and bad news, its share of good guys and bad guys, as well as quick ones and slow ones. Each is vital for the world to work. On an individual basis, what makes the biggest difference is fitting a person's *brainstyle* to the requirements of the situation. It's amazing how, especially in families, we continually expect things we want rather than what the other can actually deliver. The fit between expectations and the other's strengths is missing, and that's all it is. Nothing personal.

- BrainStyles don't make boxes, they eliminate them.

As soon as people hear "you can't change" something, they get afraid. The fear seems to be "I'm being held back—stuck with a label that will limit my future." Your *brainstyle* stakes a claim to a vast territory. You may never discover how expansive it is; you will know that you are comfortable there. By understanding the limits to that territory, you can begin growing in limitless ways. You will probably feel an immediate sense of relief as you give up all the effort involved in trying to lay claim to another's turf, where you have to compete unfairly against someone who's better or quicker. You will learn how to be more patient with yourself. You can stop waiting for others to appreciate and recognize your real gifts. You can give up trying to please everyone, if you get into that sort of thing at times, and teach them what you can really deliver. Open up those *brainstyle* "boxes" and reveal the gifts inside.

- If you can't change your brainstyle, you *can* change how you explain or "sell" the benefits of your strengths and limitations to others. You can create more realistic expectations, honest relationships, and fewer conflicts by using timing.
- You don't have to be good at things you are lousy at. Doing so means excelling at things you learn quickly and easily. Trying to master non-strengths can produce results, but takes much more time and effort. When attempting to *master* a non-strength, you can experience much more inner conflict and dissatisfaction with everything—starting with yourself.
- You can create understandings with other people that will allow each of you to use your natural strengths and timing responsibly. This can produce commitments built on the personal worth of each person.
- The goal of *The BrainStyles System* is personal mastery of natural gifts over a joyful, fulfilling lifetime.

HOW TO DETERMINE YOUR BRAINSTYLE: A PLACE TO BEGIN

There are psychological assessments (tests) that you can take, the results of which offer you interpretations that help define your abilities. When you read the interpretation, it makes sense to you and captures things that you may have felt, suspected, or wondered about. *"Ah ha!"* you think. Sometimes the interpretations are surprises; more often they are confirmations of what you already knew. *The BrainStyle Inventory,* following on the next several pages, is of the latter variety.* Taking

* See Appendix C and D for validation data. Further copies of the *Inventory* are available from *BrainStyles, Inc.* at 1-800-374-9878.

it will start you asking the right questions to find your place in *The BrainStyles System*. It will give you an idea of which brainstyle chapter to read first. About nine out of ten people taking it feel comfortable immediately with one of the four descriptions for how they approach new situations. But many change their minds about their *natural* strengths and only really get a clear understanding of their gifts *after* reading further. Remember: all paper-and-pencil tests are self-fulfilling —even though the questions are designed to get past your preconceived self-image, you can still answer the way you'd *like* to be seen instead of *the way you are in new situations.*

After you take the *Inventory*, some questions are offered to help you sort out any remaining confusion. After finding your own description, don't stop! You'll then need to learn about *others'* strengths in their own chapters—which *define the boundaries of what you do well.* When you learn about another's thinking and what it provides, you, like Beth and many others, will be able to stop competing and enjoy the best from them.

The BrainStyle Inventory®

Version 1.42

This *Inventory* was designed and tested by Marlane Miller of *BrainStyles Inc.* and Lawrence H. Peters, Ph.D., of the M.J. Neeley School of Business at Texas Christian University, Fort Worth, Texas.

INTRODUCTION

The BrainStyle Inventory is not like other "tests" you've taken. It was designed to help you identify your unique *brainstyle*. To do so, you must distinguish between your *brainstyle* response to *new* or *unfamiliar situations that require you to think through and decide about information* versus situations you solve by *recalling or remembering.*

Brainstyle is difficult to recognize because of our ability to remember rapidly. In a new situation we can recall so quickly, it is hard to tell what is memory and what is our actual thinking process. In addition, all of us have had a great deal of experience in reacting to many new or different situations. We have learned that in certain situations, we *should respond* in a certain way—different from the way we naturally respond. We have jobs that put pressure on us to behave in certain ways—ways that are inconsistent with who we really are. In addition, all of us have an image of ourselves which we want others to see. Many times our ideal self-image is what we have learned to cover up, things we want to change, be better at or admired for, but which are *not* our *natural gifts.*

When presented with new or unfamiliar information, you behave in a way that is *natural* for you. Prior learning, job demands, and self-image have little effect on how we naturally respond to *new decision situations.* The problem is that by the time we are adults, there are fewer and fewer completely novel situations for us to face. As a result, it is not easy for us to identify our *brainstyle* by looking only at our response in new situations.

Fortunately, *brainstyle* always shows up as a pattern of strengths *over time.* You will be most comfortable over the long term when responding in ways that are based on your *brainstyle.* You will also be most natural and add your *best* work with the *least* effort. When we behave in ways that are inconsistent with our *brainstyle,* we know it. We must strain to learn. We are anxious, tense, careful, take longer, and generally must concentrate all the time if we are going to decide or produce. When we behave in ways that are consistent with our *brainstyle,* we simply do what comes naturally, effortlessly—without forced concentration.

When completing The BrainStyle Inventory try to distinguish:

- between what you have learned, or remember, and *what comes naturally*
- between what situations demand of you and *what you are most gifted at doing*
- between how you want to be seen and *how you really are*

THE BRAINSTYLE INVENTORY, VERSION 1.42

There is no one best *brainstyle*—therefore, there are no right or wrong answers to the items on this inventory. Your score will reflect your own perception of your strengths.

To identify your unique brainstyle, respond honestly to each item.

This inventory has 18 pairs of statements. For each pair, choose the alternative (**A** or **B**) that best describes you. Use the following scale.

A = if **A** is **more descriptive** of you than **B**

B = if **B** is **more descriptive** of you than **A**

N = if **neither** statement is descriptive of you

In the example below, many people are aware of having *both* reactions to different situations. What is significant is which comes *first* or most naturally—especially in an unfamiliar situation *before* we draw on what we might have learned to do. If neither sounds like your natural reaction, choose N as the alternative for that pair.

Sample Item

Put an X for each pair of items on the answer sheet.
   A. *Initially, I tend to react logically in new situations.*
   B. *Initially, I tend to react intuitively in new situations.*

<u>ANSWER SHEET:</u>   **X** A   ___B   ___N

This person marked A on the answer sheet meaning that the first statement, A, is most descriptive of her natural response in new situations. B is not true until later, or only sometimes.

Choose one statement in each pair. Put an X on the score sheet for your choice.

   A = A *is* more descriptive *than* B
   B = B *is* more descriptive *than* A
   N = neither *statement is descriptive*

1A. In a new situation, my first reactions are feelings about things. Only later do I become more objective and think things through.

1B. In a new situation, I first consider things. I may be aware of my feelings, but I almost always think before responding.

2A. I am naturally inventive. I develop brand-new and complete solutions to complex problems more quickly than I can develop relationships.

2B. I am naturally friendly. I develop relationships more quickly and easily than I can develop brand-new and complete solutions to complex problems.

3A. Typically, I do *not* make a decision quickly in new areas. I remain tentative in order to assess more information regardless of my feelings.

3B. Typically, I decide quickly in new areas and seldom reconsider the decision.

4A. My new decisions are a result of good logic that has pinpointed what's wrong. I'm not easily swayed from a simple, logical answer by feelings or intuitions.

4B. My new decisions result from "seeing" how to solve problems. I test mental pictures in ways I can't easily describe to reach two or three complete, *new* solutions.

Mark the score sheet with your choice.

Choose one statement in each pair. Put an X on the score sheet for your choice.

> A = A *is* more descriptive *than* B
> B = B *is* more descriptive *than* A
> N = neither *statement is descriptive*

5A. Although I can give an answer to a new problem, I am best at *working out and refining a plan* to solve it, including the necessary details.

5B. Although I can give an answer to a new problem, I am best at creating a *new direction* and not as skillful at thinking through the details of the plan.

6A. I am best at solving complex, tangible problems with simple, practical answers. I'm better at figuring out what needs to get done than in getting others to do it.

6B. I am best at solving complex people problems with feeling and insight. I'm best as part of a team or when I'm including others.

7A. In general, I react *before* I think. I may be aware of the facts, but my first reaction almost always reflects my feelings.

7B. In general, I react *after* I think over the facts. I may be aware of my feelings, but my first reaction almost always reflects facts, not emotions.

8A. I am naturally efficient. I reach conclusions quickly, especially in *new* areas.

8B. I am naturally thorough. I collect information in new areas to ensure accuracy before deciding.

9A. When I deal with an unfamiliar problem, I typically come up with new ways to apply what I know. The solution is practical and makes immediate sense.

9B. When I deal with an unfamiliar problem, I typically put contradictory information together to go *beyond* what is known. I then provide a general direction on how to solve it.

10A. At first, I am more aware of nonverbal reactions than the facts in a new situation.

10B. At first, I am more aware of facts in a new situation than the nonverbal reactions.

Mark the score sheet with your choice.

Choose one statement in each pair. Put an X on the score sheet for your choice.

$$A = A \text{ is more descriptive } than \text{ B}$$
$$B = B \text{ is more descriptive } than \text{ A}$$
$$N = \text{neither } statement \text{ is descriptive}$$

11A. Initially, my *new* ideas are so unusual or conceptual that people have a hard time supporting them. I can create a new direction regardless of their support.

11B. Initially, I want everyone to feel good about me and about my ideas. I am best creating a new direction when others support my ideas.

12A. I am best at coming up with new solutions that are practical and easily understood.

12B. I am best at coming up with new ideas that may be unclear at first, but essentially redefine the problem so solutions come next.

13A. I contribute most by methodically comparing a *new* problem to a past situation before setting goals.

13B. With a *new* problem, I contribute most by mentally seeing and testing several new solutions to establish an overview before setting goals.

14A. I am often concise, even abrupt, because I rarely notice or consider emotions. I get to the bottom line quickly.

14B. I take time because I *feel* others' feelings. I often notice or consider emotions to reach an agreement where everyone feels good about me as well as the idea.

15A. Since I immediately assess others' ideas, I am best at adding more rational solutions based on my expertise.

15B. Since I react spontaneously to my intuition about people's feelings, I am best at adding solutions based on my empathy for others.

16A. I am at my best inventing strategies and long-term directions unlike any I already knew about. It takes me longer to explain my ideas so that people get excited about them.

16B. I am at my best getting other people excited about possibilities for projects once they've been *defined*. It takes me longer to define strategies and long-term directions.

17A. I quickly form unemotional solutions to new situations without much study. It's typically all that's needed.

17B. I form thoughtful solutions to new situations by methodically assessing them first, then breaking them down into pieces for further study.

18A. With a new problem, I analyze what went wrong by carefully getting all the facts and comparing them to past or known right answers before trying to solve it.

18B. With a new problem, I must see and test several mental images that either solve the whole problem or change entirely how the problem is defined before trying to solve it.

Mark the score sheet with your choice.

THE BRAINSTYLE INVENTORY 1.42: SCORING SHEET

Record your responses from *The BrainStyle Inventory* on this sheet. For each item, put an X in the space next to your choice (A, B, or N).

When you have completed all 18 items, count the number of Xs you made in each column and record this number at the bottom of the page.

	Col 1	Col 2	Col 3	Col 4	
1.	___ B			___ A	___ N
2.			___ A	___ B	___ N
3.	___ A	___ B			___ N
4.		___ A	___ B		___ N
5.	___ A		___ B		___ N
6.		___ A		___ B	___ N
7.	___ B			___ A	___ N
8.	___ B	___ A			___ N
9.		___ A	___ B		___ N
10.		___ B		___ A	___ N
11.			___ A	___ B	___ N
12.		___ A	___ B		___ N
13.	___ A		___ B		___ N
14.		___ A		___ B	___ N
15.	___ A			___ B	___ N
16.			___ A	___ B	___ N
17.	___ B	___ A			___ N
18.	___ A		___ B		___ N

	Col 1	Col 2	Col 3	Col 4	N
Totals:	[ ]	[ ]	[ ]	[ ]	[ ]

The column with the largest total score should reflect your unique *brainstyle*. Turn to "Highest Score Interpretation for the BrainStyle Inventory" in Appendix B for an explanation of your highest score followed by answers to commonly asked questions about *brainstyles*.

3

The
Knower

"When you know about *BrainStyles*, you can be friends with
everyone."

Author's closing statement at a book signing

"Why would anyone want *that*?"

Immediate response by a woman Knower in the audience

THE KNOWER BRAINSTYLE: A SUMMARY

The gift of this brainstyle is to bring clarity and focus to a decision.
Being logical, measurable, and practical in solving tangible problems is
the arena a Knower can enjoy most in art, medicine, math, law, business, or the home. Structuring systems and making rules to get things
"fixed" is satisfying for people with this gift. "Flow" is easiest with
focus. A laser-like focus is a natural strength this brainstyle brings to
activities. Using challenging activities to solve problems means real
enjoyment for the Knower. Those in this brainstyle can be the most
independent and self-contained as they go about their daily business.

A Knower is:

- A person who accesses the upper left brain first, fastest and most strongly, giving this brainstyle an advantage in making logical, unemotional decisions or reaching clear conclusions quickly.
- A person who naturally sees structure, form, key pieces or elements, and the process that will focus the mess into something do-able, sorted, summarized to its main causes because of the way his brain uses mostly concrete information, without emotion, to get to the bottom line.
- A person who can see cause-and-effect relationships between things, actions and outcomes, symptoms and causes, broken parts of a thing and how to put them back together.
- One who wins by having and achieving things. Achievement is a prime motivator.
- One who can make something sound inevitable by pointing out the negative consequences for not following their plan.
- Knowers use information sparingly, do not tend to be socially chatty, but are verbal, articulate, and persuasive.
- Knowers rarely express strong feelings or sentimentality verbally or physically. Feelings are considered deeply held and private. Relationships can be entered into for a specific outcome, only later do loyalties develop.
- Guilt and regret about decisions do not seem to last as long or play as large a part for Knowers as for other brainstyles, who have more access to emotional centers in the right brain.

In the database of over 1,235 people observed and tested for brainstyles, we found 13 percent of them to be this left brainstyle. Of these, 32 percent are women, and 68 percent are men. (For further comparisons, see charts on pages 234 and 326.)

THE KNOWER AT TIME ZERO

At Time Zero the Knower is quickest at being definite and staying with a decision on a *new* subject. This left-brain response sorts incoming sensory information to a simple pattern, finds a "bottom line" or cause, and quickly evaluates and states a response with rapid-fire timing. *It's A or B.* Boom. After some time has elapsed, the right brain alters that pure left-brain response with feelings or awareness of others' reactions. But it doesn't alter it much.

At Time Zero the Knower doesn't spend much time with people explaining why, or dealing with reasons or needs. The Knower delivers an answer.

This is the Knower's *brainstyle strength*. He, or she, gets things moving. When properly deployed, the streamlined elegance of a *logical* response (*If A, then B*) to a new situation affords almost instant clarity and direction. This is vital for survival, with daily problems, and especially in business. The Knower can take complexities, simplify them, and nail them down to something do-able.

Sort Facts	▶	Focus on a Cause	▶	Solve the Problem

THE STORY OF TWO KNOWERS

Dick is writing a book. This book, he says, will make him an expert in his field, the top of the heap. The manuscript is due in three months. His contract says the book must be 216 pages in order to meet printing parameters. The topic of the book is the nonpunitive discipline system he has developed and has been teaching to companies over the past decade on *Discipline Without Punishment*. He teaches people in business how to take the revenge out of punishment of the bad guys so that problems are solved and there are better relations. Period. No pound of flesh. Even Dick admits this is hard to do sometimes when feelings run high. But that's because Dick perceives the world with the gifts of a Knower.

According to the dictionary, *to know* is *to perceive or understand clearly and with certainty; to have fixed in the mind or memory.* An apt description of what this brainstyle does with new information and the source for the brainstyle name.

He is a teacher and human resources consultant by profession. When I ask how he came up with his material, his answer, as well as the way he goes about what he does, reveals his strengths.

"I saw a problem in a manufacturing plant with the way people were being treated. I was called in because workers were sabotaging the product by writing obscene messages with markers on the final units. Management wanted to know what to do. So I figured it out." His solution is one in which people learn how to change *behavior* in a logical, measurable fashion (note: *not* change their *attitudes* or learn some vague *concepts*). He doesn't want to tell me about how he reached the answers. The path on the way to the goal is just not that interesting to him, so he may not really even recall all the steps. He really wants to present the results of his work and how his solution solves the problem. He shows me a flowchart where each behavioral symptom is listed and then diagrammed through specific actions to a resolution. It's clean. It's clear. It looks *flawless*. It's breathtakingly simple for the seemingly complex and mysterious dilemmas posed by humans at work. What relief his clients must feel to see someone with the answers!

To write his book, he arrives at his office at 5:30 A.M. every day for a month, and leaves about twelve hours later. He has organized his writing into daily goals of five thousand words, minimum, each day, having, of course, already computed words per page. He hands me a card with a column of figures. They are the number of words completed each day for the past week. Each number is greater than five thousand. The manuscript goes out one day before the deadline to the publisher and Dick leaves on a prescheduled vacation the next.

At fifty, Dick is a ruggedly handsome six feet plus, his blue eyes and gray hair quite distinguished with the navy suit and yellow tie he wears when teaching. He is not beyond wearing summer shorts when writing all day in his office, however. His office is a surprise, though, given that he is a logical juggernaut in his work. Personally decorated, the space is warm and plants lush and abundant. (He has solved the problem of raising those sensitive African violets, of course.) There are few clues to his personal life. One picture of his wife is on his desk to discreetly face him. Carpeting and art from countries where he's traveled give character; books and furniture give personality. He is, he says, very visual.

Knowers seem to enjoy visual beauty in the environment because their brain-based gifts don't include creating inner images in any quantity.

He is also, I observe, very tidy. There is no real clutter anywhere. Dick is attentive and makes a point of noticing personal things. "You look wonderful in that suit. The colors flatter you." He pays attention when you speak, laughs and comments on what you say. He writes about and teaches communications skills, I remember. He is a skillful communicator, which is not uncommon for those with his strengths. He can focus.

The magic occurs when a problem arises that needs fixing. I ask for advice. The dial goes way up on his Interest Meter and there is no more of the only-slightly-noticeable effort at answering other questions with his polite conversation. He pounces on my problem, like a duck on a June bug, as they say in the South. He is a problem-solving machine that loves the joy of diagnosing, sorting, evaluating causes, and nailing an answer. This time the answer is for me. He is helpful, clear, and to the point.

What imaginable problems could this organizational problem-pouncer possibly have in *his* job, I ask?

"I explain why a client needs my system. The client agrees. And then," Dick pauses and his face screws up with puzzlement as he recalls the incident, "to my utter amazement, the client says he's just not sure." Dick shakes his head in disbelief. He says that the more questions the client raises, the more persuasive he becomes. "My logic is irre*fut*-able!" Dick says. He admits that he cannot understand why his un-doubtedly clear A-then-B-then-C proposal could leave *any* stone—I daresay any *pebble*—unturned on the way to the inevitable decision to buy.

"People are *baffling*. Illogical." Dick admits defeat. He becomes intent once again when I suggest some new alternatives for handling his client, based on brainstyles. He openly admits that he could never have thought of an alternative approach "in a million years." He is excited. I am excited. I want to tell more. He's not interested. He doesn't want more information for a *possible problem,* or to just explore a new topic just out of curiosity as other brainstyles might. He is interested in things to *apply,* to solve problems—one problem at a time. And we'd just solved a problem. That was enough for now.

As we've talked, Dick's attention has been totally focused on our conversation. But after a topic is covered, there are few transitions or small talk. A restlessness and briskness surface. I become aware of the time. If there is not a specific point to be made or resolved, it is time to move on.

Dick is an excellent example of a mature Knower, confident of his abilities and articulate about what he can deliver. Why he got in the people-consulting business seems to be explained by his need to use his gifts: he loves to solve problems. What he likes about doing his work seems to be captured when he explains the difference between the kind of consulting I have done (team-building) and what he does: "It probably takes me a good deal longer to get a contract for work with a customer than it does for you. I get complete agreement and endorsement for my program from senior management before I do a single thing. They sign up for a very clear program that they agree to publicly endorse. So when I'm leading the seminar, and Joe doesn't

like the rules or what's being said, I don't have to 'facilitate' or negotiate with Joe. I can tell him that if he doesn't want to go along with
this program it's just fine with me, but he also doesn't have to work
there anymore either." Dick has control. The program has structure.
The answers are clear and the boundaries even clearer. You're in the
program or you're not. He gets results in a very focused, structured
way.

When you meet Peg, and as you learn more about Knowers, you'll
understand why this strong, direct, attractive lady seems just a bit
phony when being social, why she enjoys the company of men more
often than she does lunching with ladies. Actually, Peg often picks
women friends who take the task at hand seriously, from raising children or playing golf to talking politics. Peg and other Knower women
have gifts that go largely unappreciated because of the cool impression
they make initially—if you only look at the surface, that is. They are
also members of one of the smallest minorities around:* the female
Knower.

Peg is an artist and a very attractive brunette, with flawless skin,
brown eyes, and eyelashes that all Southern belles would envy. What
most of the ladies don't know is that she's also a cancer survivor who
has looked rather unflinchingly at life and death. Her response was to
take more control of her life with her natural strengths as a Knower.
She now works full-time at what she always enjoyed doing—painting
—and makes money from portraits in oils, including a recent commis-
sion for a prominent Washington, D.C., personality. Her "asser-
tiveness" is actually her ability to focus—on anything.

A former flight attendant, she left officework, first, because it was
boring, and second, because she couldn't stand the "politics" ("time
wasting") or the impositions on her own sense of how things ought
to be run. She loved the efficiency, the opportunities for problem-
solving when "flying thirty-five thousand feet up in the air in a box
with four hundred angry people." (I note her delight in working with
"angry" people—a nightmare for other brainstyles.) It was also a very
practical solution to the problem of being stuck in a small, rural home-
town in Texas. The clincher: "I was in control and I *loved* it." Her

---

* Only the female Conceptor population is a smaller group.

view of the job most assuredly differs from that of the majority of her colleagues.

The family "joke," from the time that Peg was three years old, is that Peg is a "snob." Even Peg's sister has always maintained that Peg is "cold." Yet her sister calls her every time she has a personal problem and admits how valuable Peg's advice has been. She admires Peg a great deal, and sees Peg as smarter and better able to solve problems than she can. Peg was aware from childhood that her sister valued her own opinion too little, and Peg's too much. The death of their mother at age forty-six of cancer forced them together in their grief, and they are very close now.

Peg tells how she took charge, "out of necessity," of her father after the funeral. "I didn't have time to feel. Dad was in debt. And he was so shattered by mother's death that he wasn't good for much. He'd moved out into the country all by himself. We always understood each other, so I could talk to him very straight. I went out there and said, 'What are you going to do, die out here? You're forty-eight years old. You've got to move back to town.' I took over his mortgage payments so he could pay off his debts. It took a year. I postponed my grief. The day I sent him the last check and got the title to the house—the home they'd always lived in together—I went to my apartment and started crying. I cried every night for several months."

Logic first, feelings second. What for others would take enormous discipline and effort was just what had to be done for Peg, the Knower.

Peg privately thinks that she is a "rotten mother." Why? Because all the other mothers she knows are more "feminine," entertain and socialize more, show and talk about their feelings more than she does. They nurture. They're warm. They call their husbands when the plumbing fails and call friends to discuss problems—their own and others'. But Peg doesn't. "As a young girl I was never in trouble like my sister and brother. They always were doing things to stir things up and get a licking. I just wasn't willing to do those things. I didn't *enjoy* all the storms and trauma." Peg pauses briefly and gives me a level gaze. "Some people can't stand the calm. They don't seem to feel *alive* if there's not some thunder. My brother could screw up any chore there was and create the biggest problems for my dad. And then he could split your sides telling you a story about it. I think he relished the excitement."

Peg's husband is her "rock," but in a lot of ways drives her crazy. He loves seven-course meals, lingering over wine. She prefers fast food, or at least a quick and easy meal: heat it, eat it, and go. He keeps closetsful of newspaper clippings, she hates to save anything. "You can always call Information," she laughs. He takes forever to address Christmas cards to make sure that all the children's names are there and the card is personalized; Peg would just as soon have prestamped cards and address them "M/M Smith *and family*."

Peg has never called her husband at work with a problem. She doesn't like going out to lunch with the girls. She isn't big on entertaining. She doesn't like "chitchat." She gets the job done. As an artist, she has taken what was an interesting hobby and made it into a profitable vocation. She took some art classes, but found that many teachers tried to teach her to paint in a way that was "bor-ring" to her. When I asked her what was so boring, she explained, "They want you to do endless sketches, color charts, black and white studies, or put your feelings on canvas. I just couldn't relate to that. I don't paint feelings. I don't need a lot of time to sketch and plan and think about a painting. I enjoy painting real things, still lifes, or portraits that have a right way and a wrong way; and *then* incorporate mood and drama. The bottle is *there,* not there. You can see it. You can get it exactly." Since she learned about what being a Knower involves, she says it's a lot easier to accept the fact that her focus and literal, realistic scenes are just as much art as the abstracts. "My work has gotten a lot better because I'm freed up to do what I do best. And sales are better than ever!" she exults, chuckling at her own delight in the "bottom line" that is so typical of her brainstyle. She's also more understanding of the different approaches her students take to painting. ("But I'm *still* not very patient," Peg admits. "I just go to something else while they take forever to plan out their drawing.")

Peg is different from America's Model Woman. Not less sexy. Not less attractive. More controlled and efficient. She has, for example, a left-brained approach to being a friend. I explained that it was difficult to get to interview a Knower for this book. Knowers don't seem to want to give an interview in order to help other people or to contribute to mankind's understanding. "No they won't," Peg says. "It's inefficient. Time-wasting. There's got to be something useful in it for them." "So why are you giving up your precious lunch time and changing out of your paint-grubbies to give me this interview?" I asked. A perfectly legitimate question for Peg. Probably a bit indelicate for some other brainstyles. "Because it's my way of being a friend. I respect you and what you're doing. I don't make phone calls or send cards, but I know this is important for you, and so I'll do it," she says, in a matter-of-fact, so-there-you-have-it tone of voice. No sentimentality, but *just* as touching. You get the point: she gives what's important to ME, not what's important to *her.* I don't know other people (or, to be more accurate, other *brainstyles*) who do things with quite as much practicality. Or impact. Peg leads one to conclude that for a Knower the ultimate gift is one that money can't buy, the gift of self. Personal time is the sacrifice hardest to give for this brainstyle.

Think about it. How many zillions of gifts have you received that reflected more of the giver's tastes than your own? How many thoughtful expressions of caring have you sent or received that were for no real reason at all? Hallmark executives get down on their knees and kiss the earth in gratitude that Knowers are not the majority of Americans, because they don't think this way.

When Knower husbands give their time for someone else's inexplicable goals, it is the ultimate gift. One man told me that after he learned more about how his wife thought, he understood why she a) loved to go shopping and b) couldn't make up her mind. To him, her seemingly endless trek from store to store looking for the perfect gift that she could only pick out with some mysterious voodoo ("I'll know it when I see it") was painful at best. "But now I've decided to give her that time because I know how important it is to her. I had to just give up *my* way of getting the job done. I could've taken the first thing we found. But it's a way to spend time together and we don't have that much time during the week."

THE INVISIBLE (FOR MOST) SIDE OF THE KNOWER

So is this the *real* Tough Cookie in our midst?

Yes. If you listen only to their conversation.

Peg tells me of a family portrait she has just completed in oils. Three months after she was commissioned, the family's beautiful teenage daughter was killed in a car accident. The parents, in their grief, began to split apart; the remaining two younger brothers were numbly helpless as their family dissolved around them. The family itself was in real danger of dying. Peg created the painting from individual photographs. She then wrote the following letter to accompany the portrait:

Dear Rob, Marilyn, Robbie and Kim,

First I would like to say thank you for the trust and confidence you have placed in me to produce your family portrait. Each of you possess a special beauty which made my work even more of a pleasure.

Obviously by painting this portrait, we have placed Betty forever in your family in a physical way, just as she will forever be in your hearts and minds. But there is more symbolism in this painting which I will offer as an explanation of why I chose the final composition.

I placed Betty in the center of the grouping for many reasons. She is the only daughter. She is the middle child. I always thought of her as the center of your family unit, touching each of you in a different, special way. Technically, her personal dramatic coloration and beauty require her to be centered, just as the most dramatic and beautiful flower is always placed in the center of a bouquet.

Rob and Marilyn, I took the liberty of painting you in Betty's embrace. [Betty is standing behind her parents with one hand touching the outside shoulder of each. In one hand she also holds a pink rose.] This brings her into the painting as an active and integral part of our group the day we did this sitting. If she had been there with us, this is what she would have done; embracing you physically then, just as she embraces you spiritually now. This action also symbolizes the two of you as the core of her life; the source of her existence, the source of her sustenance. The three of you form a triangle of strength. Her embrace holds you firmly together, urging you to cling to each other, now and always, for your source of strength.

It is my hope that when you view this painting through the years, you will feel not so much the pain that your beautiful Betty is gone from your bouquet; but rather the joy that she bloomed in your garden.

With deepest affection, Peg

Marilyn, the grief-stricken mother, framed the letter and put it next to the painting. Peg's letter, direct and factual, easily becomes a personal and spiritual message that reveals an inner sensitivity and deep understanding of people that Peg's everyday demeanor may not. I found it very moving.

Some weeks before the next Christmas, Peg's doorbell rang. Marilyn, in a poetic gesture of her own, sent a symbol of the healing that had taken place for her family. The florist delivered a dozen pink roses with a card that said only "With love, Betty."

Peg tells me the family has moved, and are closer now as a foursome than ever before. The portrait of the five is at the center of the home.

Logic put into personal service is profound.

There is the *least* understanding and sympathy for this brainstyle. This may be partly true because they are so few in number. It is also true because their *non*-strengths—warm, open, and spontaneous relationships—are the coin of the realm to be popular. Popularity is not on the Top Ten for the Knower.

THE STRENGTHS

Whether Knowers are entrepreneurs and turnaround specialists, engineers, or professional artists, their primary gift is in making very clear, unemotional, factual decisions—usually about how to "win" the sale or the argument first and turn to relationships or feelings later, and to a lesser degree than those who can access their right brains more easily. They do not get passionate about their decisions. They are just certain, factual, and logical, even from the time that they were kids. First comes the logic, then the quick analysis, usually in a very impersonal way—*even about very personal subjects.* As Peg says about her portraits and realistic paintings, "When I start my day, I have to get the business out of the way first, then I can have fun painting. It's no good if you never get paid—even though I don't always [get paid]. I get involved with the people side *later.*"

One Knower twice tried running retail businesses that were dependent on people and their selling skills; he went bankrupt both times. An interesting fit occurred for this Knower when he could leverage his ability to streamline systems in a field where complexity can drown you. He is now providing computer-based financial collection services to the health care field. Another interesting aspect of this business: collecting debts is onerous work for people who hate confrontation. The Knowers' *gift* is confrontation—*directly facing* an issue or problem. When someone can streamline a system to get the job done *and* the business comes right out of the founder's strengths, the chances for success are enormously improved. In the case of this Knower, his staff has increased from five to twenty-two in three years with profits to match.

In a discussion with industrial psychologist James Hörger,[1] who had spent years interviewing successful entrepreneurs, I found his profile for those who made it successfully through the first five years of start-up ventures to be about a 90 percent match with the Knower brainstyle. The problems he'd seen these Start-Up Experts have? Staying on after the start-up phase, and playing by Other People's Rules. The ends justify the means more often for the goal-driven Knower. Those who have not moved beyond their own need for control or for the personal thrill of victory to the needs of others, cannot seem to get over the hurdle of having all the answers themselves. No enterprise is a One-Man Show.

Knowers rarely choose careers where forming close personal relationships is critical to success (in their view). Relating to others is most often a task with an end in mind. When "relating" means to sell, to negotiate, or to manage, okay. When relating means to build a relationship for its own sake, not okay. A *personal network* for Knowers means primarily a network of business contacts. Knowers can be natural power politicians when they focus on it. The ones to beat. The Power Brokers. Climbing a career ladder = solving problems for people. Why not claim the rewards?

Peg rounds out the real reason for her career choices, "What's most important for me is to do what I enjoy doing. I don't think Knowers will do what they hate. There's no amount of money available to pay you to do something just for the esteem thing. I see other brainstyles keep after something that may not be working for them just for the glamour or to get esteem from their job. I couldn't do that. I *wouldn't.* No way." Career choices seem to rise from the inner confidence in the Knower's problem-solving abilities. "Whatever comes up, I know I'll handle it," says Peg. "And what if you can't?" I wonder. Peg explains, "Then I say, 'I tried my best, I used the data I had at the time. It's time to move on. It's over.' "

SELF-ESTEEM AND SELF-CONFIDENCE

Pat Pearson, Dallas psychologist and author, makes a distinction between *self-esteem* and *self-confidence* that is useful here. She defines self-esteem as caring about who you *are,* unconditionally, no matter what you do. Self-confidence, on the other hand, occurs when you know you are good at what you do; you have expertise and respect yourself for it. The right brain is aware of the former, the left brain the latter. Self-esteem does not predict self-confidence, however. For instance, we've all met successful or wealthy people who don't like themselves very much but know they are very good at what they do.

For a Knower, only self-confidence makes sense. Self-esteem? It's vague. It's not on their screen. *Other* brainstyles seem to know what this means, after all, they talk about their feelings, get upset, and discuss "self-esteem" all the time, while the Knower looks at life as a place to either solve a problem or not, to get things done or not get things done. Life is that much simpler, more provable, and has less fuss.

Peg doesn't go to anyone else for advice about how to solve problems, nor does she see her painting as a source of self-esteem. "I don't get up every day and check my happiness index: Am I happy? Am I not happy? I think *other* brainstyles do this, but it just doesn't compute for me," Peg observed. Peg feels secure because she can solve problems that come up without a fuss.

Peg continues, "My Conciliator son asks me a lot, 'Didn't you ever worry about this? Didn't you ever worry about that? How did you know what you wanted to do?' I told him, 'Look, I was a kid growing up in the country. I just knew I didn't want to be there. So I left. I made a change. If there's something I don't like, if I have to put up with it, I will as long as I have to—until I find a way to change it. I'm just going to do what I do. If there's a cliff out there, I'm either going to skinny down it, go around it, or jump off it, but I'm not going to worry about it. Whatever's there, I'll handle it. And it'll be okay.' "

The experience of self-esteem is not a left-brained experience. You either do things or you don't, solve problems or you don't. The worry and doubts and regrets of the right-brained are foreign to those whose lives are dominated by the logical left and who do not have as much access to the information processed by the right half of the brain. Perhaps if the Conciliators who do so would stop labeling their natural, feeling way of processing events *"a crisis in self-esteem,"* they could reach the same level of acceptance I heard in Peg's explanation of how she goes through life. Peg doesn't spend a lot of time labeling *herself.*

Knowers rate themselves lowest of the four brainstyles on a scale that measures Managing the Impression You Make on Others. That is to say, the world of *taking things personally* is rather mysterious to this brainstyle. So when they say something that to the other three brainstyles is "offensive" or "obnoxious," you can bet that most of the time it was not intended to be so. Knowers are just being factual. It's no wonder that many Knowers see *other* people as the ones with the interpersonal problems, with all the reactions and introspections and analyses. As one older male Knower put it, "When someone told me that I was being obnoxious, I always saw it as *their* problem."

COMMUNICATIONS. Get to the point. Out with it. Nail it. Move on. *Don't just talk about it.*

Knowers draw from the part of the brain that excels at speech. Focused, clear speech is the gift, and that speech is most often used to decide and tell rather than ask and explain. *Need-to-know must* be a phrase that was thought of by someone with the Knower brainstyle. Certainly military in origin, information that gets shared on a need-to-know basis is information that is controlled. And if the focused, structured Knowers were in charge, all which appears personal, blabby, detailed, circumlocutious, too abstract, or repetitive would *not* be needed and no one would ever have to know the extraneous, extra, time-consuming, long way around to get to the point. And that includes this paragraph and anything like it.

Remember the old saying? *Clarity is power.*

Knowers hate ambiguity and excel at the kinds of things that require precision like math, mechanics, law, diagnostic medicine, accounting, systems (computer and otherwise), and business logic, rather than handling vague and abstract tasks like diplomacy or management. As consultants and small business owners, Knowers are best giving answers and directing the action. Over the long run, most have a tough time working for others and do very well working on their own. From art to electrical engineering to business start-ups, a Knower will condense, structure, and focus. Peg says, "The hardest part of a painting for me is the background. It's so vague. I hate doing them." Peg, a mother of two boys who is primarily a homemaker, has always managed the home finances and was the natural choice in her family for executor of her mother's will.

INTUITION. Perhaps you're surprised to see this word associated with this brainstyle. Knower readers are probably smiling rather smugly. Knowers are most likely to have an aptitude in foresight (see Appendix A). Coupled with a moderate ability to generate ideas, Knowers often predict future outcomes for a project. When experienced, the mature Knower can spot trends quickly, perform analysis at lightning speed, and make that little leap into *what must be.* "Decisions are by nature predictive," says Philip Goldberg, author of an enlightening text called *The Intuitive Edge* (see more information on intuition in the next chapter). And who makes decisions faster than the Knower? That there is an intuitive or illogical component to the conclusion after the facts have been assayed is commonly understood by most Knowers.

Goldberg names six types of intuition. At least two of them would seem to be the playground for those with fast logic: *prediction* and *discovery.* Prediction is an extrapolation from the facts that continues to venture out into the unknown, to include the unexplained feeling or illogical leap. "At the very least, a forecaster has to use intuition in gathering and interpreting data and in deciding which unusual future events might influence the outcome. Hence in virtually every prediction there is always some intuitive component."[2] Knowers who *just know* can tell the difference between times when they want to have the right answer (from their left-brained logic) and times when they are making a genuine prediction about the future, which includes the unknown. Keeping track of hits and misses will develop this ability. Leaving the world of the nitty and the gritty to veer into the oncoming traffic of maybes and might happens is a fine line we've all crossed. However, where others guess, Knowers easily get their story and stick to it. The Knower can sound persuasively sure at these times, but is gambling his personal credibility if he's wrong.

The intuitive process called "discovery" is "the sudden leap to understanding, the spark of insight, the precipitous penetration to the truth"[3] that comes *after* lengthy analysis. Answers to specific problems after hard, rational, and solitary work can produce incremental *ah has!* that finally synthesize all the preceding chaos into a new solution. Goldberg cites examples of how the scientists who discovered DNA did so in the midst of arduous, logical thought. The breakthrough was generated by review and analysis in the left brain, then repeated from slightly different views to track down the answer. Intuitive process can "reveal verifiable facts," as Goldberg says, and the Knower's gifts certainly fit the bill.

▼

THE KNOWER

- Diagnoses the cause
- Sorts the facts
- Analyzes

- Decides
- Concludes on A or B
- Simplifies
- Solves

- Sets up structured answers
- Runs the plan
- Confronts the problems

- Simplifies and resolves chaos
- Starts a business
- Is a communicator
- Directs the plan

TIME ZERO ▶ SOON AFTER ▶ WITH PRACTICE ▶ EXPERT

- Knowers are least apt to change their mind at Time Zero and so can come to a rapid, factual, unemotional decision. Later the right brain provides awareness of feelings and intuition and the impact their decision may have on others. *Influence them early; talk about the goals.*
- The Knower decides or concludes rapidly, based on facts, about practical, usually tangible things.
- The Knower's primary strength is seeing cause-effect relationships between unrelated things, allowing them to figure out solutions to complex and difficult problems.
- Knowers are excellent at directly addressing issues in order to reach a desired end with the least amount of emotion, worry, or regret.
- Knowers are clear and logical communicators. They do best with structure and not as well with people.
- Knowers look for opportunities to:
  - be in control
  - achieve by solving practical problems
  - work independently
  - make things simple and efficient
  - create new solutions that make immediate sense
  - see it and tell it "like it is"

▲

NON-STRENGTHS BRING CHALLENGES FOR THE KNOWER

PEOPLE. Illogical, irrational, and emotional people and events are challenges for this brainstyle. The strengths mandate a direct, straight-line approach. Simplicity in style often gets interpreted as brash, rude, or aggressive.

How *does* a left-brained person operate in a forest of touchy-feely right-brainstyles?

As one woman confides, "The first year I dated [a Knower], I cried at about half the things he said to me. He was so . . . so *brutal.*" She learned about brainstyles. "I had a revelation. I understood how he cared *by giving me direction,* solving my problems when I asked, and helping me anytime I needed him. He just didn't say things like *I wanted him to.* Then we got engaged."

The mental process of sorting facts to focus on a single, most likely cause sounds exactly like BLAME to the other brainstyles who keep their options open and attend to How Things Proceed. "The thing that frustrates me more than anything else," grinds out a Knower executive through clenched teeth, "is people who cannot stand to define the problem by telling the Truth." The *Truth*? "Either he did it or he didn't. Either he's smart enough or he isn't. When you get to the real nut of it—*then* you can go about finding an answer that'll solve the real problem," he says forcefully, intensely.

AMBIGUITY. Ambiguity drives a Knower nuts. Working or living around a lot of chaos without being able to fix it, organize it, or get someone else to take care of it is as irritating as listening to the sound of fingernails being dragged across a blackboard. Knowers can feel compelled to take charge.

DIPLOMACY. SUBTLETY. People who get emotional or vague are in some ways scary or painful for the Knower. They can dismiss all the fuss by calling right-brainers "weak." Knowers keep their distance and, as a result, get labeled *cold* and *insensitive.* Situations requiring great delicacy, sensitivity to nuance, and awareness of subtle play between people—negotiating with the Japanese comes to mind—would be the least favorite assignment for the results-oriented bull in a china shop that a Knower can be. Knowers are better at persuading, going for a goal rather than massaging the process.

OPTIMISM. Considering the *upside* (as opposed to the downside) comes second for the Knower, if at all. Knowers drive the optimistic right-brainers nuts with their so-called negative outlook. At least the Knower's assessment of what can go wrong and the risks attached sound negative to their opposite brainstyles, who pride themselves on their sunny view of possibilities. The Knower's strength is drawn from the factual, structured left side of the brain. Optimism comes from the imaginative right side.

CREATIVITY. "Thinking out of the box" is a challenge for this brainstyle when it means to think in *abstract* or *feeling* terms. When it means thinking of new ways to *do* something or to *use* something, then a Knower can use their own special problem-solving ability to come up with eight new uses for the old brand of soap. They can Reinvent the Corporation, restructure, remodel, and redirect the overblown, outworn, and sloppy to be new, efficient, and useful. Others feel free to go into unknown territory after talking with a Knower who outlines the issues, sets up a plan, and addresses all the potential problems in the future to get somewhere new. Knowers *innovate.* They come up with new applications and synergies for known ideas or things. Creative play, random associations, and open-ended explorations are too loose and unformed, unreal, and purposeless for this brainstyle.

PATIENCE. This is often a challenge for this brainstyle when they see or think of the obvious answer and everyone else is mulling over the information, the relationships, the implications, the possibilities. *Let's get going!* could be the motto of the Conciliator, who has a similar, quick, impatient response to get started; *Just do it* the motto of the Knower. These two brainstyles can look alike, but their focus—and contributions—are quite different. (That's why, dear reader, you need to read about *all four* brainstyles.)

A prime motivator for each of us is to employ our strengths in our daily lives. Look for underlying strengths as a cause for Knower behavior rather than digging out the old cliché analysis *It's a need to control* to explain Why She's So Bossy. You'll be opening a gold mine of direction, focus, and unemotional advice. If it's off target, you'll see better what *not* to do.

TO SUMMARIZE THE NON-STRENGTHS OF THE KNOWER

Quick or strong feelings. "Multitasking," or doing several things at once. Making relationships with many; being tolerant and accepting, open-ended and nonjudgmental, diplomatic, subtle, tactful. Dealing well with ambiguous or ill-defined situations where there is no clear structure and no one in charge, no rules to follow. Being optimistic. Using random or illogical associations to create new, "out-of-the-box" solutions. Patience.

Knowers Need Other BrainStyles

Knowers need the Deliberator in order to:

- assess the plan to see what's been overlooked
- present ideas diplomatically, thoroughly, patiently
- bring in the rules and precedents
- build a consensus of ideas, gathering information and support
- steady things, ensure continuity, bring in new information, and put personal plans into action *(See Chapter Six)*

Knowers need the Conceptor in order to:

- create a winning future; they'll see things differently and give a new framework for systems and solutions
- be passionate persuaders, excellent at introducing why change can benefit the whole person, system, family, etc.
- review communications for impact on people (Conciliators can be helpful here too) *(See Chapter Five)*

Knowers need the Conciliator in order to:

- get people involved and excited about the idea or plan; they can add personal meaning to the factual necessities; they'll be strong public relations support
- help see the personal, social, or political implications of the plan
- resist the idea because of their own personal interest; talk about how they see things, thereby keeping "communications" open with others *(See Chapter Four)*

DECISION-MAKING

Confronted with a new and unanticipated situation, the Knower has a formidable advantage in being quick, decisive, and to the point. Since language, quick analysis, as well as deductive logic are the strengths from which they draw without having to take illogical and random feelings into account, the delivery has a certain punch. In verbal battles, Knowers tend to "win."

Think about it. When do you hesitate to voice an opinion? When you think you might hurt someone else's feelings? Create conflict? Be wrong? You can complain all day long about a Knower's decision and it won't affect him in the slightest because he is unencumbered by right-brain restraints in new situations. The response comes out automatically without emotional baggage to slow it down. This facility puts the Knower in control and often keeps him there—the first and most conclusive answer most often rules the day, especially in a time crunch. This is the gift of the left brain: to sort, to judge, to organize.

Reactions to this brainstyle for those with different brainstyle timing can be to feel defensive, on edge, "slow," or just plain inept around all that decisiveness. This is the pitfall of looking only at *superficial* behavior and not at the underlying brainstyle. Learn to value the timing of your *own* brainstyle as much as any other and to eliminate the comparisons you may feel the urge to make. (Read about how a Conciliator did just that in the next chapter.)

BrainStyle Clue:

Knowers get into trouble expecting others to make decisions as quickly as they do. Still, don't ask a Knower to "be patient." Influence him early. Spend time on the bottom-line result (goal) you're after. Tell it; sell it. It must be logical. Once the decision is made, it's made.

For the Knower, results appear *before* the process or the people involved. The Knower's formula for doing business is simple: See the problem. Identify the cause (fix the blame). Define the answer. Make a plan. Remove the barriers. Get it done *or preferably have* it done.

Most of us have a problem with step two. To fix blame is personal and antagonistic. To the Knower, it's merely a vital step in problem-solving. It's Getting Real.

The Knower can be decisive, take action, take control, and drive toward a clearly defined goal faster than any other brainstyle. Why? Because reaching a goal requires a series of decisions, and at each juncture the Knower reacts decisively. The clarity and speed of the left-brain computer at each Time Zero along the way processes mainly facts and data, undisturbed by feelings and imaginative detours. This brainstyle gets where it sets out to go. The key is that the Time Zero response is the *definitive* one for the Knower—more so than for any other brainstyle.

Case in point: A good example of a Knower using his strengths came from a Knower salesman. A customer was describing his relationship with the Knower: "I got so mad at him, it wasn't funny. I told him his product was the worst I'd ever used, he was the most obnoxious sales guy I'd ever dealt with, and when that didn't faze him, I threw him out. But he kept coming back. My tirades didn't seem to bother him. It was incredible. He never moved off the goal. He took all the abuse I could muster and never reacted. No other salesman would have— *could* have—stood it. He just kept coming back and telling me how he was fixing our problems. And darned if I didn't give him back the business."

The lack of feeling in an emotional situation was the Knower's strength. His structure of the situation was to solve the problems and get to the goal. He "won" (as a Knower would say).

CONFLICT

Knowers, by definition, are absolutely clear on their goals: they want control; they want results. They appear inflexible. They often are, but only because they have personally worked through the problem so logically that to them there is no other plausible way to achieve the goal in question. And so, once they have committed to an idea, they will use their powerful logic to argue their view. Such a defense is not "confrontation" to the Knower. A critical point to know about this brainstyle is that they respect people who respond directly. The eyeball-to-eyeball presentation of your case is what they desire and you don't have to think like a Knower to do this. Just be direct with information. Often, they will stop and listen. They will attend to an approach that is as straight from the shoulder as is their own. The Knower calls it being *direct;* at least two other brainstyles call it "steamrolling." The only problem is the *interpretation* ("steamrolling") attached to the behavior by a different brainstyle.

A division president of a major airline is a Knower. He described meetings with his boss in which exchanges were heated. In one such meeting, his volatile boss threw a wristwatch against the wall. The Knower smiled while recalling the episode and said, "Everyone else ducked, looked at their shoes, or got up and left. I didn't mind. I just looked up and said, 'Good, is it time to start the meeting now?' " There was nothing scary in the outburst or his confrontation to the Knower. He had already decided the wristwatch thrower was a) not serious, or b) not a threat. When this brainstyle has decided something, they are gifted at not allowing emotions to influence them.

BrainStyle Clue:

Knowers rarely get into "conflicts" or "attack" others. These are the perceptions of other brainstyles. Knowers are direct. They use left-brain language, which measures and evaluates. To discuss an emotional subject with a Knower, rehearse it so it is not so personal for you.

The Knower comes to the table with logic, judgments, and facts so tightly packed around an argument that there seems to be no soft spot left for negotiation. Through reading or interviewing others, she builds arsenals of facts selected to make the best argument possible—a winner. Often for the Knower it is only win or lose, right or wrong —because the left brain operates this way. Indeed, the brainstyles-illiterate Knowers may evaluate right-brain activities, such as consensus and compromise, as losing. In fact, without some of the latter no plan gets completely implemented.

By not recognizing that "being right" so fast means literally *interfering* with the timing of other brainstyles at Time Zero, the Knower misses opportunities to influence effectively. Other brainstyles need time to process, react, or listen. This most basic interaction is defined by brainstyle, *not* "intelligence."

> *BrainStyle Clue:*
> There is only one turf on which to engage in battle with a Knower: the goals.
> As long as you try to fight on details, you can't win. The Knower will get
> locked in. Change the arena and move the discussion to the big picture or
> desired result.

AT WORK: MANAGEMENT

The Knower may quickly reach the top management team. Why? Because he is able to make his views sound *inevitable* in the left-brained, measurable world of business. The Knower can be indispensable. He is a forceful negotiator who uses a solid line of logical details to defend his vision and its monetary value. As long as doing business equals getting results, the smart Knower can climb swiftly up the career ladder.

Vision and creativity for this brainstyle can be defined very differently than for those with other brainstyles. It should be apparent by now that the leap into the future for the Knower will be a more practical move than for most of the rest of the group. By collecting disjointed facts or examples, the hard-charging Knower can convert a synthesis of information into a fairly rapid number of future possibilities. The thing that characterizes the Knower's vision and distinguishes it from the Conceptor's, for instance, is that there is a consistent *practical* theme to future solutions. Right or wrong, the vision is one that applies existing technology or current ideas in ways that *make sense,* apply what is known for *use* by someone, and *minimize risk*. Ideas are new, and they are usually specific. *Brainstorming* for a Knower will be tossing out ingenious new ways to solve old problems in the future— an invaluable resource for any enterprise that wants to move forward. In contrast, the visionary Conceptor may preach future breakthroughs that won't sound as workable, be a great deal more risky, with a plan that is initially vague and not nearly as clear or rational.

Management systems (as in Management by Objectives) that value and reward *results first* promote this brainstyle. Unfortunately this gives the Knower no real preparation for management, which requires skill in the Knower's *non-strength:* dealing with people and their irrational, nonlinear emotions.

Knowers who include people in the plan have a better chance of having plans implemented. They will not naturally do so. "Relationships take tremendous effort," says the Knower. And when your efforts are naturally focused on the task at hand, you do not have the time to be a friend. Relationships have a purpose—just because everything has a purpose for a Knower. More often than not, they do not have the need for a friend just to have a friend, even though they can *be* a great friend—the one you call when you need something. Several Knowers interviewed had stories of wild parties in their youth, when being a friend meant acting crazy, often as a ringleader in some contest involving booze and rule-breaking of some sort. They do not deal with people by "empathizing" or "understanding" in the way that other brainstyles do. As one Knower recalled, "I've learned to call in the 'sweepers'—they clean up after I've put my foot in my mouth. They listen and talk nice and I keep my mouth shut." This Knower knew he couldn't pretend to do something he wasn't good at.

Knowers help others see where they want to go. They challenge plans—in words others say can come across "like a hammer." Hurt feelings can result for those who focus on the words. Knowers get past the right brain—into focus with the facts, with organization, and with words to make it happen. They demand *action* in service of a *goal*. "I'm willing to be screamed at. It doesn't bother me, and I'm never afraid," says the turnaround specialist who first fires former employees before restaffing in the new image.

The Knower gives unquestioned loyalty and support to his subordinates *after making an initial decision that they are on his team.* Then he must leave them to do their best, ask for results, and hold their feet to the fire on meeting targets. "Once you get through the bark, the guy's a 'softie' " is the kind of comment made about Knowers on many occasions. In fact, Knowers see themselves as tenderhearted and most often misunderstood as "tough," when in fact they care deeply and are just trying to bring logic to a messy situation without all the extra emotion of the Conciliator or the extra steps of the Deliberator.

When the Knower supports *your* goals, he is a powerful ally. If he has another agenda, watch out. He will go to the mat for a goal of his own. This brainstyle is a focused, conclusive one.

Often, the Knower makes a better consultant or expert (nonmanager) than manager. Dealing with people by providing direction is most natural; this brainstyle is best equipped to provide inputs that are logical and lend themselves to the laws of thermodynamics. As a result, the Knower makes the ideal turnaround officer. He is the one who can come into a troubled company, review the plan, separate the wheat, fire the chaff, and come out with a fresh loaf. Then he may need to move on to another "field," where gifts for swift decisions will be appreciated. Once the chaos is stabilized with logic and a firm hand, the resulting equilibrium will require different strengths. Drawing from other brainstyles is a must for daily management when the Knower cannot move on.

DELEGATION

The Knower sees what needs to be done but has a hard time getting people to do it. The gift of the pure left-brain response is that she who possesses it can cut to the core and figure out what needs to be *done* faster than anybody else. But that does not thereby make her a consensus-builder. Basically, the Knower doesn't naturally trust people who are slower to understand what (in the Knower's perception) the job involves. As the Knower might judge, the Conciliator is wishy-washy, the Deliberator slow and indecisive, the Conceptor off-the-wall. Another Knower is, as often as not, just wrong.

The danger lies in the Knower's trying to sell the whole package at Time Zero. Other brainstyles cannot assimilate it at the beginning. *Human interactions require timing and that timing must be based on their brainstyles.*

Because Knowers, like all other brainstyles, give trust to those they are comfortable with and because they are comfortable only with a fraction of those with their own brainstyle, they do not trust many people, hence do not delegate well. Many say they never understood that others *thought* differently, they just assumed the others weren't very competent. Moreover, the act of delegation, which requires both trust *and* release of control, is doubly classified as a *non-strength*—albeit a skill basic to managing people and running a company. True, a Knower will take charge faster than any other brainstyle (remember Secretary of State and former General Alexander Haig's famous statement: "I'm in charge here," which came *too* quickly after President Reagan's attempted assassination?). He structures. He orders. He tells you what to do. But *telling* is not the same thing as delegating.

The Knower does not naturally delegate well. Why? Delegation involves giving another person both authority and responsibility. It means giving someone else *control*. Delegating starts with the words "You be in charge of . . ." It shouldn't be confused with an assignment, which includes no authority and possibly only a little responsibility. An assignment starts with the words "You do . . ."

For the young Knower, limited skill at delegating creates few problems. Traveling fast and alone means traveling light. But as she is promoted, there is more to attend to than the systems she has devised and the goals she's after. Typically, the high-ranking Knower can assign the work on a project to others, with assessments along the way, until the time of the final reckoning. The question is whether the Knower ever releases control. Developing others' strengths is the Knower's weak suit. As a result, others in the organization fulfill the Knower's prophecy: they really *can't* do it as well.

Peg tells of how she successfully "delegated" responsibilities at home to her two sons: when she determined they were old enough, she presented them with challenging assignments to allow them to overcome their fears and demonstrate their own competence to themselves. One son had not ridden his bike beyond his own block. Peg thought he needed a "boost from the nest." Peg told him they needed some things from the store—including a treat for himself—and asked him to take his bike to get them. "He looked at me with eyes as big as saucers and said that it was a 'long way.' I just told him I trusted him to make it." Her son told her later he was "quite scared" but figured if she'd asked him to do it, he could. Now in his twenties, he says his mother continually gave him a push beyond what he thought he could do himself.

Knowers provide a learning climate by teaching what they know best: how to solve problems. They do not necessarily provide all the explanations and right-brained comforts to go along with the challenges. The benefits are no less substantial.

BrainStyle Clue:

A Knower lives to make ideas real—to see the results—in systems and with people. The drive from the left brain propels the Knower to clear a path for the shortest distance between start and finish. Ensure that the Knower's agenda includes a broader vision and the values that demand all contribute as a team.

The Knower is a natural leader, but rarely a "popular" one. The brainstyle commands respect, not adoration.

Using natural strengths, the Knower can spend time in the Knower's version of *coaching* about what the goal is and how to reach it, systematically. Allowing time for others to change means patience is required for this part of the job, and it is often in short supply for the Knower brainstyle. Moreover, people with other brainstyles will have different approaches to getting the job done as well as different ways they like being *coached*. Knowers are not empathizers. Conflict can start when time and brainstyle timing are not taken into account. The Knower needs to remind herself that quick does not equal competent.

You can always tell a Knower, but you can't tell her much.

LEARNING

The Knower summarizes great chunks of information with breathtaking efficiency and, like Dick, is often excellent at writing or speaking about them. This is how he does it.

When a Knower sets out to learn something, he does so by sorting data, which he files in memory as conclusions or summaries. Put another way, he files or remembers information in left-brain, logical "chunks," not individual details. And so when the Knower remembers (retrieves) the *information, it comes back up the same way:* as conclusions. The information gets stored quickly and comes back in rapid, concise summaries. This ability to learn and remember "conclusively" gives the Knower the appearance of being a "quick study." The fact that most of the process goes on privately can create the impression that he is "arrogant," which is not necessarily the case.

The Knower looks very much like a "closed loop" because of the way this brainstyle processes information. Once the Knower has organized the supporting evidence into his (internally consistent) conclusions, there is initially very little that anyone can do to persuade him that another system—much less another conclusion—might be superior or at least just as good. Two other brainstyles have the most difficulty with this: the Conciliator and the Deliberator. Both of these brainstyles process information by constantly getting new inputs and other opinions. This is why you hear comments like "He just won't *listen*" and "I don't know how to influence her. She has a closed mind." The way people process information determines the way they relate to their environment. The internally "complete" Knower does not *need* people *for information* (approval, decisions, new data) the same way that other brainstyles do.

The capacity to be persuaded—and be a part of the crowd—depends a great deal on right-brain input, and the Knower has no ready access to that input.

The young Knower characteristically will be the first one to take a stand on an issue—and not care who supports it. More than likely he is interested in technical or practical considerations for his own reasons. Knowers are not the social butterflies. They do not care about others' opinions except as those *opinions affect their own achievement.* They are respected as leaders, or for their independence. If the teacher or coach or classmate can get across the idea that how they act or dress will damage or enhance their chances for getting to their goal, they will listen. School can be a place to win for a Knower when results are prized. But most often sociability and adaptability are the Citizenship Requirements and lots of negative assessments get made about the Knower, who doesn't care about fitting in for the sake of fitting in.

The bookstores are filled with books on how to change the Knower who "abuses" the sensibilities of others. Brainstyles that process information differently care greatly about how things are said, and how feelings are considered in the saying. We can get out of the victim-persecutor dialogue with respect for *both* brainstyles by keeping the following in mind: the Knower is not being "insensitive." In his own left-brain world, he is being direct and factual. Others learn to stop taking it personally or give themselves time to prepare ahead or react after a Knower encounter with a sympathetic friend. It doesn't work to try to change the Knower's brainstyle.

RISK-TAKING

A Knower doesn't risk, he covers his flank. He improves the odds. He reduces complex situations to formulas, logical strategies. Each brainstyle defines *risk* as "possible loss." The Knower's most personal risk is that he or she will be *wrong*—devalued because he is no longer the expert. Winning and losing are part of the game. No problem. But the Knower will take precautions not to be proved wrong. And this seems to include not paying too much. As shoppers, Knowers seem to minimize the hunt and focus on the "kill": the best value for the lowest price.

It may sound strange to say that someone who is right out there delivering opinions with expert authority is not a risk-taker—especially of the damn-the-torpedoes-full-speed-ahead school. That takes much more emotion in the regular course of things. The Knower is logical. And as with each brainstyle, this is both the good news about risk-taking and the bad news. Look at a recap of Knower brainstyle traits:

- takes in literal, measurable information naturally
- makes fast decisions by sorting and judging quickly
- uses information that is encountered later to support initial conclusions
- stays "in control" (doesn't re-sort the information readily)
- knows exactly what needs to be done according to plan
- likes to work and decide alone
- learns by getting the conclusion first, then adding the facts to support it
- works in the future by combining today's ideas in new ways to come to innovative applications for tomorrow

Here's how the Knower brainstyle acts in response to risk:

- He looks to the future and then formulates goals or new synergies of ideas based on things already known. Here the strengths of logic come into play. Dealing with risk means dealing with the unknown. The Knower tries to make the future a logical certainty, if not a verifiable one.
- After the initial brainstorming and leap into the future, the ability to assess and structure means a plan to *prevent things from going wrong.* The left brain does *not* plan *for what can go right.* Compared to Conceptors and Conciliators, there is little optimism in the Knower's system even though there may be a great deal of confidence and positive support for others. The Knower would say there is *realism.* There *is* focus and a drive to the goal. *Most Knowers' systems are grounded in practicality as well as problem prevention, not possibility thinking.* Success is often defined as "staying ahead of the game." Other brainstyles want the leap into the unknown to have some (emotional) "hope." Knowers don't deal comfortably with a vague "dream." They are too practical.
- Risk requires flexibility, the willingness to change as often as change is required. Knowers will change *tactics* on a dime. When better options are available they will take them. But major directions are hard to redefine for this brainstyle. It's easier to stop, cut bait, and start over. *Structure* and *change* are contradictory. And structure is the strength of this brainstyle.

- A Knower prefers working alone partly because he distrusts the processes others use (slower or less logical = less competent for many Knowers). Trust is what allows a leap into the unknown. Trust is what attracts a network of support to deal with mistakes. *Collaboration* is a non-strength of the Knower.
- The Knower makes fast, logical decisions that eliminate having to deal with emotional input. *Risk is profoundly emotional* for most. If the logical answer doesn't carry the day, Knowers cannot influence outcomes.

BrainStyle Clue:

Let the Knower tell you what kind of system you'll need to get from here to there. Ask the Knower to critique the latest new idea. He'll tell you what can go wrong. When it's time to decide the future, call in the Knower when you want "realistic," innovative ideas that will prevent problems and apply solutions in new ways.

BEING THE KNOWER

Being the Knower *can be the most difficult of all.*

The following is an interview with a mature Knower:

Q. *What are you most proud of?*

My biggest contribution was foresight in selecting the company's computer systems. I evaluated one that went against IBM's recommendation. This was a major factor in the successful acquisition of the company. We were running with the lowest data-processing costs in the entire new corporation. (Knower *contributions: foresight based on fact, taking an unpopular stand, creating efficiencies.*)

Q. *How have you changed over your career?*

When I was younger, I worked everyone eighteen hours a day. I worked all the time. It was all I cared about. In the last ten years, I opened to look at what impact I had on people. I didn't have the words, couldn't see what I was doing. I had heard feedback before, but it just seemed like they were always being defensive. I got new feedback in an atmosphere of trust and support and I took it in—probably for the first time. And I was over forty-five. Self-consciousness dropped away and so did the fear of being rejected. I found out that I overwhelm people with logic. I didn't know I did this. I thought about winning—being right. My self-esteem would suffer if I couldn't win—logically. I was more willing to fight than to be affectionate. I now choose another behavior—not at Time Zero—but later. I get my answer quickly. I have started asking the others for theirs too. When I fire out quickly, I clean it up right away. I try to think about it for a while.

Q. *What are your strengths?*
I am best at goals, systems, and controls. I'm most effective in planning and organizing for implementation—to make ideas real. My strength is coaching people in being logical in their approach and solutions. I can question for detail in the steps to implement. The difference between me and a Deliberator is *speed and relevance.* They get to the point by going around and around. They use a staff to get all the bits and pieces they can and then synthesize it them- selves. There is a lot of overhead. I tend to cut to the chase and limit the problem in the first place. I would be good in a turnaround situation, but I still tend to be authoritarian as a leader.

Corporate Comptroller, Knower

As a Knower, if that is your case, you recognize that you are often misunderstood. You know your ideas are good, and you know that most of the time you are right about things. You know that you can work a system quicker, faster, more efficiently than anyone else. But sometimes you have trouble persuading other people that your ideas are the best way.

These are your trouble spots:

APPLYING OTHERS' STRENGTHS. You may assess your personal worth by the strength of your left-brain speed. Most Knowers who do are locked into competitive overdrive where *fast* beats *best.* This can lock you out of relationships because you'll come across as "arrogant" when you judge others as slower and therefore less competent. In a results- oriented world, you *are* faster with an answer. Problem: you *need more than one* (your) *answer.* And you need commitment to the answer that is reached. Realize that your strength in the left brain means you are *not* strong in the right-brain strengths of others, which inspire, enroll, bond, and create commitment. To make the whole plan work, explore the bright-side possibilities, create personal motivation by getting *others* involved—especially other brainstyles. They will be faster and better at how to get the *whole* picture.

By recognizing that having the right answer first means literally *interfering* with the timing of other brainstyles at Time Zero, you can influence others much more effectively. Other brainstyles need time to process, react, or listen. This most basic interaction is defined by brainstyle, *not* intelligence or competence.

One Knower marketing director said, "I never really understood why there had to be two political parties. I mean there's really only one set of answers [that makes sense to me]. The big *ah ha!* of brainstyles for me is that people actually think differently in a way that can be useful to getting the job done." He was genuinely amazed not so much at the differences, but at the *value* each brainstyle could bring. Then he set about applying what he'd learned to take advantage of the different strengths of his team. The team results increased dramatically.

TELLING PEOPLE WHAT TO EXPECT FROM YOU.   Explain the benefits you can provide with your focus, solutions, and direction and tell them they will probably be better at building relationships than you will.

Explaining what you're good at is very useful in the early stages of a relationship. For example, the woman Knower who, for one reason or another, must volunteer for the local hospital committee might offer: *I'm probably not as good at socializing or being as diplomatic as some of you. But if you need someone to help organize the meetings or work on the goals and plans, I'd like to offer help in those areas. I'm good at focusing things. When people don't understand this, they think I'm being abrupt or don't care as much as they do. That's not true. It's just that I have strengths in other areas.* Getting expectations clear can do wonderful things for the whole group. Others can talk about their *own* strengths. A volunteer group, a family, or a new team at work can start off on the right foot for a change.

MANAGING YOUR TIMING.   The reason people have problems with Knowers is that Knowers get to the part of the topic *first* that the others (Conciliators and Deliberators for example) get to *last*. See if you can negotiate a role where you get to act as consultant or facilitator for others so you can contribute while they massage the ideas and information. Help them get what they want. Even so, Conciliators and Deliberators will still want time to arrive at their own conclusions, thank you. So making the game of getting to your goal one of *timing* with others can make all the difference. And that includes knowing when to quit and letting someone else with different strengths take over. (See how one Knower achieved this at the end of this chapter.)

Create a team by leveraging different strengths to contribute to the overall goal. Participate in meetings selectively—to structure them, to bring focus, to challenge ideas—at the beginning and end, if you can. Let the talkers and interactors have time to feel comfortable discussing, proposing, and assessing.

When considering a new project or idea where a lot is at stake, let others pose the upside potential and think about it for a while. Reconsider. Don't decide at the moment. Come in at the *end* of brainstorming free-for-alls to add practicality or application.

To get others to listen to your logic, you may need a personal story, explanations, details, or a description of possibilities to include in your presentation. Other brainstyles will not be sold on pure, cool logic alone.

Prepare the person presenting the details, or telling the story at the beginning, so you'll have a win-win: you want focus, they want to think things through or have an audience. How can you *combine* the goals in a way that allows the "sensitive" ones to feel "safe" with you? Their feeling of "pressure" has everything to do with your timing. Timing works better than flattery, logic, or even having the right answers.

COACHING OTHERS.   Focus on coaching others to do more of what *they* do best. Eliminate your judgments about their pace, or your comparisons of one to another. Keep the focus on the goal and how each can contribute to it.

MAKING THINGS FIT AT WORK

If you are a Knower, here are some tips for marketing yourself—and starting a constructive collaboration—to an uncomprehending business world.

- Don't claim to be a "team player." This is not your strength. Explain that you are most comfortable working alone or in charge of a piece of the work. With your cards on the table, you are ready to negotiate a real role for yourself as a team member.

- Position yourself as the one on the team who can see through the clutter, define the end result, and simplify the strategy in Time Zero situations. *However,* one answer, derived alone, is *not* the one that is going to get the most commitment. *Use your quick answer as a focus for the team, then get other input.*

- Exploit your individual contributions. Explain to others that as long as there is a system in place, you can work faster than anyone. But be sure to build in a way to get some help—or input—if the system derails or must be adjusted through negotiation.

- Add practicality to the dreams of the risk-takers. And add it after those other very sensitive brainstyles are past their initial Time Zero offerings. Any earlier is the time when every brainstyle is the most vulnerable. Mature Knowers are able to use their experience and quick judgment to both visualize the future product as well as identify potential potholes as a way of getting to the desired result. Critiquing another's new idea for being impractical because you can see all the potential negatives must be carefully timed.

- Think of the other brainstyles as creating a possible arena for you to perform in. They need *you* to make their dreams work.

- Publicize your progress and completion targets. People will bother you less if they know exactly when you will make your report. You probably already build in slack for those who use deadlines as reminders.

- Acknowledge and *use* others' expertise in your areas of non-strengths: people, detail, follow-through, or concepts, for example. Being realistic about your non-strengths creates the basis for honest delegation.

- Make sure you understand *their* version of the goals before you spend your valuable time devising systems to achieve them.

- Your left brain delivers quick critiques and conclusions. More than anything, this interferes with others' timing in reaching their own conclusions. Allowing them a little time to say their piece and then building on *their* words can make a difference.

- Remember, when people in other brainstyles frustrate you, it's because their brains work differently and at a different speed than yours. Figure out what brainstyle they are in. The problem is *time.* The solution is time. It will help others if you tell them you want the strengths they bring. You can work out a way to time your problem-solving instead of asking that either of you change.

- Your non-strength is listening for detail or listening empathetically *without* quick interpretation. Develop a minimum of skill in listening to exactly what the other person is saying. Others speak often in terms you may not relate to. Help yourself focus and keep in communication with them in short meetings. Most importantly, an honest statement will help others understand: "I'm not as good with the process or background as you are. If you start with the results first, I'll be able to track better and give you a better response." This is *not* the same as "Just cut to the chase."

A KNOWER WHO APPLIED BRAINSTYLES

Mel is in his thirties. Tall (six feet four), brown-haired and brown-eyed, he is still boyishly good-looking but, because of his height, can be somewhat imposing. Mel has moved up the corporate ladder in the first eight years of his career, but has recently stumbled. Corporate mandates in the human development field have hit Mel right in the breadbasket. "My performance assessments over the past five or six years always read the same thing: 'Great results, outstanding salesman, good leader, but tends not to improve on the people skills.' And when my people are asked, there have been some on the edges over the last few years who've been unhappy." He looks annoyed. "But the people I worked with directly, closely, had a great time." What is the problem? "They say sometimes I'm 'abrasive, a know-it-all, not interested in what people think, [that I] come up with the answer real quick and won't let us get there at our own pace'—and all that kind of stuff."

After Mel learned about brainstyles, he told a story about how he applied his strengths to boost teamwork.

One of the things that happened for me came out when our team was preparing a big presentation for senior management at our major customer. We'd been at it for three hours or so, because we didn't know how to work together yet very well. So finally I said, "Give me five minutes to put together a structure for this meeting. You guys all come back in and I'll explain it to you and we'll be off and running." That was something that came easy for me: "We have to do this, this, this, and this." It was like three hours of the meeting just happened in five minutes—because we had people who wanted to listen to *everything*. But from then on, what tended to happen, once we understood what comes naturally to people, it got to be okay what we each could deliver. I really was freed up.

Mel is getting better feedback. "But Mel will always be Mel," a colleague chuckles. "He *is* more understanding now, though. And easier to work with."

But the real win for Mel came in his marriage. Mel explained, "I started to figure out why my wife and I hadn't been able to communicate for the last eight years as well as I'd like us to." He continued, "I'd want to handle everything practically. 'Let's sit down and just work this out' [*now* was always implied]. She always thought about the emotional side first. She thought I was trying to steamroll her, and we never resolved an issue." So Mel read about brainstyles, especially about *her* brainstyle. Now he tries things like, " 'I really want to talk about the way we are raising the kids. I have a difference with how we are going about it.' And she usually bristles up a little bit, so I say, 'Hey, let's talk about it tomorrow, over lunch or go to dinner or something like that. But think about it.' This gives me a chance to handle the practical ideas, she gets all the emotions out of it, and it's been amazing how we've been able to improve the quality of how we talk about things."

CHAPTER 4

The Conciliator

"I'm *not* mad. I'm passionate."

*Asserted by a Conciliator after hitting the dinner table with his
fist to underscore the point he'd just made to his boss on the ill
treatment of his employees.*

THE CONCILIATOR BRAINSTYLE: A SUMMARY

The gift of this brainstyle is to operate in the world of the immeasurable and intangible. The imaginative, emotional, fanciful, or the spiritual is comfortable for the Conciliator, who can easily see what is common among differences. "Flow" is achieved by developing an *inner* focus, often through meditation or some inner discipline. A Conciliator is a person who is best in relationships with people, who seeks to overcome disharmony, who brings together, wins over, and strives to mediate differences.

A Conciliator* is:

* Pronounced Kon SIL ē ay tor.

- A person who looks for harmony everywhere—either with people or through sound (music), color, aromas, or touch. Because of the way their brain takes in sensory information, Conciliators often feel compelled to establish harmony around them in order to feel comfortable. They are naturals at overcoming distrust and hostility by verbally bonding, touching, or making eye contact.
- They access the right brain first, fastest, and most strongly, which gives this brain-style an advantage in reading or understanding the unspoken or *nonverbal* (recently assessed to be 90 percent of the real impact of a message).
- By looking for similarities, they achieve accord using humor, touch, or eye contact or by expressing empathy. They are natural peacemakers.
- Strong feelings are quickly available to them through strong connectors in the lower right part of the cortex, so these feelings are often expressed spontaneously by action or with a lot of emotion-laden words. Later, thought or logic temper or revise the initial quick response.
- Conciliators *associate* ideas to learn or remember things with their own personal connections rather than use the logic of cause-effect more natural for the left-brained.
- Putting feeling into words or the need to connect with others comes first. They must learn structure, sequential logic, strategy, and decisiveness. Plans balanced with downsides come later because of the slower connection to the left brain.
- Outcomes are of major concern for this brainstyle. The plans or process to get to a goal are often discovered along the way. "Winging it" is easiest for this brainstyle.
- Fueled by a personal mission, this brainstyle can do well at many precise and detailed tasks, bringing greater meaning to numbers or plans. Career choices vary depending on energy level and specific talents; however, most prefer to work with people.
- Thinking of imaginative ways to get to a goal, empathizing with several points of view (playing devil's advocate, playing *what if*), brainstorming disconnected ideas, or making exciting verbal or inspirational pictures to persuade others are strengths of this brainstyle. Sales and service professions are a natural fit for Conciliators.
- At their best, Conciliators are charismatic.

In the database of over 1,235 people observed and tested for brain-styles, we found 36 percent of them to be this right brainstyle. Of these, 58 percent are women, 42 percent are men. (See charts on pages 234 and 326.)

THE STRENGTHS

Inside, Conciliators have a whole dramatic universe of pictures, ideas, impulses, and feelings swirling around, overwhelming the restrictive, limited, precise, and the time-bound outlet of mere words. Fantasies. Insights. Distractions. Starting a zillion things. Being late. Changing their minds. Falling in and out of love. Being romantic. Dramatic. Touching. Outrageous. As a barometer indicates a tornado, so the eyes, face, hands, and gestures try to indicate the internal weather map of the Conciliator. Other clues for spotting this brainstyle are colorful or insightful language, natural friendliness, and storm cloud moodiness: from sparkle to sizzle to lowdown depressed and back again. A Conciliator gives off a natural warmth, even charisma, and often idealism, playfulness, or a sense of drama when doing what they do best. And most Conciliators can't hide what they feel very well for very long.

The gift of the Conciliator is to bring instant intuition—a right-brained *sensing of the immediate environment,* a *knowing,* an awareness of what's going on with people, right now, this minute—to whatever they're doing. To be aware of their own feelings, and *oops!* say or show them in unplanned, uncontrolled, spontaneous ways in a *new* situation is part of the gift (depending on how you look at it) and provides lots of Embarrassing Moments or, once mastered, witty remarks and snappy comebacks. For Conciliators, the logic, the analysis, a clearer view of the big picture comes *later*—though never as fast or as easily. Conciliators are the inventors of the LIFO (last in, first out) system. They cannot but help attending to the squeaky wheel—it screams to their sensitivities, overriding all those classes in Getting Organized to Get In Control. The right brain, remember, is the part of the brain that can't measure, can't make distinctions like time or numbers or names; it has no real language ability. The Big Engine of the Conciliator can't talk. It looks out past the language of the left brain for the spiritual side—unity, harmony, and unspoken meanings—in order to make *connections* with things and people and interpret what is happening with images and stories rather than words, numbers, or sequential logic. Then the Conciliator can really get wound up and talk endlessly, to recount and explore ideas out loud as the brain begins to make connections by hearing its own words.

The right brain operates with different rules than the left: it's the part of us that *thinks with feeling* and remembers our experiences. If this sounds confusing, remember how you respond to an advertisement with pictures that, in an instant, convey more than the ten thousand words of the announcer. There is instant recognition—knowing without words just exactly what is implied yet unstated. And so the right brain has an instant mechanism for translating an experience into "knowledge"—a conclusion, a summary, a belief that this is the way it is and it *doesn't need proof* or *your* logical explanations, thank you. If there is damage to this side of the brain people repeat mistakes and make very poor decisions, unable to benefit from their experience. Emotional memory, then, is critical to good reasoning.[1] Conciliators have an easy access to emotions, both past and present, but because of the heavy access to this side of the brain, often are stubborn (slow to change direction) and want new conclusions to fit with past experience. Seasoned Conciliators reach a balance between habit and the need for new stimuli.

"He seems to know what I'm thinking." "She can walk into a group/client/party and tell in a very short time who has a problem and who doesn't—but she can't tell me *how* she knows what she knows." Conciliators are very aware of what's going on around them. Their hardware picks up nonverbal cues, moods, and unspoken words, seemingly in greater magnitudes than other brainstyles. This doesn't mean that everyone in every brainstyle cannot pick up nonverbal cues to some degree. Conciliators are not more gifted at accurately *interpreting* nonverbal cues; however, they are more gifted at sensing them. Conciliators don't have to work at or learn how to read others. They just know how.*

More than any other brainstyle, the Conciliator seems to seek *comfort*. As the right brain looks for synthesis, convergence, or similarities, this brainstyle seeks to create relationships with others so all will be in harmony (everyone is *comfortable*) in their world. The Conciliator has the best chance of encouraging people to be comfortable working together and *liking* one another beyond the job. Conciliators apply their strengths most naturally with people in joining networks, creating teams or support groups, or making friends. Conciliator kids love

---

* An excellent resource to expand this ability is by Marcia Emery, *The Intuition Workbook: An Expert's Guide to Unlocking the Wisdom of Your Subconscious Mind* (Prentice-Hall, 1994).

parties and friends, are more likely to know everyone in the neighborhood, and tend to be more outgoing.

Conciliators learn early that nothing bonds like laughter, sometimes turning difficult situations in their favor. Stop the fight by starting the laugh. And that's how many comedians are "born." Besides laughing and giggling, Conciliator children love visual games (like playacting or dressing up), with rules made up as you go along. Conciliator boys, however, are encouraged to be more left-brained. There may be more pressure for boys to channel their sensitivity into aggressive action, to be a gang member or a bully. Or, click—new channel—a natural storyteller, team leader, pilot, or athlete.

"Personalizing everything" is the tool of the successful actor, according to Oscar-winner Shelley Winters. Who better on stage than this brainstyle? Feelings can dominate the Conciliator as they are growing up, taking things personally their major hurdle. As they mature, Conciliators can turn emotionality into dramatic ability, intense empathy, and commitment to others, or have extraordinary persuasive abilities, a passion for learning, humanitarian ideals and causes to become inspiring leaders, spiritual counselors, actors, musicians, athletes, or artists. As leaders, Conciliators most often build consensus rather than take unpopular stands. They respond to polls, trends, and fans personally with empathy and responsive action. Critics may hate too many changes; fans feel important.

When a Conciliator goes into a more left-brained field like medicine, business, sales, or law, they are the ones who take a more personal interest in patients and clients. Work is often *family,* clients and customers are *special* for Conciliators. The right brain asks "Can't we all be friends?"

Front-page stories around the nation opened the new year in 1996 with another scientific breakthrough in the field of genetics. This time it might be the explanation for another of the Conciliator's attributes that make them so attractive and fun to be around:

A specific kind of genetic variation makes people more likely to be excitable, fickle, thrill-seeking and quick-tempered, according to two studies published Tuesday.[2]

Two teams of researchers have reported detecting a partial genetic explanation for a personality trait called "novelty seeking." People high in a novelty-seeking quotient tend to be extroverted, impulsive, extravagant, quick-tempered, excitable and exploratory—your flamboyant Uncle Milton who shows up with an armload of presents, bellows out hellos, pretends to pull coins from your ear, knows all the latest disaster jokes and then sits around after the family dinner looking faintly bored.[3]

Research over the last decade has promoted a great deal of interest in and new information about the turf the Conciliator calls home: *intuition, imagination, thinking out of the box,* and which promotes the swiftly changing actions and reactions of this brainstyle. W. H. Agor is the director of the Global Intuition Network and author of a book on the role of intuition in decision-making. His research tells why business is finding "that traditional analytical techniques such as Management by Objectives and straight-line forecasting are not always as useful as they once were" to make decisions because "*totally new trends are emerging*" that make the old methods "inaccurate or misleading." He underscores the need for intuitive skills to help "guide major decisions in the following settings:

- where there is a high level of uncertainty
- where there is little previous precedent
- where reliable 'facts' are limited or unavailable
- where time is limited and there is pressure to be right
- where there are several plausible options to choose from, all supported by 'factual' data and you have to choose one of them."[4]

The strengths of this brainstyle are especially obvious when logic is not enough to solve a problem. "Winging it" is their gift, results are the focus. Plans? No. Caution? No. Pioneers are those in a field who are in over their heads, who must rely on their intuition. Conciliators are at home here, making contributions where *breakthroughs* can occur.

As we learn about the brain, or what Agor terms the "last great frontier," and how to use its gifts, we will know a great deal more about how to draw on the gifts of the right-brained Conciliators.

THE CONCILIATOR

• Makes spontaneous decisions	• Makes logical revisions	• Sells	• Teaches
	• Criticizes	• Inspires	• Is charismatic
• Harmonizes	• Takes action	• Makes personally meaningful plans	• Is a persuasive organizer
• Feels	• Is demonstrative		
• Imagines alternatives	• Talks about the experience	• Creates options	

TIME ZERO ▶ SOON AFTER ▶ WITH PRACTICE ▶ EXPERT

- The Conciliator is greatly influenced at Time Zero by what is said, seen, and felt. The initial reaction is with the right brain, which has very limited language ability. Feelings and images are processed fastest and give an overall hunch. Later, logic and language clarify or revise the initial reaction. Decisions are often changed.
- Conciliators react quickly and spontaneously, usually conveying how they feel.
- The Conciliator's main strength is in building relationships, bringing harmony to different elements, people, or things.
- Conciliators are excellent mediators with conflict, with a natural ability to "read" and empathize with people.
- Conciliators look for opportunities to:
  - start things
  - support others, make things happen
  - add the sizzle
  - bring meaning, add the spiritual, the personal
  - try a new way, imagine options
  - make relationships count
  - participate in things
  - communicate by talking, writing, drawing
  - see it and tell it as it could be

THE RIGHT-BRAINED GUY WHO'S MAKING IT

Brad is a marketing executive with an influential job that has evolved directly from his unique right-brainstyle strengths. His success is unusual in the buttoned-down, measurable world of corporate America, and especially the major company he belongs to, which is particularly fussy about systems and data and financial reports.

He started his career in the military as an air force pilot in the 1950s. From there he went into sales and has worked for the same company for over eighteen years. He knows the business, the products, and Who's Who inside out.

Brad has an easy laugh. He has a *way* about him. He's easy to like and easy to talk to. With short brown hair, blue eyes, and a solid build, he's fifty but looks forty. He makes conversation easily, openly, giving a great deal of information and anecdotes about the people and products he knows so well.

Currently he is in charge of a unique sales staff who perform more as consultants and counselors than salespeople. Brad has hand-picked and created a team of people who have leveraged the Art of the Relationship to deliver service that sells. People on the team talk of themselves as a kind of Dirty Dozen in the corporation—the folks that had gotten stale in the same jobs have turned into Chairman's Council Sales Superstars with Brad's help. How did he do it? "He saw potential in us that other bosses couldn't," says one of his supportive subordinates. Brad has a special gift with people.

"I'm a troubleshooter," Brad says, when I ask what he does best. "I'm able to sniff out problems with people—political problems—way before they hurt us." Brad explains how he can "read the signals a customer gives off," interpret them, and extrapolate the implications for a sales strategy very rapidly. So rapidly, his boss sees him as a "firefighter." Brad figures out a rough response and acts on it so quickly that he has kept very complex relationships alive and well for more than seven years, relationships that are full of land mines.

Brad's "customer" is actually executives based all over the country, each of whom can cancel major orders worth millions of dollars with a phone call. Brad's job is sensing a potential wound before any damage gets done and administering just the right vaccine. "I have antennae for possible trouble: a buyer gets under pressure and then someone from our company says the wrong things at the wrong time. I hear something small here, get a call from there and *bam!* I'm on a plane. I make sure my people are there too, smoothing, helping, making things work—putting those complex data systems to work for the customer. The whole notion came out of simple strategy: my company would act as a *support* for the customer rather than a supplier. It was a breakthrough.

"Their founder and my former boss took a walk together after one of those stuffy business dinners. They got along well. They came out with an idea that set the stage for a new way of doing business that was right up my alley—people driving the business rather than the systems driving the people. I can't tell you how revolutionary that was for our company. We've always been *very* structured, *very* much by-the-book.

"In this job, with this customer relationship, there *is* no 'book,' no rules, nothing but my intuition and personal skills and my ability to coach my people in doing more or less what I do. I could never, in my wildest dreams as a young salesman, have predicted I'd be doing a job like this. It's pure invention every day. I *love* it." He looks and sounds jazzed. Brad continues, "In fact, three years ago I had a serious heart attack. I'm sure that if I didn't love what I do so much I couldn't have recovered so fast or kept at it since."

Brad's job is more than a job to him, it's an opportunity to put his spontaneous feelings into service that makes an enormous impact in sales dollars. Brad says he was "in the right place at the right time" to get this position, which points up the strengths of the right brain right along with its limits: without words, the process, the *control* of things seems to just happen.

Yet having strengths in one area naturally excludes equal strengths in others. Brad's gifts in the realms of insight, intuition, imagination, and action mean he's not as good at planning and organizing, for instance. To be effective, Conciliators need to keep in touch with people. To produce results, they need to connect with people that balance their strengths. "He's so spontaneous that he can derail one of our staff meetings with the latest 'hot item,' " moans a subordinate. Brad wants to talk things through to reach consensus on issues he knows are sensitive, and that he will have to push with senior management back at headquarters. "There's only so much we can massage the issue," says one somewhat frustrated but loyal salesperson. "We've dealt with the issue and now it's up to Brad. Some of us are worried, though, that at the next meeting he'll bring it up again."

But Brad *has* heard them. He's only too aware of the conflicting personal needs of a field staff that travel 80 percent of the time. "I've got to give them recognition, you know, feed their egos and get them in front of the room to keep them happy. At the same time, they want to be told what to do sometimes. I'm their only link to our company for most of the year, and when they get together they need time to talk through their own agendas," he explains. He says he knows he's frustrating some of those who want him to be more decisive, but he knows he's best as "a coach and a facilitator." He gets asked in a meeting to settle a dispute. He refuses. He tells the team that they've got to "figure it out" themselves, to learn to solve their own problems. There is grumbling about his lack of leadership. He doesn't fit the mold or the expectations of those who work for him who want more structure and direction. The structure and direction they seek is from the more typical strengths of a left-brained business executive. That's not Brad, and he knows it.

THE CONCILIATOR AND INTUITION

Intuition is a word bandied about by everyone; it's hunches, "gut feelings," ideas that pop out of nowhere. What *is* intuition, really? A definition from one brain researcher describes how many scientists explain how the right-brained "read" people or just "know" so much about them. "*Intuition* is an immediate knowing of the environment"[5] through the senses.

Another researcher explored the topic by going beyond what the five senses pick up to extrasensory awareness. Philip Goldberg describes six different types of intuition and how they each affect our rational, decision-making processes.[6] Books on the subject[7] would be very useful for Conciliators and Conceptors to read as well as some Deliberators who have more right-brained access in order to start developing *natural* gifts where it'll be fun and useful, not to mention easy and natural. Brad has successfully applied his intuitive awareness to take relationships to a new level in his company.

Goldberg defines intuition (with the dictionary's help) as "knowing directly without use of rational processes." Intuition is nonsequential, disordered, effortless, unexplainable, and, he adds, it's more than a guess; the idea or hunch turns out to be correct—verifiable—and cannot be derived from available cues or clues. Conciliators seem to pick up and tune into more nonverbal cues and use them internally to "know" what's coming in unexplainable ways. Brad calls this ability his "antennae."

In brief, there are three types of intuition this brainstyle might watch for to develop further.

1. A Conciliator has a way with hunches. The first type of intuition Goldberg describes is one in which the brain makes a leap after studying facts to discover some verifiable truth or the underlying cause of a problem ("discovery" as mentioned in Chapter Three). Where the Knower will get the answer with logic and analysis, Conciliators have an edge in following through with hunches about people because of a natural ability to sense and read nonverbal and emotional cues. When, for no logical reason, you suspect someone may be untrustworthy, check out the facts available before dismissing the idea or the person. One woman Goldberg interviewed reportedly had that feeling about a salesclerk who worked for her. Because the clerk was so friendly, she kept putting her suspicions aside, attributing them to other causes. Finally she decided to check the books, "just in case." She found, to her amazement, that cash was missing over a long period of time. This confirmed her *intuition*. You can expand your own ability with simple exercises: guess who is calling before you answer the telephone, guess what strangers do for a living or something about them before you are introduced at a party—tune into your own awareness in situations that can be easily verified.

2. The "little voice" that tells you to go or stay, take the job or not, is probably telling you the truth. How often do you find yourself saying "I *knew* I should've gone. I felt it would be best and I just didn't listen—even when something *told* me to do it." Keep track of your wins until you can tell the difference between real intuition and opinions or emotions.

3. On a bit more sophisticated level, consider the idea of what Goldberg calls "operative intuition" rather than writing off events as "luck." Being in the right place at the right time, having amazing "coincidences" where things come together just right for no apparently logical reasons might just be the result of your preconscious awareness and access to an inner guidance system that does not use logic or words. Conciliators who are skilled in listening to this rich source of data from within gathered at a national conference to tell how intuition worked in their business lives.[8] From Silicon Valley to the U.S. Postal Service, Conciliators who just "knew" they could

"find a better answer" shared remarkable solutions to very difficult situations using their natural optimism, sensitivity to others, an open spirituality, and trust of others. Most were clearly pioneers in their areas.

The sense of being attracted or drawn to a situation or a place is an example of this type of intuition, as is the kind of certainty that we are meant to follow a "calling" or carry out some mission.

An assistant who worked for us for over six years told me a few weeks after she started her new position how she found the job. She never read want ads and had no reason to because she was then in a fine job. "One day, for no real reason, I picked up the paper and felt almost *compelled* to look in the classifieds." There she saw our ad and instantly "knew" this was the job for her. She said it seemed "eerie" to interview and have almost a feeling of certainty that you were "meant to be there."

Urgings to go in strange directions, sometimes in contradiction to the facts, and at the risk of seeming silly or illogical, can serve the Conciliator well. As author Goldberg says, "We play guessing games with life. Those who guess well are called intuitive, those who are intuitive, however, don't think they are guessing."[9]

Describing types of intuition within this chapter does not mean that Conciliators have a lock on being intuitive. Other types of intuition are described for all four brainstyles. Everyone has access to the right brain to a greater or lesser extent and can learn to pay more attention to their inner *knowing*. But the particular set of gifts that includes the ability to make spiritual connections seems to come very easy and naturally to most Conciliators (this is also true for those called right-sided Deliberators—see Chapter Six), and for those with this brainstyle it is a path to explore for further growth.

THE BRIGHT GAL WHO PRIZES WHAT SHE KNOWS (NOT WHO SHE IS)

Leslie is in advertising at a Fortune 50 company you've heard of and at twenty-eight is making big bucks.

A pretty woman, Leslie's trim figure and bright blue eyes frame her sparkle. That's the only thing you can call it: sparkle. When she lights up, she tends to light up everyone around her. No doubt about it, Leslie is an outgoing Conciliator, with an engaging way about her.

"When she's up, she's very, very up. And when she's down, she's not down for too long," says a friend. "But she *can* get in the pits," adds another. "Though she's *mostly* fun," the first wants to emphasize. Having done very well at Johns Hopkins University, speaking German and Italian, she went to work in Italy in the U.S. firm's overseas marketing group, and was promoted back to corporate headquarters to the junior rung of the fast track in marketing. She describes the pressure and competition of the advertising group as cutthroat and fast-paced—where *you better get the numbers right;* or even better, *get the right numbers.* She describes herself as an achiever, coming from a family of "professional achievers," and her view of life is you "feel good when you're on top." Leslie wants very much to succeed in this job.

She confesses she often tells herself that "This is Corporate Life. Fake It Till You Make It. Button Up and Be Buttoned Down. Never Let Them See You Sweat." She says she didn't expect a bed of roses. She's willing to work hard. She's heard grapevine statistics: only about one third of the "freshmen" will make the cut. She had very high hopes when she started; she has impressed a lot of people.

But something is just not right. Leslie's closest friends, who think she is the most "together, strong, and successful" of all of them, are puzzled by her sudden outbursts about something. She even *cries.* Just isn't like her. Tsk. Tsk. Must be the pressure.

Leslie is beginning to wonder whether she is in the right job, the right field, or for that matter the right *life.* She has little time to think about it with the long hours she works. Will she be single until she's forty? She has no time to socialize. *Other* people's lives sound soooo interesting to her. She wonders what it would be like to *lead* the corporate seminars she now must attend, what it would be like if it were *her* up in front of the room being admired. But she must attend endless meetings where she's just one of many junior hotshots politely trying to *win,* to come up with an idea that other people will resent through their compliments and hope to outdo as soon as they possibly can.

Whether it's the wrong job, the wrong "corporate culture," or just that *(oh no)* she can't cut it, Leslie's feeling more and more unsure of herself. She questions, for the first time in her life, what she's after and why. She wonders what she needs to do to get on top of her own life the way that she got on top of the last market analysis.

Leslie is a Conciliator in a job that demands her non-strengths as a top priority. Everyone around her is more gifted than she at doing their jobs because she's not doing what she can do *best*. She's gotten as far as she has because she's competent enough, even in the things she's *not* very good at, to pull them off. Luckily for her, she's still only twenty-eight and learns fast from her experience.

NON-STRENGTHS BRING CHALLENGES
FOR THE CONCILIATOR

How does *a right-brained person operate in a left-brained world?* How do the sensitive, empathetic, creative ones withstand the pain of criticism that they, more than others, tend to personalize? How does someone without a poker face play poker?

BEING NEUTRAL.   One of the biggest challenges Conciliators face in the rocks-are-hard, water's-wet world of measurable realities is tolerating politically incorrect name-callers who do not care one whit about another's personal *sensitivities,* and who find the Conciliators and their feelings distracting and painful to be around. Conciliators can get told in a variety of ways to *get over it,* to stop making their feelings such a big issue by their personal reactions. This is because a Conciliator's strength is a quick and personal reaction. Their *non*-strength is to respond coolly, objectively, or neutrally. Leslie is playing up her unnatural response in order to succeed and the personal cost is getting higher by the week.

Conciliators are their own worst enemies. Perfectionism to a Conciliator means becoming a person whom all will admire and applaud. Frequently the young Conciliators are the most vocal about their own importance, achievements, and talents—the spotlight equals success for the most extroverted among them; yet the Conciliators often lack objective measures for their conclusions. The right brain sees the world through a lens of personal interpretation: the latest good word is a high, the "bad" is a "slap in the face." Conciliator athletes are the ones who will be affected by their last shot. Only *later* will they learn to "roll with the punches."

Because they subjectively compare themselves to others with different gifts, Conciliators are the first to moan about being unappreciated. Constantly looking outside for affirmation, their feelings interpret what they see as personal gains or losses. Consequently, Conciliators decide they must adapt—button up, sound tough—or feel out of place in corporations (or families) where performance and achievement get all the attention. Getting recognized and appreciated for their unmeasurable gifts is always an issue for this brainstyle, so they often avoid corporate life and pursue their own venture where people skills count most and others can't tell them what to do or how to feel. Or Conciliators rebel, overadapt, act out, or leave families where they hate the measures of their worth through others' eyes. Conciliators like Leslie who join corporate ranks can go through a lot of struggle, resenting others who get the nod for the quick logic or steady analysis.

Conciliators who are born into families of different brainstyles can go through early lives of thinking they are never loved or understood for who they really are.

STRUCTURE. ORDER. BEING ON TIME.   As we learned from Brad's and Leslie's experiences, Conciliators' *natural* strengths include spontaneity, playfulness, being imaginative, feeling deeply and showing it to others. Their non-strengths are structure, order, tidiness, routine, following the rules, and saying no—these are gifts that get things done in order, on time, and within bounds. Conciliators *can* be prompt and efficient —in bursts.

Often, Conciliators want, even demand, visual order and predictability.* A neat secretary or mate can be a godsend. A number of mothers with Conciliator children have told of their spontaneous, playful toddlers crying or getting very upset when something is changed in a room arrangement, or when an unexpected event or change occurs, like starting school, moving, or when parents argue.

Later in life, Conciliators make up their own visual filing systems according to categories *personally meaningful*. Additionally, they start many fabulous projects that are briefly stimulating, and then get *boring*. Most Conciliators are strong in ideaphoria, the ability to rapidly generate new ideas with visual or nonlinear thinking (see Appendix A). When combined with a high energy level, they are more outgoing, they demand more new interests and new people. So more stacks of stuff pile up to crowd the memory—which can only be found with

---

* This may provide external control when the internal right-brained images do not. Creating visual harmony is a gift common for this brainstyle.

an increasingly complex personal retrieval system. It's overwhelming. It's "burnout." It can be a mess.

In the growing ranks of professional women (45 percent of all the women in our database test as this brainstyle), there are increasing numbers of women with this strength who will be *damned* if they will allow their emotions to get the better of them (at least at work). They make "cold calls"—selling to strangers—without batting an eye. In this regard, they join their Conciliator brothers—the macho men— who have acted invincible most of their lives. These Conciliators become the structured, overachieving, tough cookies who make a point of competing with the left-brainers by acting more quickly, showing no reactions, and talking numbers right along with the best of them —until, that is, they get promoted to a level that keeps demanding high-speed, *fact*-based decisions until they hate the work and just can't deliver. As many ambitious Conciliators have found, their incompatibility with the job becomes stark and painful during sleepless nights wondering what kind of job would really make them happy. Nursing ulcers from the pace and stress of unending deadlines, left-brained demands for clear priorities and fast analysis overwhelm their natural gifts and leave hollow stomachs and low self-worth behind. It is at the peak of frustration that Conciliators may become aware that their gift requires achievement through personal connections with people in some form or another and that those connections are a better measure of personal success than success defined by left-brain measures.

Those who decide not to feel anything at work, or who put their lives into boxes so they can at least have feelings at home, may become painfully separate from their strengths and become dissatisfied with themselves. This is the lesson Leslie is struggling to learn.*

Case in point: May is a striking woman, about five feet seven, with intense blue eyes, fair skin, and salt-and-pepper hair. You're aware of her eyes first because she tends to look you directly in the eye. She is a department manager in a large retail chain store, recently picked as

---

* The Conciliators' inability to identify their natural strengths would seemingly show up on personal assessments like the Myers-Briggs Temperament Indicator. When cross-referencing the MBTI with *The BrainStyle Inventory*, Conciliators had more mixed results than any other brainstyle (see Appendix D). This is why we suggest it takes time to identify the difference between natural and learned behaviors—especially when the environment does not measure or, often, reward the natural brainstyle; self-tests reflect the personal confusion.

the *best* department manager of twenty-plus stores in her region. In her mid-forties, May discusses the long climb she has taken to get on top of her feelings and the interpretations she's made of her experiences since she was young. She puts it this way, "It's taken me a very long time and a lot of thought to know that if I pass a group and there's a lull in the conversation, it doesn't mean they're talking about *me*."

May talked about a lifetime of taking things personally, subjectively interpreting outside events emotionally, with *herself as the target*. She changed jobs a lot because of these feelings. She grew up, she now realizes, with a sister and father who were left-brained Knowers. She compared herself to them, then judged herself as just not good enough. She interpreted every incident by comparing her quick feelings to her sister's quick, cool logic. "My sister was always so good with words. I'd feel like such a dummy in comparison," she says. May took event after event and stored negative feelings with them in her emotional memory because of the *decision she'd made about herself* without logic or objectivity and filed away under I'm Unacceptable. Now when people stop talking when she walks by, feelings of fear and shame laid down in her right-brain experience are automatically called up to create a perception based on that old mental file that has no reason and no words, but seems to prove over and over that she's unacceptable just for being herself.

At least this happened until she began feeding information that contradicted those old beliefs into another part of her brain. She started getting tired of all the drama, the upset, and arguments, and considered changing the way she saw herself. By reading about her natural brainstyle strengths, *she opened a new file in her brain for her self-image*. This process enabled her to start paying attention to some *new* experiences based on things she did that were natural and easy. She compared herself to others less frequently. She then started having a number of "realizations" when new information hit those old memories.

One day, when walking by a small group of people who were talking until she came by, she recalls being vividly startled by her own "brainstorm" as she thought, *they're not talking about* me—*and if they are, I don't care!* She remembers thinking *what dumb ideas I used to have.* May had taken charge of her hardware by using her left-brain thinking to do what some scientists call "extinguishing a feeling attached to an event," or what psychologists call "emotional intelligence." She discovered how to reprogram her feeling-based thinking about an event that no longer fit her new self-image.*

Projection creates perception. This statement means that what has been filed inside our brains creates our perceptions of reality. Conciliators are particularly gifted at empathy. Conciliators can also project their internal states onto others. This brainstyle especially needs to have a clear, factual description of their gifts in order to avoid seeing the world as a mirror. The natural hardware that sets up a Conciliator to intuit and understand is the very same hardware that sets them up to be distracted by the mood of every person they encounter.

We can *think* logically (in the left brain, where we are conscious) and be aware of *feelings* (in the right brain, where we're not always aware of *why I feel this way*) at the same time. Conciliators can use this information as a way to manage their feelings, rather than be managed *by* them.

May describes getting over her past feelings as the mysterious process of "just growing up." She really doesn't know how it happened, but she is now coming across as more confident, even-tempered, and helpful. As she told me, *"Brainstyles* came at just the right time for me." Now she knows why, in the past, she'd just get mad and quit job after job *even when she was quite successful.* No one would work harder or longer, but then she'd bridle at the least sign of correction or authority telling her what to do. "I took things personally all the time —the *wrong* way. I'd feel out of control when someone would tell me what to do, and I wasn't going to stand for that." She has a new way of looking at herself that puts her in control and makes her feel good. She now takes direction because she feels more sure of her *own* direction.

---

* According to the most recent research, emotional learning goes on without our conscious awareness, in a separate part of the brain. We commonly remember things we are not conscious of learning. "For example, if someone is injured in a car crash in which the horn gets stuck, he or she may later have a reaction when hearing the blare of car horns. The person may remember the details of the accident, such as where and when it occurred, who else was involved and how awful it was . . . [and] also become tense, anxious and depressed." The feelings come from a different part of the brain, and unlike the conscious images we are aware of, are much harder to get rid of. Joseph LeDoux, a professor of neuroscience and psychology at NYU, reports that *another* (prefrontal) *part of the brain*—what we are referring to here as the left brain—must be involved in actively learning to *control or prevent further emotional associations.* He adds that this takes a lot longer to do. "Emotion, Memory and the Brain," *Scientific American,* June 1994, pp. 50–57.

When a strongly right-brained person gets the whole picture, by finally, accurately, putting feelings into words, it is a wonderful thing, an "epiphany" or peak experience. Getting this clarity can feel like "change," but is actually just another step closer to mastering who you really are. The next step, giving the benefits to others, follows automatically.

When May got clear on her own gifts and stopped comparing herself to others—particularly her very left-brained family—she started using, and valuing, her hardware in a whole new way.

CONFLICT. Most Conciliators *hate* conflict, except when they are the ones dishing it out.

Conflict, in everyday terms, involves discomfort, disharmony, and new (Time Zero) decisions. These are the non-strengths of this brain-style. Emotional or intuitive responses are the strength. To most Conciliators, the first reaction they have to left-brain judgments, confrontation, or strong emotion is to feel that they are being "attacked." They then defend. The most important thing for Conciliators to recognize is that they have an instantaneous response, and, rather than attempt *not* to have one, to focus on the one they have. The good news *and* the bad news for the Conciliator is that they *personalize* information. In conflict this slows down the process of reaching a solution considerably.

A Conciliator would rather lie than get involved in a conflict situation. As a builder of consensus, she takes conflict as rejection of everything she does well. Conciliator managers are deeply invested in how people *feel* about doing their work. Somehow, conflict is a sure signal that the Conciliator has failed to communicate or to understand well enough. It is easy to see how a "tough" Conciliator can avoid all conflict by stubbornly defending and sticking with a decision.

Rather than deal with a situation that he cannot cure through good will, the Conciliator will go along with a decision he disagrees with or will fail to give critical feedback to another who has made a mistake that must be corrected. In the matter of going along, the Conciliator may say yes and then go off in another direction as if he had never heard the order in the first place. As for giving feedback that is not positive, the Conciliator may prefer to "fix it himself" (stay in control) rather than confront the one who got it wrong to correct the mistake.

Conciliators use personal influence to short-circuit conflict. This brainstyle is the master of selling and persuading to reach a consensus without conflict. Deliberators rely more on facts and explanations, Knowers and Conceptors may use confrontation to get their way or to get to the truth. Not the Conciliator. Phone calls, personal meetings, and anything to build rapport are the tools of the Conciliator's strength. The ever-present and unstated potential of the *constructive* Conciliator is to use their strengths for building harmony at home and with the team. That is why it's essential for a Conciliator to be at peace with himself. Volatility or moods show up instantly as thunderclouds in the face of the expressive Conciliator. And thunder precedes rain. The feelings within can boil up and spill all over everyone nearby. Conciliators are often the eye of many a storm.

May's sister says, "I swear when she was younger May had to be traumatized to feel alive. Contentment was boring for her. She either created problems or married them." Emotions sometimes seem to become an addiction for those who naturally are aware of their feelings. The Conciliator's gift for empathy can be the path to everyone else's soap operas and their own source of stimulation. Getting excited, anxious, upset, or angry is natural and has the added benefit of getting attention. Conciliators seem to explode rather than confront. They demand, argue, then give in rather than discuss. It is for this brainstyle that so many training seminars were created. Emotional management is an industry that makes billions. *Timing* has got to be too simple an answer, doesn't it? Or, like Brad, more Conciliators can get centered in their strengths, understand their limitations, and just be themselves.

▼

TO SUMMARIZE THE NON-STRENGTHS OF THE CONCILIATOR

Focus. Setting priorities. Structure. Getting things organized in a sequence and keeping them organized. Time awareness. Thinking strategically and logically for the longer term. Conciliators can quickly imagine the future complete with whole scenes of dialogue and action, but not with the left-brained analysis and structure of the other brainstyles. Being neutral, dispassionate, or impersonal is rare. Being accurate or attentive to details in new areas is difficult. Confrontation and conflict are avoided. Neither steadiness nor evenness in disposition last for long.

Conciliators Need Other BrainStyles

Conciliators need the Knower in order to:

- provide focus on one or two goals
- bring in the cold, hard facts
- prepare for the pitfalls to their dreams
- reduce the complex problems to a simpler plan
- state the limit and outline its boundaries in order to finish and move on
  (See Chapter Three)

Conciliators need the Conceptor in order to:

- define their philosophy more broadly
- see where to go in the future
- invent things that are do-able
- plan for more than one outcome *(See Chapter Five)*

Conciliators need the Deliberator in order to:

- get organized and get realistic
- carry out the plan thoroughly
- analyze the numbers
- lend accuracy to their ideas
- provide calm or reassurance and come back to earth *(See Chapter Six)*

▲

DECISION-MAKING

Conciliators make quick decisions based on feelings—subject to revision. On any given issue, the Conciliator will most likely make two decisions, not just one. Left without the immediate, critical influence of the left brain, the feeling, right-brain response wants to say "Yes!" and often does.

The difficulty is that once the structure-bearing left brain has a chance to catch up with the spontaneous right, the decision gets modified. At Time Zero the Conciliator responds with, "Sure, I can do that." At Time Zero + X (maybe as soon as an hour later), the Conciliator may redecide, "That's a bad idea." As a result, the well-meaning Conciliator—the great doer, list-maker, and consensus-builder—can look like the Great Intender. The quick responses can be regarded as indecisive or, worse, unreliable, inconsistent, and undependable: "He says one thing and then does another!" "She never follows through." "The squeaky wheel gets all his attention." Conciliators can be called liars and their integrity challenged, when their intentions are just the reverse and they want the best outcome for *everyone*. Quite paradoxically, Conciliators work overtime on their *nonstrengths* in order to be more reliable and consistent. Making promises that will be kept is a major commitment for this brainstyle.

MAKING DECISIONS JUST AS YOU ARE. The Conciliator is the mirror image of the Knower, who makes a quick, left-brain decision and sticks to it (feelings processed later for the Knower only serve to support their "logical" conclusions). By contrast, the Conciliator just needs to hold off on making that first, quick nondecision until the left brain has had a chance to enter and put pure feeling in balance with reason.

A handsome, fortysomething Conciliator who has been quite successful in travel and real estate sales for over twenty years explains why his credibility is greater since understanding about his own timing when decision-making: "I realized that even though I always *thought* I made fast decisions, it's usually because I'd *pre*-made a decision without realizing it and so I didn't listen to what was being said. What I do now is try *not* to make a decision until I've slept on it. That might be one night or three nights, but it always comes together. I don't beat myself up for taking the time or for changing my mind after I've slept on it.

"You know, I *always* slept on them anyway—and then I'd just go back and change them. I know myself better now. I've gotten used to my own timing since learning about my brainstyle. It works so much better for me. I'm more reliable and consistent than I'd been in the past. It's a more honest way to be." He continues to tell how his marriage has been helped by understanding his own need to think something over compared to his higher-energy wife who decides more quickly. "There's a lot more harmony in our marriage over important things." He adds, "We can fight about the *fun* stuff now."

Timing becomes particularly important for the Conciliator as he makes decisions—especially major decisions that concern life plans and long-range goals. Often, the initial period after a new event is a time for "second-guessing," and emotion-laden doubts and fears are disguised as analysis. The most desirable state for making the best decision is a *neutral* one: to be objective takes time, talk (discovering what's stored in their own right brain), and factual, logical input in several reviews for the subjective Conciliator. Those who just "trust their gut reaction" and make consistently "good decisions" are rare, but they also have the best chance for doing so in areas that require their natural strengths and experience, where past decisions as well as their own *intuition* are stored.

CONCILIATORS CHANGE THEIR DECISIONS QUICKLY BUT NOT THEIR MINDS. "Isn't she just the sweetest person?" "Well, when she's in a good mood she is one of the most charming people I've ever met. But watch out when she's not. She can be hell on wheels!" This gossip could most likely describe a Conciliator because emotional steadiness is not their strength, nor is predictability. The emotional highs and lows of a Conciliator's behavior are caused by the very gift that creates them: the response of the right brain to its immediate environment.

Once a Conciliator has made the intuitive decision that you are a friend, or can be trusted, then they can be the greatest ally in town. At least until they have another experience that tells them differently; i.e., if you say something that "hurts their feelings," they will change their feelings again toward you.

Connected as the (lower) right brain is to the activity centers for fight or flight, it is primed for instant action. Sensory input from the eyes, ears, nose, or skin can be turned into immediate reaction: striking out, tears, a brilliant smile, a phone call, a to-do list—just like *that*. The instinctive response at Time Zero to a request for a decision pours out of the right brain and, most often, aims to please. When that instant response has no outlet, however, it can get *blown out of proportion* and become an *overreaction*. The reaction needs an outlet and it needs *timing* to make the real impact the Conciliator is capable of making, which is an insightful, far-reaching decision.

In working with other brainstyles on new decisions requiring a lot of left-brain facts or structure, the Conciliator may feel and appear "slower." The Conciliators' strength is contributing rapidly to the possibility of future applications—often freely associated. *What about this? What about that?* Imagination is so much greater for the Conciliator that more time is needed to sort out and organize their game plan within the rules. Homework, rehearsal, and preparation are essential to the Conciliator so he can do his thing with confidence and all the spontaneity and fire of "winging it."

BrainStyle Clue:

Conciliators have trouble with others' strengths because of their own *timing:*

- The Conceptors' need to talk through their own *images can be distracting and disruptive to the main job of the Conciliator: finding words for feelings or hunches.*
- The Knower's fast logic doesn't even take the right brain into account for a while. The Conciliator can take the interruption, or the black-or-white conclusion, personally.
- The Deliberator's factual and thorough approach can look initially like impossibly detailed tasks and standards way too demanding to reach for a Conciliator's gifts.

Conciliators do not perform well when making *new* decisions under pressure, especially *time pressure.* For example, students taking tests feel "under the gun." Test questions in math or chemistry can be real threats, scaring the wits out of the Conciliator seeing them for the first time. Taking sample tests (a rehearsal of sorts) can calm some fears. Outlining answers for essay questions ahead of time will help structure written responses.

The Conciliator can easily be left behind in a discussion in which fast, logical decisions are imperative. What a Conciliator *can* do is give quick reactions, consider both sides of an issue and its possibilities. But logical decisions need preparation.

Steve, thirty-one, dark-haired, brown-eyed, with a dimpled smile, known for his winning ways with people, is a manager of distribution for a major soft drink company. In a planning meeting he was pressed by his boss to come up with new shipping routes. Before that moment, Steve had never thought about coming up with new routes. He was faced with a Time Zero (new) event.

True to his Conciliator brainstyle, he turned several colors, his mouth became set in a grim line, he frowned, got mad, then shut down the conversation: "We can't do it. No way." Later, after cooling off and giving himself a chance to think it over (and to let his left brain get into the action), Steve was able to come up with several options for new routes. "I just didn't like the pressure," he admitted, "and I guess I flew off the handle a bit. I work a lot better when I have more time to think about things."

Steve now asks for a break for a few minutes when "meetings get tense or emotional" and cause him to get tense or emotional. "When I feel comfortable, I perform better and give a lot more to the meeting. And I don't just react, as in the past. I let the first response 'sit there' until I can see some alternatives. It's working well for me and my team."

In fact, Steve has handled teamwork and planning so well he's been promoted several times. He's developing expertise in more than just timing with people: he's excellent at developing whole systems in delivery and transportation where people and timing are the major element for success. He has translated his knowledge of his own strengths into excellent coaching and managing skills. "I know my limitations," he says, and adds, "so I guess I make it okay for other people to have their own timing needs and limitations."

BrainStyle Clue:

Conciliators need time to "think about it"—whether they know it or not. If you want a final decision or a true commitment from a Conciliator, don't ask for an immediate response. A Conciliator decision made under pressure is too fluid to depend on. The Conciliator needs to figure out how the thing can be accomplished. Their picture needs to match your goal. Once that's clear, the decision is made.

THE CONCILIATOR INSIDE VERSUS OUTSIDE

Three Conciliators were described by their associates as "stubborn, quick decision-makers who need a lot of control." Conciliators can be mistaken for Knowers. In fact, *anyone* who acts decisively or gets bossy can be *labeled* a Knower. That'll teach you to use labels. Further conversation with these three about their *first* responses to *new* situations *off* the job revealed a real right-brained, *natural* brainstyle.

Jim, twenty-nine, and Bill and Wendell, in their late forties, are three examples of men who have learned a set of technical skills—accounting, technical drafting, and manufacturing. In working in their specialties each comes up with rapid decisions that they will not change easily. Each can act tough, then tender. Which is the true brainstyle?

The difference between these three men and natural Knowers is this: the Conciliators get an image, an intuition, or a feeling response first, *then* they attack a job and start making decisions and giving orders. The Conciliators, unlike Knowers, all feel most comfortable, and are at their *best,* working with others, even though they have chosen careers where the daily emphasis is to solve left-brained problems and design and implement solutions. Each has *decided* (stored in memory) that "changing your mind is wishy-washy"—not what a strong person/leader does. They each admit to being stubborn. They have *learned to adapt* to hard-edged situations by putting feelings in support of their decisions. They stick to their ideas in the face of disagreement, but at a certain price: "I guess I explode sometimes because I have a lot of feelings on a subject," says Wendell, who admits that he must learn to control his temper. Better that Wendell focuses on his feelings *as an asset.* Brad has learned to do this. Leslie, now with a new company, has just begun to focus on her emotional side and has applied for a job in human resources as a trainer. "Teaching is what I really want to do," she says. She will do well. She's a natural.

AT WORK:
MEETINGS MEAN NEW DECISIONS AND CONFLICT

No other brainstyle has the natural ability to *read* people and respond more immediately to a human situation than the Conciliator. *Intuition* begins with the fine-tuned sensing of emotion, posture changes, and nonverbal information available right now. The Conciliator takes a very personal interest in knowing what other people need in order to feel good about a decision. In a meeting, the Conciliator is able to know or sense what everybody else in the room *feels* about the subject at hand. With this immediate and continual supply of incoming data, it is often hard to keep focused on the task at hand.

Whether the Conciliator is leading or attending a meeting, the most obvious, yet the most neglected, thing to do is to *prepare* for *decisions.* (This can apply to "meetings" at home as well.) Time Zero is a time of spontaneous reaction for the Conciliator. This is where *inconsistency* comes from for this brainstyle. To talk through possible reactions of others ahead of time is an excellent way to make the event a Time Zero + 1. Good meeting structure, with a goal, agenda items for decision, and a process for discussion, is an enormous support for this brainstyle, which will put him in a position to listen and facilitate agreement much more effectively.

Case in point: Dan, a Conciliator who knows how to use his strengths, is the product manager for a manufacturing firm. He is ideal for this job because he is gifted in appreciating, liking, and thereby establishing relationships to influence people who see things differently than he does.

Part of Dan's responsibility is to coordinate information and keep it flowing among individuals involved in sales, finance, and technical research. People in these areas have their own "language" and their own ways of getting the job done. Asking a salesman, who thinks in terms of *customer,* to agree with the financial director, who thinks only of *cost,* to agree with the technician, who thinks of the *product,* holds great potential for all kinds of disagreement.

On those occasions when Dan has to call for a formal meeting to set a course of action, he follows a procedure he designed to reduce potential conflict.

- He meets participants one-on-one well in advance of the meeting.
- He sounds out all the players to get a feel for their personal agendas.
- He tries to influence each individual toward an alignment on common goals.
- He arrives at the meeting well-prepared and knowing pretty much what to expect.

Once the meeting starts, Dan has one more hurdle: his own impatience. Contrary to his urge to summarize and pull together a consensus for a quick and well-orchestrated conclusion, he has to force himself to hold back, allow disagreements, and observe the group dynamics at work. Things can get messy and uncomfortable. Earlier in his career, he reports, he tried to "structure every minute" to control the conflict (and his own discomfort) and move the group along. Now he tries to bring out more open dialogue and build on what people say. Deliberators and other Conciliators like this method and don't mind the longer meetings because everyone gets some air time.

All people have some need to control. *How* they do it—what the right and left brain give them to work with—is what we observe as a brainstyle. Dan works easily with group dynamics, which is his brainstyle strength. Without awareness of brainstyles, however, Dan might easily use those same strengths to try to control the group for his own agenda and soon lose their support.

Short, spaced meetings on the same subject can help the imaginative

Conciliator sort and synthesize the continual options that come up, decide on one, and flesh it out to be a whole plan rather than just a great project idea. Often impatient, Conciliators in charge don't want to wait around for details—what may be considered the "grunt work" —even when it is the details that spell success. Staying on track may need others to follow up, but they will resent the Conciliator boss who finds certain tasks "beneath him" to attend to. Conciliators' quickness to show disgust for jobs they're uncomfortable with have earned many the title of Egomaniac.

Another use of Conciliator skills is to seek out the opinions of others, and formulate their own presentation to reflect a consensus. Conciliators who have built on their ability to find common ideas and bring agreement often prepare by lobbying for their position ahead of time to neutralize the opposition (and confrontation). The Conciliator is the natural networker and politician, and depending on the personal values he has committed to, either a "constructive" (longer-term, more mature) or "destructive" (short-term, self-centered, immature) influence on the team.

Conciliators can structure a meeting with the best of them. However, their natural bent is to "wing it," to "go with the flow." This can mean overlong, rambling discussions based on a natural gift for brainstorming—getting the new idea right in the middle of the old one. It can mean *fun*. In a structured setting, everyone gets irritated or lost, but it is *exactly* how writers create scripts: they play off one another's ideas to create the product. Those who can best apply their own outrageousness are the masters.* Conciliators in corporate life often try to force-fit their amorphous gifts into a tiny, square goal. It's always a squeeze.

WARNING! Don't assume that a Conciliator will never fight in a meeting just because he prefers to avoid conflict. Hell hath no fury like a Conciliator who is fed up with putting his right brain on hold for too long. Feelings have a logic of their own, especially on issues

* Larry Gelbart, a seasoned Conciliator writer who started writing for radio at age sixteen, tells of creating scripts for one of the funniest TV shows ever: Sid Caesar's *Your Show of Shows*. Larry worked in a "meeting" with Neil Simon, Woody Allen, and Sid Caesar, among others, where they would just "tell gags, have fun, and play around with an idea until we could make each other laugh." A specially trained stenographer took notes; the scripts emerged from their creative play. (Larry is the writer who took *M*A*S*H* from the movies to TV and wrote the script for *Tootsie* and the Broadway play *City of Angels,* among other home runs.)

held dear or values close to the Conciliator's heart. When resentments get stored away, when others don't attend to feelings as well as the Conciliator would, the volcano may explode. Out pours the passion of the past—all freshly felt in the present moment, filled with personal, molten conviction. Conciliators are fierce warriors—slow to ignite, slow to calm down once on fire.

BrainStyle Clue:

Help the right-brainstyle stop storing up feelings: ask the Conciliator how she feels. Allowing short outbursts prevents forest fires.

Remember, conciliating is rooted in heightened sensitivities.

AT WORK: MANAGEMENT

Having a Conciliator for a manager can be a rewarding experience, particularly if you value relationships and like being part of a team, and providing the particular Conciliator is *aware* that he or she has a natural gift for noticing and responding to everything. No other brainstyle will be more generous in giving feedback for all jobs—well done, or not. Although less likely to be pessimistic (anticipating what you might want to hear), the brainstyle is a continual awareness-reaction machine. One downside is that Conciliators get so interested in what's going on now that they can get very picky about distracting details. Add emotion to pieces of a project and you get twenty separate fascinating issues, ever expanding, which get started, but not necessarily finished. Thus it is essential that the company's or team's priorities—the vision, the mission, the overall direction—be clear for the Conciliator to implement.

As long as your team has a clear vision of its future, the Conciliator couldn't be better at giving you the support to get there. On the other hand, if the priorities are vague or shifting, the Conciliator may not be very helpful. This brainstyle does not *readily see* where to go in the long term. Ideals or outcomes are not the same as whole strategies, which need more analysis. Both Knowers and Conceptors look ahead with more clarity than do Conciliators. The Conciliator generates imaginative options, brings meaning, personal dedication, and commitment to the job by staying in touch with people, making long-term company goals do–able as well as personal for himself and his people. He does *not* come up with the goals in *new areas*. As one new Conciliator vice president put it, "We're working on the right values, and struggling a bit to hit profit targets. Our people are *involved* and *cared for*. Focus will emerge over time." The VP is well-liked, though described as confusing to others, especially when he talks about the job priorities. Meeting profit targets was more difficult than establishing rapport for him. He was asked to leave after eighteen months. He talked only of his disillusionment with "company values for people."

BrainStyle Clue:

When asking a Conciliator to lead, be sure you ask for what he can deliver. The Conciliator is a builder, not an architect. He comes through best when plans are well-defined. Where there is no context, the Conciliator can procrastinate, get distracted, want to discuss the process right up to the deadline, and take a long time to bring in results. The right brain is not disciplined.

One reason the Conciliator is a good manager for the good employee is that he himself hates to be managed—when being managed means being told what to do and how to do it. What the Conciliator wants is support. Personal support. He thrives on being listened to, praised, and encouraged. Conciliators require "high maintenance." They also provide it for others. In short, the mature Conciliator manages as he would like to be managed: with praise, careful listening, and attentiveness to feelings. That is why this brainstyle is a natural for service-oriented businesses. A good boss asks the Conciliator for constructive criticism to keep the working relationship free of resentments because the Conciliator hesitates to share for fear of creating conflict. It also helps a Conciliator to unload after taking care of everyone else. Their natural empathy makes caretaking easier than setting limits or working through conflicts, martyrdom more desirable than holding others' feet to the fire. Conciliators can burn out for lack of their own attention to themselves. They can make a good case for the mental health potential of Happy Hours. They need time to vent, that is to say, unload their right brain.

When put in a management position, the Conciliator can become a great builder and healer of old wounds with these same gifts. So why don't Conciliators rise to the top of all corporations, using their supportiveness and intuition to keep industry humming along? Business by definition is a breeding ground for conflict and change—neither of which is managed particularly well by one who quickly and keenly senses the problems and then adds personal meaning.

The Conciliator can be a barometer that cannot read itself. The result: conciliators are most often found in the middle of large companies. Their success comes in customer-oriented or retail ventures where they provide great, quick service by staying in touch with people.

Case in point: John joined the company as a mail clerk right out of the marines. From the mail room, he worked his way up through production, logistics, and a variety of other jobs before arriving as VP for human resources at a major chemical company. He brought to his job a tough yet reassuring Conciliator brainstyle for dealing with people. Never a technical manager in this technical company, he was someone who could put people together to get a job done.

At the time John arrived, the department had just been reorganized. Many people had been fired, and morale was low. His job was to come in to rebuild and strengthen a department that was fragmented and without direction.

What John did was settle the situation by taking three steps: 1) he surveyed the department's "customers" to find out what was needed; 2) he formulated a simple, understandable direction that reflected the larger company goals; and then 3) he built teams and coalitions.

Once the department had been re-formed as a working operation, he networked outside it in an effort to restore its credibility and reputation, as well as inside it to build teamwork and respect among peers.

More projects of larger impact were initiated and followed through by subordinates under four years of his guidance than were accomplished over the previous decade. Conflicts between sections were addressed by using outside consultants in team-building sessions. John followed up the confrontations brought out in the offsite sessions with his own personal support. His brainstyle management was a good "fit" for the situation: people-building rather than confrontation and the creation of a new direction.

DELEGATION

The Conciliator does not delegate new projects easily; it's too personal. After some experience has been stored, it may be easier. Like all other processes, delegation for the Conciliator begins in feelings or in feeling-based memory. It is difficult to give up control—as good delegation requires—when the attachment to that control lies in the feeling side of the brain that "knows but doesn't speak."

Under the friendly or informal handshake lies a great need for control and structure. After all, it takes time for the Conciliator to attach left-brain conclusions and reasons to right-brain feelings. And once logic has bonded to feeling, the reasoning for action has been marked PERSONAL.

So what does right-brain feeling have to do with delegation? Everything. Projects have emotional meaning for the Conciliator. Everything is personal to the Conciliator. These people search for meaning in work, form attachments easily, and don't like a great deal of change. So delegating a project—or even a piece of one—is a very personal issue.

In contrast to the Deliberator, who has trouble delegating because nobody else is smart enough to get it right, the unseasoned Conciliator hesitates to delegate because nobody else will *care* enough. As a result, for the Conciliator *trust* becomes the central factor in delegation. Trust can be a heavy burden for the one entrusted with a task in the Conciliator's name. And even with the trust factor firmly established, it is likely that the Conciliator will not be able to resist "casually" checking in, just to see "how things are going." If the one delegated to do the job doesn't come through, the failure can be felt as rejection or even a betrayal.

Consider the boss who became frustrated with his secretary. He was as pleasant and personal as he could be in assigning work to her. In fact, he often worded his requests as *favors,* like "Could you do me a favor and get this out right away?"

Yet as considerate as he was to her, she often put off his work. He would show his annoyance and let her know that he was *hurt* by her lack of concern for his projects and, by extension, hurt by her lack of concern for *him.* As a result, he ended up having to do a lot of the work himself.

After the boss learned about brainstyles, he realized that in delegating he had left out the specific details regarding project priority and time schedule: both left-brain functions. Every request he made, therefore, was regarded as a personal one, *separate from the work* his secretary did, so she put them aside in order to "do her job."

> *BrainStyle Clue:*
>
> *When you have been delegated a task by a Conciliator, keep in mind that you have accepted a precious responsibility. Reassure by keeping in touch. Give feedback. Explain that you understand the Conciliator's sense of the project's value. Then do it.*

LEARNING

The Conciliator learns by storing experiences and their meanings, often visually.

He learns especially well on two fronts: from books and experts. People in this brainstyle are often voracious readers. They read for inspiration. They read a lot—finding words for their feelings. They love conjuring the mental images, and reading often becomes a "flow" experience,* like armchair travel. And while often they cannot recall the specific details of what they have read, they can come up with a good rendition of the main idea. Like the Knower, the Conciliator often remembers only conclusions, except that a Conciliator's conclusions make personal or *emotional* rather than logical sense.

When it comes to reading, Conciliators do not store information "as is" in memory the way it is written. Nor do they store concepts as the Conceptor does. Instead, this brainstyle must relate the information to a familiar experience: "Something like this happened to me (or I can imagine it happening)." Once he has made the personal connection, the information can go into memory. Then when it is time to be recalled, the whole package comes back up, personal experience and all.† Memory programs for students (and others) work on this type of recall: store people's names by associating with a mental picture (if you can make them) or remember chemistry formulas by

---

* "Flow," as we saw in Chapter One, is that time when you experience a state of "effortless control," lose your sense of time, and forget your problems while being totally engaged in an experience.

† A real breakthrough for the nonlinear thinker was created by Tony Buzan to facilitate recall for students. In his book *Use Both Sides of Your Brain* (E.P. Dutton, 1974, 1983), he calls the technique a "mind map." Buzan defines a nonlinear way to take notes that helps focus on key words and associations that will be most useful for those who don't naturally think in a linear fashion.

creating a personal association with the first letter of a list. Many Conciliators enjoy word games that require making associations. A good vocabulary is built on this aptitude. You'll probably have Conciliator friends who enjoy crosswords and word games. Their playmates will most likely be competitive Deliberators who also like words.

The Conciliator can appear to grasp new ideas more slowly than others with different brainstyles do. Brainspeed is always the factor for all brainstyles. A Conciliator with a slower brainspeed takes even longer to process information because he is personalizing every major piece of data. That's why memory games and visual cues can work well for this brainstyle; it's a way of personalizing information since they do not file information in a linear way. On the fast end of the scale, there are Conciliators who are *so* fast, *so* spontaneous, *so* responsive, they've been classified with attention deficit disorder (ADD), which is an inability to focus and learn because a person can't physically shut out incoming sounds and sights, and their feelings and sensitivities are extreme. Their natural speed inhibits the quick digestion of lengthy ideas, but is an ideal fit for fast-paced jobs and activities, like managing a restaurant, for instance.*

For Conciliators it is often hard to remember *on demand,* within a test structure or on time. The right brain has a seemingly "random access" retrieval system. Facts and stories pop out of nowhere. This method of learning (storing, filing, and retrieving) makes people in this brainstyle gifted teachers and storytellers. They have an uncanny ability to make even dry facts (at least the ones they recall at the moment) seem interesting and accessible, something an audience can personally relate to. They are often, when extroverted, the joke-telling life of the party, the natural actor and comedian.

The other source of learning for the Conciliator, and perhaps the preferred source, is others. Unlike reading, talking with others pro-

---

* A July 18, 1994, *Time* magazine cover story on ADD updated the latest medical treatments for the biology of the disorder as well as the research on brain activity and genetics as causal factors. Some of the advice for the hyperactive might translate well to higher-energy Conciliators:
• establish a predictable schedule of activities
• learn to use a date book
• have consistent places to keep possessions at school or home
• sit close to a speaker or teacher to minimize distractions
• take tests or do work in a quiet area
The article stressed that others should use lots of praise and support in dealing with the hyperactive.

vides an instant personal experience to bond with the information. The highly energetic Conciliator is always looking for and learning what will work with the most people—a natural at public relations.

On any given topic, the Conciliator is likely to have a network of people who are experts on the subject. Because the Conciliator is so skilled at establishing a rapport with a great variety of people, he can rapidly come up with answers and information on a variety of subjects from his personal network. His approach is a personal one. Deliberators are also excellent at collecting and managing resource networks, but only a few are close *friends*. With apparent effortlessness, the Conciliator considers a network of experts to be personal friends.

Like the Conceptor, the Conciliator learns by teaching, often understanding what was a vague right-brain feeling as he *puts it into words* —an inspired and often inspiring process. These people are natural communicators. The drive to communicate is both to influence others *and* to gain their *own* insights into what they *know*, which is stored in the right half of the brain, and which has no words.

It may appear confusing to watch how the Conciliator learns, "slow" to pick up new ideas, and "fast" to generate reactions and imaginative—sometimes disconnected—alternatives. Which are they? Fast or slow? And do you then judge them as *smart* or *stupid* or *scatterbrained? Left-brain measures don't apply to their right-brain answers.*

Beliefs a Conciliator hold to be true change very slowly, requiring repetition of new information, especially as a visual or emotional *experience,* to dislodge or change the old belief. Grudges. Painful memories. How many of us still hold resentments toward our parents or childhood friends that we should have gotten over twenty years ago? Think of someone who is terribly afraid of snakes or won't fly in an airplane. By the time that person is an adult she has plenty of information to know that it isn't rational to fear these things—the facts show that many snakes are not poisonous or that air travel is safer than travel by car. Even though the rational left brain may have the facts, the right brain—so in touch with the environment—stores the senses, feelings, and images. The experiences remain and logic can't reach them easily.

Conciliators learn more easily than other brainstyles from experience and their rapid interpretations about the experience. As a result, they have to work much harder to change their beliefs, like quitting smoking or giving up a favorite habit. Providing a picture, a story, or an experience may be worth *many* logical explanations. Moreover, for the Conciliator, a request, an order, or a shift in a new direction takes time to move through the senses and doesn't immediately translate into the action *you* asked for. This is why they can be so spontaneous when acting on an *inner* impulse, but resist your requests until you "say it right."

RISK-TAKING

"Taking a risk" is *taking a stand or making a decision in the face of possible loss*. When risk is discussed, *considered* risk is assumed. No person in any brainstyle considers what they're doing as "risky" at the time they are doing it; instead, they see a problem to which they are applying their strengths.

The Conciliator operates best from feelings and acts impulsively—behavior that may look to others like risk-taking in its purest form. In fact, the Conciliator tends to *ignore* left-brain *risk and consequences* in the short term and, after thinking about it, to look for support and a fallback decision for the long term.

Case in point: Mike became a pilot in the marines because of the sheer challenges involved. As he puts it, "Where else at age twenty-three could I be responsible for millions of dollars' worth of equipment, and have as much fun?" What he enjoyed was testing himself to the limits. The "high" was getting back to the bar with all the other pilots, being the star who had overcome all that (left-brain) technology with sheer (right-brain) guts.

"Sure, there was all the macho stuff—who could wear the darkest sunglasses, drink the most, fly the best. But competition wasn't the whole story, although I was in there to excel. The *real* game was to see how far you could go and not get 'caught'—not screw up—to push the edge of the envelope and invent the whole game while you were up there. Flying upside down under a bridge was not scary for me, although other pilots said it was stupid. For me, it was something I knew I had the skill and the problem-solving ability to do." *Risk* was not the issue to Mike. The emotional high of testing intuition and reactions against the laws of gravity were all that counted. *Right-brain impulse + left-brain skill = quick, skillful reactions without regard for consequences.*

The Conciliator will take interpersonal risks often. The Conciliator on a roll can be outspoken and beyond decorum, buoyed by his passion, out of touch with cause-effect logic. He can stride into any superior's office and demand an answer. He will confront leadership in ways that will leave his co-workers trembling. He is working from strength: knowledge of relationships, conviction and passion about values or goals.

Yet what the Conciliator is doing and what constitutes real risk are two different things. The Conciliator *does not consider the consequences of his actions until later.* In fact, what you get at Time Zero are emotional fireworks, not considered action. Consideration belongs to the left brain, and when the Conciliator acts at Time Zero, the left brain has not yet joined the process. Given some time, the Conciliator can become aware of consequences, pull back, change his mind, or re-group for an effective presentation, or longer-term commitments.

BALANCING STRENGTHS

Taking advice or direction from others who think differently can be especially difficult for Conciliators even in small things. A recent argument I overheard at a health club between a man and his wife went something like this:

Husband: "You're going to fall if you keep running like that!" (She is running fast on a treadmill with her knees almost hitting the upper bar. He looks concerned.)

Wife (angrily): "Stop saying that! You'll *make* me fall! I'll run any way I want to!"

Husband: "Don't blame *me* when you fall! You're so stubborn, you won't listen to anybody." (His face is red and his mouth sets in an annoyed line.)

The husband and wife kept an icy silence for the rest of their time on adjoining treadmills. Talking to her later, I determined the following:

- She is a Conciliator.
- She hates her husband giving her "negative ideas—because they *might* just come true!" She actually thought that once she took in the words, her actions might follow *whether she wanted to do them or not!* She reported being "manipulated," "feeling helpless," and "bossed around" by her husband. The problem? Her focus was totally on the other person's words and her own feeling reactions to those words. She allowed no time for a conscious (left-brain) thought to form that might reestablish her *own* logic—not just a retort—but a *use* for the idea behind his words.
- She quickly defended running *her* way with the only tool at hand: heated, emotional words.

What options does she have? Her husband was pointing out a negative possibility for her behavior. If he could put it into words, he would undoubtedly admit that he was concerned for her safety and took her defensiveness as a *rebuff of his caring*. She, on the other hand, after a moment of thought (when they'd stopped speaking) realized this, and, she admitted, "got embarrassed."

She was so afraid of *his* words, *his* control, she forgot who was in charge of *her* feelings! She missed his concern, and his warning for her. She feared giving up *control,* she "lost it," as she put it. She lost control of herself, control of the relationship, control of her goals, and outside input that was meant to help her get her job done. All she was fixed on was her feelings, and her feelings told her to *resist control.*

When control is the issue, it's always a tug-of-war. You focus only on yourself. The results get lost. It's personal.

Conciliators can be quite successful but can have a tough time taking on a partner or following orders for the same reason the wife hated being told what to do: *his* words interrupted *her* experience of *her* inner controls. Conciliators need to take in information through feelings or experience. This means they demand control in order to have time to process their *own* information through their *own* internal system and then resist taking someone else's word for how to do things.

Conciliators, in general, like *good* news, *good* results, and happy endings and get upset with bad shots in golf, tennis, or any game, get uncomfortable with negative financial news, or negativity of any kind. Realizing that "bad" information is only *one* possible interpretation, a *useful* one that can prevent problems, is a left-brained decision Conciliators need to make again and again. Those who know this have a wider circle of people they can listen to and influence, have better plans, and are more effective in the Real World.

BEING THE CONCILIATOR

Being a Conciliator means having the hardware to make a very special contribution to others. Your brainstyle brings people together, and can do so with insight, imagination, and open concern that no other brainstyle can match. Here are some tips on how to be more effective from the wisdom of other Conciliators who have studied brainstyles.

- "Accept your feelings because they are what lets you get along with people. You can call a *time-out* if you get overwhelmed. Everybody will appreciate it. But *don't* spend time telling yourself to 'stop being so emotional!' as so many Conciliators do. *Use* your feelings to contribute to others. People count on you for your empathy, caring, support, and enthusiasm. Let off steam by *talking it out*—not *taking it out* on somebody else," advises a Conciliator in her thirties. Another Conciliator in her twenties offers suggestions for getting feelings to become her own personal support system: "I know I'm real emotional, but I can also be very upbeat. When I get down now I give myself the pep talks I used to give my boyfriend. I set a new goal right away to get around what I thought was a failure. I also have learned ways to calm down so I don't just 'pop off' to cracks people make that I think are negative. I've started meditating and after a tough meeting or hard day I exercise. I feel good about myself much more of the time now."
- "Conciliators are your best friends. Don't expect anyone else in any other brainstyle *especially family or spouses* to understand you in the way a Conciliator can understand you."
- "Conciliators can be incredibly self-involved. If I don't have someone to listen, I'll blab about my life until people turn off. Friends are survival for me, and counseling is a life raft sometimes."
- "Watch out for trying to be the 'rescuer.' I've fallen into political traps in the family and at work trying to empathize with others. I'm a natural spokesperson for everyone *else's* problems and hidden agendas. I'm always trying to help and wind up getting all the flak. It's because they *know* I'll sympathize." Use your passion for a cause by furthering the progress of the *whole* team or family—*including* the boss, your parents, or the teacher. See if you can get everyone together and you be the facilitator. A win-win spokesperson takes time for balanced preparation.
- "When I talk too much about me, it's boring. When I talk too much about you, it's fascinating."
- "I've stopped trying to take care of everyone without being asked. It'll kill you. I let people ask for what they need. It's better for both of us."
- A counselor offered, "I try to think about what I'm feeling when I'm with friends so I can be more sensitive to them. I used to think I knew what they felt before they said anything. I ask them now,

and I've learned to separate my feelings from the ones I project onto them. People tell me I'm very empathetic. They trust me."

- "I've learned to accept that other, left-brainstyles are *faster* at *logic,* not 'insensitive,' 'uncaring,' 'smarter,' or 'better.' I try to use them as resources now. When they are negative, I try to privately translate their statement into a possibility. I ask myself, *If what they're saying were to happen, can I deal with it?* Yes or No? It helps me to think things through just a bit more to include prevention of the potential disaster in the plan. A Deliberator taught me this."

- If you feel stymied because you can't choose which job to take or choice to make, you may, like one Conciliator in her mid-twenties, be stuck because you fear you'll make a mistake, choose the wrong thing, and lose an opportunity to do something else "forever." You may fear the confinement or limitation of focusing on just *one* thing by setting the priority. A career counselor wisely advised her, "You don't have to find the *perfect* job; you are developing your skills. You can try several options in order to find a more perfect 'fit' for you. You don't have to choose just this once. What you are discovering is more about your natural gifts, one experience at a time. Focusing on one thing can *add* to your abilities, not limit you." Conciliators who do not naturally focus or envision the long-term future readily —*especially* when it's personal—feel constrained when they settle on one option. Mature Conciliators say they have only gotten somewhere in their lives when they *had* to work on just one thing at a time. Most confessed that they hated doing so at first.

- When it comes to "getting the job done," favors (and good guys) can get moved to the bottom of the list. Recognizing your strengths, you will be better able to separate the business from the friendship, the task from your attachment to it, and find a neutral way to ask for a desired result from others.

- Manage your impatience by learning about others' timing. You are not necessarily smarter, just quicker to get out of the starting gate. "My idea of smart was an 'ego trip,' " says a hyper-Conciliator who "finally got told off by a friend" for being too impatient. Impatience comes across as arrogance, puts others under stress, and you will lose the benefits of their best thinking.

- Watch for how you can *time* your influence with others so you won't get your feelings hurt when being spontaneous, only to inter- rupt *their* new idea and get put off. Only other right-brainers can follow your rocket bursts, and only if they're calm that day. Pause.

Use *timing before* responding to others: "Let me think about it." "Give me a minute." Ask for time to "sort the issue out" rather than simply resist the new idea or the direction. Ask for more information.

- It may appear to you that those you live and work with will not live up to their commitments with the spirit you expect or the understanding you need. You may start feeling very alone or misunderstood, especially if your partner has a different brainstyle. Discuss your goals, even at home. A couple whose marriage was little more than weekends together (one was commuting out of state to work) sat for an hour and talked about their priorities. It cleared the air, and allowed for a first look at *common* goals—difficult to do when individual work was 90 percent of each person's life. It broke through the isolation. You may need to reconstruct your goals together without *assuming* your partner should already know what is important to you. Look for open empathy and understanding from *other* Conciliators.

- Look for ways to use your great capacity to make friends, build coalitions and teams, and bring the family together, no matter how uncomfortable it is to get started. You have the very best abilities to get others to turn in their best performances. Use other left-brainstyles to help keep the focus on the goals, the time schedule, the priorities, or the plan. Your strengths aren't there, so you do need more time and energy in these areas to bring in results.

- Look for assignments where the goals are clearly articulated. Check your natural response to "get it perfect" or you might wind up doing it *all,* working too long and falling down on the job. Use your natural gifts in selling and negotiating to delegate by getting others inspired.

- Understand that you do not have to be in touch with the future (be a visionary) because you *can find out who is* and take your lead from him or her. Your natural networking skills put you in touch with where the leading ideas are. As Henry Ford said, "I don't have to know all the answers, I just need to know who to call."

- When at work, distinguish between coalition-building and just plain socializing and gossiping by avoiding all negative gossip. "Watch out for making friends by telling someone else's secrets," counsels a Conciliator who says she has had to "learn the hard way."

- When you know conflict is unavoidable (like confronting someone about their mistake), rehearse the scene. Ask yourself, "What's the worst thing that can happen?" Then ask, "How can I handle that?" Anchor your emotions in a reasoned, clear, and caring delivery. Compare them to *their own* best efforts—not someone else's.

- Watch out for projecting into the future based on one or two positive—or negative—events. Many Conciliators become alternately very ambitious, then very depressed because a few events point to success or failure. Get input to define a longer view.

- Keep a journal, or take notes that you can review about your progress, plans, and dreams. Writing can help you get more objective as that right brain finds the words. It'll slow down the spontaneous wildly optimistic hopes and give you time to balance passion with logic, to get real self-esteem.*

- Don't get a job where the primary demands are repetitive and you need to be structured and organized, unless you love accounting so much that balancing the books and getting things tidy is a real joy to you. You might notice what you truly love about the work is the people. Why not make them the *whole* job?

- Take time periodically to check that all your activity (all those lists) adds up to your real purpose or top priority. You can lose the larger picture with all the distracting input you get plus attempts to respond to it all and please everyone.

- Your mental hardware sets you up to make emotion-based, subjective decisions. No matter how objective you think you are, it will never hurt to get a second opinion from someone in another brainstyle. Don't buy hot stock tips or invest your money without an objective assessment. Sleep on it. Stay in control by knowing how you work inside. Go for the best answer outside.

BEING RIGHT-BRAINED IN A LEFT-BRAINED WORLD

Combine a great deal of energy with any of the four brainstyles, and you get an *extrovert* who can process ideas rapidly and think fast on their feet. Others with slower brainspeeds call them "overbearing, obnoxious blowhards who *never shut up.*"

It's especially amazing how Conciliators can talk—even at young

---

* Dr. J. Pennebaker, a psychologist at Southern Methodist University, reported in a study in 1993 that those who kept journals, writing about past emotional experiences, especially when they "described in story form how they had worked out their problems," were "more likely to be in better health." He published his results in the journal *Behavior and Research Therapy.*

ages they're chatty. One theory is that the inarticulate right brain with all that sensory input fuels the left-brain speech centers continually to find out just what's going on in the right-side image machine. *As you talk, you literally find out what you know!* Another theory is if you can't bond or touch physically, you can reach out with words, *lots* of words, stories, personal revelations, and on and on.

Imagine this: You are sitting next to a man on a plane. His face reminds you of Jack Nicholson, the actor, with his brown eyes and hair and intense gaze. Only his face is rounder, somewhat softer. He is wearing a very bright shirt and carrying a lot of packages to get to the window seat. He starts talking before he even sits down, apologizing for all the packages. His energy is so intense, it's like sitting six inches away from a turbocharged fan, a "fan" blowing right into your brain.

COMMUNICATING.   He starts talking by introducing himself. "I'm an entrepreneur. A cheerleader. A dreamer," he starts out, reeling out a seamless stretch of ideas, aphorisms, anecdotes, insights, poems, and visual depictions—all about him and his remarkable life (very much the topic of this internally able, introspective brainstyle—*me, my* life, *my* insights, because Conciliators learn from their own experience). He tells you of three marriages. "I've been *abandoned* twice," he pronounces. *Abandoned?* He grins, enjoying the punch of using emotionally laden, attention-getting words. He is excited, dramatic, even riveting in his language and speech. He's a natural storyteller, jumping around from event to event without chronology, joining ideas with the internal logic of his imagination. It makes sense when he tells it.

INSPIRING.   He tells you of climbing the highest mountain of each continent around the planet after he was fifty, then co-authoring a book about the adventure to inspire others to do the same. In order to do this, he tells you how he mentally mastered his body to get up those peaks. He admits that he had never, nor does he now, exercise physically. He used affirmations, aphorisms, poems, all his mental muscle to pump up his prodigious dream machine of a right brain to distract his feelings and overcome the physical realities of the mountains. He also, I hear later, had a supply of bottled oxygen available, to the disdain of a Deliberator mountaineer, unaware of the lure to the Conciliator of the test of his inner mettle. (The Deliberator, in contrast, measures his conquests more tangibly, and never really boasts of them. Meetings on the slopes among the experienced climbers are acknowledged quietly, without a lot of "hype," he says. "We know who's climbed," the Deliberator says significantly.) Whose accomplishment is greater? Who can tell?

LEARNING.   He learns visually (by remembering pictures) and aurally, often repeating what he hears. He listens intently on occasion. Most Conciliators use the same methods. Some learn by "getting a feel for" new ideas and then getting a picture and talking out the idea until it's "clear," i.e., they can mentally envision it.

TALENTS.   He sings harmony and has had natural rhythm since childhood without any training. *This can be another natural strength for those with strong connections to the lower half of the right brain.*

DREAMING.   His name is Bass, the same as the ultrawealthy Texas family. "But I'm not one of that family, and *I'm* seventy million dollars in debt. People get me confused with their money when they hear my name. The difference is *I* need investors. Oh, I've made tens of millions of dollars in my day, but now I need *hundreds* of millions."

His first dream was to be a boys' prep school English teacher and inspire his students to greatness like Robin Williams's character captures thirty years later in *Dead Poets Society.* "I've seen it [the movie] over and over. Cried every time about the 'what if's.' " His eyes mist even now over that long-ago lost dream so clearly formed from his natural gifts. But when he went to Yale to become a teacher, he "woke up" about his junior year and decided he'd "better make some money." He tells you how he "grew up in a hurry" when he realized what money and success could bring. He then went into geology so he could join his father's oil drilling firm. *He* takes on the "people side of the business" because his brother, who is "all left brain," handles the financial side. He brags, "My brother knows the price of everything and the value of nothing. He deals with people and just makes them mad." In contrast, he talks about his own gifts: "I can make a deal because I love people." He becomes the salesman and key negotiator for the business, which he loves. (Extroverts in all brainstyles love making deals.) He learned enough about the oil business "not to be anybody's fool." (Did you detect just a hint of defensiveness there about his non-strengths? He, like other Conciliators, is concerned about appearances.)

SPIRITUALITY.   He is deeply religious and believes that divine inter-
vention has saved him financially at the last minute several times. He
believes that "applied skill and opportunity create 'luck.'" And he is
actively looking to use all the "luck" and prayer he has to save the
current deal that his dream is riding on.

He has narrowly escaped death several times and attributes the fact
to a grander Plan for his life than he can comprehend. "The great use
of a life is to spend it on something which outlasts it," he quotes. You
may, by this time, have a hard time keeping up with his stories spilling
out one after another, one reminding and taking off from the next in
the *random memory stacks* stored in that illogical, picture-painting right
brain of his. But the power of his message is clear. And the impact on
his life is also clear. He *is* inspiring. You realize *this is charisma,* effortless
and full of passion. He is a teacher and a preacher and he can't help it.
He has access in full measure to the part of the brain that creates
meaning and philosophies. He is emotional and spiritual as he speaks
of his gratitude for the opportunity to live such a full life and how he
deserves none of the credit. His dream ties it all together. He wants to
develop a skiing area that caters to "body, mind, and spirit." Thus the
necessity for the $70 million—*not* for mere "personal gain," but to
create, in his vision, a dream to enrich *others.*

MANAGING STRENGTHS.   He tells you of the problems he has had
because he thinks of things faster than most others—along with the
added difficulty of always needing to explain or understand *in pictures.*
He talks of the struggle it takes to be patient. Oh yes, he has *had* to learn
numbers and the language of business. But it's not his native tongue. He
resolves these struggles by continually recalling his larger purpose for
working with others. *It helps him most to recall that he likes people.*

He overpowers fear, the paralyzing agent for all, by taking on life-
threatening mountain-climbing situations and showing himself he can
survive. He has taken this into his daily life. He feeds positive images
and words into his thoughts continually. "What the mind wills, the
body follows" is his mantra. *Conciliators need to stoke their own furnace
with positive self-talk* to overcome fears and free themselves from approval of others.

He uses his strong, hardwired connection with the unspoken and
intuitive to read people and sell his ideas, but tempers his persua-
siveness with an awareness of a higher purpose—a reason to *serve*

others rather than manipulate them. Conciliators who do not find a larger meaning or purpose for their lives have little focus—the essential condition for "flow" or mastery—and can be left with self-involvement so intense we see them as their "egos" and not much else. Or they are left with no sense of their true value—because a Conciliator's contribution is largely immeasurable.

A focus on facts is ultimately unrewarding for a Conciliator. You hear how this Conciliator has found his answer. Projecting his inner resolution on the world around him, he feels comforted by a universe he chooses to see as benevolent. "Faith is the reservoir for action" is another aphorism he uses to capture the meaning and direction for his life. He has a strong faith as the source of his ability to go against the odds, and the norm, the stereotype of what it means to be a business-man or just a normal guy. *He has made it okay to be different.*

Unusual in his energy level, his frontal-right-brained powers of visualization are intense. As you listened to all his stories, you may have been aware of his excellent recall, likely to be a result of his inner filing system of vivid images that can retrieve the words along with the pictures that were stored together.

RISK-TAKING. Like many Conciliators, he plunges into what others would call "risky ventures." He sees them as simply doing everything he can to pursue his dream. The inner view can create the world's greatest risk-takers—heroes and death-defiers—because they don't at-tend as much to the measurable, the facts, the reasons not to.

You may ask: *But can he get the job done?*

He readily admits to you that he "needs someone with a left brain." He concedes that he needs to leave the room while his new CEO, "a fantastic numbers guy," in his view, calms down the crowd and explains how it's going to work. Obvious solution? Not really. You realize that he didn't understand this simple strategy for most of his career. So he's just recently hired someone with different strengths to complement his own. It's been hard to give up control when you have so much on your side: the passion, the dream, the energy, the faith, the reasons, the incredible persuasive communications at your command.

We each need to realize we don't have it all. Conciliators need to balance their strengths with those of the left brain in order to have a whole answer. And that means taking advice, getting input, sharing control, and keeping their word.

CHAPTER 5

The Conceptor

"I've always felt *different,* ever since I was a little girl. I get 'flashes' all the time, like when I'm driving or when I first wake up. I see the answers in my head to problems I've been working on. I tried to describe it when I was younger and people thought I was strange, so I just stopped telling them."

Confession of a woman Conceptor, crying, in a BrainStyles seminar.

THE CONCEPTOR BRAINSTYLE: A SUMMARY

Conceptor: a person who forms general notions or ideas by mentally combining all the characteristics or particulars. The gift of this brainstyle at Time Zero is to *invent,* because information is collected by both right-brain intuition and left-brain judgment. This can lead to rapid conceptual "leaps" about future possibilities that are hard to articulate at first. *Foresight* is the dominant strength, and at their best Conceptors are visionaries. "Flow" is experienced when mentally inventing the new and untried. Conceptors are often intense, passionate, and illogical during their thought process.

A Conceptor is:

- A person who naturally creates global and comprehensive hypotheses which set the stage for decisions that draw from both facts and insight. Talking is usually more comfortable than listening because the Conceptor, gifted in ideaphoria, can get passionately involved with the information. He or she can't listen well or take in very much data because it sets off an internal, random search for related concepts that follow a logic known only to the individual.

- Conceptors access a rapid left-right-left-right brain exchange in the present and therefore memory or experience is not accessed well or logically. Conceptors live in the world of ideas and inner images, yet are also critical thinkers who can focus and reject ideas quickly. Often, they can express ideas with the passion of the Conciliator and the logic of the Knower, making them formidable proponents of their ideas.

- Conceptors have clear priorities for their ideas and seek real applications for them. Conceptors can be labeled "too global" or "too general," their direction-finding too random or "blue-sky," yet their contribution can be to provide new, previously unseen possibilities.

- Conceptors are the most open to change, seeking new experiences and outside stimulation as a resource for their internal vision machine.

- Achievement is more important as a motivator for Conceptors than for the other brainstyles. To see their ideas in action and to be the best is what drives them, rather than the award or fame.

- Many Conceptors seek to be the one in charge, to make room for their visions at the top. While not as outgoing, their happiest times are when left free to invent in a protected place where their stacks of files and materials won't be rearranged, where their ideas are listened to, and they have an opportunity to try and fail without censure.

- To grow, to take on the new, is vital for the Conceptor. Undefined and ambiguous situations are comfortable, and rules and policies starting points for creating. Conceptors are best in the beginning of things, worst after the project is developed and needs maintenance or nurturing.

- Conceptors are the inspirational visionaries, groundbreakers who love churning things up just to see what they can do with all the chaos.

Conceptors, according to the data we have collected, are even scarcer to find than the Knower brainstyle. Only about 9 percent of the sample of over 1,235 we observed or tested were Conceptors. Of this small group, less than one third of them (31 percent) were female. (See charts on pages 234 and 326.)

THE STRENGTHS

"People either love me or hate me," a young Conceptor woman says, "but they don't ever just say I'm 'nice.'"

If the Conceptor brainstyle suits you, you're probably used to being told this by now. The standard definition for being "nice" was put together by those who see the world using a different set of hardware. You use the parts of the brain that see patterns, make images, deal abstractly, and quickly sort, test, diagnose, and eliminate possibilities. That's how you invent, or how you get to a new understanding of an issue. And *new* usually means personal discomfort for the listener. We only hear applause for the Conceptor mavericks who have earned their superstar stripes by creating breakthroughs that change an industry. But if you're not at the top of the list yet, you know you could be. You think *differently,* perhaps backward to most. And you've suffered for this difference socially, no doubt.

At a party, you may not impress many unless you get to hold forth on something you want to talk about. Oh, dear. You care more about your ideas than making impressions or keeping friends. Your fun is inventing—on the spur of the moment—making things up, based on your rapid re-sorting of observations, intuition, and your own mental slide show. *New* is easy, *traditional,* difficult. As a deductive thinker, you either prove it later or drop it.

If you are reading this to figure out if Conceptor is your brainstyle, take note: many with other brainstyles have a unique approach to life using different strengths. As soon as we say that Conceptors are different and a small minority, some who have felt "different" automatically identify with this group. However, it is not the topics that the Conceptor addresses that make them different, it is *how they put things together* to get someplace new *first* before analysis or anything else. Whereas others who have unusual ideas are usually articulate about them, the Conceptor most often is not—especially about ideas in the formative stage. They must translate random internal images into words and put those words in sequence. With most of their ideas about the future, and with little organized recall, they are at their best with intangibles, theories, and concepts that can unify and redirect the specifics. At first, this can sound like thinking out loud. "He sounds vague, bounces from idea to idea. He's hard to follow," says a fact-based and structured brainstyle about a Conceptor. When at a new or Time

Zero event, the Conceptor is at his or her busiest, talking, formulating, and associating ideas, a most distressing event for the more thoughtful family member or listener who needs time to *think*. A fact-based Deliberator describes a Conceptor this way: "He takes off on a subject and never connects with what I said or what was done previously. He goes from idea to idea and doesn't STOP. He never wants to *rest,* he just wants to *think—in my ear.*"

Although *anyone* can be demanding and unruly, when the Conceptor takes over, his or her strengths create an *original* synthesis of ideas—leaving precedent behind—that can move a project beyond the next steps. The Conceptor is capable of real *creativity:* making *something* out of *"nothing"* (not very many hard facts). In a world dominated by the logic and sensitivities of the two most numerous brainstyles (the Deliberators and Conciliators), the Conceptor minority does things differently, and because this is true, their contribution is often overlooked.

Conceptors score highest in risk-taking behavior by their willingness to try out new ideas in the face of contradiction, resistance, or the threat of loss. They also have the greatest need for achievement of all the brainstyles. Conceptors will move mountains to see their ideas made real, from plays to buildings to computer programs to lightbulbs. Conceptors have the hardware that compels change.

The Deliberator can lead by example, with organization, planning, incremental, even dynamic, strategies that move forward logically. The Conciliator can generate new alternatives and ideas while bringing along the team, and the Knower can envision applications and drive them home—but only the Conceptor is detached enough from yesterday's rules and conventions, while informed by today's feelings, to freely create. The detachment comes naturally because with both sides of the brain in action from Time Zero, the Conceptor does not have to refer to the linear past with the left brain in order to know what to do next.

Conceptors use random associations to create something new that often rejects your idea or smart research at first. The whirling machine inside needs time to spin off possibilities, sort and test them, all before they can join those around them for other ideas. Thinking aloud or in doodles, the more extroverted can even try to talk with indescribable ciphers and wiggles on whatever surface is handy, to tell you of the emerging brilliance being woven as they talk. They are enamored of relationships within and among ideas first. Later come facts. First come a few priorities. Later come the steps. First come conclusions that can shift to new and broader directions, then hop to specifics, then back to the overview again.

This *isn't* like getting an idea and going to see if it can be done or has been tried. It *isn't* like imagining a new way to do something, then painting a whole verbal picture right before the amazed crowd's wide-eyed stares of what the theater could look like with new paint and curtains. The Conceptor might invent a new use for the theater entirely. He might include a halting, rambling, sometimes blurted out, new jumble of questions, diagrams, disconnected speculations, and, after a time, perhaps outlandish assertions about what the product could be or how all the furniture can fit into a smaller space—*without any proof, precedent, or preparation.* They can *start* in left field with only their *own* view that they want to get to home plate. Their brain is working with symbols or pictures, they are trying to put subtitles to them aloud while seeing a changing scene. This can be quite taxing. It can also be quite funny for the viewer. Conceptors can laugh at things that no one else finds funny—it is the silly image on their inner screen that is so amusing and available only to them.

When addressing a complex problem, the holistic approach of the Conceptor can name critical issues, sort priorities, and come out with several strategies for getting to the future. The Conceptor speaks in a personal "code" (which is how he took in the information—as a concept or symbol) in which words are charged with many associations and assumptions. One Conceptor boss told his employee to go after "the truth" when calling on sales reps. He had to be interrupted and asked to explain just what "the truth" was. He stepped up to a board and talked for ten minutes from an outline and squiggles he generated on the spot. Conceptors often speak using a deductive process—they know the outcome and don't know why or precisely how they got there—and work backward to the present. People and systems are all a part of their mental musings. The future is the most comfortable playground, and creativity in approach and solution is the outcome. Controversy comes next.

Just as soon as we say that the Conceptor is creative, everybody wants to be that brainstyle. Like "bottom-line thinking" and being a "team player," being creative has become one of the "shoulds" for everyone. The Conceptor has the brainstyle best suited to supplying creativity and vision. That's just how it goes—but it's not how everyone can or should go.

In fact, early in their careers Conceptors look less like creators than troublemakers. They tend to take rules as starting points instead of stopping points. They can be difficult: "Quiet! I'm doing the talking here. This is MY . . . !" (idea, plan, whatever). Picasso was no picnic to live with. Neither was Thomas Edison. When less secure, rejection of their ideas is a personal rejection and the Conceptor can retreat into a personal shell. They can insist on creating (using their gift) when all that is needed is replication. Their gift is *lateral thinking*—idea generation that can sail away from experience like a weather balloon into the stratosphere of possibilities. Ask a Conceptor to build a moveable container, and she is likely to devote valuable resources and time inventing a wheelbarrow that could readily be purchased off the shelf for much less money.

A Conceptor's gift is drawn largely from the continual access they have to the random intuition machine in their right brain. Intuition of all types is their stock in trade, spirituality their solace. Most interviewed have been embarrassed by their mental flashes, unable to explain how they occur. Consequently, a Conceptor's communications skills are flawed because of this ability to know something without knowing *how* they know. Conceptors describe their own mental fireworks as puzzling even to themselves. "I surprise myself lots of times," said one Conceptor. "I don't know what I'm going to say before I say it."

Conceptors often tell of an ability to hold two opposite ideas simultaneously. Such a gift, termed *Janusian thinking* by Yale psychiatrist Albert Rothenberg, occurs "when seemingly opposite components are seen to be equally valid or complementary."[1] When Conceptors merge opposites and translate the fantastical right brain into left-brained words on the fly, they apply "creative intuition" to invent brand-new solutions to practical problems and make decisions. Their ability to generate alternative ways of viewing situations has led to the creation of everything from packaged cocktails, to wrist-size heart rate monitors, not to mention the lightbulb. What distinguishes this brainstyle from the intuitive machine-gun fire of the spontaneous Conciliator is the immediate practicality of their ideas.

Author Philip Goldberg credits "intuitive evaluation" for feelings of certitude. The Conceptor is notably *arrogant* for being so cocky while so completely bereft of proof. Einstein, for example, was "unreasonably confident" that his theory of relativity was valid, a very typical posture for Conceptors. As Goldberg recounts, Einstein's biographer reported that when confirmation of the theory was received from a British Lord, a student of Einstein's "was somewhat surprised by the Master's apparent indifference. 'What if the theory had not been confirmed?' she asked. Einstein replied, 'Then I would have been sorry for the dear Lord. The theory is correct.' " Even the biographer is taken aback by this Conceptor, Einstein, when he comments, "I have never been able to determine whether Einstein was referring to Lord Eddington or the Almighty. Either way, he seemed awfully sure of his theory." [2]

Conceptors can be passionate, overbearing, overwhelming with the need for their own ideas, but tend to have more personal distance from their business families than Conciliators. Conceptors' organizations tend to be more balanced, emphasizing both analysis, discipline, and strategy as well as teamwork and close relationships. The Conceptor's gift is in supplying the vision and the strategies as well as building a team around ideas, delegating well and being more comfortable with real change than others. Those in other brainstyles are better at evaluating them, attaching costs, getting support, and then implementing them.

Katie is a Conceptor who has learned to focus her strengths and provide direction. An entrepreneur who started and built an interior design firm from scratch in the recession of the early 1980s to two offices with some sixty staff members by 1989, Katie found a few things she could do better than others and pushed only those things. She says she "tries to discipline her interactions." Actually, working from two or three priorities is her natural strength. She has been told that she has a way of initially focusing *all* her attention on the client's needs in a project—both personal and professional—to design new directions for the solutions that fit their situation. She began by problem-solving quickly to get maximum creativity for the lowest cost. How? She says she is best as a "hands-off" manager who provides direction, goals, and even training but allows the professionals to "make the details work." She adds, "I'm best at inspiring others— being somewhat clairvoyant, as in, reading what they're *not* saying, then putting it into a controlled solution." Katie assesses her strengths with an overview, good in some broad areas like drive, delegation, setting priorities, and not good in others, like execution of details on a daily basis. Other brainstyles get to the overview, but not as early or as easily.

Conceptors thrive in ambiguous, ill-defined situations. The NEW is their playground. This is where the Conceptor is at home, where they are free to create as they go along from their own internal images and concepts of what would or could solve all the problems for everyone. They look for patterns in things. Unifying concepts. They look for what is *not* there. "If all the facts point in one direction, I assume the opposite is equally true at the same time," says a Conceptor chemical engineer. An exceptional inventor, Nikola Tesla invented over a thousand things like transformers, amplifiers, switchboards, and alternating currents, to name a few.[3] Gifted with the ability to see three-dimensional objects with his mind's eye, he could envision a new tool and rotate it on its axis *mentally,* then put it aside, only to recall it at a later time to see what improvements he could come up with *without consciously thinking about it.* Tesla said it was both a blessing and a curse to have this gift; a blessing to "see" in such detail, a curse because the image wouldn't go away until he actually built it. The gift for "structural visualization" (seeing in three dimensions) is a genetic gift more common in men than women. It is not unique to the Conceptor brainstyle except when it is combined with foresight and ideaphoria (see Appendix A). These abilities generate multiple, workable possibilities into the future. Many Conceptors "see" concepts in their minds, not things, and are compelled—cursed if you will—to get them to happen. They are happiest with the freedom to be in charge. "Growing up can be very painful," says a Conceptor in her fifties.

Case in point: Carol is a mother of four whose youthful plan for her own future was to be married and have children. "College was too much like high school," she says, "and I really wanted to be away from home." Her small town was too confining for her opportunities. A dreamer, Carol escaped from what she felt was an oppressive small town by sitting for hours envisioning imaginary cities, and designing all the buildings. She would return home and build models of the cities in her room with cardboard and newspaper. Carol can visualize in three dimensions and always thought everyone else could too. She started feeling "different" when she found out they couldn't.

When the plumber called Carol at work to say that he'd have to put in a new set of pipes for her laundry room, before she knew what she was doing, she'd discussed his solution and why it wouldn't work. She then described a new configuration of pipes that would. "How can you do this over the *phone?*" he wanted to know, clearly skeptical. Carol told him she could "see" it in her head and to "go check it out."

He called back in an hour. "It worked," he reported, with a hint of amused envy and new respect. "I never had someone be able to solve a problem like this by telephone before," he said.

Carol liked being in control. As a child, she loved playing "cowboys and Indians, because I could always get the Indians to win—and manipulate the other kids who I didn't think were as smart as me to go do things." Carol chuckles at her childish arrogance, a not-uncommon trait for the brainstyle. She was always fairly independent, never really belonging to any one social group, preferring to move from group to group. She either had "friends or enemies, and not much in between," she recounts. She left school to marry an older man, an engineer, who brought stability and the promise of a good income to make up for a small-town upbringing where there was never enough money or opportunity. She laughs heartily as she tells of how her kids call her "crazy" for doing things differently than other moms, pulling practical jokes, talking more on their level than some of the more "proper" moms in the neighborhood. She creates a very individual and creative environment in her home with special projects and interests. As a homemaker, she has used her visual abilities to landscape large garden areas, remodel the house, and decorate and design new layouts for projects her husband would construct in his business. She gets quite involved with her kids' creative assignments for school. She liked "being at home, without schedule or structure," where she could "get a lot done on her own."

Carol is far more sensitive about what you say about her work than what you say about her pleasant appearance. Well-groomed, she's never been one to spend the kind of time on hair and makeup that her Conciliator daughters do. At five feet eight, she even had her share of physical fights before adolescence set in. She's never minded confronting others directly, "but I gave up fighting when the boys got too big," she grins.

Now in her forties, Carol had to return to work when her husband's venture into his own construction firm went bankrupt. Along with the downsides of having to work ("I'd still rather be home with the kids having *fun*," she moans), there have been some real wins. Having goals to accomplish has meant a source of self-confidence Carol never had before. She completed a two-year college program in one year, with honors. After fourteen years in the home, she got a job as an administrator over twenty other applicants. Going through a personal bankruptcy meant a loss of everything they owned and the family had to move.

She has discovered a great deal about her strengths by starting a career. *Brainstyles show up when there are decisions to make.* Now that she has learned of her strengths in conceptualizing projects, she says, "I think my ability to keep focused on the big picture has enabled me to keep moving forward and finding worthwhile goals when faced with those disappointments." She's been the one to create new synergies and efficiencies in how co-workers use their computer database in responding to customers.

She still struggles with sharing the credit for and control of the information she's working on. Unused to working on a team, Carol is self-sufficient, both in brainstyle strengths and from years of being her own boss. Even at home she struggles with her engineer husband who "asks me to justify and prove everything."

Conceptors as a brainstyle are naturally suited to running the show —especially their *own* show. Their problems arise from not having all the strengths to carry things through to completion. Carol is not the natural collaborator other brainstyles can be. These skills come later and have to be learned. The ideas come first.

▼

THE CONCEPTOR

• Invents a theory	• States possibilities	• Decides quickly	• Contributes as a visionary
• Sees the patterns	• Generalizes	• Gives the global view	• Articulates details on one or two subjects
• Gets the overview	• Reframes, makes a new approach	• Discusses strategy	
• Associates the idea randomly	• Reacts with feeling or an unusual argument	• Reinvents the approach	• Invents, creates, makes breakthroughs
		• Explains in more detail	
		• Changes the entire plan	

TIME ZERO ▶ SOON AFTER ▶ WITH PRACTICE ▶ EXPERT

- The Conceptor takes in selected information at Time Zero with both the left and right brain. They are best picking out the patterns, themes, or underlying concepts in what is said.
- The Conceptor's main strength is inventing—seeing mental images that redefine reality or making up a future possibility, regardless of what has gone before.
- Conceptors use random associations, and are best at generating new possibilities in practical areas.
- Conceptors thrive on change and ill-defined situations where they can sort out the principles and establish new directions.
- Conceptors look for opportunities to:
  - start things with a vision
  - lead others, assembling the skills in assessing, planning, and execution that they lack
  - solve problems in new ways
  - achieve, be the best at something
  - take chances by going beyond what is given
  - see and tell it as it never was before

▲

NON-STRENGTHS BRING CHALLENGES FOR THE CONCEPTOR

The Conceptor is often best with chaos, wonderful in making big changes or getting things started. The Conceptor can be a natural leader. Their strengths do not, however, predict success. These are the reasons why.

COMMUNICATIONS.   It is said that the Conceptor and physicist Albert Einstein did not speak until he was four, nor could he do simple math. Conceptors' gifts are limited by communication.

A pretty young woman, blond, delicately fair with lovely blue eyes, was crying. "I've always felt *different*," she said, "ever since I was a little girl. Then when I came to work here, this woman took me out to lunch to tell me 'We do things differently here. You are proposing ideas that people can't understand. You get very excited in the beginning of a project and no one can follow your ideas.' She was telling me I was weird." The tears, she said, were in response to her first exposure to the description of the Conceptor brainstyle. "All I've ever heard was how I was strange or different. This was the first time I've heard a description of how I think—and more than that—what was *good* about it."

Her job was to integrate several software programs with a variety of computer hardware, troubleshooting problems that arose when the hardware wasn't cooperating, and come up with new ways to coordinate the sophisticated informational needs of a customer service staff of about twenty people. She was hired to keep the glitches out and the wires humming, so to speak. She was good enough to be hired by Procter & Gamble—even without a college degree. She learned her job through sheer interest, and her gift for visual problem-solving. "I get 'flashes' all the time," she says, "like when I'm driving or when I first wake up. I see the answers in my head to problems I've been working on." This was something she was trying unsuccessfully to tell others because her answers appeared in a personal, indescribable code. Translating the "code" was when the heavy lifting started. This Conceptor was trying to create the impact for others that those blasts of insight and views of the future had on her. That was when the blank stares and the rolling eyeballs took their toll. She had been slammed by people who pride themselves on their precision and skill with words. She had not developed enough self-confidence or trust in her own abilities yet to overcome the others' standards, for communicating in a way that "made sense." Now, with brainstyles, she can explain things to a much more receptive audience.

Conceptors, more than other brainstyles, are dependent on others for information. Poor data collectors themselves, they spend more time constructing ideas, tending to rely on only a few sources for their input. It seems that they take in a great deal about a few subjects, but in a rather random way so that the quality of information is crucial to quality outcomes. But it's the thought process they enjoy more than anything. As one Conceptor said in his own modest way, "Even when I get inaccurate facts, I can still get someplace worthwhile."

You might think, then, that Conceptors are natural team players. This is not necessarily the case. Others who want things more "organized" and interactions more "equal in give-and-take" mistakenly label a Conceptor's behavior "manipulative," "demanding," or "egotistical" because their thinking is so different. The Conceptor is very aware of her own thinking and may lose track of yours at first. Their focus is able to narrow to a few priorities, however, which brings focus. Initially, they may try to control the conversation while trying to translate their inner random searchings into a workable solution.

PLANNING.   When the Conceptor is working on a plan, he needs to "percolate" with others who are willing to support his idea long enough to unfold it by talking it through. Conceptors are dynamite at the biggest issues for the plan: the long-term goals, the strategy in outline, the key milestones. Others are best at how to go forward. When collaborating, the steps and strategy are excitingly reorganized by the Conceptor's thinking, but not according to traditional planning mandates or the other kids' rules.

A Conceptor often has "Ah-ha!" realizations alone or in conversation. He can get excited about these insights. He'll want to talk about them—maybe diagram them, maybe build them. They *may* lead to something wonderful. In business, they depend on the right data and testing. For this, the Conceptor needs to sell the idea over time, while others get "comfortable," applying their *own* timing to the new idea.

ASSESSMENTS.   The Conceptor doesn't set out to collect data. He gets an idea and then searches for the connections with other concepts. *Data come later,* and most often is accessed randomly. Collecting data is this brainstyle's *non-strength* and can best be supplied by Knowers and Deliberators. Often interviewing candidates or meeting new people produce a fit with a Conceptor's preconceived ideas rather than a more objective assessment, which takes longer and comes much later for those with these gifts.

At first, a Conceptor's ideas may seem muddled and incoherent when the issue is large. For simpler problems this is not the case; they can readily make grand pronouncements or reach quick overviews, seeing and testing the ideas quickly. Yet Conceptors have to repeat their big ideas several times before they know *exactly* how to say *exactly* what they mean to say. The repetitions *can* help others understand and sign up for the program if they don't let their own way of saying things cut off their patience. Conceptors take time to formulate things into understandable directions.

STABILITY.   For the Conceptor, there is no idea or plan so good that it can't be changed. This means a flexibility that opens possibilities to a flood of ideas that overwhelm. New ideas and their revisions need to be limited by time and available resources. Overcommitment to too many new ideas will limit effectiveness and overburden those who do the work.

FOLLOW-THROUGH.   The Conceptor delegates well and naturally. His preference is to start things. His non-strength is executing the plan. Early on he, like Henry Ford, may sound like one who is simply getting everyone else to do the legwork, by making all the right calls to all the right experts. As he matures, he needs to truly delegate in a way that values the expertise of others. Creativity without execution is nothing but dreaming, and the unseasoned Conceptor can be poor at stopping the creative process and settling in on an idea to carry it through to completion.

Case in point: A Conceptor in his early forties was on the fast track in a large chemical company. He was dynamic—great with ideas and people. Put in charge of a new acquisition, he had a number of ideas about how to move things faster and more effectively to new levels of profitability. Within six months he instituted two major reorganizations, one of which moved the field marketing offices. Any change is disruptive. He followed one change with another and didn't get *input from the team.* Accounts were scrambled and sales lost. Too much, too soon. The Conceptor outpaced the execution, which was deadly for the organization. He got the ideas himself and told the marketers. He needed to spend time helping the organization follow through on one change at a time—offering his flexibility and vision to the problems that arose. He needed a dialogue. Instead, his timing was off. The marketing group stopped listening to his "idea for the day." He lost credibility within the team. Then he lost his job.

A Conceptor will never be as good as the Deliberator at executing an idea or as adept as the Knower in "cutting to the chase." And for all of his people skills, he will not have the Conciliator's gift of building the relationships once the goal has been defined. Once the Conceptor has determined: "There is where we will go to camp," he might easily forget to pack the tent poles, gas the car, or check with the Park Service to make sure there's space. He delegates those parts of the trip to others. Relieved of the chore of picking the destination, those with other gifts can determine what's needed to get there in style.

Once it becomes clear to the Conceptor that his gift involves looking to the future and seeing what the possibilities are, he stops making excuses for not following through and ensures his non-strength will be covered by support systems and those who are naturals at running the plan. He also learns that no one can execute an idea as fast as he can come up with them. The effective Conceptor learns to discipline his own timing of new projects and ideas, the ineffective Conceptor does not.

RELATIONSHIPS. When in a social setting, what you see is largely learned, not spontaneous, behavior. Conceptors are not as interested in learning how to impress others for the sake of having a friend as they are to have someone to share ideas with. Many have spoken of somewhat isolated childhoods, especially if they were not good at sports or didn't like playing the games the same way the other kids did. Friends were most often picked for their ability to follow and listen. Beginning as intuitive thinkers, Conceptors develop a different way of combining and sorting the information they get. They learn early that they'll have to get fairly pushy if they want to be listened to by others.

Without a doubt, Conceptors are passionate people about ideas as well as people. They also seem to form long-term marriages and wonderful friendships. They just will not participate in a steady, predictable way, which is, of course, why you either "love 'em or hate 'em."

▼

TO SUMMARIZE THE NON-STRENGTHS OF THE CONCEPTOR

Assessing the details. Following through on the plans. Organizing the vacation, party, or project into a step-by-step process. Communicating by explaining thoroughly. Collecting all the facts. Acting or performing *evenly*, since Conceptors cannot "maintain an even strain," without internalizing a lot of stress. Routine and stability are the Conceptor's nemeses. Relationships develop over time for Conceptors.

Conceptors Need Other BrainStyles

Conceptors need the Knower in order to:
- discuss future risks and make their strategies practical
- confront others without the passion
- edit correspondence and/or communications
- move them to action or start the action *after* they get the overview
  (See Chapter Three)

Conceptors need the Conciliator in order to:
- support them personally
- represent them or explain their ideas to others
- play imagination games with them
- know who to include in the plan
- build and keep the team or family together *(See Chapter Four)*

Conceptors need the Deliberator in order to:
- evaluate the big ideas for what was missed
- interview people they want to hire or partner with
- balance their ideas by making them realistic
- organize and follow through with a plan
- explain their ideas to others
- handle the politics, neighbors, and family follow-up *(See Chapter Six)*

▲

DECISION-MAKING

Given very limited information, the Conceptor makes new, complete decisions. He may be no match for the Knower at the starting gate, but he is first with a global *response that can set the stage* for making several decisions on a brand-new topic. Once the broad direction is stated, or the hypothesis formed, a project can roll out quite smartly. The Conceptor's decision-making process *begins* with both sides of the brain rapidly supplying input, rather than one hemisphere dominating the other. Intuitive analysis is what distinguishes Conceptors. It is important because, ultimately, long-term decisions require the best of what the left and right hemispheres of the brain can offer. A complete decision must include the imagination, sensitivity, and passion of the right brain with the logic and articulation of the left brain to go beyond what existed before.

People in the Conceptor brainstyle often move more quickly to bigger decisions than other brainstyles can reasonably and emotionally follow. At Time Zero the Conceptor responds with reactions generated by an instantaneous left-brain/right-brain processing. He is general, sweeping, and often arrogantly sure without any proof for backup.

The fact that the left-right brain exchange happens so quickly for the Conceptor gives this brainstyle a distinct advantage over other brainstyles in the matter of making decisions *that others can enroll in.*

BrainStyle Clue:

The Conceptor starts broadly, so others must *contribute.*

- *Unlike the Knower, who quickly makes decisions based strictly on left-brain facts and logic, the Conceptor derives decisions from a blend of reason and feelings. The human factor is always a part of the process.*
- *Unlike the Deliberator, who builds agreement for a single decision, a Conceptor can easily redecide.*
- *Unlike the Conciliator, who can create a future drawn solely from his imagination, the Conceptor tests fantasies for practicality, with or without dialogue and the affirmation of others.*

To get to the future, the Conceptor cannot go into memory stacks as ably as the Deliberator to see what worked before; and he doesn't attend as closely as the Conciliator does to what is available or known on the subject, nor can he be as unemotional as the Knower. The Conceptor has a self-contained system that creates a whole future scene, testing it and reviewing the possibilities by using both feelings *and* critical analysis. Memory is accessed as whole "thought balls" of experience. Rules or precedent be damned.

Conceptors continually redefine, resort, and re-view a problem. The Conceptor can arrive at a number of solutions to a single problem. This capacity to generate multiple solutions is unique, and gives this brainstyle natural flexibility to modify, incorporate, and integrate others' ideas. It also means that when a change occurs, a Conceptor is ready to move. After all, there is no reason to stay with a bad decision when there is another decision waiting in the wings. The Conceptor creates broad-enough decisions with specific plans of attack that can be changed easily. The difference between the Conceptor and other brainstyles is that the Conceptor's strength resides in the inventing stage. Only the Knower is best on the front end of a project and in a very different way.

BrainStyle Clue:

To arrive at a decision, the Conceptor talks around a problem conceptually, using diagrams, metaphors, and images as support. He will probably exhibit a variety of moods—from excitement to negativity and back. He can envision several solutions and how to deliver them without getting attached to just one. This is flexibility, not necessarily a lack of commitment.

One final word on decision-making: it is important to remember that *the ability to make a decision quickly has no particular value.* Most of the things in life that are meaningful really don't happen in a split second. What is important is that *a good decision with long-term value needs the contribution of both sides of the brain.* That way it will be comprehensive enough to deal with inevitable changes. The Conceptor is best at coming up with "umbrella" decisions in a complex area the quickest. *He needs others to make it do-able,* and that takes an appreciation of their timing and strengths. To lead, you need different views to reach a best, not perfect, answer.

BrainStyle Clue:

When dealing with a Conceptor expect him to "create" a decision. Ask questions about what appear to be disconnected parts of his ideas. Help draw out connections and support unformed thoughts. You can evaluate the new direction more effectively later, after the overview has produced some testable decisions.

For best results in the problem-solving process, refer to standardized rules later as points of reference, rather than as limitations or gospel.

CONFLICT

The Conceptor deals with conflict in most areas as just another problem. One Conceptor describes the process as being able to watch interactions "as though I were an outside observer trying out ideas without getting attached to any one of them. I'm simply looking for what *works*," he says, assuming you know what he means by "works." "Other people get locked on to an answer and start defending it. I stay free of that answer by continually testing out each part of an idea and *its exact opposite* in my head—and keep on problem-solving."

When attacked "personally" Conceptors can be ferocious, using their strengths to deal knockout blows by going for the other's personal vulnerabilities. Many choose not to engage in "petty fights." The more extroverted wade right into the big issues, the more laid-back challenge and discuss basic assumptions. What the Deliberator and the Conciliator define as "conflict" is merely problem-solving to the Conceptor. And so it appears that the Conceptor doesn't mind "conflict" at all. To people in this brainstyle, conflict is a part of the big picture: you have people, you have competition, you have disagreements. Most Conceptors we have met love a good "negotiation." A young Conceptor in her twenties was a fast-track consultant with Arthur Andersen's consulting group based on her ability to "wheel and deal" while putting together client proposals for new products. "I loved it when things got 'hot.' The tenser the better. That's when I was the most cool. I love being at the center of the storm."

Yet while the Conceptor *feels* a great deal, and personally enters the fray, he can be done with it and move on to the next event without rancor (unlike the Conciliator, who takes conflict personally and may have a hard time letting go of feelings once they're stirred up). Timing is the difference. The Conceptor will add left-brain logic faster than the Conciliator. Conceptors have their eyes on winning the war against whatever blocks the way to their vision of the future. If losing this or that skirmish happens, it happens.

Compared with the Conceptor, other brainstyles are limited in their natural capacities to deal with conflict.

BRAINSTYLES AND CONFLICT IN BUSINESS

Case in point: Two business partners, Jim and Bill, have worked together successfully for twenty years. One of the major factors that sustains their good relationship is the way they handle conflict. Jim, a Conceptor and the elder, takes the lead in confronting the broad issues between them in order to prevent quarrels based on hardened positions. Bill, a Conciliator, will bring up problems in operations (his area). Jim immediately looks for the larger picture in Bill's specific ideas for the future, and their potential for harming or helping the business *as a whole.* Bill contributes by not demanding control of how they work together. He focuses on maintaining the relationship, allowing his pushy partner to "get it all out, without me taking it personally, or even seriously. I just can't react to a lot of what Jim says. I look for what to build on." The laid-back approach is crucial to their partnership, as Jim will be the first to admit: "If Bill were someone who demands as much control [as I do], we'd be fighting all the time."

A particularly touchy area has been money, especially the percentage that each takes from the partnership. Bill (the Conciliator) mentioned several times that he was concerned about how the two of them handled expenses. Jim suggested lunch and started the conversation with "I don't want you to decide this today. But I want to look at how we share control of the company and how we make decisions."

After looking at the much larger issue of control, they proceeded to discuss the investment strategy for the next few years. Each item was an emotional one for both of them. Bill brought up how much they would take as salary. As Jim moved through each item with him, he kept referring back to the larger issues, looking for how he could get Bill's needs (managing operations and marketing, dealing with customers) met and feel he was fairly rewarded. They addressed salary, formalizing different roles, and a new organizational structure after *several* discussions. The issue of expenses fell into a much broader picture, once it was established. Jim, the Conceptor, says frankly, "I just don't take it as personally as Bill. And I guess I plow through the gut issues a little quicker—they just don't bother me in the same way. I can really get upset if I can't deal with the broader issue, though. And Bill knows it. I demand a lot of control to deal with the concepts." *Conceptors need control outside because everything inside is so random.* The Conciliator Bill says, "He can really get me mad at first—it seems he wants to do everything *his* way. But once I see what he's talking about, I see the logic and we negotiate from there. He gets things going for us, no doubt about it, bringing up issues that are often painful. We

> *BrainStyle Clue:*
>
> *Although the Conceptor doesn't mind conflict, it may be very uncomfortable for others. A disciplined Conceptor can direct his energy at doing battle with issues rather than the people who propose them.*
>
> *The mature Conceptor learns the difference between taking control for* my *goals and using control for* our *goals, the difference between short-term versus long-term wins.*

make a good team because I can figure out how to get things to work at the 'nitty-gritty' level beyond his big ideas."

Jim, in the example above, has studied and applied the material on brainstyles to his partnership. This is not at all the case in most partnerships. In an article in *Inc.* magazine entitled "Reconcilable Differences," a different story of a partnership is presented in which a "rapid accumulation of differences and delusions forced them to scrap the company they had worked so hard to create."[4] The authors interviewed psychologists and business consultants to get these recommendations: 1) *stay true to the goal of minimizing emotions in favor of rational thinking* and 2) *plan around a predefined business concept and plan.*

If the ideas presented here so far make sense, you know by now that the first recommendation is a constant stretch if the brainstyles of the partners clash. Partnerships explode when one or more partners have to work from non-strengths too much of the time. The way to make a partnership work is to *include* the fact that one partner is more emotional, and work *that* into the execution of the business plan. The two brainstyles written about in the *Inc.* article were a Conceptor and a Deliberator. Each brainstyle had his *own* interpretation of the goals and the business plan based on their brainstyle-based perceptions. Resentments over money and clients increased and communication stopped. The *Inc.* recommendations for focus are rational, but only a *start* toward making the partnership work. The third recommendation needs to be: leverage strengths to lead each area of the business. It is not enough to focus on clear goals and communicate regularly. Partners must appreciate what their differences can contribute (as Jim and Bill demonstrate) and communicate using brainstyle timing as a key factor in resolving them. A partnership that works is one where each other's strengths are valued by each of the partners.

THE SEASONED AND UNSEASONED

Young and inexperienced Conceptors have said they can be overly aware of others' opinions—sometimes to the detriment of making their ideas a reality. When too sensitive, they can withdraw. One Conceptor adds that she doesn't like to share ideas before she's thought them through. She also resists having to "prove" her ideas. Nothing makes her madder than hearing someone who's thought about her idea for two seconds get an equal shot at challenging something she has spent hours sorting and thinking through. Yet without the challenges or collaboration, Conceptors cannot fulfill their deep need to achieve. They must learn how to use timing with other brainstyles in order to move their ideas forward. If the goal is to be *right,* then that's *all* one gets. Battles seem to provide the seasoning for this brainstyle; politics are an arena that belongs to the strengths of other brainstyles who are more diplomatic, communicative, and know how to manage the impression they make on others.

After the Conceptor sees what must be done, he seems to fall in love with his idea, and often gets impatient with slow motion. People in this brainstyle can be excessively confident of their abilities and then must learn to be adaptable enough to find ways in and around the system. They thrive on challenge and cannot imagine that there is some task or problem they can't do or solve. The quick left brain directs action, the right side adds the spin. Rules and gatekeepers slow things up. Rules speak of the past and the status quo, two stationary concepts that the Conceptor finds distasteful. Often it is the way the Conceptor uses rules as mere starting blocks in his race for new adventures that people are attracted to. As the Conceptor and all other brainstyles realize how this works, "personality" will take its rightful place, behind strengths.

Case in point: David was a thirty-year-old engineer at Firestone Tire and Rubber Company. As a junior chemist with no track record, he got wind of a tire that kept falling apart in every test. Major resources were involved. The problem was one of international proportions. The company stood to lose money or its reputation if the tire continued to fail, yet no one was coming up with a solution. David decided it was his personal challenge.

His job did not even vaguely involve the problem area. This was the turf of *senior* chemists, engineers, and designers. David, however, was able to draw unmonitored funds for testing, so he began unauthorized tests not only in his own area, but in the design area as well. He asked questions and learned the angles of the cords and how flat the tread was. Using the tire building facilities on site, he ran experiments he designed himself. He tracked them statistically, amassing his own database. He changed the cord angles. He changed the flatness. He lined up the data and saw a new way to engineer the tire, then he hid the new specifications.

While R&D was still focusing on the rubber, David had conclusive evidence that the tire failed because of the design. He knew absolutely how to solve the problem but he couldn't show it to anybody. *He wasn't supposed to be working on it in the first place.*

It wasn't until there was a meeting of the company's international group that David had his opportunity. The tire was the topic of discussion. Its failure was still a mystery. David stood up—statistics in hand—and started his presentation on how to reconstruct the tire and solve the problem.

Silence.

No applause for the maverick.

David may have been right, but he broke all the rules.

The problem disappeared, but that was pretty much the last David ever heard from management about his work. He had to be content with a certain "underground" reputation over the next few years, and an eventual promotion into engineering. His six-year career at the company ended. He soon moved on to get more "seasoning."

It is amazing that the Conceptor ever survives in any traditional organization long enough to rise to levels of recognized authority. They generate controversy by making sweeping statements on large issues. On the way up, this is deadly. They then leave the established family, company, or institution to do their own thing—not such a bad thing—but as David reported, "I nearly lost my health when I changed careers to sales several years later." Stress is a major factor for the alert and highly aware Conceptor.

It may be true that the *mature* Conceptor is the best suited of all the brainstyles for leading, but if so, the young Conceptor is in trouble. Junior members of companies are supposed to *follow* people *and* the rules, not to *tell* others what to do. Even when a Conceptor reaches an age "suitable for leading," he may run into resistance from those who expect the leader to do what he asks *others* to do. A good leader *does not operate* the team or family but sees to it that *the team operates.* This takes years of experience. In the case of this brainstyle, there must be some track record, some explanations and positive relationships so that others can support the ideas as well as the guy who thought of them.

Throughout his career, the Conceptor appears less directed and more "blue-sky" than the Knower, less team-oriented than the Conciliator, and less knowledgeable than the Deliberator. However, the flexibility of the Conceptor's brain process allows for appreciation, if not understanding, of complex concepts like those in music or physics or organizational systems. Unstructured projects are the Conceptors' playground. They "order the universe" by controlling and conceptualizing it into their own vision of what it ought to be, while struggling to adjust/survive within any structure, particularly a corporate one.

Typically, people in this brainstyle have no trouble making reputations for themselves. If they are as intelligent and competent as they are confident and creative, then Conceptors can rise to the top and lead the way, naming new directions for everyone—including themselves—as they go along. The Conceptor is most at home when leading. Seeing what to do and telling others about it comes naturally to this brainstyle (*too* naturally, some would say). Conceptors *like* running the show, and they *can* be good at it.

Case in point: A seasoned Conceptor, "Trammell Crow, America's biggest landlord and one of its richest men, started out 40 years ago building warehouses. Crow's informal management style—intuitively picking a partner here, a partner there—allowed him to build his vast real-estate empire." So starts the cover article "The *Real* Art of the Deal" in *Inc.* magazine in November of 1988. A pioneer in office malls and trade marts, he has "built on or helped to build, more square feet of shelter, roughly 250 million square feet of it . . . more than any man in the country. More forms of it, too." The story of Crow's life, the realization of his vision ("He wanted to build a company that would be the IBM of the real-estate industry"), is the story of a man who set his own rules, figured out whole new uses for real estate, and trusted others to build the business. By 1971, according to a *Forbes* article of that year, Crow was the proprietor (solo or in partnership) of more than $1 billion worth of real estate. Hiring key people with a shrewd eye for talent, he put his vision first before anything. His maturity showed in the use of his gifts. His early partners said he worked harder than they did. Crow's value for self-reliance shows when he says, "I believe that my fate is in my hands and no one else's." He allowed himself the luxury of doing what he did best—inventing new forms of storage we know as "industrial parks" or multifunction buildings and making more and bigger deals. Crow "thinks of himself" not as a landlord but as a "manufacturer of a product—space." This was very radical in any business—but especially in the real estate business.

Even more amazing was Crow's answer to a Harvard Business School student's question, "What is the key to executive success?" "Love," he replied. Toughness and trust merged his business and personal lives as his logic combined with his unique personal warmth.

What stands out in Trammell Crow's case is his willingness to lead the way in building the company by negotiating the big deals, setting the direction, then getting himself out of the way so that execution wasn't his main responsibility. Crow explains, "You've got to know and remember that this company wasn't made by me, but by Don and Joel—and 100 others." The dialogue was continual between the chief and his followers. Talking to them today, you are aware of *their* love for their former boss.

It is important to point out here that the Conceptor's capacity—even necessity—for invention does not make this brainstyle better, smarter, or more accomplished than other brainstyles. A Conceptor's brainstyle seeks to change things, whether things need changing or not. This is a very different process from the Deliberator's rational, usually diplomatic, innovation: making something out of something—e.g., improving, or making what exists better. The Conciliator's imaginative brainstorming also relies on bringing together what is already there in

---

BrainStyle Clue:

If the Deliberator's motto is "If it ain't broke, don't fix it," and the Knower says, "You break it, and I'll break you!" then the Conceptor's motto is, "Let's break it and fix it, and then maybe break it again."

(The Conciliator has no mottos that include the word "break" except "Let's take a break" or "Breaking Up Is Hard to Do.")

new and imaginative ways, as does the Knower's decision-making. The Conceptor can naturally start from scratch. As you can see, this is the good news and the bad news for this brainstyle.

Where others are content, the Conceptor sees problems that need fixing. He is beset by what an artist calls "divine discontent."

BrainStyle Clue:

A Conceptor has the strengths to see that the system operates by:
• *establishing the game (overviews),*
• *setting up the boundaries (strategies and limits),*
• *confronting those who want to play outside of them (handling conflict), and*
• *negotiating agreements where every person can win within the game.*

The brainstyle strengths of the Conceptor fit the criteria. The variables are self-esteem and maturity level.

LEARNING

The Conceptor captures unfixed concepts that gather shape and coherence from the left-brain/right-brain exchange. More than any other brainstyle, the Conceptor needs to deal with information in overviews, punch lines, or summaries, or have the time to create them from a few key facts. This often means visual or verbal presentations. In fact, learning seems to occur for these people when they have a forum in which to articulate and thrash out ideas. As a result of their need to "talk through an idea," Conceptors are not always popular with teachers. Yet they flourish when challenged and praised. All in all, formal education for students in this brainstyle can be a frustrating ordeal—for everyone. They are just not very good at sitting still and learning what is put before them.

When Conceptors don't like doing their homework, it's probably because they don't like to sit still and read. They hate detailed analysis and reporting. They *get the drift.* They like restating or summarizing in their own way. (They may have this in common with some of each of the other brainstyles who will act similarly but for their *own* reasons.) They resist discipline, developing it later.

For the Conceptor, individual facts or details do not become a part of memory until *after* she has stored entire concepts that have been formed through the left-brain/right-brain process. Moreover, Conceptors *store only those details that support the concepts they see as important.* That's because the details have no special significance in themselves until they have been blended into the big picture that the Conceptor can give you complete.

As students, Conceptors may "test high," that is, they do not show up as very bright until they take tests, applying their ideas. It may not be uncommon for the "lazy" one of the class to score in the 90-plus percentile. In class these people may not participate the way "bright ones" do.

People in other brainstyles, particularly the Deliberator (the detail memorizer, or "bright one"), are likely to take the Conceptors' generalizations as sloppy thinking or, worse, manipulation of the facts to reach their own conclusions. The linear logic and clear explanations are missing. The Conceptor seems to discover his own meanings as he talks. This is because the right brain has a big part in his thinking and it *often* becomes clear when spoken by the left brain. The Conceptor learns best by talking things through.

Put a Conceptor in front of a blackboard with a piece of chalk in his hand, and then get ready to go tripping. The Conceptor learns most quickly at the head of a conversation with those who are willing to go on a freewheeling ride through a world of ideas. Conceptors *can be active, fast learners.* The more the Conceptor scribbles and talks and charts about what he is thinking, the more he learns what he is thinking about. The more participative classrooms of the last few years have discovered how discussions and experience-based learning works well for some and not for others. Using brainstyles as a way to structure such learning groups could promote more efficient learning for everyone.

BrainStyle Clue:

The Conceptor stores concepts, not information. As a result, he will often slow down a process of information delivery so he has time mentally to build a concept around a fact. This process sounds like interrupting. It is. But unless he interrupts, the Conceptor will lose interest or become disruptive.

This method of learning, opposite to that of the model student who can memorize in sequence, does not fit our expectations or administrations. Conceptors can be "late bloomers," who learn rules of social etiquette later in life and not nearly as well as others.

RISK-TAKING

Each brainstyle takes "risks" in its area of strength. While other brain-styles may label such actions as "risks," the person doing the risk-taking rarely sees things that way. They are merely "problem-solving."

From the outside, Conceptors look as if they are addicted to risk. They appear to consider only projects filled with the dangers of the unknown. In fact, Conceptors consider many more sides of a project than does the spontaneous, impatient Conciliator. The Conceptor who doesn't allow her own brain speed to run away with her takes in other ideas before committing everything to a project.

Conceptors love the unknown, rating themselves most prone to take chances when compared to other brainstyles (see Appendix C). "I'm at my *best* in a new situation" was said by several Conceptors in interviews. The risks taken are generally calculated risks, based on an assessment of what the future could be like if certain things can be done. In their own minds, Conceptors have determined the questions that need answers. These questions can produce a GO or NO GO with the authority of reason and intuition combined. The "risks" so apparent to other styles are manageable problems to be solved, in-stantly, over and over, for the Conceptor.

By the time the Conceptor says "Go," it is likely that she has on hand more than one arrow for her bow, not to mention plans for containment and damage control should the project go bust. If Plan A fails or runs into trouble, there is always Plan B and Plan C for action. As a result, the Conceptor is prepared to change course at a moment's notice without having to stop and begin all over again. Unlike the Knower, who can lock on to a decision as final, definitive, and unalter-able, or the Deliberator, who has labored to arrive at one and is reluctant to change, the Conceptor begins a project with two backup solutions and is able to change on the fly.

It is the *calculated* quality of the more seasoned Conceptor's risk-taking that separates people in this brainstyle into capable visionaries from "gamblers" and "prophets." The Conceptor brainstyle can make no pretensions to being able to predict what the future will be. Some may decide to do so. The strength of this brainstyle is to look at problems and envision a future state, complete with feelings and results. The end is created from a series of solutions, and is charged with the Conceptor's personal confidence that his problem-solving generating ability will make the idea successful along the way. It must be added that the difference between a Knower and a Conceptor in the life of a risky project is the part that emotions play. Conceptors are very open to the input from the right brain. A great deal of anxiety, worry, and sensitivity to others' warnings about problems will be major factors for Conceptors, taken very personally. The better they are at critical analysis—the left-brained skill of eliminating and sorting into priorities—the more they can envision the downside, especially when in a bad mood. Conceptors will bring a great deal of passion to a risky venture. Knowers will bring a great deal of drive and logic, if they decide to go forward.

BrainStyle Clue:

Conceptors may sound arrogant and be "blue-sky." Look beneath all the swagger for competence and soundness of the plan. What would it cost to get to their vision of the future? Provide boundaries and benchmarks to discipline the thought process they use.

TWO CONCEPTORS

"I used to think I was lonely. Now I know I'm just different," says Kay. Kay is, at thirty-one, on her third career. This time it's an unheard-of Ph.D. in architecture. "I've spent my entire life trying to figure out what was *wrong* with me," says John. Now in his late thirties, John has created marketing research systems that "will absolutely tell you exactly why the customer bought the product." Talking to either of them is a riveting experience.

As a child, Kay was very organized. She kept things orderly because, as she discovered, she is slightly dyslexic. Keeping things ordered outside meant staying in control of the disorder on the inside. Today, she remembers telephone numbers by their position on the keypad. She's always had trouble reading out loud, preferring to read to herself so she could skip words and get the gist. She felt "strange" and a bit insecure about this in grammar school.

Kay does not know John, but they have much in common in the way they think, although their lifestyles are very different. Both loved to read when they were growing up, although Kay was more active outdoors than John. They loved getting new ideas. Kay was conscientious and always got good grades; John only got good grades when he was interested, alternating between intense interest and activity and boredom, retreating to his room and his own projects, playing piano by ear, building things, learning photography, inventing things that he never built.

Both majored in partying early in college. Both found it easy to get back to good grades. Neither had a clear career path in mind. Kay changed majors in college six times. John, after receiving high test scores to get into college, majored in communications. He wanted to go into radio, but without the funds he ended up with his own market research firm, "because this is the information that wins, that solves the problems." Kay, with an unusual intensity level, has gone back to school in architecture, working frequently for two days without sleep after achieving all the fast track could offer in a business consulting firm. Her marriage is background music to her love of learning a brand-new field. Luckily her husband travels a great deal. She is more intense than most people, channeling all her energy into the new field. It would not be surprising that Conceptors have some area in their life they do to excess. Kay is extremely gifted. When she got her industrial engineering degree, she thought at the time that she was treated differently because she was a woman. Now she understands that it is because of her brainstyle. She could never "prove out" her work like the other students, nor could she explain it as logically. She just had the right answers. She says a lot of her confidence came from the fact that her father told her "you can do anything" and she believed him. John says he set out on his own course *"in spite of* his parents."

Kay, like other Conceptors, says, "I was never a part of any one group in school, I belonged to a number of groups. Whether I didn't fit in or whether I chose not to join is hard to say today. But lots of people have told me they see me as aloof, as different. They're wrong, you know. I'm just shy. But," she adds, "I do *think* very differently."

She loves teaching, as does John and most other Conceptors, who enjoy using their gifts to shake up others' thinking, to use their abilities to see others reconsider and puzzle over things as they do so often, as well as having an audience to think through their hypotheses with them. Both like being around others who are stimulating, who challenge them, and are not as patient with those who aren't. Intelligence for John is to "see beyond the obvious, to learn from an experience and move on." He "doesn't like being around critics or negative thinkers," and "can get very insulting to them," he says, unabashedly. Kay is much more tolerant, but spends more of her time with the brightest students. Conceptors have favorites, and may be unaware of it, as wrapped up in the pursuit of their dreams as they are.

Conceptors are quite influenced by their feelings, and can be quite passionate or sentimental about things that touch them. Memories of whole experiences can be quite overwhelming. "Somewhere Over the Rainbow" is not a bad theme song for this brainstyle who is so strongly inspired by the future.

The Conceptor's partner of choice seems to be another brainstyle, especially the one they consider their opposite, the Deliberator. Kay talks of an early first marriage. "We were from similar backgrounds with traditional families and values. His expectation was that I would be a traditional wife. But I soon realized that I could be independent financially and emotionally. We argued a *lot*. He was very narrow in his thinking." Kay left with not much of a backward glance, on to new things on her own. Her former husband, most likely a left-brained Deliberator from her description, was devastated. He'd married for life. Kay has remarried a man who is also a Deliberator, but who is a right-brained explorer in his balanced approach to life. "He knows so much about so many things," she says. "He likes to make sure things are right and in order, which is a real complement to me. He has a great vocabulary, at times he helps me say things I just can't put into words. He thinks about things so differently, so he can question me and challenge what I've missed. He supports me in so many ways. *And he cooks!*"

John has been married for over fifteen years to a Conciliator, a lovely woman he depends on to be very supportive and more stable than himself. Her job involves a great deal of conflict resolution. John respects her communication skills and intelligence. But most of all he values a spiritual connection they share. Their right brains relate easily and well here. Both read and appreciate metaphysical subjects and readily accept the unexplainable with a personal faith.

When John was a boy, he was a shy (introverted) Conceptor and was called a daydreamer. He loved the radio. He created a whole imagined world of radio stations that he would build and turn into an empire when he grew up. He spent hours and weeks going over possibilities in equipment and the impact his inventions would make, imagining what he'd put on the air and how fabulous he'd be as the deejay. He found it hard to describe his inventions to others. The words couldn't be formed fast enough, and he couldn't really contain all the magic he could see in his mind's eye. So he wouldn't try. He'd spend time alone or with those old enough to understand without much explanation.

John reports that after he'd thought through his radio empire over a period of a couple of years, met ham radio operators, and found out everything he saw as "interesting," he had a plan to buy out a radio station, funded by his dad. But his father's death intervened and the dream was put away with the personal loss. "I worked at a radio station at the time. I predicted their value would increase. Not only was I right, I couldn't afford the plan any longer." He was on to photography and then, of course, creating with a computer.

Drawing more from his right brain, John is keenly introspective and extremely sensitive to those around him. "I spend a few minutes with a problem and I know the answer. I look through very disconnected information a client will give me, for instance, and *wham!* I don't know how I do it. But I found a way to use statistical methods to prove that I'm right most of the time." Yet he has his limits. "I thought I was retarded because I couldn't do addition. Well, I hate addition, it's *boring.* And anything routine, for that matter. Teaching is fun but it's still too repetitive. I like to solve whole new problems *all the time.*"

John knows he could never work for someone else and so he started his own business. He flies an airplane and skis, plays the piano, and learned to sing "faster than any other student" his teacher had ever taught. John has had to spend the most time learning interpersonal skills for his business. Dealing well with people is his Achilles heel. "I was so arrogant when I first worked, I made presentations just to make other people look stupid—like the president of the first company I worked for. Luckily, I found a supporter who was also a Conceptor— the only guy in management, I'm sure—and twenty years older than me. He told me to quit it or he couldn't protect me and get any money for my projects. If it hadn't been for him, I'd've been fired rather than leaving eventually but on my own terms." Today he says,

"I've learned that if I were as smart as I thought I was then, I'd've engaged them instead of making them mad." John paid his way by creating new computer systems applications for the firm.

How does he stay creative now? "I have to get out of town about every third weekend," he says. "If I don't, I'm no good for anything. I get snarly and add no ideas." John needs to recharge by getting back to ideas and away from the daily details.

John and Kay expand the boundaries of the very brainstyle that is famous for doing so.

Conceptors introduce changes that get the rest of us out of our ruts, no matter how much resistance they encounter every step of the way. Conceptors are often overlooked when the credit gets passed out. It is easy to forget who started things. The Conceptor's strengths look so easy as they put things together so simply, that we often are unaware that they're doing something special. Before Conceptors get involved we're confused; after they get involved, we're resentful. Later we start to hook things together based on something they said and forget to tell them that it was really their idea in the first place.

BEING THE CONCEPTOR

Those who know say that being a Conceptor can be a trying experience. When you feel isolated, different, misunderstood, "Remember that you are not alone, there *are* others who think like you do," says Kay. "Knowing this has made all the difference for me." As a Conceptor, you may be very clear in your own mind that you have incredible insights and that you are better equipped than others to deal with the big problems that face you and others because you can see ahead faster than they can. You also know by now when the difficulty arises, and when you want to tell them your ideas. "Timing is a small price to pay," says Kay.

Here are some further tips from Conceptors who have discovered how brainstyles work in their lives:

- "When I was young, I *made fun* of people. As I grew up, I learned to have fun *with* them. People eventually smirk at my corny humor," says John.
- "I can't talk about philosophy or religion or politics early on— sometimes not at all with some relatives. But if you intend it well, stay general enough, you don't *have* to be offensive."

- "Other brainstyles may need time to sort their experiences into your new categories—especially on personal topics—and this can be upsetting for them," explains a Conceptor when asked what has helped him develop patience.
- Conceptors can generate three or four whole plans to keep things moving. Explain that this is what you're doing, so you get involved in the *beginning* of things. "If you're patient, then you're not seen as *too* changeable."
- "Keep a supportive friend or spouse nearby when all others abandon you, i.e., don't fight with everyone at the same time. You may think you can stand alone, but you do a lot better, you know, with someone you can really talk to."
- Saving and retrieving ideas is a major problem. "I get so many ideas, I get overloaded easily. If I write them down, I lose them." The doodles on the napkins and scrap papers are important, but get lost too often. Many Conceptors develop their own systems for keeping ideas available—from sketchbooks to relational databases on computers to erasable white boards at home.*
- "When you get too many ideas with no one willing to listen, it's best to blow off steam some way other than venting upon those around you. I've learned you've got to have stress relievers—especially exercise—to stay human."
- One Conceptor elder advises, "The more obnoxious *they* are, the more polite *you* must be. That way they can't dismiss your idea because of how you said it."
- "Once it was okay for me to be wrong and admit it, I did a *lot* better with everyone."

  Communications can be the stumbling block for Conceptors.
- "Sometimes I can help people in other brainstyles by describing why I don't 'chat' easily, and why that doesn't mean I'm aloof. I've learned to ask 'Is this helpful?' Otherwise, I've been told I overwhelm people with ideas and they can't deal with them."

---

* Thomas A. Edison (1847–1931), with more than a thousand patents, kept more than 3,500 notebooks. "The pages present a visual biography of Edison's mind at work: every single invention . . . as well as countless other ideas, metaphysical speculations and the multitude of projects that never advanced beyond the scribbled page. . . . An obsessive draftsman, hoarder of ideas, supreme egoist, engineer and botanist—a conceptual inventor, scientist and mathematician, Edison illustrated every step on his 'voyage of discovery into the unknown.' " "Eureka: Thomas A. Edison's Notebooks, Brought to Light," *The New York Times Magazine,* May 14, 1995, p. 30.

- "I say this, and I don't mean it to sound bad, but trying to communicate to someone else in another brainstyle is like talking to someone who drives a car when you are a pilot. *You* know what it's like to drive a car, but *he* has no clue about what it's like to fly an airplane. *You've* got to explain your*self.*"

- "I thought *every*body thought like I did, but that [we didn't get along] because I was just impatient or put people off or something. When I realized that my husband didn't think *at all* like me, that he wouldn't take a job that I'd take, that he wouldn't even look at a job or a problem like I would, well we had a most enlightening talk about *how we think* [differently]. It really helped us. I stopped thinking he was just rejecting my ideas. Now I [realize how people think differently] automatically with everyone."

This Conceptor says her hardest time is at the beginning of projects when differences are greatest, and vocabulary and experience to bridge the gaps are still undeveloped. "If they know you're not trying to put them off it helps," she offers. "Even better, tell them about brainstyles." She illustrates with the following example: "I have a professor who's a Conceptor. [Since I'm a Conceptor] I'm the only one who understands him. He speaks on several levels at once. He gives assignments that he doesn't explain, but that are clearly for a purpose, I mean I can tell that he wants *us* to look beyond the obvious and figure out the connections. I call them 'Mind Games.' I love them! But the other students get mad; they call him the 'Mysterious Prof.' They say he doesn't teach, he doesn't explain—he philosophizes. And it's true. Really, he just isn't making the connections for them. I want to explain it for him, but I don't have the vocabulary either. This seems to set me apart from the rest of the class at times.

"He [the Conceptor professor] takes *nothing* for granted. I understand that. Neither do I. In fact, my current question is *What is reality?*"

The Conceptor's gift is to see underlying patterns in *concepts,* much as a Knower sees underlying patterns in tangible *things.* This can set you apart or, as you find the words, help others see things differently.

- "Your projects need to serve others, not just make *you* look good. Deliberators especially dislike your erratic methods and the way you brag about your achievements. Conciliators, if they're not trying to outbrag you, can listen and be supportive. You've got to tell others what's in it for them. Make a point of appreciating their way of thinking."

- Conceptors agree this may be one of the most difficult lessons to learn: get allies at work who want the new and untried and have the bucks to support you. "Pause for politics, it'll pay off. You've *got* to have someone who understands you or you'll never get anything done."

- "I've got to have philosophy or something spiritual nearby when I get stuck. I don't read, I graze, but I get nourished by the concepts and can start all over again."

- "Get your hands dirty."

- You're a natural entrepreneur. Consider taking your overqualified, underappreciated set of strengths away from the boring and over-structured safe haven of corporate life (if you're there) to the continual challenge of your own company.

GETTING ALONG WITH OTHER BRAINSTYLES

In order to avoid the frustrations of being the Conceptor in what appears to you to be an ignorant and slow world, tell them what you're best at providing, then get all the concerns on the table at the beginning. Work on goals by describing ideas as actions when others get confused. People in other brainstyles like activity more than you do. Have frequent and shorter meetings. Save yourself from enormous frustration while staying in control. When people are doing what they do best, they will not find your energetic facilitation of their work either bossy or arrogant if you are working alongside just as hard.

- Supportive Conciliators are a wonderful audience when you (Conceptors) are brainstorming ideas. They can supply the imaginative support needed to take a concept from disjointed metaphors and images to a full-blown solution. Get an agreement up front with this other brainstyle about who is the leader and who is going to take the idea further. It might prevent some hurt feelings.

- Deliberators are the best partners for objectively assessing an idea, a person, or a project. You will miss the small things, be inconsistent, forget the criteria, get excited about one thing and miss the rest. They can cover your non-strengths in evaluating against criteria and planning how to get things done in a "realistic" time frame; that is, within the time frame of other brainstyles.

- If you are particularly sensitive about a project, don't let the Deliberator or Knower in on it at the beginning. They are best at critique. Also, both of these other brainstyles will want to focus on just one idea. "Don't push [them], they'll say things to get you off their back and only follow through on the one idea they like anyway."
- "Knowers are great partners in creating the future. They add the hard edge, the straight lines, the clarity."
- "If you're more shy, you may tend to get *too* serious about your ideas and their global importance. Lighten up so everyone else can too."
- "Keep your word," since follow-through is your non-strength. You need to track your projects with a system you actually use. If you can't personally follow up on projects that have been set in motion, make sure there is somebody who will.
- "You need a specialty that supports your vision with knowledge of a particular field. The hardest times occur at the beginning [of your career] when you can see where to go and no one believes enough in your idea to follow [you]. You'll need to out-talk them with some facts."
- "You're only as good as the quality of information you get."
- In order to control and reorder the universe as you know it is supposed to be, remember this: *you can always get control over others by getting them to do what they are going to do anyway.*

6

The
Deliberator

"There's Deliberators in general, and then there's me."

Response by a left-sided Deliberator after several discussions of all the brainstyle descriptions, how he fit each one and why, finally, he would acknowledge his gifts as those of a Deliberator brainstyle.

THE DELIBERATOR BRAINSTYLE: A SUMMARY

The gift of this brainstyle is in *assessing* what's actually going on around them and *remembering* what they've stored in their mental files as the best or right answer to a situation before doing other things. They can be rapid with opinions or assessments of a situation, but delay decisions to act. "Flow" is often experienced by those with this brainstyle when in hot pursuit of the answers to a challenging problem that requires a great deal of complex information, analysis, and probing to figure out and describe the solution. Creating elegant solutions, flawless systems, or striving for perfection in something is fascinating for Deliberators, whose strengths are then employed at the maximum.

A Deliberator is:

- A person who accesses the memory first, structures and analyzes what they take in, to bring their own sense of order to things. A person who solves problems with their acute observation of both people and facts, assessing and comparing to what should be, recalling, sorting, synthesizing, and giving answers in their area of expertise.
- After assessing the situation, a Deliberator uses both the left and right brain to respond to give balance to their thinking. Their gift lies in the ability to analyze or assess first before becoming emotional, generalizing, getting to the "bottom line," or making a decision.
- Deliberators do not make hasty decisions in new situations, they have an advantage in assessing more information while organizing their thoughts before acting. They use memory-based, or experienced, thinking and actions to try to bring order to things. As we now know, memory is located throughout the brain, so Deliberators may be covering more territory to search for their answers, thus the delay in their response.
- Deliberators see the world by putting together the pieces to eventually construct the whole picture. They are the Reality Minders, the ones who assess how things are as a baseline to get somewhere better.
- A Deliberator is most comfortable with precedent as a starting place.
- Deliberators come in a wide variety of speeds and sizes and are the most difficult to spot, precisely because of their strength for learning and storing such a wide variety of information. There is no standard occupation for the brainstyle. They are the ones who can *learn how* to be quick at everything.
- Some people in this brainstyle draw more from the right brain after Time Zero, while some draw more from the left. That is why many who have the multifaceted gifts of the Deliberator confuse themselves with the other brainstyles.

In the BrainStyles database of over 1,235 people, the Deliberator is the most numerous. Forty-two percent (42 percent) of the target group observed are this brainstyle, with men 60 percent of the total Deliberator population. (See charts on pages 234 and 326.)

THE STRENGTHS

When you've met someone capable in this brainstyle, you're apt to say:
She doesn't just react. She thinks before she does something.
So professional. So insightful. His questions really get you to think.
He had a way of looking at the plan that makes a lot of sense.
After talking to her, I feel so much better. She's so helpful. She takes you

one step at a time, so you feel like you're making real progress. Before this, I
felt so scattered and confused.

He knows something about almost anything you want to talk about.

In a new situation, people in this brainstyle think before deciding. It may be no more than a pause, but it's long enough to search memory banks and apply what they know to the next move. Thus, the brainstyle name.

These are the folks that, when using their formidable gifts, get us places the way we are supposed to get there. They put things together. They bring a structure to things. Even if they're messy housekeepers, they have a mental order for it all. Using their basic aptitude for analytical thinking, they can impose a logical, most often sequential (A-B-C-D) order to things that were previously random, complex, and confused. They are the mom or dad who schedules three kids, their school, lessons, shopping, meals, a social life, *and* a job pretty routinely. In fact, of all the brainstyles, the Deliberator is the one who can wade into complexity and get it organized, though not necessarily simplified. Throwing the baby out with the bathwater was not done by a Deliberator (at least on purpose). They love those files. They tend to save things in closets, drawers, on shelves and in scrapbooks to use as a reference or reminiscence. That is unless they've finally decided to clear the decks and throw everything out (before starting all over again).

Most Deliberators are also good critical thinkers and tend to assess, challenge, question, and compare what they're given before going to work on it and making it better, faster, simpler, or more understandable. They first find the holes, later the common threads. They get accused of being "negative" often by those who don't know how to use this talent. They are most often the challengers, the questioners, the ones who are never satisfied with the outcome. At their best, they always raise the stakes for achievement. There's always another issue to face, a problem to solve, and challenge to meet. They are forever explaining how things got to their present state of affairs before launching into how things might work better, and are adept at creating "models" for improvement. The descriptions are in a variety of languages, from the technical to the poetic. Brilliant Deliberator novelists and painters take your breath away with their re-creations of a scene. And those that have finely tuned sensory abilities, as many in this brainstyle have, include all the details to create a vivid and realistic picture.

More than likely, when there is an established standard for something—rules, a roadmap for getting there, a procedure for the way things should be done—the Deliberator is responsible. Deliberators can create policies and procedures, come up with how to swing a golf club, or make just the right sauce for the *poule anglaise,* and explain it so that you can understand it. Often, they are natural teachers, out of their sheer love for learning new things and explaining them to others. They *need* to use their ability to make the world a comprehensible place. When they find out *why,* you'll know.

Most have a natural talent for making a good impression on others and are the diplomats among us. Most can attend to the finer points of things in interactions (when they want to), and can make a career out of the right and proper way to do something (which doesn't mean that all Deliberators are "proper" by any means). But coming up with a set of rules for Dungeons and Dragons that aces all the other players out of their defensive weapons when playing the game is "proper" too, if you look at it from the point of view of a competitive Deliberator. Deliberators compete by being right with the facts and on top with the best comeback or smart retort. The more the left side of the brain gets accessed by the mentally active Deliberator, the more competitive they are; the more active the right side of the brain, the more inclusive and collaborative. The latter might just reconfigure the rules to make sure everyone gets included and feels good about the game before they try to beat your brains out. Whether the Deliberator collaborates or competes is something learned, not mandated. But most certainly, the natural gifts of gathering and storing information spur them to have the best answers and expertise. Deliberator leaders are at their best when they are on top of the information, and tend to demand the same of those they trust. It *had* to be a Deliberator who said "Information is Power."

In the normal course of daily events, the gift for gathering and remembering information means that a Deliberator confrontation is the equivalent of presenting information, with the assumption on the problem spotter's part that when the other side gets the facts, they'll *do* something about them. In some quarters this is called *nagging.* Ah, how disappointing it is for the well-informed Deliberator to see how casually others can treat his precious information. "But I've told him over and over what the problem is and he still refuses to do anything about it!" The Deliberator assumes that the other will think as he does and move right on to the planning and fixing of the problem. Deliberators are constantly disappointed when this doesn't happen.

Deliberators tend to avoid direct and especially emotional conflict, by far preferring a discussion—even a heated one—but an argument that doesn't get irrational (yuck) or involve messy tears or yelling. Keeping their cool is much easier for the more left-sided ones, but once *any* Deliberator is riled, the emotions tend to rise up like a tidal wave and effectively block any rational thought (see the footnote in Chapter Four, p. 110). The crash upon the shore will explode and take a while to melt back into the still, calm waters of normal conversation.

If any brainstyle likes "role models," this is the one. Deliberators learn by example. Since analytical and diagnostic abilities are the strengths, then the non-strength is foresight, or the ability to envision long-term implications and be motivated by rewards that may lie far into the future. Deliberators may become competent entrepreneurs, but their real strength is in mapping out the steps and strategies for the near term, or generating the outline of the system that can make things go more smoothly. When up against the Conceptor whose main strength is to invent in the future, the Deliberator can get very uncomfortable with the "blue-sky," futuristic leave-taking from the world of the concrete and proven. That's why an example or role model is so helpful—inventing their own models comes later and in areas they know best, so they like having someone show them the way as they go along. They can then get on with making things work, which is their real strength.

Rather than launching into the unknown as a Conceptor might, the Deliberator *innovates*. That is, she builds on and improves the known by taking smaller, more provable leaps that create whole new generations of products and ideas. Deliberators (as well as Conciliators and Knowers) tend to build on the past when using their strengths to make new things, plans, or products. You won't find Deliberators in the Change for Change's Sake Club.

The fact that Deliberators work out of both sides of the brain means an overall balance to their thinking. At their best, Deliberators are the most objective, factual, and neutral of all brainstyles when it comes to presenting or considering new ideas. Once they store information with a bias, however, they can be overwhelmingly dogmatic, leaving no detail out of the torrent of reasons why they are right and you're not. They admire consistency and get frustrated with, or distrust, those with random ideas and lots of emotion or hyperbole.

This brainstyle, which is naturally curious, possesses learned behaviors in every area. One such man presented himself to a prospective employer as a "chameleon" who could "be whatever I need to be to handle any situation." If any brainstyle could deliver on a promise like this, it would be the Deliberator. The pervasive problem is, of course, that trying to be all things to all people gets them into trouble and they can be labeled a "jack-of-all-trades, master-of-none." Deliberators are trying to get it all so they can be, do, and have it all, all at the same time. They see themselves in all brainstyle descriptions. They have the hardest time accepting the notion of "limitations" and are most likely to be confused (and confusing) about who they really are. They tend, then, to make a lot of promises about what they can deliver both to themselves, and to others. When centered on their gifts, however, they are the most realistic and reliable of the lot, and often come through with a dedication that is unbeatable.

▼

THE DELIBERATOR

• Assesses	• Is aware of	• Has the answer	• Sets the
• Analyzes	intuition	quickly	standard
• Recalls	• Wants to	• Plans, organizes	• Argues, debates
• Is thoughtful or	organize things	• Sets up a	• Teaches
shows no	• Wants	system	• Becomes the
reaction	information		expert
	• Calms things		
	down		
	• Makes a list		
	• Challenges,		
	questions, gives		
	opinions		

TIME ZERO ► SOON AFTER ► WITH PRACTICE ► EXPERT

- The Deliberator resists influence at Time Zero: nods or ignores, but doesn't react, while searching memory and assessing the situation.
- The Deliberator makes delayed decisions.

- The Deliberator can give rapid opinions or assessments.
- The primary strengths of this brainstyle are:
  - assessing things: comparing A to B, looking for flaws, seeing what's missing, what could improve
  - analyzing things: putting an order to things, fitting a piece into the whole. They have a mental order and can find things in their physical mess
  - learning and remembering: they are curious and like challenges in learning and storing information

- Deliberators seek opportunities to:
  - set up the plan
  - learn
  - be challenged
  - do the right thing
  - make the world a more rational, understandable place
  - see and tell it "like it is" accurately

▲

THREE DIFFERENT VARIETIES OF DELIBERATORS

Three sons of a Deliberator look and appear very different, have chosen very different careers and lifestyles, yet all are Deliberators. They also represent the three major groups within the brainstyle: the *more typical, steady Deliberator with analytical strengths;* the *right-sided* Deliberator, who assesses first, then draws more from the right side of the brain; and the *left-sided* Deliberator, who assesses quickly and then draws from the more structured left brain. For this brainstyle, there is *not* a one-size-fits-all description—it's just not specific enough.

The Steady Ones

About six foot two, blue-eyed and brown-haired, the middle brother describes himself as "slower and not as bright" as his brothers. He has always had a steadier lifestyle. He does not readily seek out physical adventures, preferring his own mental challenges. He loathes big changes; loves challenges that demand his talents. The conclusions he finally forms seem set in concrete. Personal losses are heartbreaks for him. A death of a friend, family member, or pet can be a quiet but long-term grief. He has a long fuse, reacting mildly and after consideration most of the time, but if he's really worked up about something, *watch out*. There can be fireworks. Deliberators are slow to ignite, slow to subside.

His high standards show up over time in his own dedication to his work. His mother helped him define his career by reminding him of a favorite childhood fascination with medicine and doctor gear. Her support encouraged him to choose a direction he might not have formulated himself. "She believed in me," he says, his voice gravelly with feeling to this day. And so he set out to become a doctor, studying very hard for very long hours to get through med school. He never got above-average grades until he really worked at it. He tells of how he had to review material over and over to remember it, and thus he came to a faulty conclusion that he is "not as bright" as others that he knows.

Although clearly a very feeling person himself, he feels uncomfortable with very much emotional expression. He hates steep emotional ups and downs. His peaks and valleys are more like low-lying hills. He avoids confrontations if at all possible. He tends to understate rather than exaggerate, and doesn't trust those who are too volatile, labeling them "high-maintenance." Most Conciliators are above his patience/pain threshold for handling rapid incoming information and giving out quantities of reassurance. He likes structure and organization to stay in control, valuing self-control very highly.

A Deliberator often proves the old saw "still waters run deep." They smolder rather than sizzle, often keeping things private until some explosion occurs.

BrainStyle Clue:

The basic strengths of the Deliberator include:
- *delayed decision-making involving more memory search, and careful consideration of data*
- *preference for a single option when deciding*
- *an ability to see what's wrong, missing, or incomplete, to generate high standards for the way things "should be"*
- *an ability to explain and discuss rather than confront emotionally or bluntly*
- *delayed anger, delayed recovery (a tendency to hold grudges)*
- *the greater the stress, the more in control*

As a doctor, he is skillful, thorough, conservative in approach, dedicated to his patients, gentle, caring, and consequently well-respected, and so has built up a large practice quickly. He has become a specialist in his field—a very happy place for those in this brainstyle to be. He is also a specialist outside his professional life, attending to a few interests: family, sports, collectibles, and friends. He does not read many books, preferring magazine articles that pertain to his field and interests.

He does not manage his own finances, deferring to another's much scrutinized, and therefore trusted, expertise. Where he can't become an expert, he leaves things to those who are.

The Explorers (The More Right-Sided Deliberator)

The eldest is more outgoing, with higher energy than the steady middle brother. He seems to inhale information about others. His curiosity means lots of new topics to discuss at dinner. He'll read up on a city he's going to visit, call the visitors' bureau, prepare ahead. He's a natural researcher. He also cares about your opinion. He's sensitive to how you tell him. He assesses the quality of a gift or a purchase almost as carefully. He's aware of everything you wear, down to the labels. He does his best to organize incoming stimuli, which is certainly critical for those who are finely tuned to the situation around them.

Brown-haired, blue-eyed and slender, at about five feet eleven, the oldest brother has always been more outwardly sensitive. He expresses his feelings the quickest and is very alert and responsive to any nonverbal messages around him. Deliberators care very much about how they're treated, something they share with sensitive Conciliators and Conceptors. In fact, many confuse their gifts with those of these other brainstyles, until they explore their own special capacities for analysis and execution in depth.

Growing up, the eldest could be very impatient, very focused on what he needed at the moment, and had lots of projects. His grades were above average in high school when he was interested, and he had a lot of interests. He is curious, open, sensitive. His higher energy means more unpredictability (some friends think him moody). He can vacillate from aggressiveness to avoidance when it is necessary to confront or conflict with others. He still hates direct confrontation and will avoid it if possible.

When the eldest brother went to college, he tried to follow his dad's mandate to be an engineer, doing well in algebra and calculus but not in trig or physics, and so ended up in general business with the feeling that he'd failed—a harsh self-criticism with a painful result. A strong, left-sided Deliberator who couldn't understand the emotional side of his son, his dad gave love and support by spurring him on with his own high standards and advice to "do the best he could." Counseling wasn't in the picture. The son heard only criticism. He tried to be "tough"; but always fell short. Yet, tapping into a natural persistence and a need to excel, he went to graduate school, where he finally found marketing and liked it very much. The field had pizzazz, which pleased his tastes, and had concepts he could understand and master. He liked new things that would stimulate his curiosity and need for learning.

The eldest brother's right-sided access means he is a very sensuous person, aware of how things look, feel, and smell. All the more reason for him to choose marketing where sensitivity and good taste count. After graduation and several jobs, he traveled abroad a great deal, hitchhiking, living with friends, moving from country to country, experience to experience, in a seemingly insatiable thirst for the new and untried. In his twenties, he became involved in the personal growth revolution of the 1970s. Philosophy, religion, and spirituality were always a part of his life and became especially helpful in giving him a more understanding and accepting view of the world than his high-achieving, demanding father could explain to him.

This brother tried two corporate jobs and didn't like them. He didn't have the confidence to start his own business. He was easily bored by accounting and wasn't that good with financial analysis. He often suffered in his own comparisons with others. He needed his own place to shine and was unclear where that was. He enjoyed work that gave him a sense of accomplishment. He would volunteer for various organizations when he had the time, but he "didn't have the patience" to be a counselor as others with these same strengths might choose to be. His preference was to work with "real-world" issues rather than all those "messy" (translation: confrontational, illogical, and scary) emotions.

Right-sided Deliberators are "good with people," because they are able to make quick interpretations of what is said, and apply their sensitivity to figure out what people want to hear. Without self-confidence, this gift can keep its owner "off-center" a lot of the time, resentful of their sacrifices or observing others and personalizing the worst possible interpretations—something many take decades to overcome.

An excellent learner, the eldest brother would read widely on self-help topics and discuss what he learned by teaching or sharing informally; an excellent teacher, he was articulate in recalling and presenting what he knew on a variety of subjects. It points up the curiosity most Deliberators use in taking in information, reading, and figuring things out. Sometimes all the new information helped; certainly it made him an interesting conversationalist. It was one-on-one counseling that allowed the real growth, however, and a stable marriage that settled him down.

At thirty-nine, after succeeding at a number of sales positions selling concepts, not tangibles, he became a general manager of a retail franchise with about twenty employees. This position took advantage of his sensitivity to others, as well as his sales experience and marketing background. It was a good fit. He did quite well for about five years. He gained in confidence and presence. Sales grew substantially. Systems were installed and improved. He hired staff, then trained them extensively in personal and group sessions. Turnover was the lowest it had ever been. He was personally involved and very challenged. He worked hard. He was good at "facilitating" in the office, that is, he didn't insist on having all the answers himself, and open about what he did and did not know. He got people involved. He was a kind and caring boss who was active in the community, marketing his company enthusiastically while enjoying visibility and status himself.

But, finally, he couldn't make it work with an "autocratic" boss who "didn't care about people" and who wanted more and better numbers with lower costs. To a Deliberator, values can make or break a relationship. He was forced to leave because his boss wanted a more confrontational and focused style of leading than he could deliver. At forty-five, the right-sided Explorer cruises the Internet working on a number of voluntary marketing projects out of his home that represent his values for people and the environment. The pace is not too pressured, there is a variety of things to do, and he can travel and keep in touch with a network of longtime friends and acquaintances, before launching his next adventure.

BrainStyle Clue:

The strengths of the right-sided Deliberator include all the strengths of the Deliberator and are:

* more openly emotional after a new event than other Deliberators
* more open and articulate about intuition, spiritual or philosophical insights and beliefs than other Deliberators
* more willing to change things around them than other Deliberators
* often impatient and focused on immediate responses and results, therefore sees "change" and "progress" in themselves and others most readily
* often the helpers, using sensitivities to take care of or teach others

---

The Whiz Kids (The More Left-Sided Deliberator)

Thirty-five years old and naturally slim, bragging that he can still fit into his high school clothes, the youngest brother is more practical than fashion plate, and hates throwing anything away that he can "still use." The eldest is amazed at how anyone could keep anything that long.

The youngest has seemingly endless energy, and a fast pace to match. Among the three Deliberator boys, he got the best grades, learned the quickest, got along best with more new people, and never really overreacted to personal slights. He is best at maintaining a cool exterior. Like his brothers, he still hangs out with guys he knew in grammar school. He is a loyal friend. He is also the family problem-solver, acting as a skillful and dedicated guardian of the mechanical and physical health of the home and all its equipment. He is the one who gets called in a crisis, personal or otherwise. You realize this is how he shows his deep loyalty and caring for his family most easily: he *does* things for them. In fact, Deliberators in general are better at expressing how they feel through deeds over words. The youngest is not openly emotional. He loves solving problems, thoroughly and efficiently. He is reliable. When the problem is brand-new, he does thorough research before proceeding.

He was the most athletic, most capable at a number of sports, and loved adventure. While in college, he drove, as a professional, a race car designed to go 250 miles per hour in a quarter mile. He wanted to continue this hobby but didn't think it was mentally stimulating enough—too routine. He never saw a risk; instead, he saw problems to solve where he'd figured out ahead of time how to match his skills to overcome the possible consequences. He figured the risk down to a fine level of detail. He was never out of control. He was on top of the odds. He took up hang-gliding, water-skiing, sky-diving, parachuting, fast cars, drinking, and dating. His high standards showed up in high performance, no matter the topic. He graduated with honors as an engineer and went on to get his MBA. Personal fears or relationship meltdowns were never dwelt upon since he would simply move on to someone else. Unresolved issues didn't "slow him down" or serve as grounds for personal counseling. Unlike other Deliberators, he didn't relate well to either "head shrinks" or books on the subject. Great with numbers, protocol, keeping focused, and working hard and smart, the left-sided brother had aptitudes similar to those of his father and so chose the same field. He was soon on the fast track at the large corporation he joined right out of college. After eight years, and receiving a substantial bit of funding from his dad, he left, much to corporate dismay, to start his own oil exploration business. He has spent the last two years with another expert developing an intricate computer program, designed to control the data and bring predictability out of complexity to reduce risks. He has learned everything he could about all aspects of the project, especially the computer analysis. He is excellent at analysis, financial or otherwise, and focuses well on any complex task, staying with it until it's completed. He can learn and absorb a great deal of information. He reads for self-improvement and achievement but not really for fun. His family wonders if he'll ever get married. Close relationships are his long suit over time, but the emotional demands of new relationships are more intense. When it comes to making a decision for a mate, high standards make it hard to get started. The Whiz Kid slows down in decision-making outside his area of expertise—especially when it's deeply personal and unpredictable.

What do all these people who live, work, act and appear so different have in common?

Overall, all access their thoughts, ideas, and opinions first and their feelings second. They first look at the pieces, then become aware of the whole. This sequence can mean a step-by-step approach to go forward, drawing on their past experience for both facts and feelings. All Deliberators are relatively more even-tempered than other brainstyles, although this evenness may not appear in the early years, espe-

---

BrainStyle Clue:

The strengths of the left-sided Deliberator include all the strengths of the Deliberator. Left-sided Deliberators are:

• less likely to have as much sensitivity in the five senses or fine motor skills, more likely to be a skillful athlete using large muscles
• the least emotional in this brainstyle
• fastest of the Deliberators to reach a single solution
• able to focus and diagnose problems more quickly than other Deliberators
• more data-based and thorough than the Knower
• generally more structured than other Deliberators
• more mathematically gifted than other Deliberators

---

cially for the more moody right-sided Deliberators. Most remain loyal friends over long periods of time. Most Deliberators value steadiness, and so long-term relationships and family are central in their lives. Most Deliberators care about the impression they make on others, are diplomatic, often have a variety of interests to talk about, and attend to the details of good communication. Men can be incredibly romantic suitors, and both sexes tend to be faithful and attentive spouses. Both try to attend to the details and keep things steady for the long term. If either cheats on their spouse, it's a costly personal decision that has undoubtedly been rationalized with a whole new set of carefully thought out standards. All tend to perfectionism in the things they care most about.

Over time, and in new matters, all assess a situation and apply what they've learned. From gardeners to goalies, computer hackers to taxicab drivers, Deliberators will be the ones to look and sound *professional* or authoritative because they can think before they speak and consider their answers. Good recall and respect for tradition—the ordering of life—is often valued. Routines, like going to the same restaurant or vacation spot with familiar friends, are relaxing. All are excellent planners and have used this strength in whatever they have done. They plan their adventures and challenges. Under stress, they all tend to get quiet, get organized, and appear more in control of themselves. They each compete by being right, having the best answers, or failing that, invest in the best of something else: a car, clothes, a home, and so on. Quality *and* style are important. Deliberators look under the hood after they admire the design. They don't brag out loud. They just own or wear the best. They don't just talk about it, they prefer to set the example.

DECISION-MAKING

Deliberators are the brainstyle most likely to make and keep commitments over the long haul. Most decisions are made by homing in on *one best answer* and sticking with it.

Weighing the pros and cons can be an endless pursuit; two or three options can provoke analysis paralysis. That is why most Deliberators prefer one alternative. They've invested the time in generating it, it has their own analysis behind it, so it's obviously the best one. Deliberators can be called stubborn by those who don't appreciate such commitment to a decision. *Patience is their virtue.* If all else fails, the best they can do is wait out those whom they see as "wafflers" who "bend with the wind." Look what happens when you change your mind by trying to be flexible: you can lose an election like the Deliberator President George Bush, who vowed, "Read my lips, no new taxes," then changed his decision in response to Congress and was defeated a year later. Deliberators would be first to point out the downside of quick responses.

The central gift shows up in the common experience at Time Zero. New decisions are delayed while considering information—facts, precedent, previous experience, others' expertise, or new alternatives —one at a time. More than for other brainstyles, experience and memory govern actions for this brainstyle, even though the right-sided Deliberator can seem comparatively impulsive or emotional.

NON-STRENGTHS BRING
CHALLENGES FOR THE DELIBERATOR

CONTROL.   Control is the lifelong challenge for those with this gift. Deliberators strive to operate in a chaotic, random world while trying to get things under control, find their "fit," and learn enough to understand how it all works. Life is mercury under the thumb—just when you think you have it pinned down, out pops another uncertainty. The Deliberator is the guy who goes to pick up a ball and kicks it away every time he bends over to snare it, never reaching his own idealized standards, even after a lifetime of achievement. From Nobel laureates to everyday folks, these are the ones with their own special brand of perfectionism. Contentment can be a mere rest stop in a career; home and family are where it's savored.

You can see the range of strengths available to this brainstyle among the examples. No single one has all the Deliberator abilities, yet each is trying to perfect something in their lives. Frustration levels reach the red zone for Deliberators who have an answer and not enough control to get things done just the way they want them.

FOCUS. Focus is the blindspot for those in this brainstyle who have trouble admitting that they have non-strengths. This isn't just a phenomenon among Manly Men, however. Women Deliberators are also in control of themselves and the chaos around them, and hate to admit to any uncovered bases. Equality in perfectionism, indeed! The strength of someone who seeks perfection, often working on several things at once, means that the non-strength is *focus*. A typical strategy of the Deliberator is to attack all priorities equally, generating lists of items, with nothing left off. Even the more left-sided and focused in this brainstyle can fall prey to their many interests, their need for accuracy, and their desire to be thorough, which after all, are only expressions of what they can do well.

GENERATING MULTIPLE ANSWERS TO A PROBLEM. This is not something the Deliberator can do very easily when it's a serious and new issue. Those whose energy is high, and who have an ability to generate a lot of ideas (ideaphoria aptitude), can think of options readily, but if you look closely, the options are really alternative steps or activities. Whole new strategies and career plans do not emerge easily or quickly out of these strengths. That's why a lot of discussion is necessary. Deliberators gather others' ideas, order and organize them, and provide the Assembly Required, but do not invent the whole package. This non-strength uniquely qualifies them for running their own business.*

Meet the left-sided Deliberator, Burk. Burk is in one of the worst possible situations for him right now, struggling for financial survival.

---

* "Most small business owners do not need charisma, flair, or strong ideaphoria to succeed" according to Brenda Smith's research in *How to Strengthen Your Winning Business Personality,* p. 170. Weak idea generation *helps* efficiency and reliability in a company.

All his previous measures of personal success are gone. But Burk shows only more self-control. He spends a lot of time reading novels. His wife is supporting them both financially.

Burk has a very precise way of figuring things out: alone. He thinks about a problem for quite a while and doesn't talk it over with anyone until he's got it resolved in his own mind. He only consults his attorney in private. Burk frankly admits that he wants to be in control. When problems get too many, Burk just clams up.

He started working in landscaping (mostly yardwork at first) right out of high school. He was so diligent, and learned so well, he was promoted up through his company to be head of the landscaping division as the company grew. He didn't go to college. Didn't need to. He learned quickly, was excellent with numbers, even taught himself, then developed computer schedules for over seventy-five workers. As a manager, he didn't delegate readily or trust easily. He believed in maximum accountability, assigning tasks that must be done according to his exacting standards. "I've seen what happens when other people take over, they screw things up." Burk was a strong overseer. After he trusted someone, he'd leave them alone.

Now Burk is responsible for home landscaping and maintenance. Recently, a new man was hired to run the commercial side of the business, which has had a great deal of turnover lately. Leo was hired as a "people person" to keep workers motivated and on the job longer. About a year after the change, Burk went to his boss about the new guy: "He's a pain to deal with, not a real businessman." Burk knew he could do things more efficiently and profitably his way (which was probably right) and tried to get his boss to fire Leo (which turned out to be wrong). Burk wanted to run the whole thing. The boss's answer was no. But Burk wouldn't stop there. He boldly presented a plan to consolidate both departments under his control, with Leo reporting to him. Leo, of course, went ballistic and mounted his own very effective counterassault, which cast Burk as a loner and troublemaker. Leo put forward some pretty hard news from employees who didn't like Burk. In hand-to-hand combat with Leo in front of their boss, Burk was tough—too tough—and lost his temper. Leo was justified, Burk fired. Burk went for the whole pie and got no pie. But Burk lost more than his job, he had no other career. He wouldn't go to a business competitor for a job. Pride? "I'm sick of the landscaping business," he said. And he probably *is* sick of a business where the only real challenges he'll deal with are those that he can't control. His strengths don't apply to people. He needs a partner for that.

From Burk's conversation, you learn that he's bored. Reading between the lines you realize he has no plans or any money. So, Burk's lifestyle has been substantially *downsized,* as the saying goes. He is using his computer skills to work on some small projects out of his home. He is not looking for a job in the computer field, however, which is "useless without a college degree."

There is considerable strain within his family. His teenage son quit school; his daughter, ten, told her friend that she wanted to go live with them "to have a nice family, like ours used to be." Her grades have fallen and she wants to move. Burk is using his single answer to step up the controls at home too: more homework, more rules, less play, less talk. His wife is having more frequent illnesses. Burk appears unruffled in public, but isn't sleeping much, has intense headaches and significant outbursts of temper at home from time to time. One thing is for sure, no one is telling him what to do. His ability to set a course and stick with it is awesome. In an age where values and tastes are fleeting at best, Burk is a rock.

Burk's non-strength is generating multiple answers to a problem; his strength is carrying out a plan. Under stress, he only gets *more* controlled implementing his plan. He is not a typical "entrepreneur" but is a perfect candidate to run his own business.

Burk is a decisive commander, driving toward a goal with his strong analytical and critical thinking. He would find a military culture comfortable, one that has clear rules for implementation. All good generals know you have to have the loyalty of the troops. Burk has shut down on incoming information in order to be in charge. He will not be a good partner, especially now. When he is in charge, an organization will dictate goals that Burk can oversee. He will challenge others with his demanding standards. However, Deliberators who are strong and decisive like Burk can simply decide—one time—to include others' ideas in their plans. "America's Toughest Bosses," a regular feature of *Fortune* magazine, portrays men and women who have these gifts and have driven their companies to great success with, of course, a high body count along the way. Employees either learn to use the boss's high standards as a personal challenge and the goals as learning opportunities—or they quit.

Currently Burk has to settle for a much smaller playing field than he used to have: there are not businesses that can make you rich and still be one-man shows with his level of expertise in a new field. Finding loyal lieutenants can be done, but sooner or later negotiations must occur. Burk, playing from strength, trusts his own answer more than he trusts anything from anyone else right now. His own business will be the basis of his self-confidence. Employees are another more troublesome matter. His solution: a computer consulting business he can run out of his home. The business is a natural fit, yet obviously limited in scope and earnings potential. Using his own labor, he's finally making enough to pay expenses after three hard years. He probably has plans for expansion, but those plans are, of course, private. If he chooses to work for someone else, he would be a valuable asset —*if* he could drive another's agenda the way he drives his own.

FORESIGHT. Foresight is the major limitation of the brainstyle. The Deliberator gets to the future with planning and experience. Foresight is an ability to live and think in the future using minimal clues and random indicators from the present. Foresight leaps to the future without a Deliberator's ruler. Deliberators predict trends, as any good economist will tell you, based on the past. When foresight is a strength, possibilities can leap and solutions unhinge from previous experience and data. Those who are the more right-sided members of the crew will use insight and inspiration funneled into the realism of their analysis. They will parallel the creative process of the Conceptor, but they will use different strengths: more facts, more analysis. It takes longer to get to the future for those who have their feet on the ground. When with Conceptors or Conciliators, the Deliberator usually feels uncomfortable with the overoptimistic and unsubstantiated futures the others describe so easily. Deliberators are at their best planning and implementing for the near future, or beyond the next few years, by a path you can follow all the way from the past.

Leonard is a nice-looking, sandy-haired man of about medium height. His eyes are large and gray and filled with intensity and near-despair. As a college student, Leonard made the wrong decision. He didn't know how to choose a career after flunking out of his first choice. Some buddies told him of a "cinch major"—guaranteed, easy B average—and, even better than that, he'd come out with a *title:* "You know," he drawls, "doctor, lawyer, *engineer. Oh, boy.*"

When Leonard, who is a right-sided Deliberator, made the decision in college to switch majors from landscape architecture to packaging engineer, he did so out of a lack of foresight, along with a lack of appreciation for his real strengths, which would have allowed him to ask more questions and think things over longer. He took one highly critical look at how he had already failed to meet his own high standards, flunking cost accounting and landscape design classes, and so took the first suggestion someone else offered. He generated no other options. So he ended up setting out to master things he couldn't master—pitting perseverance against the obstacles.

As a result, Leonard ended up working twice as hard as his peers, taking too long, arguing a lot, and being generally defensive in each new job he took. He was trying to grow into his non-strengths—basing his whole career on them, in fact.

Now thirty-five years old, Leonard has been fired, or nearly fired, from every single job since college. *Five* good jobs in the last ten years. Today he is understandably in real pain. "I'm at the end. I'm at the wall. I'm so fed up . . ." His voice breaks. His self-control is strained to the limit. His whole body is tense as he paces, sits, grabs a chair, then stares out the window. His eyes fill with tears more than once as he grimly recounts each miserable experience, sparing himself nothing, having excised the blame and explanations in months of outplacement counseling sessions.

"I finally had a job with the biggest company yet. My title and résumé seemed to work." He grimaces. "After about six months, they let me know just what they thought of me. I had to give up an office for a *desk*. And not only that, my desk was assigned to be in the corner of the basement—the *basement*—analyzing compounds I couldn't care less about. And now that I was in a research group, it was even *worse*. If you weren't a Ph.D. or an M.D. you didn't count for anything. I was told over and over that I was *just an engineer*. It was like being told to *go sit in the corner*."

He *knew* he could do better. He said that during the first three jobs he blamed his boss, his management, or the situation. Something just out of his reach needed to change for him to be happy and get his due.

After ten years, he still couldn't master the mathematical analysis—even though he could analyze the ideas. He didn't have the ability to get the precise and detailed accuracy required to satisfy the bosses, even though he was able to be specific and detailed in his observations.

He only recognized what he might be good at by seeing it in action —marketing—where he could coordinate more ideas, rather than be the expert, and deal with people more frequently, persuading them with reason, which he knew he could do. He still couldn't pass the statistics courses required to get another degree. He was stumped. Leonard was misapplying his strengths to lose five jobs, one after another. He was running into dead ends in pursuit of a bad decision made a decade before. Sometimes to their detriment, Deliberators seem to persevere longer than other brainstyles.

Deliberators can organize their world according to high standards. This can be tough to live up to. It can be debilitating when you are quite sensitive to the world around you, and short on the foresight needed to see how to make your strengths work for you. The less the aptitude for foresight, the greater the need for short-term encouragement or feedback. Yet high standards accompany bigger challenges that have longer time frames, infrequent acknowledgments, and, as a result, bring more stress.

FIT.   Given their brainstyle's sensitivity to the environment around them—their desire for appreciation and direction, their own respect for role models, and the need to reach their own high standards, it is quite a painful experience for the Deliberator—*especially the right-sided Deliberator*—to be in a situation where their strengths are not specialized or don't match what is required of them. Families, where one or both parents are Deliberators who have succeeded because of their high standards and hard-driving competition, can create a very demanding climate for children who care so much about others' approval and who also have high standards for success of their own. Parenting a Deliberator child has a lot to do with helping them manage personal and family expectations to build real self-confidence on their actual strengths.

FEELINGS.   Talking to some Deliberators, you might find out how aware they are of the details of an interaction: who said what, to whom, and when—especially if it's in a field they know about. But you wouldn't be able to "read" their faces while it was going on. Most Deliberators, *male or female,* are good poker players because they do not have a lot of access to emotion. They do have access to sensory information and physical control. In fact, most sports that requir-

focused, consistent execution favor this brainstyle. Look at top golf and tennis professionals and you will see mostly Deliberators. They just do not have as much emotion to factor in as they compete. A computer analyst was being told to "open up and show his feelings" by his co-workers. In his case, he's being asked to do what he cannot do in order to make his colleagues comfortable. Deliberators feel challenged when asked to get emotional. Feelings can stop all engines. This same man's eye begins to sparkle when he talks about his computer projects. He just may need to find a better job fit.

BEEN THERE. NOT DONE YET.   Deliberators resist stopping points, finishing things, being "plateaued," or moving on. They are at their best in the middle of things, following up, finding things out, planning, improving things. They are Doers who love being busy. The challenge can become frustrating when faced with an ambiguous situation where they can't see what to do over the long term and can't get "their arms around the problem." Discussions can last for a long time in sorting out a complex issue, because their gift is in collecting and organizing first, simplifying later.

Because the Deliberator brainstyle is great at taking in and sorting out information, sometimes by seeking answers to tough problems, they constantly need new games to play. The more right-sided Deliberator will want variations to their favorite toys and the latest models of everything. Depending on the energy level and aptitude for generating ideas, if something new doesn't come along often enough, brace yourself for the complaints, requests, or the job hunt to start. The nightstand will be loaded up with new books. A steady doctor may have an apparent stable life, but mental, emotional, and technical challenges are his soulfood. Deliberators love mastering the game—the harder the better—but not inventing it. Investigating things, but not necessarily resolving them, is the domain of the left-sided Deliberator. The more the left brain is accessed, the greater the glee in fixing, solving, and finishing things.

If a Deliberator tries out your idea, then they want to revise, edit, expand, refine, amend, and include whatever you left out. By that time, *they* own the idea and they want to improve upon it. Deliberators are often loath to share credit, focusing more on their own hard work in improving the original. The initial idea seems less important as time goes on, which is not much of a problem for the Deliberator but can be a real pain for the originator.

CONFLICT. Direct and irrational, full of new and spontaneous decisions—if it is to be win-win, that is, and not just bulldozing—conflict is *not* the turf of the Deliberator. A Knower or Conceptor will stab you in the front; the Deliberator and Conciliator, who try to avoid conflict, are most likely to stab you in the back. Deliberators prefer reason to fighting it out, discussion to heated battle. This brainstyle's strength is to get more self-controlled under stress, to never let them see you sweat. They are often idolized by many in other brainstyles who are not as much in charge of their feelings. The Deliberator's non-strength is to hit the issue head-on and negotiate on the spot to a new and unprecedented outcome. The Deliberator is often at a loss in a conflict situation with constant Time Zeros. Too many *new* decisions and a great deal of flexibility are required.

BrainStyle Clue:

Conflict resolution requires Time Zero decisions. Deliberators must expect this and use time accordingly: prepare ahead for the issues, build in time to think, prepare the other for a rational, delayed—not emotional, not uncaring—response.

Francie, a very able entrepreneur in the custom jewelry business, had a customer that hadn't paid his account for nearly a year. As she described it, she spent a lot of time rehearsing what she was going to say, then "let him have it." In re-creating the scene, Francie said the customer saw the showdown this way: He knew she was "very upset," her eyes were flashing and her cheeks got red. But *still* she chose her words carefully, calling the *company* (not him) "cheap." She never really raised her voice or got out of control even though she was totally "fed up." Francie had tried to prevent her fireworks by all means possible. She acted reasonably, appealed to her customer's sense of fairness, was persistent, and used a great deal of patience, just waiting to see if he would figure out the "right thing to do" by himself. No such luck. She hated the whole situation, but once warmed up, armed with the facts, she just "went on adrenaline." Only *later* was she really mad "at the situation" (feelings come later for Deliberators). She regretted not confronting him sooner, hated even having to confront him at all. It was not a happy ending, and it took a while to get over. He offered a settlement and she took it. "I had bills I had to pay, so I took the short-term answer. I didn't have time to think," she admitted. She wrote off the account, "cutting her losses rather than get obnoxious." It "wasn't worth it" to her to pursue any further—the pain outweighed the gain.

A crucial issue was central in Francie's dealings: the ethics of keeping your word. Surely, of any brainstyle, Deliberators have a natural ability to be aware of and assess whether ethical standards are met or not. Francie decided a long time ago that if she said she was going to do something, she would do it. The man on the other side of the desk in the dispute, another Deliberator, had not made this decision. He used all the same skills to assess the situation and justify his own position, but disregarded their agreement. Deliberators are the ones to see all the shades of gray in a dispute. They can end up using facts to support *any* position. What can be crucial, then, is to have enough time to clarify what is really being decided in the beginning and, as Francie says now, "get it in writing."

When a Deliberator executive in management found out some time later about the lapse in ethics, Francie's adversary was fired and her entire bill was paid.

Another Deliberator, Ann, had more time to prevent problems. Ann served a term as president of a major Dallas charitable foundation for a year. As with most volunteer organizations, there were many political subgroups with different agendas and positions already in place as Ann took over leadership. Ann was very worried about potential conflict as she went into the new position. However, she used her strengths to plan ahead:

- She met individually with each board member and established mutual interests up front.
- She prepared well in advance for every meeting.
- She focused on a specific fund-raising goal with key team members.
- She dealt with conflict indirectly, over time, by facilitating several potentially heated discussions until all opinions were aired and a consensus was reached.

"I know we took longer," Ann assessed, "but I was comfortable leading this way. We reached our goals with everybody on board and that was very important to me."

Ann took care of the politics by including the agendas of others over time with planning.

For the Deliberator, there are few, if any, sudden surges of overwhelming emotions without some reason for them. Where there are no imbalances, there is evenness. Equilibrium represents a steady state: perfect balance on the highwire of life.

When faced with a conflict or a hurry-up situation, the Deliberator may get tense but not mad. This disinclination to get hot and bothered does not mean that a Deliberator will walk away from a fight. He *will* fight for what he thinks is right *but only after trying to defuse conflict by explaining, discussing, or reviewing things with you.*

Nobody learns the rules better than the Deliberator, and no one is better at playing hard and staying within bounds. Emotional conflict is out of bounds—but a hard-hitting debate to prove who is right—according to the rules—is appropriate for the Deliberator. As a Deliberator must have said, "Don't get mad, get even."

Unlike the rules of grammar or tennis, which change once a millennium, rules in negotiations at home or at work are quicksilver. "Rules" can apply in different ways on different days where people are involved. Now you see them, now you don't. What's more, other brainstyles play by their own rules. There is no universal standard, a fact that drives the Deliberator nuts. How is it possible to compete to win without clear rules? When a Deliberator cheats to win it's with an explanation and a system. They make up their *own* rules.

It is the Deliberator's great sense of orderly competitiveness that drives him to achieve. The greater the achievements and influence, the more people to deal with. As the Deliberator succeeds, conflict is inevitable. Not all people want to be reasonable or fit into the systems constructed to prevent problems. Knowing his strengths, the Deliberator must use other brainstyles as resources in order to respond to "unreasonable" conflict and prepare in order to minimize the number of Time Zeros. Or, as the Deliberator nation Japan has taught us, use time as the ally. Stay with it until all the conflicts are aired and a consensus is reached.

Confrontation is a natural non-strength of the Deliberator.

BrainStyle Clue:

The Deliberator will choose among three strategies to resolve a conflict: avoid it entirely, pronounce the right answer, or discuss it at length. You can offer choices for the Deliberator to choose from to take the heat off and move things along.

TO SUMMARIZE THE NON-STRENGTHS OF THE DELIBERATOR

Vision or foresight. Quick decisions. Focus. Being able to reformulate and set new priorities in a new situation quickly. Generating multiple answers to a problem. Flexibility after deciding. Delegating or trusting others readily until they prove themselves. Letting go of control. Letting go of the data. Conflict and open expression of feelings. Creativity that *invents* rather than the Deliberator's brand of creativity, which *innovates to improve solutions that already exist.*

Deliberators Need Other BrainStyles

Deliberators need the Conceptor in order to:

- provide long-term direction
- suggest broader possibilities
- include new ideas for overcoming obstacles
- challenge assumptions
- confront the bigger issues *(See Chapter 5)*

Deliberators need the Knower in order to:

- provide focus to the end result
- reduce the possible options
- sort the facts into a simple plan
- provide efficiency
- push, challenge, break through obstacles
- say it directly *(See Chapter 3)*

Deliberators need the Conciliator in order to:

- clarify the feelings involved
- promote the idea
- determine self-interests
- make it exciting, give it sizzle
- say it nicely, caringly
- make things comfortable, warm, and friendly *(See Chapter 4)*

LEARNING

Teachers, especially those in public elementary schools, can only dream about classrooms filled with happy Deliberators waiting to read, absorb, analyze, and retrieve, free from overly sensitive Conciliators, disruptive Conceptors, or stubborn Knowers. Deliberators can be so receptive and, well, reasonable *if* they haven't already formed an opinion on the subject. American public school education was modeled on orderly progression: first grade, learn how to print; second grade, perfect printing; third grade, learn script. The Deliberator likes this sort of predictability and this brainstyle has an extremely high tolerance for the logic of the linear.

Difficulties arise when:

- The pace of teaching is much faster or slower than their own learning pace.
- There isn't enough stimulation from new ideas or activities (for the more right-sided) with realistic challenges for them to master.
- There is a lack of respect for the teacher's expertise, or to a lesser extent, the teacher's presentation. Deliberator students can spend hours "trashing" a teacher who can't present information in a way they can take it in.

Unlike the Knower and Conciliator, who store information in logical or emotional chunks, or the Conceptor, who stores atomic "thought-balls," the Deliberator stores in order. The Deliberator balances information and files it the same way. This means that Deliberators remember (retrieve) things in a balanced, rational way. At a Time Zero event, the other brainstyles can come up with an immediate response. The Deliberator comes up with questions or, even better, information read the night or week before.

Since knowledge is power for the Deliberator, knowledge precedes action. They set up companies and institutions based on this value for knowledge.

Since the Deliberator looks to outside sources for knowledge, the working environment is critical as a source of input. There is great importance placed on who they work with and whether they admire or respect their opinions.

Deliberators create cultures in which the ability to provide information—the right answer —is a major criterion for success, a culture in which knowledge of the rules and standards is critical to survival. School systems, highly technical companies, specialized firms of experts like attorneys or CPAs, and government agencies are examples of Deliberator cultures. Depending on the values, the brainstyle can measure and evaluate so relentlessly, the competition fostered can be ruthless, and status the prime goal.

RISK-TAKING

Of all the brainstyles, the Deliberator is least inclined to take risks despite what other people may think he is doing. Risk-taking requires an unusual amount of optimism about future prospects, and when anticipating the future the Deliberator can be too aware of all the things that can go wrong. If the Deliberator cannot identify and neutralize risk in a new situation, forget it. He will not give it a GO. If you recall the left-sided Deliberator Whiz Kid, whom you met earlier in this chapter, his adventures in race car driving and hang-gliding were not "risks" for him, nor were they new or unknown. He conquered them step by step. When he entered a new business, he used a similar, thorough, well-analyzed process.

Taking a risk requires making a decision now about something that may happen in the future. When a Deliberator can't assess the current problem against a previous and similar one, he will slow way down or not take the risk at all. If the situation is completely new to him, he will need time to collect information and come up with a plan to deal with it. A cautionary strategy is a typically safe and preferred one for the style. Fortunes can be lost when greed or time pressure demand a quick decision and they cannot assess and plan. Deliberators can be thoughtful, even successful, gamblers when using their brainstyle to assess the system and odds. Then they author books on their system to beat Las Vegas,* and of course, advise others with a model on how to do the same.

For most, the natural response of this brainstyle is to assess and be cautious. Risk, even calculated risk, denies the risk-taker direct control over the outcome. The Deliberator hates to give up control.

---

* One of the early texts on the subject was by a UCLA Ph.D. in mathematics who wrote *Beat the Dealer: A Winning Strategy for the Game of Twenty-one,* Blaisdell Publishing, 1962. Edward Thorp translates mathematical probability theory and statistics into strategies for playing blackjack with detailed stories of how his successful system got him banned from the casinos.

> *BrainStyle Clue:*
>
> *If you want to coax a Deliberator into taking a calculated risk, compare it to something the Deliberator is familiar with and that has proven successful. Plan with him how to keep him in control and minimize surprises. "No surprises" is a* Deliberator *motto.*

AT WORK: THE DELIBERATOR

At work the Deliberator either wants to be and do everything, or wants to be left alone to be the expert in just one area.* Most of the time, however, it is very difficult to keep people in this brainstyle from simultaneously signing up for karate, singing, and language lessons even if they have only slight aptitudes in these areas. A Deliberator with good physical coordination and above-average intelligence is especially vulnerable to being trapped in a tangle of conflicting interests, overcommitments, and expectations for himself.

It is a paradox that the multitasking Deliberator is most productive, effective, resourceful, and competitive when his boundaries are most closely defined. Give people in this brainstyle sidelines and a goal and you literally set them free from the tyranny of their own ambition, interests, and many-sided projects. Get a Deliberator to focus and the flashlight becomes a laser.

Case in point: Tom, a financial manager, appears assertive yet warm and charming. He looks his interviewer directly in the eye when explaining how excited he is about his work. People have told him he is one of the best at his job—a "real leader." He is articulate, describes business situations thoroughly, with lots of facts about his excellent track record.

He describes his strengths as "being bright, flexible, a good people person, able to spot a good business deal, creative, bottom-line-

---

* One of the founders of the nonprofit organization Aptitude Inventory Measurement Services (AIMS), based in Dallas, Texas, after administering aptitude tests to over 10,000 people estimates that 25 percent of the population are *specialists who "achieve* success in careers that emphasize individual effort over people skills," where developing expertise means independence and respect "regardless of their people skills. . . ." "In other words, these are the folks better with things than people." Brenda Smith, *How to Strengthen Your Winning Business Personality,* Career Press, 1990, p. 15.

oriented, and highly ethical." He finds the whole idea of having a single set of strengths ridiculous. This is not what he's been told. He believes he is good at most things, or could learn them if he didn't know them already. He's a one-man show, and proposes business deals accordingly.

He says, "A particular strength of mine is an ability to appear as the other person wants me to appear. I'm a chameleon." Tom wants the freedom to consider all proposals, which he alone assesses, and act according to his own decisions. He is looking currently at a "pipeline of sixteen to twenty opportunities."

Tom is trying to get investors to set him up in a firm that screens and funds small businesses. He fails to get backers because, he is told, he has *too little focus but wants* 70 percent *control* of others' money.

When Tom finally took a position inside a firm as an investment banker, he executed several projects quite successfully. He had to focus, be more thorough, and share some control.

One of the best and most common "fits" for a Deliberator's strength is where calm, incremental change is desired. When additional strengths at *overview* and *focus* are available from those who have different brainstyles (Knowers or Conceptors)—not just other, more left-sided Deliberators—real progress can be made. Deliberators who stumble most are those who cannot admit to their limitations, try to plan their way out of trouble, and get the right answers too late for the opportunity.

DELIBERATOR DILEMMAS: THERE'S DELIBERATORS IN GENERAL AND THEN THERE'S *ME*

If you suspect you may be a Deliberator who can't seem to find your fit anyplace, here are a couple of people who had the same problem and who can, perhaps, help you with your questions.

Since a Deliberator's gift is one that sees the uniqueness in things, the details, the steps, the pieces, they are most naturally the ones who often a) see themselves in all the descriptions of the brainstyles and b) find it hardest and take the longest to accept and use the concept of a single, core strength to leverage with others. Deliberators want to get on to the specifics. "Just exactly what does this mean? Give me an example." "Where's the backup? the proof?"

The Right-Sided Deliberator

Some Deliberators are easy to confuse with a responsive, imaginative Conciliator brainstyle; others with the visionary Conceptor.

The distinctions become more important as we grow older and, according to genetic researchers, there is "an increasing genetic contribution with age and a decreasing effect of shared environmental influences."[1] In other words, the older we get the more important our genetics become while other people have less impact upon us. Life choices based on strengths can make the difference between ultimate success or failure to find fulfillment.

A great many Deliberators have a strong right-brain connection to their senses, quickly becoming aware of people and things around them. This is the definition of *intuition* Robert Ornstein, a noted brain researcher, prefers. Environment, therefore, is especially important to this group. As kids, they color inside the lines, they value personal boundaries, privacy, or the right phrase or sensitive sentiments from others. They tend to *take things personally.*

Yet the right-sided Deliberators like to deal at work with concrete problems by selecting a course, getting things organized, fixing problems, then moving on, using patience and experience with people to solve problems. Projects are often personalized, self-worth hinging on the success or failure of doing a job.

Receiving feedback is an acquired taste for these folks, and is most often called "criticism." They often want an appreciative audience to applaud their brilliant ideas, not correct them. They have the hardware to be more objective than the Conciliator, though it takes a personal decision on the Deliberator's part to *use feedback as information* rather than a put-down.

A Deliberator who has trouble deciding whether feelings or analysis come *first* for her in new situations is a woman who keeps her family and other people's concerns at the center of her work and home life. Completing *The BrainStyle Inventory* the first time, she scored nearly 100 percent in the Conciliator column. Her name is Sharon. She feels a great deal of pressure at work. She is not as much in control these days. Everything, it seems to her, is changing. There's been a reorganization. Old touchstones in her environment have been removed. She has a new boss, which means new policies. Rules are fluid. More importantly, the situational cues she's relied on to define success are all

BrainStyle Clue:

To distinguish between the right-sided Deliberator and a full-fledged Conciliator, the most important difference is an even or steady approach to life. Deliberators access emotion as just one element in their analytical arsenal; Conciliators access emotion and intuition as the first and major elements in theirs, with more spontaneity and emotional peaks and valleys.

Both can promise in order to please. Both personalize.

Conciliators like instant action and can act more decisively and quickly than most Deliberators; later, initial right-brain surety can be replaced with doubt and decisions changed. If the Deliberator commits, they can stick with their less impulsive decisions longer.

Both can be "psychic" and imaginative. Both can be great with people. At times both can be scattered and disorganized.

gone, replaced with uncertainty. He is asking for *numbers,* cost cutting, in particular. Sharon feels invalidated. It is unclear whether Sharon's twelve years with the company will count with the new boss as much as they once had. She is running into "communication problems" with him. She doesn't know if they can work it out. Is it because she is a woman? Black? An engineer? Too emotional? Too analytical? Or is she in the wrong job? Defining her brainstyle is a way of reconnecting with the anchors in her life. Applying what she learns about her gifts is a way to get back in control.

Sharon, when asked whom she admires, thinks about it for a while, sorting through many memories. She has two answers: Martin Luther King and her mother. What does she admire about them? "King saw possibilities. My mother has always been [a] very feeling [person]. I've always admired that," she pronounces. Is Sharon good at these things? She is unsure. She looks at her team's feedback for confirmation of what she can do well. The answers tell her that she's "good with people." As Sharon reassesses herself, her "models," or the way she "should be," come to mind first. She decides she is a Conciliator.

The next step is to figure out how she can use her natural gifts to solve the problems at hand. She is unsure. How can she establish a relationship with her boss first and set the stage for negotiation and further influence? We discuss how she might sell her ideas by inspiring others, tap into her personal "charisma," and be more of a team member.

This discussion takes longer and longer for Sharon to understand and respond to. She isn't sure she can come through with the requisite Conciliator relationships, she finally and reluctantly admits. Why the reluctance? She has "very high expectations" for herself "for doing well in *all* new things." I notice that she is not spontaneous with answers in new areas as we talk. She reports that she doesn't make new friends easily. She finds collaborating difficult, she likes to decide alone, then work with others. Conciliators like to talk things through, often reaching a new decision *with* another's input, and then get things moving on their own.

To explain her confusion further, Sharon says other tests she's taking show strengths in analysis, yet statistical and cost analysis are very hard for her. She doesn't know what things she's learned through her training as an engineer versus what comes naturally for her. She finds introspection difficult.

I ask what, over the long term, her family counts on her for: steadiness and reliability or openly showing her feelings, like her mother? Without a pause she replies, "Oh, being steady. I've always wanted to show my feelings more, I admire my mom for just that reason."

With that, everything fell into place to determine her brainstyle.

It was no accident or just a bad decision that Sharon learned to become an engineer. "I'm very good at project analysis—but not cost analysis like my boss," she continues. "I love planning and scheduling. That was my favorite job, taking a lot of individual systems and approaches from a lot of different departments, and organizing them to make a single, coherent, step-by-step plan for everyone."

Sharon is a Deliberator who relies most on her right-brain *after* Time Zero. She doesn't have the foresight, the kind of focus for decision-making, or math abilities of those in her brainstyle, like her new boss, who use more of the left side of the brain to process and store information. She is very uncomfortable with an undefined situation, preferring clearer structure and values similar to her own. She takes time to form relationships because it takes time to learn about another's values and find common ground. The more introverted, the longer it takes. Were she a Conciliator, she'd make friends more easily and quickly. The relationship would come first. She has *other* assets.

More often than with other brainstyles, *values,* which involve previous, often emotional decisions, can make or break a relationship for a

Deliberator. The continual draw upon past decisions is the strength. Solidity, steadfastness, and continuity come from this ability. Personal boundaries come from an ability to access values readily. Sharon's view of her boss as "someone who doesn't value people" was over the line of personal acceptance for her. When values clash, relationships can't really mesh, especially for this brainstyle.

The next step, and biggest challenge, is for Sharon to use her gifts to help her boss. The breakthrough came when she began to accept her strengths, then considered allowing her boss to be "an okay guy who can't deal with people as well as I can!" She took a complex project that focused solely on people and asked for his help in running the numbers. She went to a new colleague and got some cost input as well. The barriers to teamwork began to fall like dominoes, one toppling another.

The Left-Sided Deliberator

What makes the difference between a left-sided Deliberator and a Knower? Decision-making is the key distinction among brainstyles. The sharp, focused, decisive Whiz Kid you met earlier gets in a *new* situation and wants more information. He handles risk by getting more facts. He assesses first. The youngest brother boasts about having the facts and prides himself on having the facts *right*. "I don't shoot from the hip" is a statement of pride for him. He absorbs, remembers, and can use a broader range of details on more subjects than a Knower can. And he hates conflict or anything that smells like a relationship problem. He'll try to reason it to the ground, but when it proves unreasonable, he backs off. If he were a Knower, he could most easily present the tough stuff first. He is more dependable, steady, hardworking, and reliable than a right-sided Deliberator, most Knowers, and certainly anyone on the right-brain side of the scale (such as Conciliators and Conceptors).

Joe, twenty-three, a student in medical school, has heard some material about brainstyles, but is confused about what his real gifts are. His new wife (a right-sided Deliberator) is convinced that he is a Knower, "because everything he said the first year we were dating made me cry." She says that he comes up with answers very quickly and solves problems with a single solution. After I talk to Joe for an hour, I am convinced that he is a left-sided Deliberator. Joe's central gift is also *assessment*. Here is how I reached that conclusion:

Joe describes how he approaches *new situations:*

"I have always liked the sciences because they are so *challenging*— but not easy. I like to *learn complex new things* that *challenge how much I can keep track of.*

"I grew up in a small town and knew everyone in town. When I went to college, I had a real hard time meeting people. So before I would go out, I would sit and *plan what I should talk about, and how I could go about meeting people.*

"I have kept a journal, kept track of things I have difficulty doing. I *revisit* it from time to time, and *decide what I need to get better at. I then work at those things."*

Question: Joe, given the following sequence, which do you prefer: *Assessing, Predicting, Deciding, or Acting?*

Answer: "*Assessing.* I like going over what's happening and *coming out with one answer.* After that, taking action is boring. Figuring it out is what's fun. *If I revisit the decision* once I've made it, *I go into a real spin.* That's when my stomach hurts. Too many choices. Like choosing med schools, I only applied to one. And I've already figured out the specialty I want. I'm not sure it's the right one, but it'll be *stable financially.* That's real important to me. If I think of reconsidering a specialty, I feel real uncomfortable.

"When I was a kid I broke my arm. It was serious enough to need surgery. Everyone was real upset. But when the doctor walked into the room, he had such an air of confidence that I instantly felt better. He knew the answers. He knew what to do. I decided right then that I wanted people to feel that way about me. I want to be respected. I care a lot about how people think about me."

Joe wants to be an expert who is respected for what he knows. This is key for most Deliberators. Joe builds on his strength of making up his own mind—alone. If you remember Burk from earlier in this chapter, he is another left-sided Deliberator who stays in control of the information by deciding alone.

"When I listened to the tape explaining brainstyles, the part that made me feel the best was when you said you didn't have to be good at your non-strengths. When I work on things I don't do well, it does take ten times longer, and it's a relief to know that's okay." Now Joe finds relief from his perfectionism. This allows him to focus. This kind of focus often comes faster and easier for a Knower when doing things. Nor do Knowers worry as often about perfection; more often they work on winning, or resolving the problem. Knowers want an answer that works. They *learn* that it takes more patience and control to get one. Deliberators enjoy the ride more. A better answer is worth their time.

"Success, for me, is getting the right answer—in the short term. In the long term, it's having a family and a stable career."

Why is Joe a Deliberator and not a Knower?

- He likes exploring, collecting information, and assessing situations as much or more than he likes coming up with the right answer.
- He tends to be a perfectionist, gets into subjects in depth, and adds to the list of priorities for himself, rather than whittling them down. He likes to be good in many things.
- When he revisits a decision, it is upsetting because then he has too many options. It is not simply an opportunity to make a new decision as it would be for a Knower. Moreover, Joe doesn't enjoy *Deciding* and *Acting* as much as he enjoys *Assessing*. He isn't aware of an ability to forecast or *Predict* in the future. That seems to be a part of *Assessing* to him. *Assessing* seems to be his gift; later he comes up with a single solution to get the right answer. Joe will, no doubt, become a wonderful doctor, especially as he learns to get second and even third opinions.
- Under stress, Joe plans and organizes. Knowers tend to act.
- What distinguishes Joe from most Knowers is when (so his wife says) he does not confront people if they challenge his initial thinking.

Similarities between the left-sided Deliberator and the Knower:

- When his wife told him she didn't like the way he came up with answers for her problems, Joe decided he just needed to listen, and that's what he has done a lot more of, even though he says he comes up with quick answers in his head. Joe is a problem-solver. He likes to repair things—or people, as both these left-sided brainstyles do. Neither the left-sided Deliberator like Joe nor the Knower evaluate themselves as strong with people. They are *both* excellent diagnosticians and advisers, however, on complex problems.
- Joe tends to come up with a single, unemotional answer. If he hears about a personal problem, he quickly has a solution. Knowers can come up with more decisions, more quickly.
- Joe is good at establishing effective plans, routines, and procedures to bring stability; he honors traditional values.
- He follows through.

- He weighs consequences before acting.
- He enjoys clarity and closure before he moves on.
- He enjoys working in a situation based on facts, within a given structure, and having challenging problems to solve.
- He relates with a formal, more impersonal style until he knows you well.
- He may be more impatient than many Deliberators for a decision and decide too quickly, yet *not* be very responsive to a need for *new* ideas and *new* decisions that go against precedent, as a Knower might.
- He may also see more risks than possibilities in new projects and take too long worrying about and preparing for the worst. He'll spend a lot more time at this than a Knower will, however. A Knower tends to decide Yay or Nay and then move on.

BrainStyle Clue:

Left-sided Deliberators and Knowers make practical, unemotional decisions very well. Both are logical and structured and honor tradition. Knowers are quicker to decide and act in new areas than Deliberators, and they tend to see issues as black or white more of the time. Deliberators are more thorough, like more options before deciding, collect more information, and attend more to planning in order to get something done.

BEING THE DELIBERATOR

In the Family of Humankind, you are, so often, the center to the eye of the storm. Others count on you. You deliver. You are the Rock. Sure, you have ups and downs, make mistakes, say the wrong things, but how many times have you calmed things down with your realistic appraisal and thoughtful responses? Your consistency and perseverance to make sense out of nonsense, to make things just that much better, gives a continuity to the seasons, even to the daily crashes and clashes of fleeting passions.

Following is some advice to you from seasoned veterans in your brainstyle to help you better get to what you do best—and let others in on the fun.

MAKING DECISIONS. The unseasoned in this brainstyle get defensive about their need to think things over before deciding. This can mean hoarding information, then telling the answer or stalling for time by "yes-ing" people into leaving you alone. Here are a couple of tips from others:

- "I've learned to get input into my decisions *especially* when I know the answer. I was coming across as aloof—a 'know-it-all'—and unapproachable. I was just trying to hurry, so I lost out on getting any support. Finally, I was in a job so isolated, I was desperate for input. Since then, I learned to use others' ideas, especially now that I know what strengths to look for."
- "You've *got* to focus on two or three solid priorities. I was trying to get it *all* done and loading everyone up with tons of paper."
- "If you think about it, it's as easy to generate three plans instead of just one to build in flexibility and have a fallback position instead of a crisis. A Conceptor taught me this."
- "I use a planning process at home that I learned at work. You need to chart a path for yourself—just like you'd plan a project. I always jumped for the new and interesting, but I got so confused about what I really wanted to do that I had to just finally stop and plan it out. It's made all the difference in my career even though it took quite a few hours of discussion, with my husband and several friends. Earlier I just 'fell into things.' I forgot how I could really plan when I take the time."

Seasoned Deliberators have learned the difference between relying on their past experience to come up with a single favorite solution and build upon the future with serious input from others. Your strength is in organizing, improving, and refining. Seek out others who will work with you on defining the big picture. Include Conceptors who can address people *and* communication issues.

- "Control the process, not the results."
- "Get others under control by getting them to do exactly what they can do best. They'll always deliver."
- "Give up trying to excel in everything, to be perfect. That's just your ego talking."
- "At first you might judge the value of the whole thing by the accuracy of the pieces. If you take the time to think it over you'll

be in a much better position to see the whole picture. Even so, there's others who can jump faster to the end. I used to hate their nerve, but now I use them for clarity. They really help me see what to do."

BEING YOURSELF WITH OTHER BRAINSTYLES.   (See Chapter Eight)

- "When all you do is challenge, you can't move ahead. I know I get into arguments about how we're going to get someplace. I don't trust people who give you quick answers or talk about some glamorous new future without explaining how they are going to get there. But I realize I need help in this area—you know, seeing out ahead. I'm best when I'm planning and doing, thinking how to get things to work. My *best* boss was a Conceptor."
- "I can get in a bind sometimes. I keep comparing things to the *way they should be.* When I point out the gap, all others hear is criticism. I'm just making observations, challenging *them* the way *I* like to be challenged. They hear negativity. I try to explain. We get into an argument. I've learned to give an overview of what I'm trying to do and show how it'll help get them where they want to go. I use what *they* offer to close the gaps in *my* plan."
- "When I notice how others think differently, and sometimes help them to actually make their wild ideas work, they've been more willing to listen to me."

Right-sided Deliberators who are more people-oriented and less technical suggest that if you feel restless, dissatisfied with work and the challenges that are failing to stimulate, you may be searching for a "better fit." When Michael Crichton went to medical school and found the process wanting, he left on a personal journey that started with traveling all over the world, then writing, which eventually led to enormous success as a writer and film producer. To get to your real contributions, you must stop occasionally and look for the patterns in what you love to do.

- "When I lost my job, I was very depressed. Don't make the mistake of thinking you are valuable because of *what* you know. Losing a job can be devastating because the information is all outdated, instantly. You are valuable because of the *way you think*. Not everyone *can* take the time to really be thorough like I can."

- "You'll get bored and want to learn new things right in the middle of something. But remember that you're best when you're the expert on a subject. Stay with the boredom just a bit longer and see what it's about. I find I have a few of these 'spells' but they pass quickly as I go deeper into the project or subject or person."
- "Working on several things at once is fun. Reading several things at once is stimulating. But you won't really learn or complete the thing as well as you could or as well as you need to, to feel good about any of them. You may just need a time-out to refocus. Too much of everything is not much of anything."
- "You can't help everyone. You can't really even help those you love the most. I try to help them help themselves. I tell them how much I care. They don't always know."
- "I have to plan ahead how to say NO. I find it hard to set limits, to draw the line. I try to think of it as a discussion, rather than a confrontation. The most important time for me in dealing with another is at the beginning. I prepare."

AT WORK.   Being a Deliberator becomes uncomfortable only when there is a bad "fit" between your strengths and the demands of the job. Until that time, you are the one who gets rewarded for your reports, your innovations, your professional calm. There may be a few who grouse about your "people skills," but you can be diplomatic enough to get over these hurdles.

- Work on your desire to criticize (point out the "gaps") by using the very same strength to compare another to their own best efforts. (Wrong: *Sam did this faster than you.* Right: *You did this faster last time. What's going on now?*)
- You value reason and the harmony reason brings. The bad surprise is that the higher in management you go, the less people seem to make sense. When rationality does not prevail, you are asked to make fast decisions without the necessary information. Confrontation increases. You are also asked to install solutions with more people involved who bring up more options and decisions. Teamwork is your answer and will require, as you know, the majority of your time.
- When figuring out the right team or company for you, see if you can "fit" your *pace* to the basic business. If the business needs contin-

ual quick-action decisions to succeed, you'll constantly need to sell your strengths to faster, less thoughtful demands from others. Watch out. Stress comes from the pressure for faster decisions than are natural for you to make. You'll go for more control, make more decisions by yourself, and ignore others' concerns. This can be a disastrous way to run a family or manage people.

- Set up systems that will allow you to deal with information in the time frame you need to make timely decisions. This means some planning before well-structured meetings kick off with clearly defined goals. There is no rule that everyone present should discuss every subject. You can get distracted by past history or an analysis of someone's behavior. Get a Knower to facilitate if you can. If not, take a time-out, restate the goal, and reassess who is essential to move things forward.

- Alert those who work above and below you (especially the Knowers in your life) that your responses to requests for decisions may not be as quick as others can make them, but they *will* be thorough and carefully considered. Then work for win-win deadlines. If you're constantly pressured, you're probably in a bad fit and should consider another job that has more structure and a longer time line for producing results.

- Those in other brainstyles want some responses from you, e.g., "Good morning," "I'm trying to understand how you feel," "I'll get back to you in an hour with a next step" to keep informed about your thinking because you don't show your feelings as much as some. Bulletins help.

- Don't make the mistake that other Deliberators have made: people do *not* separate your ideas from your actions. *You* may have just engaged in an interesting discussion, but they may expect you to implement the ideas you were talking about. Clarify what you are committing to and what you are not.

- No one's perfect. As you discover your own perfection, you'll see it in everyone. Start by looking for your own strengths.

CHAPTER 7

Test Yourself

The KNOWER

The CONCILIATOR

The CONCEPTOR

The DELIBERATOR

WHY KNOW SOMEONE'S BRAINSTYLE?

- To look beyond obvious or social behaviors to the strengths behind them, so you won't take things personally.
- To bring out the best in others.
- To know what to rely on them for; to give up expecting things they can't deliver.
- To get them in the right job where they can contribute and grow rather than play "politics" by trying to look good.

WHAT DO YOU LOOK FOR?

- Decision-making in new or unfamiliar situations.
- The key things they can be counted on to deliver over a period of time.

- You may initially be aware of a person's *non*-strengths, which is another way to back into their strengths. The popular media and the tabloid press spend most of their time describing non-strengths when reporting about the famous. Sometimes it's easier to tell the brainstyle of the person from the criticism leveled at him or her.

Quick Review of Basic BrainStyle Strengths:

The Knower: *Rapid (left-brain) unemotional decisions in new situations; clarity, structure, focus.*

The Conciliator: *Rapid (right-brain) emotional decisions in new situations; imaginative, spontaneous, or unstructured solutions.*

The Conceptor: *Rapid (left-brain-right-brain) "overview" decisions in new situations; invention, reformulation of basic assumptions, vision of future possibilities by combining logic and imagination.*

The Deliberator: *Rapid assessment of the situation based on memory to reach a delayed decision in new situations; analysis, planning, and delivery of the plan; overall steadiness.*

TEST YOUR UNDERSTANDING OF BRAINSTYLES:

Here's some practice in identifying brainstyles of famous personalities.
A warm-up:

- Britain's Prince Charles, a classically trained Deliberator, who lives by tradition and rules—except when he makes up his own—has constantly been called "stiff" when compared to the Conciliator, Princess Diana. Their brainstyle differences have been exaggerated with their lifestyle, their relationship eroded by Charles's loyalty to another woman. Their marriage sums up the tensions between these two brainstyles. The daytime talk show host Regis Philbin, a Deliberator, found national success, on the other hand, when he partnered with the spontaneous Kathie Lee Gifford, a Conciliator.
- The Conceptor Donald Trump has explained publicly why he got fed up with his very competent Deliberator wife, Ivana. "All she could talk about was business," he moaned. He chose his new wife, Conciliator Marla Maples, for her support and personal attention, among other things.
- And then there's Knower Sam Donaldson, famous for being an annoying journalist, yet acclaimed for pursuing the question or issue, no matter what.

- Deliberator Clint Eastwood demonstrates mastery of his craft, his depth of experience, and his wide range of interests, for example, in the film *The Bridges of Madison County*, in which he directs, stars, and composes and plays part of the musical score. His brainstyle is particularly suited to a disciplined approach to many subjects.

(For more information on how brainstyles can pair successfully, see the next chapter, especially pages 245–49).

1. Former President George Bush invaded Panama with a planned, clearly articulated, "Four Point Program" after an initial raid failed to achieve the objective. His strengths are said to be his thoughtful, thorough approach to decision-making and his high integrity. He was also recognized for his skills in diplomacy. On the other hand, he was criticized for being indecisive, and labeled "unresponsive" during his reelection campaign.
*What is his brainstyle?*_____

2. President Bill Clinton's campaign for president as well as his leadership in office have been characterized as highly responsive, warm, and personal. He has been characterized as a highly influential communicator who can establish a personal rapport with an audience. He is criticized as being erratic, changing policies and decisions too frequently.
*Given the above information, what is his brainstyle likely to be?*_____

3. First Lady Hillary Rodham Clinton has been an attorney throughout her career. She is often characterized as focused, professional, and very analytical. When initiating the health care proposal, she organized a complex process of data collection, bringing in a task force of experts from all over the country. The recommendations were compiled in a report of over a thousand pages. She has been criticized for being unfeeling, cold, and detached.
*Given the above information, what is her brainstyle likely to be?*_____

4. Current House Speaker Newt Gingrich told a freshman colleague entering Congress with him in 1969 that one day he would be speaker of the House. He talks, according to the futurist Alvin Toffler, about a vision of the future based on a real breadth of knowledge and understanding of trends. He is criticized for dropping verbal "bombs" —making explosive, global statements about traditional institutions or political figures he disagrees with, disregarding the sensitivities of others in his search for "truth."
*Given the above information, what is his brainstyle likely to be?*_____

5. What is the brainstyle of each author likely to be?

The Book Title	The Author's BrainStyle?
A. *Thriving on Chaos*	_____
B. *Love and Profit*	_____
C. *Thriving on Order*	_____
D. *Winning Through Intimidation*	_____

From the following descriptions, guess the brainstyle of the person described:

6. "[Steven] Jobs is at his best in any brainstorming session. A core group of eleven employees is discussing what goals should be, how best to build up the company. Jobs dominates the room. Even when he's not talking, he's moving, exuding energy, guiding the discussion through sheer body language. When he likes something, he gets visibly excited. His eyes light up. He bounces in his seat, paces, gestures. He talks about what NeXT [Jobs's new company, after Apple] will be like. Jobs shows himself a master at defining priorities, exciting others with his vision of what NeXT can be, clarifying the company's ultimate goals as they move from research through production to the actual marketing of the new computer."[1]

*His brainstyle?*_____

7. "Steve Bostic explains how to run a business: 'I don't agree that growth has to be chaotic. I think that's a total myth. There may be chaotic moments and times of crisis, but it's completely unnecessary to deal from crisis to crisis. In fact, that way of managing undermines your ability to grow. If you want to achieve significant growth, you need order, not chaos. You need to have things well planned and well thought out. Everybody has to be singing from the same hymnbook. You have to take your vision, think it through, and turn it into consistent strategy. And then you have to get it on paper. That's key. I maintain that if you can't put your vision on paper, you can never do it in the real world.' "[2]

*His brainstyle?*_____

8. "Frank Lorenzo was the ideal person for coming in as CEO to turn around the troubled Continental and Eastern Airlines. But problems surfaced with people, unionized people, at that, as he tried moving the old culture to a more hard-line, measurable, fiscally viable one. Others could not change in the time frame that Lorenzo directed. His Waterloo was not being able to get enough people to enroll in his vision of the future. The veterans saw only that he operated 'without care' for their agendas or established hierarchy; they didn't get included

in setting policies or goals. Fast and early decisions established an inner circle vs. outsiders who became enemies. The company became a battleground where you either won or lost. As the head of Texas Air, he did it his way or no way at all, and was willing to go out fighting."[3]
His brainstyle? _____

9. The dramatic portrayal of Oskar Schindler in Steven Spielberg's film *Schindler's List* shows a man who says he is a "businessman," but cannot run the operation day to day. He hates the routine, the schedules, nor does he understand accounting. Schindler tells his business manager that he brings the "sizzle," he knows how to wine, dine, and entertain. He knows how to promote the business by understanding and empathizing with the German high command so that they trust him and confide in him. He argues passionately for his Jewish workers by knowing his audience. He gets into trouble with a spontaneous, unguarded kiss of a beautiful Jewish woman in front of the Nazi high command.
His brainstyle? _____

10. Jacqueline Kennedy Onassis has been described as "an American icon" for her dignity as well as other qualities, such as being a very private person, respecting tradition, being a faithful, loyal wife and mother with a gracious, low-key style. Her consistently high standards showed in her taste for clothes, her extensive knowledge of literature and the arts, as well as her thorough and diligent work as an editor.
Her brainstyle? _____

11. Margaret Thatcher led the British electorate as prime minister for over a decade. The "new direction" she defined for the nation was actually a traditional free market. Her brilliance was in presenting ideas rationally, steadfastly, and driving home the execution of her plans against many coalitions. She delivered on her word. "Iron Maggie" was not known for being personable, collecting her share of enemies along the way, although she was respected. She was publicly derided for her "lack of femininity."
Her brainstyle? _____

Now try some harder ones:

12. Mary's problem, the career counselor tells her after sixteen hours of extensive testing, is that she has *too many* aptitudes to ever really settle on one thing and feel fulfilled. "Oh great," she moans. "I suppose I'll be restless all my life. I was always a rebel," Mary glints out of sparkling brown eyes. "I loved to argue. My dad said I should've

been a lawyer. I seriously considered it—but couldn't stand all the hours alone in the library, so I married a lawyer at age nineteen instead."

Her career counselor told her her greatest strength was in analytical thinking. She's employed that strength for over a decade as a licensed professional counselor, sorting out personal and marital problems for hundreds of clients. She brings order to the chaos of lives of those unable to sort out their own. She's a wonderful listener: practiced, sensitive, alert to the cues of her clients and able to match what she hears and sees rapidly to her experience as well as the years of study she's put in on a multitude of psychological topics. She's good at listening and summarizing constructively with "professional detachment."

Her brainstyle? _____

13. Martha is a fast-reacting, high-intensity office manager who gets into all aspects of a project quickly. She anticipates frequently interrupting what you're saying. She wants to get there first. She runs into trouble sometimes when she tries to anticipate what's coming next based upon what was done *last* time, which she quickly recalls. She often assumes others will understand her urgency or her goals. She can get "bossy" because she gets so focused on the goal. Relationships suffer when she tries to create efficiencies wherever she can. She decides slowly yet tackles several things at once. She is active. She makes lists. She does best in a structured environment with clear policies and procedures, with lots of new projects.

Her brainstyle? _____

14. Mike, head of a customer service group, spends a lot of overtime on personnel issues, and never turns away someone who needs to talk. "He *cares* about people," his staff say, "but he takes forever to make up his mind!" Mike wants to help others, to realize his ideals, and apply the management model he knows can make his department a "great place to work." His peers say he's created a *family* of his work team. Mike says he's making up for past autocratic, impersonal leadership and using all of the human technology he knows to do so. Mike is getting things right, thoroughly, and with care. Mike never fights the system. He's a great lieutenant and doesn't like taking charge or making a decision until he's *sure* of what he's doing. Mike rests his integrity on knowing the facts.

His brainstyle? _____

15. Kevin McCarthy is a widely popular radio talk show host in Dallas. Listeners tell him they agree with his opinions, but most enjoy his jokes: "He's a great storyteller," his fans say. They are attracted to the casual, friendly atmosphere he creates. He is known for his "personality" and is able to discuss a wide range of social topics and people very comfortably.

*His brainstyle?*_____

16. Bob Crandall, CEO of American Airlines, uses his strength for detailed analysis to "obsessively" go after details in a way that looks, sounds, and feels a lot like confrontation—at least as *Fortune* describes him in "America's Toughest Bosses."[4] Crandall's perception is that he is pursuing facts, not confronting people. "His willingness to scrutinize the tiniest details, plus the encyclopedic knowledge he has acquired from that scrutiny, puts extraordinary pressure on executives to do likewise." Crandall is reported to use "an intimidating mixture of energy, verbosity, profanity, and bluff," reports *Fortune.* As the head of today's number one airline, he gets results through people who also focus on details in a highly structured corporate system.

*His brainstyle?*_____
(This also defines the brainstyle of those preferred in the company culture.)

17. A comedic master like Johnny Carson has used his talents for observation and understated delivery to deliver a rare thirty-year career. How? By drawing on other writers' expertise to ensure that he could deliver consistently. Carson's gift was polished and perfected, he drew from a vast repertoire of experience. He became a real star by putting the guest in the limelight. He was known as the "professional's professional."

*His brainstyle?*_____

18. Two women are candidates for Mary's secretarial position. Mary is a high-energy, rather disorganized Conciliator.

Candidate A: When asked what her skills are, she lists *highly organized, a good problem-solver,* and *efficient* as her top three abilities. A is very personable, enthusiastic, and charming during the interview and says she can get along with anyone, especially on the telephone.

Candidate B: Mary had to ask a lot more questions of B to get her list of top three skills: *very organized, likes to solve computer software problems,* and *reliable.* B is quiet and does not enjoy telephone or personal interviews as much as being left alone to get her work done.

From the limited information above,
1) *What is the brainstyle of Candidate A?* _____
2) *What is the brainstyle of Candidate B?* _____
3) *Which would be the best choice for Mary?* _____

ANSWERS FOR TEST YOURSELF:

1. President Bush fits the Deliberator profile.
2. President Clinton seems to be a Conciliator.
3. First Lady Hillary Clinton is most likely a Deliberator as well.
4. House Speaker Gingrich seems to fit the Conceptor profile.
5. The authors' brainstyle is most likely:
   A. Conceptor.
   B. Conciliator.
   C. Deliberator.
   D. Knower.
6. Steven Jobs fits the Conceptor profile.
7. Steve Bostic fits the Deliberator brainstyle.
8. Frank Lorenzo fits the Knower profile.
9. Oskar Schindler fits the Conciliator brainstyle.
10. Jacqueline Kennedy Onassis fits the Deliberator brainstyle.
11. Margaret Thatcher is most likely a left-sided Deliberator.
12. Mary is a right-sided Deliberator,
13. Martha is too, and so is
14. Mike.
15. Kevin McCarthy is most likely a Conciliator.
16. Bob Crandall is a (left-sided) Deliberator.
17. Johnny Carson is a Deliberator.
18. Candidate A is a Conciliator, Candidate B a Deliberator. Mary will very likely get along best with A yet be complemented best by B who can cover more of Mary's non-strengths.

CHAPTER 8

Getting Along When Nobody Changes

Part One: At Home and At Play

"When my wife chose to stay home to have a family, I feared we wouldn't grow together. The power of *BrainStyles* is it gives you a common language that transcends what you do—entrepreneur, housewife, corporate person. It relates you back to a central purpose; it makes you two partners who can rely on each other and grow together. I believe this can keep marriages together."

MARK BREDEN, Marketing Manager,
The Procter & Gamble Company, Fayetteville, Arkansas

THE FOUR BRAINSTYLES IN ACTION

"Heeeyyyy! Come *on!* We're waiting!" Dave was red-in-the-face mad. All six feet three and two hundred twenty pounds went into the bellow directed at the swarm of men scattered like an unruly platoon over the green and sandtraps ahead. There were seven men in various states of rumpled golf attire playing as a group: an absolutely forbidden number within the code of Proper Golf Etiquette—three over the limit. Dave, a Conceptor, saw a breach in the order of things, principles being violated. Worse than that, they were slowing up his golf game. He was hot and letting them know about it.

Startled, the entire group looked his way. They were guys out for a good time on a Saturday afternoon, having a few beers, and taking their time. *Obviously.*

The Knower in Dave's group, Chris, a blond former beauty contest winner, was standing on the teebox with Dave, impatiently holding her club, also waiting to tee off. "Let's *go!*" she shouted, right after Dave. Now they were really startled, hearing the attractive lady, dressed in a matching taupe and white linen golf outfit, holler at them. Looking at her, hands on hips, she was squarely confronting their merry band. Chris likes playing golf efficiently, quickly. And there were bets at stake with the other couple. She was very annoyed to be held up by this messy crew of disheveled rule-breakers. She was similarly and overtly confrontational.

Chris's husband, John, a Deliberator, contained his six-foot-four frame in the golf cart, giving the distinct impression that he was trying to blend in with the seat. He was annoyed too, but he expressed his annoyance much more privately. Talking to Chris and Dave, John said, "Who the *hell* let these guys on the course in *this* size group? This is *outrageous!* Never in fifteen years of golf have I seen *seven* people . . . *look* at what they're doing to the green!" John saw every rule in the book being broken. He was even more annoyed than the other two, but was embarrassed by their outspoken confrontation, and was unwilling to say anything directly to the group ahead.

Dave's wife, JoAnn, the Conciliator in this foursome, completed the collection of brainstyles. Quite vocal during the round, she was now quietly watching the scene from the relative security of her golf cart, appreciating everyone's feelings. She could, she thought, see both sides of the issue: the fun the group ahead was having, and the impatience of her husband and friends. Nor did she particularly care if they had to wait a few minutes for the gang ahead. She could use the rest, she thought. They'd been in too much of a hurry all day, as far as she was concerned. Then, watching the mess they were making by not raking their sandtraps, she concluded that the guys *were* rather selfish to be so messy, which put her squarely on the side of her own team. So she also sat uncomfortably in her golf cart, not wanting to be the target of the retorts and unsubtle gestures made by the stirred-up-herd of golfers in reaction to the Conceptor's and Knower's annoyance. She began to wish that the more outspoken pair hadn't said anything.

Everyone agreed that they should complain to the management when they finished. But Dave said *that didn't take things far enough* "We need to get our money back or they won't change anything. They'll *never* fix it in the future," he pressed. Dave talks about the future as an absolute that he's very familiar with. *Always* and *never* are common to his speech.

Upon completing the round of golf, the Conceptor and Knower, Dave and Chris, made a beeline for the golf course management in the pro shop. John and JoAnn, the Deliberator and Conciliator, making sure their clubs were secure, carried on various other fussings with their gear, before walking into the shop right past the encounter at the desk initiated by their spouses, and straight into the appropriate locker rooms.

"There is NO EXCUSE for letting SEVEN play together on ANY COURSE," Dave said into the face of the pro shop manager. "I've played all over the world, at some of the finest courses, and NEVER have I seen this kind of thing! We can't play or recommend playing on a course like this. Our fees should be refunded." Chris added to his sentiments with comments like "It was disgusting! We had to wait fifteen minutes to tee off on hole after hole!" and added, "You really should give us our money back for such a lousy round."

John and JoAnn had already proceeded to the lunchroom and were chatting amiably, with a great deal of relief, about how their spouses were handling this problem so directly. The Deliberator and Conciliator, finding comfort together, knew where they stood and were clear that neither was willing to do anything nearly as confrontational.

The Conceptor and Knower returned triumphantly, comrades-in-arms, having secured the promise of the manager to refund their green fees. "Dave got him to tear up his credit card slip. I certainly hope you are going to get that accomplished, John," pronounced Chris after declaring the win, yet leaving the trophy for her man. The shyer, more conciliatory pair was suitably grateful and appreciative.

On the way out of the shop, in a quiet and diplomatic voice, the Deliberator asked for and received his credit card slip. The Conciliator was already in the car, refurbishing her makeup.

Each of this foursome acted true to their brainstyle in a confrontational situation where decisions were required. The Conceptor took charge of naming the issues, the Knower pushed for the win, the

Deliberator named all the rules being violated and was putting together a plan on how to resolve it more diplomatically, while the Conciliator was seeing the personal sides to the issues, desiring harmony before getting angry, but unwilling to confront anyone directly.

How can different brainstyles get along when they have such a distinct way of thinking and acting? These two couples have a nice collaboration going, one partner covering the other's non-strengths. This is working well, you might observe. Each of the partners seems to accept the other's gifts. Problems arise only when they don't.

HOW EACH BrainStyle IS SEEN BY OTHERS

When we are COMFORTABLE with another BrainStyle, we DESCRIBE them in this way:

KNOWER	CONCILIATOR	CONCEPTOR	DELIBERATOR
Direct,	Warm,	Challenging,	Deliberate,
Straightforward,	Enthusiastic,	Visionary,	Systematic,
Decisive,	Accepting,	Optimistic,	Neutral,
Aggressive,	Supportive,	Sees the big picture,	Objective,
Shrewd	Imaginative,	Experimental	Private,
	Spontaneous,		Thoughtful,
	Empathetic		Cautious,
			Methodical,
			Tactful,
			Professional

When we are UNCOMFORTABLE with another BrainStyle, we LABEL them like this:

KNOWER	CONCILIATOR	CONCEPTOR	DELIBERATOR
Dictator-like,	Self-absorbed,	Manipulative,	Rigid,
Cold,	Defensive,	"Blue-sky,"	Self-interested,
Bullying,	Pushy,	Unrealistic,	Overextended,
Pushy,	Personalizes everything,	Controlling of ideas with no follow-through on details,	Unfocused,
Inflexible,	Cannot take feedback,	Weird,	Paralyzed with indecision,
Insensitive or unfeeling,	An idealist,	Incomprehensible	A perfectionist,
Type A,	Moody,		A loner
Political	Wishy-washy		

BRAINSTYLES AND CONFLICT

Conflict arises from expectations. You can count on each brainstyle fighting according to its strengths. Therefore, understanding brainstyles is critical for understanding expectations, then finding the basis for mutually satisfying solutions. Recalling that the source of a brainstyle is *brainspeed*, it is a simple next step to use your knowledge of each of the brainstyle's timing in situations replete with Time Zero events to enter them with more self-control and confidence. Emotional fastballs pitched in heated home discussions or tangled professional meetings are called *conflict situations* by Deliberators and Conciliators, *taking care of business* or *problem solving* by Conceptors or Knowers.

The following chart is the formula to start you using the timing

---

TIMING WITH The BrainStyles SYSTEM

TIME IS THE PROBLEM.   TIMING IS THE SOLUTION.

Observe for BrainStyle timing when there is a new event:

KNOWERS	CONCILIATORS	CONCEPTORS	DELIBERATORS
Conclude first.	Respond/react with feeling first.	Reframe into a concept.	Assess first.
Sort into 1 or 2 categories.	Imagine possibilities.	Simplify, test, and generalize.	Sort into elements.
Simplify into a system.	Are aware of relationships.	Create in a random way using trial and error.	Compare to standard.
Decide now. Feel later.	Feel now. Decide now.	Decide on a hypothesis.	Do the right thing.
			Don't react or decide now.

Allow time for their strengths. With a:

KNOWER	CONCILIATOR	CONCEPTOR	DELIBERATOR
Realize the first decision will come fast, and won't change very much.	Refuse a quick decision.	Allow time for specifics.	Don't ask for a quick decision in a new area.
Offer your goals early.	Allow the left brain to input.	Get interim decisions.	Offer goals, alternatives early.
	Expect changes.	Ask questions.	
	Be supportive.	Fill in details.	

unique to your brainstyle to prepare for those Ground Zero time bombs. You can feel and be more in control of yourself inside when everyone outside seems to be uncontrollable. When you use timing, you don't have to make demands on someone else to change or try to only do things *your* way.

WHAT YOU'LL FIGHT ABOUT AND HOW YOU'LL FIGHT

BrainStyles can help you predict, and then prevent, what you'll fight about. Timing is initially the problem. Timing is also the solution. The following principles apply to home or office, given the brainstyles of those involved:

The *Conceptor* wants to take over quickly in order to establish the overview. He doesn't mind a good verbal tussle, and sees an argument as an opportunity to sort things into general principles, or bring underlying assumptions to the surface. Conceptors go for the win by defining the game itself. These *are the issues. Don't bog me down with the details!* Other brainstyles get caught off guard if they can't decide quickly on the new issue or want to point out the specifics the Conceptor is disregarding. Negotiations can be fun ways to get to new places for Conceptors. Remember how Dave, when angry, took charge by attacking the big issues: the broken rules, his own delay, the future cost, all of these instantly translated into future action in his mind—demanding satisfaction at the pro shop.

The *Knower* will respond to conflict by delivering *rapid left-brain* solutions. These can come across as edicts. Other brainstyles, having no time to sort out the issues that are so very clear to the Knower, may either shrink from the conflict or resist what appear as "controls." When Chris got to the pro shop, there was only one right answer: the return of her money. Although both the Conceptor and the Knower were very combative, their tactics were distinct. The Conceptor was more willing to negotiate early, the Knower was not. A direct confrontation *(No, that is not our policy)* or a time delay *(I'll get back to you)* plus a specific solution of your own *(but I'll tell you what I'll do in the meantime)* can shift the Knower's logic to new ground and open the discussion further.

The *Conciliator* either tries to bring harmony and negotiate around a fight, or becomes defensive to avoid conflict. These responses are ways of slowing down the speed of the exchange to allow time for a lot of right-brain processing. Other brainstyles may feel "manipulated" by the indirectness of the Conciliator who needs preparation, or "time-outs" to cope. JoAnn, for example, was initially uncomfortable with confrontation. After listening and thinking about it, she got indignant. Conciliators are unpredictable in the face of conflict. An initial outburst is followed by apologies and regrets, or a calm, avoidance response while a volcano brews underneath only to explode later.

The *Deliberator* avoids conflict when it contains emotions because emotions do not make sense. There are Time Zero events in a conflict situation. This brainstyle will slow down the exchange, then sort and organize the issues in an attempt to find logical solutions that can be discussed rationally. This strategy can either calm or infuriate others.

Fight-Starters:

"Why can't you support me like Chris does? She's not shy. You just disappeared." (Conceptor to Conciliator)

"You certainly embarrassed me out there on the golf course, yelling like that." (Conciliator to Conceptor)

"Well, you sure disappeared when things got tough. At least Dave stood up for getting our money back. If it was up to you, we'd be out all our money and nothing would change." (Knower to Deliberator)

"Do you have to make such a scene? Can't you act more like a lady?" (Deliberator to Knower)

Fight-Preventers and Marriage-Builders:

"I like it when you stay back and let me do my thing, then get people together afterward, like in the lunchroom where you congratulated Chris and me." (Conceptor to Conciliator)

"You certainly took over in an area I couldn't handle well at all. I appreciate how you got our money back." (Conciliator to Conceptor)

"John, you always smooth things over. The man almost looked pleased to give us our money back after you talked to him. Nice touch." (Knower to Deliberator)

"Chris, you were great, taking it to the mat like that. You're our fighter." (Deliberator to Knower)

> *BrainStyle Clues:*
>
> • *Knowers "fight" early over who is going to win.*
> • *Conciliators "fight" later over personal issues of fairness when they can't avoid it.*
> • *Deliberators "fight" by arguing and discussing what is right, based on value and precedent.*
> • *Conceptors "fight" early over the big picture, philosophy, values, and future impact.*

MEN, WOMEN, AND THEIR DIFFERENCES

"That was a fine report, Barbara. But since the sexes speak different languages, I probably didn't understand a word of it."
Drawing by Handelsman © 1995 The New Yorker Magazine, Inc.

When we fall in love, we fall in love with differences. When we love for a lifetime, we draw from our differences to sustain each other.

Yet those same differences can become the source of all our problems with another.

Most of us have a heightened awareness of gender when we are sexually attracted to someone or mad at them. In the first instance, no problem; in the second, *oh dear.* The battle between the sexes is an ancient debate. The updates by neuroscientists will be used for the same old battle unless we wake up and put chemistry in the service of more loving ends. Alas, recent scientific scoops dramatize differences in sexy headlines like "Men and Women Truly Don't Think Alike."[1]

The best-selling book *Men Are from Mars, Women Are from Venus* is a wonderful guide to resolving conflict in marriage, explaining how, in general, men's and women's differences work in relationships. Author John Gray explains, carefully and kindly, how to heal rifts that develop out of the woman's need to feel, to think out loud by talking, and to be listened to when the man simultaneously needs to be alone, to solve problems, to achieve results, to settle into himself in order to contribute. Gray sums up: men need "to be free," while women want "understanding."[2]

Gray and anthropologist Deborah Tannen[3] have undoubtedly captured the language we *learn to speak* as women and men. The latest brain research is discovering differences in the hardware between men and women that can account for specialized skills as well. The language we have learned supplements our natural way of responding in new situations. Moreover, of those who have assessed their brainstyle, most Conciliators are women (by 60 percent to 40 percent), which means, as you know by now, a natural gift for feeling and expressing emotionally. It is even likely that women in all brainstyles have paid more attention to the emotional side of their lives—or at least learned how to express their feelings more openly in Western cultures than men.

However, if you find that, as a woman, you also have a need to achieve *even when* your emotional needs aren't being met, to solve problems, to go to your *own* cave to think things over, perhaps you can now build upon what you have learned about a need to express your own natural brainstyle strengths.

If you find that, as a man, you strongly desire to be understood, to express your feelings, to be heard, or think out loud in order to solve a problem, perhaps you can consider a fuller measure of what it means to think things through with your unique mental hardware, regardless of your gender or that of the person across the table from you.

The following chart shows how those identifying themselves with *The BrainStyle Inventory* divide by gender among the brainstyles. There are enough exceptions to gender generalizations to pay attention to what's going on *inside,* it would seem.

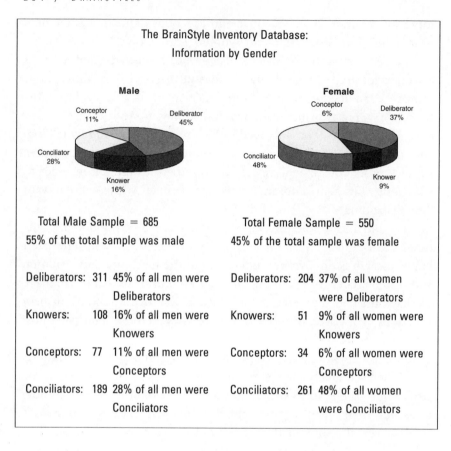

The BrainStyle Inventory Database:
Information by Gender

Male

Conceptor 11%
Deliberator 45%
Conciliator 28%
Knower 16%

Female

Conceptor 6%
Deliberator 37%
Conciliator 48%
Knower 9%

Total Male Sample = 685
55% of the total sample was male

Total Female Sample = 550
45% of the total sample was female

Deliberators: 311 45% of all men were Deliberators

Knowers: 108 16% of all men were Knowers

Conceptors: 77 11% of all men were Conceptors

Conciliators: 189 28% of all men were Conciliators

Deliberators: 204 37% of all women were Deliberators

Knowers: 51 9% of all women were Knowers

Conceptors: 34 6% of all women were Conceptors

Conciliators: 261 48% of all women were Conciliators

ENJOYING A PARTNER WITHOUT CHANGING WHO YOU ARE

What brainstyle is best for you to marry or partner with? The opposite? Different but similar? The same? There are three possibilities with good news and bad news for every pairing. The peril in all cases is that you allow the situation or the lover to define *you* rather than staying centered in your own strengths.

COMPLEMENTING. Fay and Bill, two Deliberators, went through a rough patch in their marriage when working on their new direct mail business together. Each naturally took a very structured, logical approach. It was helpful that as Deliberators each wanted to proceed in a step-by-step fashion. Their marriage and their business were based on similar and compatible natural strengths—a real plus. However, when finances were tight, Bill used a different approach to their problems than Fay. Fay became more emotional and Bill more quiet and

The KNOWER wants to	The CONCILIATOR wants to	The CONCEPTOR wants to	The DELIBERATOR wants to
EACH BrainStyle (REGARDLESS OF GENDER) LOOKS FOR OPPORTUNITIES TO APPLY STRENGTHS			
• Control the outcome	• Build relationships	• Create, invent	• Determine the process
• Achieve results, fix things	• Coordinate, bring together	• Influence others	• Gain knowledge
• Think independently; work smart, not hard	• Do, be active; respond to problems quickly	• Solve problems in new ways	• Work at intellectually meaningful tasks
• Hit measurable targets	• Bring meaning to tasks and people	• Achieve recognition for ideas	• Be the expert; to do the right thing
• Solve problems that bring order and efficiency	• Solve problems in areas where people and ideas come together	• Solve problems by posing new ideas that redirect all elements	• Solve problems that make things more rational or understandable; to capture the issue with a model that explains and enlightens
• Make things simple		• Lead by creating a new vision of the future	

Do Not Reproduce without Permission from BSI © 1993.

withdrawn. They saw themselves as two very different people. According to Fay, "He's acting *just* like a man, and I guess I have a woman's point of view that's more feeling, more sensitive to these things." The more emotional she got, the more she moved away from her natural deliberative strengths, the more their differences in communications became center stage. "He's so stubborn. He won't talk to me. *He* won't show *his* feelings; he walks out of the room." Fights were bitter; blame and resentment were winning the day. They considered splitting up. When differences become accentuated, common ground disappears. And of course, the most visible difference is our gender and all the trappings that go along with "being a woman," or "being a man." The stereotypes roll in like a big fog bank and clarity disappears.

Can you hear *60 Minutes'* Andy Rooney saying, "Did you ever notice that the only times we get so darned aware of how he's acting just like a man is when we don't agree with him?" It's handy. It's quick. There's lots of studies to show us how the sexes are different.

But Fay and Bill worked out a resolution by focusing on what they had in common: a step-by-step approach to getting the job done. They had overlooked the fact that each has a similar brainstyle to focus on their differences. *Trouble.* When they boiled their disagreement down to a single issue: when to hire an assistant they could afford, they then agreed to postpone that matter until after they allowed feelings to settle down and their compatibility to reemerge.

As an ancient Greek philosopher said, "Right timing is in all things the most important factor." Bob Hope says, "Timing is the *essence* of life." Can you think of any time when timing *doesn't* matter?

COMPETING. "Just because she's a woman, she thinks she can . . ." You fill in the blank here, but you know that the next statement is going to be one based on competing to win at the expense of the other. The goal is to "get your two cents in" and "show her that (choose one) a) I'm right" or b) "I can figure out better answers" or c) "She's a _____."

When there are differences between us, and I am unsure of what I bring to our relationship, one of my ongoing objectives is to prove my worth by triumphing over the one person I think is better than I am. It's a problem that arrives in adolescence and then stays with us the rest of our lives.

How much of your time is invested in one-upping? Must you have your say? Correct others' dumb ideas? In too many meetings, this motivation wastes at least one third of the time with unneeded presentations (for impressing), questions (for poking holes and making someone look smarter), and general resistance or subtle sabotage of someone else's ideas. And that's just at *work.* How many divorces have begun by redecorating the den?

Typically, competitive behavior is too unpleasant to deal with or admit. It generally gets tucked under a blanket of *poor communications* so that Communications Skills training or How To books can be spread over everyone from time to time to further confound the problem with tactics and techniques that keep us busy, but distracted from the real cause of problems in the relationship.

ADAPTING. We all want to fit in, more or less. We all find ourselves going along to get along at times. So when the new in-laws, the new company, or the new school has a way of doing things that is their set-in-cement tradition, well, it's adapt-or-die time all over again. You become *flexible*. In fact, learning how to do things you are not naturally gifted at is vital for start-ups at work and at home. If *all* you do is employ your strengths, no one might get invoiced, or fed, or off to school on time. That's common sense. What *isn't* common sense is making versatility the single goal. Becoming flexible can so easily become trying hard at everything or going along so often that it's hard to tell when you cross that little double yellow line to defend something you just flat out can't do very well or know a lot about. You may then have head-on collisions with people who just might be better than you in some things.

"I size up the situation, and if there's a need for a funny one, a serious one, a good mixer —I try to fill the bill." This can be fun or demanding, depending on your abilities. Too much flexibility, however, and focus is *kaput*. And focus is the path to "flow"—and mastery.

"I can't stand people saying 'You're *just* like your sister'—so I act differently on purpose." Sometimes we go against others' expectations in order to establish ourselves. This young woman has adapted at the expense of herself, exaggerating her differences with her sister, setting up distance between them.

Besides this, there are real reasons to learn to do things that you aren't good at: the situation is such that there is no one else, and you get the opportunity to stretch your limits. Isn't this growth? Isn't this life?

"I do whatever it takes to run my business—and I have to do everything. I don't have the luxury of only doing whatever I *feel like* doing. I just can't afford to hire someone else." "I'm a single parent and I'm not very good at telling bedtime stories and listening to the things my kids need to tell me, but I do the best I can because there isn't anyone else."

It is true that we must often perform reasonably well outside our strengths. But that's no reason to beat yourself up for not getting it all done, not handling change well enough, not taking enough advice or, *omigod,* making mistakes. Take a breath. Are you forgetting who you naturally are? Whether complementing, competing, or adapting to get through the daily grind, sooner or later something breaks down. Basically we fight to reestablish an equilibrium. Our equilibrium comes from "what our brain already knows"[4] to be a match between our inner and outer selves. When that equilibrium is based on acting a certain way to please others we can never really feel worthwhile. When we depend on someone *else* doing things our way, we can never learn who we are.

USING BRAINSTYLES TO SORT OUT THE CONFUSION

GETTING LOST BY ADAPTING.   "I'm not sure what my *brainstyle* is," she opened. "But I *am* sure that I'm two different people. I'm one person at home and another person at work. A *lot* of people have told me this. I know how to adapt to the situation."

"What's different?" I asked.

"At work I'm decisive, bottom-line, you know, I take charge of things. I tell my partner what to do. At home I let my husband more or less take over. I defer to him on things. I would never do that at work. I guess at work I'm pushy."

Jeri is a woman in her forties, a graphic designer in a partnership of some fourteen years, talking about her understanding of and confusion with *brainstyles,* or to be more accurate, with her own understanding of who she is. She quickly moves into some of the problems she's had on the job. She is animated as she talks.

CONFLICTS.   "My partner and I have worked out a good relationship —she stays in the office and works without a ruffle. I go work with clients. But recently our business was very slow and we had to take in another woman to be a liaison for two accounts. She was good with corporate clients." The word "corporate" was said like it had just four letters that spelled something with a bad smell.

"Diane" (said like a bad taste)—"Diane the *Dreadful,*" she rushed on—"Oh, that's terrible, isn't it—I'm not supposed to say that, am I?" She looks down, embarrassed.

"Diane" (the name seemed to purse her mouth) "was this woman we *had* to take on as an account rep to handle these corporate accounts because she was the one who spoke their language. God forbid *I* should ever speak *their* language.

*"Any*way, she couldn't speak to *me.* Or we couldn't communicate. Or something. Anyway, she would *not* tell me what I needed to know. Everything was so structured with her. I was going crazy. In fact, I went so crazy, the only way I could handle the situation with Diane was to make things funny. I drew a cartoon of Diane, duplicated it

three times (!) and showed it to her." Jeri stops and laughs out loud. She laughs deeply. Her eyes water. She says, "Gosh, I haven't laughed in *weeks.*"

What happened then?

"Well, Diane laughed too. Then we talked. Things got a little better. At least I could hear what she was saying."

UNCOVERING STRENGTHS. Jeri found an extraordinary solution for her problem with Diane. It is one taught by some of the wisest teachers and most ancient of traditions: to heal with humor, or laughter. "That was quite a profound thing you did," I said.

She settled in her seat. We were eating lunch. She took a few bites. She looked more confident and less guilty as she chewed over my comment, which focused on her strengths rather than her self-criticism. She continued more forcefully, while at the same time she seemed almost to be discovering what she thought while she said it out loud.

"Well, I finally decided that I had to get away in order to be myself and do what I do best. I told my partner that I hated corporate structure and corporate reports, even if they *had* saved our bottom line, and *anything* [that had] to do with Diane. I was going to move my office into my home, have less structure, and try new things. Maybe this is all just a midlife crisis." She looked abashed. "She would just have to choose between Diane and her approach, and me and my approach."

The conversation continued, picking up on what her spontaneous solution using humor had done for her and how it might be useful to illustrate a new project. The illustrations themselves would show images transformed from the initial perceptions through a new understanding, on paper. Wow. The discussion topic (healing of perceptions) seemed to bring up a whole new layer of concern.

BRAINSTYLES AND EXPECTATIONS. She plunged on. "What this is *really* about is my marriage. I feel like I solved one problem at work to come home to another set of problems that my husband is having. He's very worried about his boss and the fact that they don't see eye to eye." She got into the problem a bit more, sounding more and more irritated. "So now *I'm* going nuts trying to start this new business in my home. My computer gobbled two weeks of work. Then my husband comes home and all he can talk about is going nuts over his own stuff at work and *I'm tired of hearing about it.*"

She looked anxious, guilty, and worried, one feeling right after the other clouding across her face.

"Let's sort this out," I said, "starting with your natural gifts and go from there. How does that sound?" She nodded yes. "What do you do at work that your partner counts on you for?"

"Oh, she's the steady, quiet, stay-in-the-office-all-day-happy-as-a-clam type, and I'm out making contacts, going to lunches, making friends, selling. I'm the sales part of the business," she offered. She said it in a matter-of-fact tone.

"So you might characterize your partner as a Deliberator, then."

"Yes."

"What do you love to do best on the job?"

Without hesitation, Jeri spelled out her love of the imaginative time at her drawing board visualizing to make ideas come alive. She talked of how good she is at making friends with some clients, the "people people" that she feels most comfortable with. She talked about how she is able to put people's feelings into words or pictures for them, or so she is told. She is a good and funny storyteller.

"I'd love to do more of that, if it weren't for those damnable corporate reports that have to be done—just for the money. My life is slipping away and I'm not doing what I could be, should be doing." Jeri's pain was obvious as she said this.

"Your brainstyle is most likely that of a *Conciliator.* And your central gift is to bring intuition and empathy spontaneously from the right brain to situations to solve problems. The further you get away from the gift in yourself, the more you feel out of touch with who you are, and the more you start demanding that others around you supply what you're missing. Like Diane. Like your husband. From what you have described about both of them, they are *Deliberators* who do not, cannot, give you what you want *in the form that you want it.* Beyond this, no one else can ever supply the satisfaction you feel when being your natural self. The strengths inside you give far greater satisfaction than the problems outside you can drain away. Your job is to know, nurture, and stay in touch with them so well that you can always use them to contribute to others. It's in this way that we naturally give and receive all at the same time."

"So what should I do with my husband?" she worried out loud.

NATURAL STRENGTHS. "Your *real* gift is not in solving new, left-brained, hard-edged, fact-based problems. You are feeling stressed because you are trying to solve problems with your non-strengths. To others, this looks like you are pushing to take control. You have *learned* to be factual and assertive in your area of expertise where you have over fourteen years dealing with similar issues. You can be decisive and bottom-line in sales and design as you *remember* what to do from hundreds of previous experiences. That's how you are actually different between home and work. At work you decide from familiarity, with comfort in having seen the situation, or one like it, before. You are confronting many more situations with your husband that are *new* to you. That's when your *brainstyle* shows up—your brain-based way of deciding and responding, in the moment, to new situations. When you can't remember what to do, you are free to be your natural self, *if* you know what that natural self is and how to honor it.

"Your gift, your natural way of responding, is to *first* respond with feeling and intuition. And that means that you are naturally a loving support, an enthusiastic complement who feels for and can help others, including your husband, understand their own feelings, just by your own knowing intuition. His job is to solve his own problems, for which he is more than equipped. If you want to be involved, you might give him insights into relationships with people by putting yourself in their place and imagining various reactions to his proposals. He can try things out on you *if* you want to do so."

She thought about this. She said she knew he should solve his own problems, but that it was hard to relate to him these days. She admitted that she really wanted a little attention herself and did indeed feel resentful of all the time she was spending on him.

"Why do I keep doing this, this attending to someone else's problem when I really want attention myself?" she asked, not really expecting an answer.

"Because of your natural gifts, your mental hardware, which is a fabulous sensing device of your immediate surroundings. Your *brainstyle* picks up on the moods and feelings of others around you. It's your gift and, if you don't pay attention to it, your curse. People will drive you crazy with all you pick up about their problems—*if you let them*. So of course it seems like you must try to fix their problems just so you can have some peace, when all along the real problem is that you are not at peace within yourself. You're trying to get comfortable by fixing the *outside*. You cannot use your gifts except to support another in being more of who they really, already are. As you are more of who *you* are, you will do this naturally.

"Now, as for Diane, I have a premise: Painful People give us much more than our friends give us to grow from. It's not news. But it sure feels like news when you have a red-hot special Painful Person in your face who seems dedicated to making you miserable. The wonderful thing about PPs is that they keep reappearing in new versions until we've learned how to resolve the problem within ourselves."

THE BENEFITS OF GETTING CENTERED. "You're going to tell me that that . . . that *witch* was a gift," she said quite sarcastically, undoubtedly congratulating herself on her restrained language.

"Well, from what I've heard, she prompted you into redefining and clarifying what you love the most in your work, for a start. Then, to deal with her, you used your natural gift of spontaneity and imagination to come up with and start exploring a whole new approach to how you do what you do using humor. And you seem *quite* interested in pursuing this. Then she got you rethinking your relationship with your partner of fourteen years so that you have redefined that relationship as well. After that, you are looking at your marriage in a new way in order to see what you can do to make it more deeply meaningful for you both. I'd say she started you doing some very profound things for yourself. You just used her as a reason."

I was very touched when Jeri called a couple of weeks later. Her "life was different," she said very quietly. She called to tell of her renewed romance with her husband: "I'm getting back to just listening," she said, "and he *loves* it—it's helped us get a lot closer." Then her voice smiled, "*and* I'm using several cartoons to illustrate my current account. I'm excited!"

SPECIAL RELATIONSHIPS: WHEN SOMEONE ELSE IS YOUR SOLUTION

ENEMIES. Enemies are the real opportunities in our lives. They, more than anyone, show us who we are and what we fear. They can appear in any brainstyle to push our buttons. They can also help us more clearly define our own gifts. Conquering an old hurt is the surest sign of maturity. Trying to understand a present wound is another path to finding out who we are.

We can lose ourselves by fixating on an *enemy,* someone who gossiped about us, who hurt our feelings, who betrayed us, who did a mean-nasty-meant-to-hurt-us thing.

Enemies provide the illusion that the problem is *out there* where the answer can never be found. Someone else holds the cure.

How much pain does it cause you when you can't see beyond someone else's pettiness or viciousness? When focusing on another's smallness you in turn can become small and self-righteous as well. You lose the source of your own energy by losing sight of what you want to achieve or master.

ROMANCES.   There is another kind of special relationship in which we lose ourselves: special loves. These are not just teenage romances. These occur every time we assign the other person the job of making us feel okay. We *need* them. The other must say what we need to hear or they just don't care enough. They are selfish, insensitive, or, ratcheting up the scale, sexists, racists. They hurt us. Their words are torture. We are victimized. Words become sticks and stones to break our bones. We lose our strengths by defining theirs so carefully.

Have you ever heard someone say something like this? "Frank's awesome. He does things I could never do. I like watching him. I like the way he thinks." You notice the subtle imitations, the mild envy in their eyes as they describe how special that teacher or role model is.

How far can you go to learn from someone else before you become the cheap imitation?

What kind of gem might you be? You might never find out. Nor might you find the one for you.

One afternoon, according to an old Sufi tale, Nesradean and his friend were sitting in a café drinking tea and talking about life and love. "How come you never got married, Nesradean?" asked his friend at one point. "Well," said Nesradean, "to tell you the truth I spent my youth looking for the perfect woman. In Cairo I met a beautiful and intelligent woman with eyes like dark olives, but she was unkind. Then in Baghdad I met a woman who was a wonderful and generous soul, but we had no interests in common. One woman after another would seem just right but there would always be something missing. Then one day

I met her. She was beautiful, intelligent, generous and kind. We had everything in common. In fact, she was perfect." "Well," said Nesradean's friend, "what happened? Why didn't you marry her?" Nesradean sipped his tea reflectively. "Well," he replied, "it's a sad thing. It seemed she was looking for the perfect man."[5]

OPPOSITES ATTRACT. We all know this. It must be a law of nature. You can almost fall in love just watching someone do something that you can't do. You marvel at them. You want to learn from them. You want to be around them so some of what they've got can rub off on you. Add to that the chemistry of sexual attraction and it might sound like this:

"Judy is wonderful, but she's like a sister. Now Fran, she turns me on. I guess most people would say they were about equally pretty— but the chemistry is just there with one and not the other."

He talks easily with Judy. They have a lot in common. Fran is his opposite—quiet, controlled, methodical. "I don't *have* to talk much with Fran. I talk all day. I just love being around her. I can't get enough of her." Fran makes him feel *complete, whole.* This is the bottom line of romance, filling up all the empty spaces in our souls: precisely why romances go wrong so soon.

Can we learn from role models? Should we marry our opposites?

Learning from people different from you can make communications easier between you, can show you shortcuts to getting along with others, and can open new avenues of thought. You can also get focused on being who you're *not.* Marrying someone who is quite different covers all the bases, and is undoubtedly a primitive mechanism to ensure our survival. It is also extremely exciting in the beginning to pair up with someone so unlike ourselves that they seem a continual mystery to unravel. Later, when the falling-in-love chemicals wear off, there's a relationship of real differences in thinking to manage. And that's when the gender and racial (or whatever is most obvious) differences can become "irreconcilable."

The Knower, Mel, whom you met in Chapter Three, was concerned that he and his Conciliator wife were drifting apart. His career was time-consuming, her life was about their three children. Mel explained, "I started to figure out why my wife and I hadn't been able to communicate for the last eight years as well as I'd like us to." He continued, "I'd want to handle everything practically. 'Let's sit down and just work this out [*now* was always implied].' She always thought about the emotional side first. She thought I was trying to steamroll her, and we never resolved an issue." So Mel read about brainstyles, especially about *her* brainstyle. Now he tries things like, " 'I really want to talk about the way we are raising the kids. I have a difference with how we are going about it.' And she usually bristles up a little bit, so I say, 'Hey, let's talk about it tomorrow, over lunch or go to dinner or something like that. But think about it.' This gives me a chance to handle the practical ideas, she gets all the emotions out of it, and it's been amazing how we've been able to improve the quality of how we talk about things now."

All relationships, regardless of the situation, involve brainstyles. All people are looking for ways to apply their strengths from a deeply felt need to succeed. People *naturally* seek to do what they do best and *will not be denied*.

Following are a few tips on what happens when brainstyles partner. Maturity, and a willingness to work for goals beyond your own, are the context necessary for workability. A similar energy level (pace) helps enormously to blend differences between two people.

SOME TIPS FOR PAIRINGS AND THEIR POSSIBILITIES

The Knower–Conciliator Pair (the original Mars and Venus pairing)

This is a marriage of opposites in which all the bases are covered in solving problems. The potential for competition and adaptation is very high. The relationship must be managed continually. Conciliator tactics can be indirect (getting even, complaining to friends instead of the spouse, *assuming* the other should understand when he or she doesn't), then stormy Knowers can be brutally judgmental, then withdrawn, which is punishing to the Conciliator. Time-outs help to settle things down and recall that you cannot change each other.

- Conciliators must accept that they will best manage the relationship, the Knower the tasks. When tensions develop, the Conciliator probably needs to take the lead in resolving his own feelings before discussing the issues. The Knower can take the lead in defining issues and allowing time for the Conciliator to consider them.
- Knowers who are often quite tolerant of the Conciliator's "foibles" include their partner's needs and solutions. Conciliators reciprocate with reasoned delivery of requests.

- Recognition for a Conciliator's right-brained gifts will often go unnoticed by the Knower. Most Conciliators learn to build their own esteem in these areas.
- Conciliators need to supplement the relationship with supportive friends and expect delays in personal understanding and attention from their partner.

The Knower–Deliberator Pair

This is a marriage of complements in which the common bond is a gift for analysis and rational decisions without a lot of turmoil. The home or business is, most likely, thoroughly managed. Business partners will spend more time and have difficulty with people issues. Bringing in a third brainstyle helps. *Values* and *procedures* will be two likely sources of conflict between the pair. Most couples enjoy travel or variety in stimulating activities that can be organized or well-planned.

- Common interests are critical.
- The Knowers' patience with the more thoughtful decision-making of their partners is continually tested. (See Peg's story and how she gets along with her Deliberator husband in Chapter Three.)
- Fights can be win-lose with both partners sticking too closely to their own agenda.
- Deliberators need to respect the values of the Knower and have an opportunity to influence them.

The Knower–Conceptor Pair

This is a partnership of exciting possibilities when Conceptors are free to get results in their own way. The Knower brings practicality and structure, the Conceptor the new and the possible.

- Conceptors may want more intimacy and openness on a daily basis than the Knower is comfortable with. Scheduling private time and small vacations can provide the setting.
- Depending upon the left-brained access of the Conceptor, the relationship can deal well with future plans, but not as well with social friendships. A few friends can be developed over time and will matter the most, as will close relatives.
- There is high potential for conflict as business partners if both are strong. Agreement can be reached on goals. The Conceptor will be the relationship-minder.
- Control of separate turf is desirable.

The Knower–Knower Pair

When two of the same brainstyle pair, competition is most likely to occur. It would be highly unlikely for two Knowers to partner. If so,

* Two Knowers need a common cause and separate turf to manage.

The Conciliator–Conceptor Pair

A union of exciting potential: both are visual, imaginative, and dramatic.

* Fights can occur simply to create breathing space between the two —most often when things get too personal.
* Conversations can get wildly conceptual unless there is an agreed-upon framework or desired outcome stated: Conciliators often want *inclusion* and Conceptors *control* in projects. Both respond well to openly expressed *affection*.
* Both resist control, which represents a problem when deciding who will lead. The Conceptor is best equipped to do so when starting new projects, the Conciliator in the social and entertainment arenas as well as with the family.
* If the pair agree to support new ideas without worrying about who gets the credit or takes the lead, breakthroughs in new territory can occur. The Conceptor is most often the idea-leader, the Conciliator the supportive and imaginative action-oriented implementor.

The Conciliator–Deliberator Pair

This is a union of strengths that complement each other well. The Conciliator brings the pizzazz to the Deliberator's steadiness, analysis, and laid-back style.

* Problems can arise when conflict is avoided for too long. The Conciliator can be branded "too volatile" or the Deliberator "too cold and stone-faced." Regular communication with clear and agreed-upon goals is needed to stay intimate at home or focused in the office.
* Both can be explorers, bringing many interests to the relationship that keep it stimulating.
* Fights can occur over small things and get complicated early, *if* the Deliberator engages in an argument. Both demand lots of air time. Values are often the breaking point for the Deliberator when dealing with the Conciliator's hot projects and changeability.

- At work, meetings can be endless for these two brainstyles. This pair does well using a neutral third party, especially a third brainstyle, to help move them to decisions with focus.

The Conciliator–Conciliator Pair

This pair is likely to be best friends—or worst enemies when feelings get hurt. If there is such a thing as getting "too close," it could happen here. Meanwhile, neither is minding the store. Left-brain jobs can go undone with fights about who is responsible.

- To avoid competing or adapting too much to the other takes frequent and honest discussions. One couple made three lists at the beginning of their relationship: Things I Like to Do, Things I Hate to Do, Things I Can't Do. They worked out a schedule to take turns on the first two, and hired experts (CPA, office manager) for the third.
- Maturity is required for this pair to openly negotiate and avoid personalizing too much. Often time apart can allow objectivity to set in.

The Conceptor–Conceptor Pair

This pair, as described by one Conceptor, "thought so much like one another we could finish each other's sentences. It was spooky." Issues similar to those for Conciliators would be expected (see above). The problem with same-brainstyle relationships is that similar strengths tend to compete with each other, non-strengths are crucial to survival, and one or both may feel they are sacrificing too much for the relationship. If both Conceptors are coming up with new ways to do things, who pays the bills and makes sure the cleaning gets picked up? Only committed and mature couples survive in the more erratic and emotional lifestyles of the right-brained.

The Conceptor–Deliberator Pair

This is a partnership of opposites in which all the bases are covered in running a home or business. When both have a similar energy level, work can go smoothly. (See examples in Chapter Five.)

- The Deliberator needs to appreciate all the changes the Conceptor loves to promote and bring into their partnership in order to value their time together.
- The Conceptor must value the steadiness and organization the Deliberator brings to ensuring that things get done and not expect a

passionate or enthusiastic audience. Conceptors tend to be demonstrative or talkative, Deliberators like to do things to show they care. Each needs to continually appreciate these differences and have a friend in their own brainstyle to talk to.

- In a union of opposites, neither feels deeply appreciated over the long haul. Appreciations need to be openly and consciously expressed.
- To work smoothly, opposites need breathing room. Stressful situations for the pair occur after moves or new jobs where each needs a great deal of personal support and the partner is ill-equipped to provide it in the language of the other. Each needs their own outlets or supportive friends for personal support.

The Deliberator–Deliberator Pair

This is the union that tends to stabilize early over common values and last the longest with the least conflict. Partners tend to have discussions rather than arguments. Shared interests and beliefs are central to a lasting partnership.

- Plans, budgets, and projects can stretch out endlessly unless another brainstyle is brought in to move things along, and provided either will take an outsider's advice.
- Serious conflicts can consume endless discussion in business or, in personal relationships, create irreconcilable rifts. Each will have a right answer, while neither party deals well with conflict. If there is a real commitment to the relationship, individual counseling can help.*

Consider this: It only takes *one* to heal a relationship.

The following chart outlines *typical, initial reactions* of each brainstyle in new situations. You can use this information to get past differences to the longer-term relationship beneath the surface.

---

* *Science News* (February 23, 1991, p. 118) reported a study conducted with forty-six couples in marriage counseling over twenty years. The couples who participated in behavioral counseling for marital problems (they changed things they did and said with one another) had a significantly higher divorce rate (nineteen of twenty-three) than couples participating in insight therapy. The latter helps individuals resolve past emotional issues (previous decisions) that block communication and has much longer lasting effects, promoting autonomy for each person. (Only one of twenty-three couples divorced after this type of therapy.)

HOW EACH BrainStyle WILL BE INFLUENCED BY OTHERS IN NEW SITUATIONS

The KNOWER	The CONCILIATOR	The CONCEPTOR	The DELIBERATOR
• Is least influenced by others' reactions	• Is most influenced by others' reactions	• Is somewhat influenced by others' reactions	• Resists influence initially
• Is most definitive	• May sound sure early, then change	• Takes in limited information	• Asks for lots of information
• May not readily share information	• May not have words for a quick response; needs to talk	• May need time to digest main points	• Needs time to assess
	• Has spontaneous reactions		

To INFLUENCE The KNOWER	To INFLUENCE The CONCILIATOR	To INFLUENCE The CONCEPTOR	To INFLUENCE The DELIBERATOR
• Challenge the decision or goal directly	• Use stories or examples of success	• Use several shorter presentations	• Remove time pressure
• Propose another solution of your own choosing	• Ask for their reactions; help them to find their own reasons for actions	• Influence them after an initial event, when they are more receptive	• Offer direction or solutions to choose from
• Focus the conversation	• Help them decide by developing a personal relationship	• Don't pile on facts; use examples, show trends	• Meet or discuss a few times
• Avoid any suspicion that you are trying to take advantage or outmaneuver the Knower	• Offer personal or expert references and endorsements	• Ask the Conceptor to conclude from illustrations or examples	• Offer more information to study
			• Be prepared with information

Part Two:
At the Office

An even tougher challenge than hiring for racial, gender, or ethnic diversity is to consciously bring together people who have contrasting brainstyles. This demands a stretch beyond everyone's most cherished assmptions about a right way to *think* and *speak*.

> "BrainStyles is a common denominator across all humankind regardless of gender, race, ethnic origin, etc. It is something that brings diverse people together on common ground."
>
> HENRY HO, Customer Business Development Manager for Asia,
> The Procter & Gamble Company, Hong Kong

BRINGING OUT THE BEST

You'll learn to recognize brainstyles with practice, often by being annoyed by a certain brainstyle's ineffective or self-serving behavior (see the following chart). This is a necessary start. By the end of Chapter Nine you'll get the formula to transform these initial perceptions to recognize the strengths underneath. The following section takes each brainstyle in turn, outlining how best to respond or take advantage of what they *really* have to offer.

RESPECTING THE KNOWER

You're probably dealing with a Knower, not just an experienced person in another brainstyle, if that person is quick to conclude the answer on *any* new subject, get to a cause, and pose A or B solutions soon afterward. The Knower does so without needing much reflection time for analysis, or emotion. He can also move forward rapidly to new issues without a backward glance.

Knowers *want* efficiency. They *need* balance to their ideas to include the irrational and messy human factor in their plans.

The issue in dealing with the Knower is *time*. The rapid left-brain response means facts up front. Most often other brainstyles are uncom-

BEGINNING STAGES OF MASTERY:

OBSERVING BrainStyles SYMPTOMS

(What you see when you get annoyed)

The KNOWER	The CONCILIATOR	The CONCEPTOR	The DELIBERATOR
CONTROLS INFORMATION by:	CONTROLS INFORMATION by:	CONTROLS INFORMATON by:	CONTROLS INFORMATION by:
• Being first with a judgment, an answer, or conclusion	• Putting a spin on it that favors their agenda.	• Reinterpreting what is said into their own idea/ scheme	• Not sharing at all (closing) -or-
• Structuring the topic by deciding and telling others	• Making up their mind, acting stubborn	• Broadening the subject	• Telling at length (spilling)—giving all the facts
• Using people to reach own goals	• Paying most attention to the idea/issue/ person that fits their beliefs/ values/feelings (squeaky wheel)	• Bragging how much they know	• Giving unedited details on paper
• Being "political"		• Selling, persuading someone, while actually thinking out loud or just testing the idea	• Working with all priorities equally
• My-way-or-the-highway presentation	• Making a case for what's hot NOW	• Rejecting questions, concerns	• Attending to the details with people; being polite, professional while deciding alone
	• Taking action/ testing it out on their own		
DOES NOT	DOES NOT	DOES NOT	DOES NOT
• Include others' ideas/feelings	• Set priorities based on facts	• Attend to details well	• Focus priorities
			• Give overview
• Spend time on fantasy or daydreams	• Give the whole picture	• Appreciate what the plan requires	• Keep it simple
• Care if you approve or like him/her very much	• Keep it simple	• Stick to the plan	• Motivate others with "charisma"/ excitement
	• Cover the facts logically, step by step		

fortable with this speed, and so call Knowers bullies. Just the way they say things, without much feeling, and so clearly and certainly, can be intimidating—especially for the Conciliator.

A Conciliator met a Knower at a party, and after chatting for a while, she shared a very tricky family situation with the very articulate and decisive Knower. "There were so many *issues* and *feelings* involved

I just couldn't decide what to do. So I asked his advice. He asked me very *penetrating* questions. In five minutes he told me there were only two options, one of which was to 'end the relationship and never look back.' " In reporting this event, she said, "I realized instantly that my feelings prevented me from considering this choice and that was why the situation got so complex." After this logical conclusion, she then continued, "He made it *so* simple, and came up with it *so fast,* I was embarrassed." Conciliators are often bowled over with the lightning logic of their opposite. It's either the pedestal or the pits for the Knower and their quick answers. Neither, however, is appropriate. The Knower feels and grows best when you apply their ideas. Adulation or envy comes from the Conciliator's misplaced wish to do something she can't and that the Knower can do quite naturally.

Other brainstyles can be put off by the Knower. The indirect and diplomatic Deliberator finds the Knower's ability to be direct as too "in your face."

The Conceptor, when rolling out their vision of the possibilities to come, can find the Knower just a bit negative, critical, or unyielding. Rather, as one Conceptor did quite often, they can take advantage of the forecasting and focus of a Knower colleague to create "tight" plans with very specific ends in mind.

If other brainstyles would not compete with a Knower's strength, but instead use their own strengths and timing to respond and build on what is offered, enormous gains in productivity will be made.* The *worst* thing to do is to judge Knower behavior as "overbearing" or a Knower response as "intimidating." Such prejudgments are the real cause of "poor communications" and will impede your capacity to hear what is really meant. You can take it personally and lose the very information that just might further your goals.

So how can you take advantage of the real gifts of the Knower?

When your brainstyle is different from that of the Knower, first find common ground, if you can. Get to know what interests they have

---

* One team, made up of eleven Deliberators and two Conciliators, had stonewalled one member of the group because they "couldn't get along with him," and worse, he was from corporate headquarters. After determining the brainstyles of the team, they realized the outcast was a Knower. They then agreed to preparatory "Deliberator discussions" the night before the meeting to "give everyone the air time they wanted." They used the newly respected Knower to facilitate their meetings. Their eighteen-month time line shrank to produce results in just five months with "a new sense of respect for one another."

besides your project. Find something to like about them and dwell on it in conversation. Then proceed. Give yourself time to react to their conclusions. Bring in the Knowers to structure the project, make it practical, or pose some answers when you're ready for critique and a plan.

BrainStyle Clues:

The ways in which interactions with a Knower get to be win-or-lose situations relate directly to brainspeeds at Time Zero:

- *The Conciliator responds emotionally at Time Zero. In business or in most arguments, quick logic "wins" or at least overpowers. Conciliators: prepare for emotional subjects with summaries. Ask for a "time-out" if flustered. Explain your timing. Have shorter discussions.*

- *The Deliberator asks questions at Time Zero. The Knower decides. Deliberators: get data ahead of time. Consider the Knower a decision-making ally. Focus on goals.*

- *The Conceptor gets conceptual and can't return detail as quickly, shot-for-shot, at Time Zero. Conceptors: discuss the long-term goals with a Knower; don't let the Knower sidetrack you with the details. Be direct about problems and put them in black-or-white terms.*

- *Other Knowers? You can fight to the death if you choose to, or you can find common ground from which to launch a project.*

- Knowers respect honesty and directness.
- Knowers get really attentive when you are saying something that will help them get to their goal or desire.

Before you get to know them, you can impress them by being up-front and honest about what you can and cannot do when you communicate with them, as Gary demonstrates.

Lou was standing when Gary came into his office. He opened impatiently, "It's been a bad morning, Gary. I hope this won't take long. I've got to catch a plane this afternoon. I just found out an hour ago." *Uh oh,* thought Gary, but showed no reaction.

Gary is a twenty-nine-year-old Deliberator plant manager, meeting with the operations vice president, who is his boss's boss, and a Knower. So far, it is not a pleasant experience for him. Gary has been in his job for about eighteen months and knows it is important to impress the man he is going to meet. Early impressions count. It would not be far-fetched to say that the impression Gary was about to make could determine his entire future with the company. And the word on this VP was *scary*. Everybody in his office said that Lou had a temper and didn't put up with much. Gary, at about five feet ten, with soft brown eyes behind the glasses, was a Clark Kent. His build didn't show off his physical strength as a wrestler in college. But it wasn't that Lou was so tall. He wasn't much bigger, in fact, than Gary. It was his reputation. It was said he could rip your guts out with a word or sear your brain with one of his *looks*. Even though Gary had met with Lou before and things went okay he thought, he'd heard that people came out of difficult encounters with Lou and *you never heard from them again*.

So Gary knew that there was a lot on the line. He had asked for an extra three days to assemble and prepare a report that thoroughly supported his request for a major expansion to his plant—the biggest amount of money he'd ever asked for. It was a serious responsibility for Gary. And now Lou was saying he wanted a one-page summary starting with the "bottom line." But Gary wanted to explain what was involved in his conclusions so Lou would understand better what the decision required. The VP was getting more impatient the more Gary talked.

The worst of all possible things then occurred. Lou actually pounded his desk and exploded, *"Damn it,* Gary, just give me the punch line! You took an extra three days! What's the decision?"

It must be said here that Gary had had a few sessions with brainstyles and had spent some time thinking about his strengths and what he was up against in dealing with Lou. He was not totally unprepared for this demand, even if his hands were, by now, quite clammy, and his stomach had settled firmly at his feet. Gary's strengths were solidly in his favor, however. He did not process the feelings as rapidly nor take Lou's words as personally as some might. He answered rather coolly.

Gary looked squarely at Lou and said in his soft-spoken voice, "You know, I'm never going to give you the decision you want as *fast* as you want it. You'll always be faster at that than I will. But I will tell you something. I will work as hard as I can and as fast as I can to make what I give you as accurate and as solid a decision as possible. It may take three days longer, but you can bet that when you get it, *you can take it to the bank.* And," he added, "there's too many 'hip-shooters' around here. You need someone you can count on."

Lou actually sat down. He looked squarely at Gary. Gary, he thought, was full of surprises. He concluded that Gary was a straight shooter, that he was not just making an excuse for delays. It was the truth. From what Lou had seen, he *was* accurate and thorough. Gary was saying what he could be counted on for, and that he could be counted on to deliver it to meet Lou's needs to the best of his ability.

Gary was playing from strength. They both knew it.

Gary walked out with a yes for $8 million. When he got out into the parking lot, he began to realize what he'd said to Lou and had a moment of absolute amazement. Then elation. It worked! He had just been factual, delivered what he'd learned about strengths, and laid it on the line. Lou was actually a reasonable guy. They had had a good discussion after Gary's pronouncement. And Gary had flipped through the stack of overheads he had prepared and with only a little embarrassment went to the last three to give Lou his punch line.

They never had another meeting like that one again. When they met, they often caught up on family and personal things, briefly, but comfortably, especially after going out to dinner the next time that Lou came to visit Gary's plant. Lou became one of Gary's strongest supporters in the organization, recommending him for several promotions in the next few years.

Gary spread the word that changed Lou's reputation from fire-breather to respected leader. He has continued to apply the brainstyles philosophy of mutual respect that requires people to be exactly who they are to get along with some half a dozen bosses and a variety of new teams as he has been promoted to considerably larger responsibilities over the past decade.

RESPECTING THE KNOWER: WHEN *THEY'RE* IN CHARGE

The gift of this brainstyle is *focus.* You can't find a better partner to tighten things up and bring in rules and order. Knowers, however, need to stay in contact with others to make their biggest contribution and to bring balance to their straight-line approach. When the rapid left-brain Knower is working on an idea, he is probably the only person who is aware that the "percolating" process is going on. He does his best thinking alone, and in control. He does not have a need to share information. He is quite sure that nobody else will understand what he is doing and that they will just mess up the thinking process with illogical input or disagreements.

Others gather information by conferring with as many people as possible. The Knower uses unilateral methods, such as reading or interviewing. When a Knower *interviews* (rather than *discusses*), the point is to gather information, not to let others in on the plan until it's 80 percent shaped and solid.

Once a Knower lets one of his ideas into the light, you can be sure that the idea is primarily up for ratification, not discussion. Only an equally strong response will cause the Knower to pause.

BrainStyle Clue:

As a boss, the Knower thinks about the task at hand before the needs of the people involved in completing them. The Knower will tend to keep final control and assign out only the work and not the decisions.

Most Knowers will do best in charge of managing systems or crises that require decisive, short-term action.

To make good use of the Knower's gifts, your best bet is to go to her first in a situation that requires quick logic and structure at Time Zero, such as getting things started, coming up with new and focused goals or projects, keeping a job on schedule, developing a strategy, and persuading with logic. At home their gifts are invaluable, whether fixing things, reordering the chaos in the closet, cooking, or cleaning (the latter activity may not be their favorite). Knowers love order and pride themselves on making a house, a classroom, or a neighborhood association hum. There will be problems for the Knower if the job expectations are for someone with right-brain qualities like relationship skills, sales, "blue-sky" thinking, strong team, or diplomatic skills. Collaboration is a *non*-strength.

Case in point: Tim owns a company that specializes in setting up new office buildings with office furniture. Once the plans have been made and all the furniture ordered, he brings in a team to set up the offices, one man to an office.

One Knower team member of the setup crew works at an incredible speed. He works alone at lightning speed. For getting the job 90 to 95 percent finished, this crew leader gets his crew to perform better than any other. But he always has a problem when the plan needs adjusting. Maybe the wrong chairs arrived. Maybe the client changes the room arrangement. Instantly the job requirement changes from *executing* the plan to modifying it and negotiating with people.

At this point, the speed wizard loses his edge. Focusing on his own goal, he moans, "This was not part of the plan!" He can't negotiate with other goals. He wants to reinstitute the plan. He is at a Time Zero event, and his right brain has no quick way to supply him with the flexibility to revise.

Imagine the potential for this man if he were given an assignment that fit his strengths. For instance, what if his job was only to handle the first 90 percent of the installations? If he could be in charge of the system every time, and then bring in the people-oriented, patient negotiators to finish up with the clients, everyone could win.

BRINGING OUT THE BEST IN THE KNOWER: WHEN *YOU'RE* IN CHARGE

Managing or influencing Knowers isn't an easy job, but it can be done once you understand how their brainspeed works. Play to Knowers' strengths by giving their gift of linear, logical thinking a chance to work. Here are some hints.

- At work, Knowers make fast, logical decisions, so go to them early to influence their plans or goals. Give them alternative solutions or goals to choose from. Don't pose problems unless you want their answer. Understand that once they have set a course, it is difficult to influence them to change.
- At home, influence works best by allowing the Knower to be in control, and make his own decisions for his own reasons that can, on personal subjects, never be fully articulated.

One Conciliator wife got her Knower husband to attend church— an activity he had steadfastly refused to do for several years—by arranging a fishing trip with their minister and his wife. The two men had a chance to talk alone. The wife stopped the "nagging" (the personal requests that implied to him that he "do things *her* way"), which he was resisting. When he felt "free to make up his own mind," as he put it, he found his own reasons to participate quite actively in church programs to the surprise of many who saw only the surface businessman who rarely, if ever, shared his more private and deeply held goals.

- Knowers can put together future plans that are easily understood, give clear direction, and combine ideas in new ways. They will not include the whole picture, however, and need other brainstyles to round out their plans. If you act as a willing partner to further the goal, you'll be more influential.
- Knowers are best at sorting information to get to a result. They can be inventive at finding solutions to problems that get in the way. Use their planning abilities.
- When you must argue with a Knower, challenge his conclusions. Knowers arrive at conclusions and then back them up with facts. When you start arguing details, you're in for a long debate that they will likely win.

BrainStyle Clue:

There is only one turf on which to engage in battle with a Knower: the goals. As long as you try to fight on details, the "win" will be very costly: the Knower will get locked in. Change the arena and move the discussion to the big picture or desired result.

- Knowers have no ready access to right-brain feelings. Put the Knower in charge of managing things first, then people. Make people assignments part of the task of collecting information and following through. They are best working with more left-brained people. One boss had a Knower employee who was great on the technical end, but whose people were quitting (two in three months). The Conciliator boss started scheduling weekly meetings to review personnel issues step by step.
- Knowers are excellent individual contributors. Delegate tasks to them that require swift, solo execution. Better yet, give them start-up or turnaround projects which require efficient and logical solutions that can be turned into a system.
- Knowers rarely take personal risks because risk is illogical. They *do* take control, and when in charge do not see a project as risky. Put

them in charge of executing plans for the future. They may hesitate when it comes to personally investing in the plans. Don't assume that "take charge" means "take the plunge."

- Finally, the Knower may not be a good team player, but he makes an exceptionally good member of the team. Do not confuse the strength of his logic with self-confidence. Knowers don't often ask, but do care deeply that they are on the right track—especially with people. Tell them when they are.

- Working with the Knower can be tricky, especially if you are a Knower yourself. Align on goals and split up your turf. You'll both want control.

COMPLEMENTING THE CONCILIATOR: WHEN *THEY'RE* IN CHARGE

You know you're dealing with a Conciliator if their sparkle is exhilarating and their energies are distracted by personal issues. Their unpredictability may get you a bit crazed—not to mention their inability to keep track of time.

- Conciliators *want* praise, support, or "strokes"; they *need* balance. "When she's up, she's very, very up—when she's down, she's the pits," he laughs, when asked to describe his girlfriend. "He's either your friend—he can be *very* nice, easygoing—or he can really cloud up and rain all over you." The Conciliator boss as seen by another, more left-brained person, is a person of apparent extremes.

   "We're afraid to tell her what we really think because she gets so defensive. I guess she gets away with things her brother doesn't, because, well, he's just easier to deal with," says a Conciliator's mom.

   Of course not all Conciliators are moody, defensive, or insecure. Everyone has bad days. Conciliators show their downsides more openly because of their gift in communicating from the right brain. They need to talk or write or ponder to get balanced and get in touch with their left-sided logic. Put their gift into action and you get the joy of reading the results of their fabulous imagination, playfulness and humor, or art, design, or creative promotional campaigns. The right brain demands expression.

- Each of the other brainstyles can delay emotional response more easily than the Conciliator. Telling them to "relax" or stuff their feelings can cause mental constipation.

"I feel sometimes like if I don't say something, I'll explode!" she explodes in the telling. *Don't* expect quick logic. Don't tell them not to be so feeling. *Do* ask for inspiration, support, and how they feel about your advice.

- When the Conciliator is at work on a new idea, everybody will know it because he openly solicits input. He does his best thinking with others, because his gift is coming up with imaginative options that need to be bounced back for logical, left-brain input.

- Unlike the Knower, who works unilaterally on the front end without need for consensus, the Conciliator works multilaterally in an attempt to build a whole plan with expertise from the right sources. On the way, a consensus can emerge. Other brainstyles can perceive this as socializing. Without a clear goal, it can be. It is also networking. Networking, a natural for the Conciliator brainstyle, needs a focus. It is also, according to research of the last seventeen years,[6] *the* "power tool for advancing up the career ladder." The Conciliator's natural need for contacts and the ability to make them has finally been recognized as a business asset.

  Other brainstyles network as well. When Knowers or Deliberators carry out what is defined as networking, they do it differently, of course, because of a more focused, left-brained approach. These two brainstyles are more apt to seek out people who can assist on a specific task. They may or may not form friendships along the way as the Conciliator does.

- Once the Conciliator has influenced a decision and gotten agreement, he wants to move impatiently toward a conclusion. Conciliators can be very pushy and demanding once committed. Feelings are driving for a resolution. This is why many in this brainstyle think they are Knowers. Drawing on this ability the Conciliator is a passionate advocate, compelling writer, salesman, and communicator.

- If the Conciliator's conclusions are challenged, he immediately incorporates the other points of view—thus neutralizing the conflict. He is the great summarizer. Others see him as a compromiser. Conciliators are often quick to admit they hate dissension and often take the role of peacemaker in the home or mediator at the office when they're in the mood.

- If you demand obedience to "your way," the Conciliator either will a) appear to acquiesce and then do what he wanted to do in the first place, or b) get very resistant, or c) "fail" at the task you have ordered him to do. The empathy for your problems is gone when the focus is on his own activities. Unless you clearly spell out the roles you'll each have on the team, or the purpose of the project, and why the Conciliator's commitment is needed, personal feelings can and often do get in the way. "His rules just didn't make sense to *me*," says the Conciliator. Remember, this brainstyle hates being told what to do (it interferes with the internal controls for his own timing and feelings). Conciliators like "direction," "clarity," and "support." You get the picture. Let *them* figure out how they're going to get there.

• When the Conciliator forms an image of the outcome, a lot of left-brain dedication gets attached to getting their way. This is the brainstyle reason why Conciliators *don't like to change* once they get committed to a direction. This is another way to describe their stubbornness.

Case in point: Don and Mary entered a golf tournament as a couple. Don, a Conceptor, had played in many tournaments over many years and had a clear strategy for play. As they set out on the first hole he began telling Mary, a Conciliator, what to do. She balked. She slowed down. Don's face went red with the frustration of his game plan. He could *see* what to do. All Mary could "see" were his orders (the relationship, right now) and his red face, and she got madder and madder at being told what to do.

What saved the marriage was the "time-out" Mary took, away from Don, as she walked to the first green. She realized she was mad and that it wasn't going to help her golf game (a focus on the goal). She then thought about Don's experience and his ability to strategize at golf better than she could. Settling down, she thought, "I *hate* the way he's talking to me (a focus on the interactions, her strength) but if I go along now, maybe I'll learn some things. I've *got* to change my focus. And I'll give him a piece of my mind *later*." Her change in response to Don's next few instructions was faster. Don relaxed. Later they agreed that he had been impatient and spoken too harshly. ("My mind was totally on the goal, not your feelings.") Mary said that she hadn't been given an overview of the game plan—and made a part of the team—so all of his directions were just his "bossiness," in her view. She resented this. He "seemed to be telling me I was stupid and couldn't figure things out for myself (personalizing the information)."

They agreed to have a brief overview on how they would proceed the next time so Mary could have a clear view of her role (be in control of how and what she did) on their team. Neither expected the other to change. They negotiated a context (being a "team") that could allow both to participate from their strengths.

BRINGING OUT THE BEST IN THE CONCILIATOR: WHEN *YOU'RE* IN CHARGE

You must be aware that everything you say will first be "heard" by the right brain of the Conciliator. The enthusiasm and spontaneity that prompt the impromptu will automatically depend on an early positive reaction and be crushed by a negative one. Feedback will register personally. Establish a bigger context when presenting negative information. Put what you're saying into perspective. *Slow down* with initial reactions or new information to give the Conciliator's left brain time to catch up and be more objective. Ask—insist—that the Conciliator take time before responding, or presenting their exciting new ideas.

Case in point: A new employee was nearly finished with a big project. She was so excited about her findings that on a chance meeting with her VP she decided to abandon protocol and give him a spontaneous preview of her conclusions.

"Do you have a minute?" she inquired. "I'd love to get your thoughts about the report before I cross all the T's and dot all the I's."

Launching into a review of her main conclusions, she watched the VP get red in the face. Finally, she spluttered to a halt. "What's the matter?" she asked.

It seemed that her conclusions were Time Zero information for this VP. Too late she realized that he also was a Conciliator brainstyle. He needed time to respond to new ideas that he instantly judged as "politically explosive," that would "put his budget in jeopardy." His reaction was not kind. To her, it was devastating. She was terribly embarrassed, and anxious about the VP's evaluation of her competence.

Afterward she realized that presenting touchy conclusions would have been much better in a planned, structured setting for both of them. She would have had time to anticipate his reactions instead of plunging in, expecting him to share her enthusiasm. Timing of her right-brain spontaneity would have done a lot to protect her feelings attached to the facts and prepare him as well. For their next meeting, she prepared a careful agenda, submitted a summary beforehand, and when the negative reactions appeared, she was prepared with alternatives. This put her in charge of facts and kept things from getting so personal.

- Rehearsal can be critical for Conciliators. No brainstyle can have higher aspirations or be more self-critical than the Conciliator. If the Deliberator wants to *be* it all, the Conciliator wants to *be and do* it all. This drive for perfection often translates into career ambition. Modify the Conciliator's drive by providing neutral facts often about performance to prevent a right-brain-defined, (rosy) internal picture that doesn't include left-brain assessments (fact-based). This will take time (two or three meetings, possibly) to allow for the timing of the Conciliator's right-brain, personal reactions.
- Conciliators want to get credit for their good work—without having to spell it out for all their "unintuitive" Deliberator or Knower superiors—when credit is definitely due. The Conciliator is ready to undertake great tasks for the greater good of the home or office. What she is not prepared to do is to be overlooked. Nothing will be quicker to pave the way to a pleasant evening than noticing her new hairdo or listening to his day.

BrainStyle Clue:

Beware: The Conciliator can be a dedicated workaholic who will do far more than he has been asked to do. Pay attention to what he is doing, because this extra work does not come for free. A Conciliator can become downright surly if he thinks he is not being appreciated in the way he would appreciate others. This surliness often gets expressed as demands for promotion or pay increases. Conciliators can quit on the spot or hold grudges.

Here are some keys to the Conciliator brainstyle that can be useful in helping those in this brainstyle find the right fit:

- Play to the strengths of Conciliators by putting them where they can deal with people imaginatively and responsively, without routines.
- The Conciliator is the great enroller who can build the coalitions necessary to fulfill a company's vision. The Conciliator activates a vision; he does not create one.

- Information is always personalized at Time Zero for Conciliators. Prepare them ahead of time for feedback, including performance appraisals, meetings, and large issues. Even after many times considering the information, they will still have more of a right-brain spin than other brainstyles.

- Conciliators make hasty decisions based purely on right-brain feelings. Conciliators are the natural "heartbreakers." Instruct them to "think on it" before they give you their conclusions or make commitments. One twentysomething Conciliator was advised by her older sister to "go home and say aloud" ideas people had given her that she couldn't make sense of at the moment. She found it helped her to hear them a second or third time, to consider them, instead of just reacting.

- Conciliators most often will either tell you what they think you want to hear or stress the positives about a project in an effort to make the day a little smoother. Allow time for their concerns and doubts to surface. Don't ask the Conciliator to tell you the long-term downside—go to the Deliberator or the Knower for that.

- Conciliators have no immediate access to left-brain logic. Don't press for answers on new subjects that require it. Use them for imaginative assignments that require influencing, coordinating, training, selling—ideas that need to be brought to life. For instance, service is a natural field for this brainstyle. When analysis and precision are required, it is best to allow time for preparation. If there is access to a Deliberator for proofreading or auditing all the better. This does not mean that Conciliators don't choose careers requiring skill in left-brained tasks. On the contrary, CPAs, professors, and technically oriented Conciliators are numerous. Watch how they bring in others to collaborate when doing new projects, and how the task is personalized to include more meaning for others.

- Conciliators can be the best of partners, the model for the nurturing, supportive spouse. If you want someone at your right hand who will promote your goals and work to make it happen, no other brainstyle is a more enthusiastic, personal cheerleader.

- Conciliators take risks early. This is because they haven't considered the alternatives or the potential downsides (the "bad news"). They are best at figuring out how to "make it happen."

- No one is better at knowing on a feeling level what is happening *right now*. The Conciliator can do better at meeting *dynamics* than (new) meeting *decisions*.

- It might be helpful if every Conciliator wore a warning sign: "Caution! Please do not confuse imagination, visualizing abilities, and irrepressible enthusiasm with creating new directions, plans, or whole visions for the future." The Conciliator's gift for visualizing endless possibilities and alternatives for action is what suits this brainstyle. The Conciliator is best as a doer and a goal-setter, and can be a real results-getter. She can certainly generate future plans in familiar areas of expertise. Conciliators, however, are not *seers* who can look ahead and see whole strategies or directions in new areas. They sense their way along toward the future, getting very clear on the next few exciting steps to come. "I was just lucky," "I was in the right place at the right time," are typical answers to the question "How did you achieve this success?"

- Do not allow the feelings of this brainstyle to run the project or manipulate you or others into doing things you wouldn't ordinarily do. Feelings pass. They are rain clouds or sunshine, but they are not the reason for taking on a project. If you are afraid of dealing with a Conciliator because of his or her initial reaction, realize that if you don't make it so important, they will be through it and on to the real issue soon enough. Time is the problem. Time is the solution. One boss, after giving some feedback to his Conciliator salesperson, "got a two-page (single-spaced) memo refuting, explaining, and defending *one* comment I'd made out of a whole hour conversation." He got very perturbed, he said, but just before starting into the Conciliator's office, "paused, thought about the brainstyle-timing thing, then I tore up the memo and never brought it up. I figured she just needed to vent. She told me later that was the case. Before I knew she was a Conciliator, I probably would have spent three *more* hours going over the whole thing again."

BrainStyle Clue:

Although Conciliators may accept being told what to do, they are less willing to be told how to do it. Remember, figuring out how to get something done and getting others involved in it are the strengths of the Conciliator. Agree ahead of time on goals and roles to enroll the support of the Conciliator and then let him loose with some clear measures and reporting dates.

- The Conciliator works best when working in a partnership with one or more other people. Partners give the Conciliator a variety of (left-brain) opinions to work with and sort out. Partners provide support. This ability to work within partnerships makes the Conciliator an ideal project manager. A well-defined project gives the Conciliator an arena, a stated goal, and a group of people to influence. What could be better? Such a setup lets Conciliators get the attention they like. They can move the project. And *that* can be very good for business.

- The Conciliator cares how you feel about your work and your life —and expects you to return the interest. If you have another brainstyle, explain how *you* show your interest differently. The working relationship will smooth out more quickly.

- If, however, you are both Conciliators, the collaboration can be difficult because of your strengths. There may be too much understanding, too much positive feedback, too much of the relationship, and not enough confrontation and clarity. Everything is personal. Either plan for regular task reviews or, better yet, have access to another brainstyle to bring in a left-brained perspective.

- Unless an important question requires an immediate answer, ask your Conciliator manager to take time and think it over. Give time for the left-brain review. The second-best strategy is to wait a little while and then confirm the response.

- When the Conciliator makes a request of you (or asks a favor), treat it carefully. Ask a lot of questions about real expectations. Try to pin down the specifics in a way that helps him get clear on what he wants. Behind the casual request often lies the friendly command.

- The Conciliator is the one who can *do* what needs to be done and is likely to expect (and assume) you will pitch in and do the same. The friendliness can rapidly turn icy if you do not fulfill unvoiced expectations. The danger here is that when the resentment is unexpressed, it feeds on itself and grows. Conciliators can shut down and then get even. You need to ask what their expectations are.

- Do not misread Conciliators as "softies." Because they are in touch with the right brain does not mean they are warm fuzzies all the time. The overachieving Conciliator can be an impatient, critical, hardworking perfectionist, attending to the smallest details with zeal. When a Conciliator is in motion, realize that you are seeing commitment to an ideal in action. The Conciliator can come across as impatient, overanalytical, uncaring, and pushy when they feel just the opposite. Chances are they're just going too fast to show their concern. They do better and are more balanced at a slower pace.

- The Conciliator has trouble giving direct, negative feedback no matter how she may brag beforehand that she can handle it. The truth is that confronting someone is personally uncomfortable and the Conciliator brings too many feelings to the situation. Rehearsal helps.
- Prepare the Conciliator for change *beforehand* by giving them a new picture of the future. Stories and examples work best to influence their right-sided thinking. Conciliators get attached to old plans and hate to let them go. It may take several conversations to replace the old comfortable favorite with new possibilities. Stress the personal benefits.

CONSIDERING THE CONCEPTOR: WHEN *THEY'RE* IN CHARGE

If you work or live with a Conceptor, you're probably already aware of their need for your consideration of their ideas. They need air time. "We had technical meetings every week. All the lab guys would get together with the production people and talk about the problems we had in producing consistent product," the technician recalled. He is talking about meetings held with a roomful of Deliberators by the general manager, a Conceptor and chemical engineer.

"Everyone would moan, 'Oh no, he's got the marker again' when the GM would get up and go to the board to lead the discussion. He'd start talking about what we'd listed as our problems by drawing these scribbles all over the board. No one could follow or understand him at first; we'd joke about it afterward. But you know, he really did listen. I remember him quoting us. And then he would jar us out of our way of thinking about the problems—*I still don't know how he did it exactly*—and sure enough, we started to look for new ways to do the job." He pauses. "It worked."

The technician, preoccupied with his own frustrations, confessed that learning about Conceptors and what they can do took a couple of years for him. "*I valued facts and data. He* talked only of ideas and abstract concepts that I couldn't really follow at the time. I wanted him to *solve our problems!* I saw those meetings sometimes as an exercise in patience, to indulge the boss. I noticed, though, that after his talks, we'd do things differently."

Today he says that valuing people with different gifts took some amount of growth on his part. "Now I really appreciate what the boss was trying to do. I guess I can't appreciate how frustrated he must have been doing it. But what he does seems like magic or something: *you can't tell what* he's *doing,* except that *you* start thinking differently."

"Now I have a grasp of how people think differently and get a lot more from everyone, right away," the former technician finishes rather proudly.

The Conceptor in question defines *leadership* in the following way:

"Leadership is when you and twenty-five guys are in a room [and] they totally disagree with you. You don't give in. You're never outnumbered. And you don't tell them what to do. You creatively present new ways to look at problems so that you all end up agreeing on a solution."

Conceptors get from point A to B in undefined ways that give other brainstyles fits. They do not follow common rules of communication. They create their own codes for words and think "backward," meaning from back to front, end to beginning, future to present. One husband says of his Conceptor wife, "I don't know *where* she gets the ideas she has. Sometimes she just stops me in my tracks with her questions. But life is *never* dull." They're going to move for the third time in four years because of her career changes.

As one very practical Deliberator advises, "It took me about six months to follow the way my Conceptor boss thinks. I think you have to see some results to believe [that Conceptors] know what they're talking about." The Deliberator explains, "I've learned to trust his [the Conceptor's] phases. First he's totally optimistic and describes all the possibilities as though they could happen. He doesn't seem to hear the numbers or downsides I present. Then I can count on the fact that over the weekend he'll think about it and come in with a complete change of mind."

The above is a very simple way of describing a complicated set of gifts that *are* hard to follow, and where much is done that is missed by other brainstyles.

Working for a Conceptor, you may not be able to get a word in edgewise at the beginning of a project. This brainstyle often requires a forum to talk through ideas. Until the concepts begin to form, there is a great need to look at the whole picture by talking it through.*

Here are some things to keep in mind.

---

* Many Deliberators and Conciliators need the same amount of air time on the front end of things to "talk it out," realizing what they think as they say it out loud. Timing, once again, is the critical factor for each one. Separate forums help enormously to get out the best ideas of each.

- Conceptors have trouble recognizing and appreciating the difficulties involved in execution and the attention to detail that is more important to other brainstyles. Their defense can be arrogance: *I don't have time for the petty details.* To get a Conceptor's attention, use timing to create the biggest impact. In the early stages of a project or new solution, questions or points about execution interfere with the creative process. The Conceptor wants to establish a GO/NO GO. It's broad-brush at first so listen and wait. Later, after some basics of the overview are nailed down, the Conceptor needs the details. Take time to offer an analysis, present problems, or critique and reestablish your plan—more than likely they'll be grateful.
- A Conceptor can act like a Knower on one subject and a Conciliator on another. Don't expect evenness. Expect passionate ideas. Expect personal sensitivities to alternate with negotiating toughness. They're at their best in the heat of a battle for the idea.

Just because Conceptors have vision when it comes to problem-solving doesn't mean life is a breeze when it comes to managing their own careers. Two women Conceptors (growing up in very different parts of the country), Karen (thirty) and Jane (forty-one), discussed career choices they had made and how they made them. Each was very good at both artistic as well as "hard" subjects like math and science. When it was time to go to college, both women wanted to study a more right-brained subject—art history in Karen's case, fashion and design in Jane's case. Each of the women's fathers counseled them to study a major that would earn money. Jane majored in business. Karen got an engineering degree. Both achieved early success in complex jobs requiring broad analysis and design skills. Karen, while still in her twenties, earned a six-figure salary restructuring a major bank and all its organizational systems. Jane was promoted for addressing organizational and personnel issues as she installed newly designed computer systems.

Both women left their fast track positions. Their reasons were similar. Bored by purely left-brain applications, they yearned for more holistic applications of their strengths. Karen is now pursuing a degree in architecture, and Jane is a sales consultant for IBM and a new mother.

Their challenge in envisioning a future that applies their gifts is as difficult for anyone else who is deciding what they *should* do. Their strengths lie in their ability to change as well as the reasons for their dissatisfaction. Karen and Jane each had a need for more balance between hard-edged analysis and creativity. Their horizons are large. Finding a fit has been easier as they have defined what actually challenges them and what kind of contribution they want their gifts to make to others.

BRINGING OUT THE BEST IN THE CONCEPTOR: WHEN *YOU'RE* IN CHARGE

We may as well lay it on the line: Conceptors are basically "unmanageable" in the traditional sense of the word. That is why in school and early in their careers they are often considered insufferable egotists or unrepentant rule-breakers.* As students, Conceptors think they know more than their teachers. (They may only be faster to see the issue.) As junior employees, they are likely to take liberties that only the VPs take as their due. They may be tossing out rules and creating policies to make new playing fields for possibilities. It is not *easy* to deal with this brainstyle.

- Conceptors need a team, yet they are *not* natural *team players.* The gift of the quick left-brain/right-brain response is that the one who possesses it has immediate whole ideas based on both feeling *and* logic. This tends to *exclude* others at first. The brainstyle constantly needs to collect acquaintances and engage them in conversation in order to detail and refine the concept. With the input, the Conceptor can invent a plan for putting the concept into action while exciting others about a new idea.
- Conceptors need the challenge of whole projects. Pieces drive them nuts and will not receive their best work.
- Conceptors need to build minimal skills in non-strengths in order to manage systems, details, and their execution. Several Conceptors interviewed in Chapter Five had set up excellent systems to keep track of files and notes. They hate to maintain them, but the discipline is "character-building" preparation for leadership according to all of them.

* Their right-brained colleagues, the Conciliators, are not far behind. The Conciliators just make more friends as they brag, rebel, and tell their stories.

- Conceptors are at their best creating new answers. They are used most effectively at start-up or at trouble spots.

- Conceptors want personal recognition for their ideas first and the ability to see their achievements.

- Natural inventors, Conceptors develop discipline by working on the nitty-gritty. By working in the trenches, taking things apart, going along on sales calls, their concepts can reframe the old and outworn into the new. Conceptors can be very specific in the few areas they care about.

- More than other brainstyles, Conceptors need to achieve to feel successful. They want badly to be the best.

- Conceptors are not adept at "playing politics" in organizations. When they are right, they make no bones about it. They get the wrong people mad. Of any reason that Conceptors give for leaving corporate life, it is "politics." Having to "put up with control battles or battles of wits" (translation: rapid, clever, verbal jousting) with others puts them over the edge. Interpersonal battles are waged for ends that are too "small," according to the Conceptors (translation: demand too much from their non-strengths in diplomacy and relationship skills). It is ironic that the solutions they come up with most frequently address people issues better than others—the Conceptor just cannot deliver them the best.

- Conceptors are excellent at direction and priority setting. They will contribute most at the front end of a project, looking out ahead to define new directions and possibilities. Conceptors develop three or four hypotheses for the future, which gives them options in the face of a crisis. These are the folks to call when the facts spell out more than one answer.

- Conceptors need other brainstyles to assess and implement their plans, yet they don't like spending time on the details nearly as much as on the ideas. Their impatience can easily be labeled "non-support" by others ("He has *no idea* of the work that went into this!"). This is simply a Conceptor non-strength showing up. You will have to make it *your* job to get the information to the Conceptor in a way that will be appreciated. Remember: you will never be appreciated by another brainstyle the way you will by someone in your own brainstyle.

- Challenge change for change's sake with a Conceptor. If there are too many new ideas, confront the fact directly. No one can work on more than two or three top priorities and do them all excellently. Don't let the Conceptor get out of touch with the project. That rapid left-brain/right-brain processing must solve problems along the way and provide follow-through, even though it is not a strength to do so.

- In meetings Conceptors demand their own outline: big ideas first and skip the details. Under time pressure, they rush to the big picture. They show stress by demanding punch lines from others. Along the way there can be many new Time Zero decisions. The demand for well-thought-out, speedy decisions in the future stresses the Conciliators and Deliberators. These brainstyles need to use their strengths to help refine and execute the Conceptor's ideas. Hold the Conceptor accountable, sure, but they need a supportive arena to deliver their best.

- Conceptors can be very warm, personable, and forgiving with people and their personal problems. They have a unique flexibility. Pose solutions after taking responsibility for a mistake with a Conceptor and see if you cannot move into problem-solving quickly.

DISCUSSING WITH THE DELIBERATOR: WHEN *THEY'RE* IN CHARGE

The Deliberator's gifts require time—and much talk—to get through a situation. If you're being overwhelmed with information, you may be dealing with a Deliberator who is trying to decide. Here's an idea of how to think along with them.

- The special gift of the Deliberator is assessing against personally developed standards for what is "right." A lot of growing up goes into learning and storing experience. That's why so many Deliberators are such good kids, wonderful students, and loyal friends. They *listen* and follow instructions. They draw inside the lines. They develop rules for their lives and like organized games and activities. The Deliberator creates "models" to describe what they've learned and assessed as the right way to do things.

- "Models" can be useful for making sense of complex businesses and life situations. Professors do just this. Mothers do the same when they outline how things need to be done correctly, by when, *or else.* A clear list of standards and values brings continuity. Models are useful for defining the *criteria* for future decisions based on past experience, not necessarily making the decision. They provide a look at existing ideas. Economists, often bright Deliberators, tell us the future with a ruler, that is, they extend the line ahead based on what has gone before. Deliberator parents provide a center for the family that honors tradition and provides stability.

- At work, the Deliberator creates systems and executes plans. He does not see over the horizon or make up the totally new the way the Conceptor does or attack the new project with the rapidity and decisiveness of the Knower. This is not to say that the Deliberator won't break new ground in their own area of expertise; they do, but they do so based on past experience.

- The Deliberator, a natural information processor, can assess a situation rapidly to determine whether it is on track, missing something, or needs attention. This can create a solid direction in which to proceed whether at home or in the office. It is not the same as the future view of the Conceptor, which can define possibilities, but which are often illogical and risky. The pictures these two brainstyles define are quite distinct. One is logical and a synergy of information; one is illogical and speculative. The Deliberator is at his best when applying his abilities to refine, describe, and work out the details of putting a vision into operation.

Case in point: Frank is a financial consultant who worked nine years for Arthur Andersen. He built his reputation on his ability to go into a company—even one with unfamiliar technology—and figure out how to make it more profitable. Frank has been extremely successful by using his Deliberator strengths to their fullest. As an experienced auditor and business assessor, Frank has "memory banks" that are loaded with the essential criteria for financial success. His database is broad and applicable to a variety of businesses. His thought process is typical of the brainstyle, his method the standard used for problem-solving in most situations.

Frank's keen and constant assessments come from his ability to collect, sort, and remember details in an organized way, details that become criteria for successful businesses. It is critical that the Deliberator have good data to assess and file away because he works with what already exists. He compares the actual situation (reflected in the company's books and employee interviews) with his previously determined and tested standards for success. Thus he applies a "model" or formula to compare the standard to the actual, name the specific gaps between the two, and make recommendations for changes. The business gets corrected, then stabilized as change is measured along the way.

The future will look like the past (other stable companies) refracted through the present. Deliberators will bring stability and measured improvements to a system when they apply their abilities of collecting and assessing. *Experience* (more chances to use their brainstyle) is *essential* for effectiveness.

Frank's aim is *not* to create a new direction for the company he is reviewing (as the Conceptor would do). He *may*, however, prescribe more efficient ways to shape things up as a Knower might. Frank's most natural approach is to question and offer counsel on how the existing system might be improved or made more efficient within the boundaries of the company's vision for itself.

BrainStyle Clue:

Once the vision for the future exists, the Deliberator can plan how to get there. The gift of the Deliberator shows up best in assessing, reorganizing, and improving.

The major management non-strength of the Deliberator is delegation. Under time pressure, this non-strength is exaggerated and the workaholic is born. At home, planning and cleaning can get excessive, lists too long, and mom or dad is in charge of too much. The Deliberator's great ability to collect data, set high standards, and then demand that those standards are realized 100 percent makes it very difficult for this brainstyle to truly delegate, or include everyone in the family. "It's easier if I just do it myself" is their mantra. Reaching perfection depends on having all of the information lined up for their personal assessment. But if some of that information has been delegated for others to work on, then there will be gaps in their plan to form a perfect future. Simply put, a Deliberator hates giving up control. When pushed to do so, the Deliberator has three options: delegate none of it ("I don't want to burden you with this"), give it *all* away ("See me when it's finished—it's up to you"), or dole out piecework assignments ("You can do this, this, and that"). The seasoned Deliberator learns how to include others in making decisions about the real work to be done.

> **BrainStyle Clue:**
>
> *Deliberators are at their best in a defined situation, worst with ambiguity. Once any project has been roughed out, put the* Deliberator *in charge of shaping it up. He will tighten what needs to be tightened and loosen what needs to be loosened according to his model.*
>
> *Warning: The* Deliberator *can be a perfectionist and tinker with last details beyond the value they add to the project. Unless you say halt, he can and will refine until or beyond the deadline and the budget.*

BRINGING OUT THE BEST IN THE DELIBERATOR: WHEN YOU'RE IN CHARGE

Here are some other ideas for the Deliberator brainstyle that will help you find the right "fit" for him or her.

- A Deliberator cannot make fast decisions in new areas. If you push him, you will only make him tense, and get a yes he doesn't mean. You won't get the real decision you want. Magic words to use for best results: *Think it over, don't decide right now. I'll get right back to you.*
- This brainstyle does not respond emotionally. Do not assume that a lack of enthusiasm means a lack of interest. Deliberators are excited on the inside. They are naturally suspicious of other brainstyles who show their feelings on the outside—unless, of course, they know about brainstyles.
- In some cases, a Deliberator can look quite spontaneous *or* intuitive early on. This can set up false expectations for flexibility later on. Barry, a venture capitalist, explained that he was able to free up his assessment of a project to consider alternatives, to go with his "gut feel," soon after realizing he was experienced in an area. Actually, he was drawing easily from his significant memory in an area he knew well. He said, "Time Zero clarified for me that I assess the facts or feelings—then very quickly am aware of my intuition. I

always thought before that I was an 'intuitive banker.' I don't compare to a Conciliator, though. I'm more 'reasonable.' And I use my intuition *after* I get the facts." He's clearer now why women he's dated have been angry when he was "too conservative" after a few months of the relationship. He's more able to explain who he is now.

- Deliberators are most likely to look like all the other brainstyles after Time Zero. They are the well-rounded ones with a variety of interests. Test for this brainstyle by watching for the real basis of comfort in making decisions.

- When a Deliberator decides to get involved, no parent is more attentive and patient. But their gifts do not naturally lend themselves to enjoying unruly adolescents or kids who have very different brainstyles; their gift is in teaching the rules. This instruction takes time and discussions and is often the way Deliberators show they care. They put in the time. Family discussions or meetings are the place that the Deliberator can set up plans *with* others, frustrating as it may be. A Deliberator mother of a young Conciliator was continually dismayed to find that her daughter was "unaware of the consequences of her actions." The spontaneous daughter took years to learn a "self-control" that came naturally to her more left-brained mother. Even then, the Conciliator daughter "acts before she thinks," as her mother says. The Deliberator's challenge comes in letting others do things their way. They most often demand explanations that require *your* patience in return for their loyalty.

BrainStyle Clue:

Deliberators are often the "naysayers" in the group. They assess first. They sound negative. The brainstyle looks for "gaps" (problems in the system) and needs time to repair them. This can delay the action. Seek them out to tell you what is or might go wrong in your plan.

In general, then, the Deliberator is happiest perfecting the system, the company, or himself. He does not like dealing with the conceptual or the irrational, especially if it isn't (or can't be) tied down to reality in writing. Thus the IBM personal computer had to be developed by a maverick group immune to the IBM corporate culture and its

Deliberator motto: THINK. To the Deliberator, being able to articulate an idea clearly in writing is a sure sign of having a good idea. Yet for all his clarity of articulation, the Deliberator's strength is not in making breakthroughs. The Deliberator's strengths kick in after the criteria of the breakthrough have been articulated.

Case in point: Gerry, a left-sided Deliberator, is a distribution manager for a consumer products firm. When management announced that reducing costs was the number one priority, Gerry set about responding to the challenge (executing a plan once the vision is established). He assessed that the first "gap" was in controlling warehousing expenses. The sales function had always managed warehousing. Their mandate was and is to satisfy customer needs. Costs came second in most decisions.

In presenting his case to his new Conceptor boss, Gerry demonstrated with facts and figures, as well as with a field trip, how much cheaper it would be to bring warehousing under his control. He pointed out how sales overspent. As he lobbied with his boss and other peers, Gerry was told he "came across negatively." His appeal to reason only sounded self-serving and controlling ("Do this because it's cheaper, and I can handle it better"). He followed the Deliberator's process: here's the standard (lower costs), here's where you're losing money (the gap), and here's the recommendation, so put me in charge. A very logical process, but not carried out with a win–win political strategy. In fact, any number of people around the company were quite upset with Gerry's "model for change."

The discussion between Gerry and his Conceptor boss quickly identified a strategy to use in presenting the excellent data that could persuade with reason and also address the bigger picture. Several functions within the company would be affected, especially sales. The solution? The Conceptor's right-brained input outlined a presentation that addressed the feelings of the teed-off sales group threatened by someone after its turf.

Once the rational and emotional reasons had been named and addressed, a strategy was developed to get support for the change, a strategy that included more people in the solution. What is important to notice here is that Gerry didn't even see the problems generated by his strategy at first. This is because of brainstyle, not because of intelligence.

Gerry learned a great deal about "politics" (a non-strength) and "networking" as a part of the task to be done, which is how a left-sided

Deliberator (or Knower) can easily approach the people issues in a complex project. These "right-brain" items need to get on the list. They won't get there for most Deliberators—especially under pressure —unless there are other brainstyles in his plan from the start.

Gerry has established a new agenda to address organizational problems based on discussions with his Conceptor boss. After learning about Gerry's brainstyle, the boss asked Gerry to address the concept of "service." Gerry defined "service" as a step-by-step program to be implemented *with* sales. The strengths of each brainstyle were maximized: the Conceptor's ability to define a problem globally, and the Deliberator's ability to define and execute an incremental, measurable plan.

As the brainstyle with the natural gift for learning, the Deliberator looks "mature" early on. He is more controlled, more rational, and less reactive than are other brainstyles. He most often excels in school and has the best grades, then the best résumés. This is both the good news and the bad news. He is expected to achieve a lot. And he often does. However, he does not *excel* in the areas of other brainstyles and this is what we often expect of him—to be all things to all people.

Keep in mind the Deliberator's *non*-strengths when managing:

- Time Zero decisions;
- Creativity;
- Spontaneity, reacting quickly with empathy;
- Flexibility to change the plan in midcourse. (This is very different from *adding new information,* revising the decision, or being open to additional information.) Flexibility is the strength of the Conceptor, who can literally start over and try out a whole new plan;
- Risk-taking;
- Establishing clear priorities in a *new area,* defining the big picture or a direction to follow in the future, distinct from synthesizing facts or previous information into a clear model of *how it can be* drawn from what exists now;
- Confrontation, especially direct or face-to-face, regarding the larger business issues.

Deliberators will not be as gifted in these areas as other brainstyles. Don't expect them to be.

DISCUSSING WITH THE DELIBERATOR:
WHEN *THEY'RE* IN CHARGE

THE INEXPERIENCED DELIBERATOR.   Ron, a new production manager, is a Deliberator not yet clear on how to apply his strengths and, therefore, unable to focus or deliver on what he promises. He spends time collecting information about the problems of his plant, which is indeed in bad shape. (Assessing gaps.) He talks a great deal about his big plans for the future. (Creating models based on past experience.) Approaching problems with a focus on detail means that all problems have nearly equal importance. He sets goals in accordance with his desire to fix everything he has assessed. There are no real priorities. There are no decisions, because there is no overall clarity, and as a result, very little focused action. There *is* a lot of activity. There *is* a demand for more information in order to keep control in the hands of the guy at the top. Getting approvals replaces making decisions. There is a line outside Ron's office waiting to discuss and get the go-ahead on a basketful of problems, one at a time. Ron's boss says that Ron is unsure of himself (a right-brain problem) and can't decide to move forward. This is an unresolvable problem for the boss. Another assessment is that his experience and background (stored memory) does not match the current assignment, so that he cannot apply what he knows —perhaps the crucial factor for this brainstyle.

With the brainstyle diagnosis, Ron was transferred to a technical function (a job he had held before), with fewer direct reports, where he could provide planning support. This job used his strengths and more closely matched his experience. In getting the product scheduled, formulated, and in line with customer specifications, he was successful. The tasks were fewer and more complex; his strengths at assessing and planning could be applied incisively to specific projects. He was no longer managing untrained people, or a system with huge numbers of Time Zero events demanding decisions in new areas. Everyone was happier and more productive. Ron stayed with the company as a real contributor for many years. Without the change, he surely would have been fired, losing both self-esteem and clarity about what his real contribution to a company needed to be.

With *this* brainstyle, a résumé is important information.

> *BrainStyle Clue:*
>
> *Experience is everything for a Deliberator. Action is based on what is already stored in memory. A steady progression of jobs is vital for incremental improvements—in abilities, and in results. Don't expect a Deliberator to handle a job with too many Time Zero events within deadlines.*

- Don't wait for action and get mad when nothing happens. The yes may have had no deadline in the Deliberator's mind. *You* manage the process if you want the results.
- Help the multitasker focus his conversation into a single *request* or a *promise* to take action.
- The Deliberator shows how. He doesn't show off. He respects the same.
- The Deliberator states the criteria for success, and then leads by example. She wants others to do their part because it's the right thing to do. Much can be assumed and not communicated. Ask questions if you want clarity.
- The Deliberator leads others by explanation. *The assumption of every brainstyle is that everyone operates the same way they do.* The Deliberator assumes that once you understand why, you are motivated. At the office, subordinates are expected to be directed by their understanding of the system or the plan. At home, things are easiest when there is time for the Deliberator to understand why. Do not expect to get broad overviews or pep talks from all but the more right-brained. They will use their kind, patient counseling to help, but in the end will expect you to understand and go along with their plan.
- Subordinates who can prove their ideas, who are not "flashy," and who support their boss by preventing surprises are the most comfortable for this brainstyle. When this is not you, you need to negotiate. Jamal, a young Conceptor, chose banking as a career. After being fired from one job as a loan officer because he was "too flashy," Jamal took it upon himself to explain his strengths in more detail to the Deliberator banker culture. "I can talk the language of our customers," Jamal said in his next job interview. "I'm the kind of guy entrepreneurs can relate to. I can be a translator—a middle man for the bank." Jamal was hired with the understanding that he was "different from the average banker" with much greater success

and longer tenure. Family members with different brainstyles can use Jamal's methods with their relatives and explain how their gifts support the Deliberator's values.

- If a Deliberator has a problem with something you are doing, do not expect him to deal with it directly or right away. Instead, he may just act unhappy, discuss the project, or ask questions. If you ask, he will give you a reasoned explanation of why his way is right and yours is wrong. He may pick some small thing and beat it to death, losing the overview. The Deliberator will not confront you directly, so *you* will be in charge of defining the larger picture. To incorporate—or dispute—his points. He will prefer to negotiate differences, step by step.

- If you are assigned a project by a Deliberator, follow directions and bring back what you were asked to bring, along with another alternative you may like better. Show what the pitfalls are in each. Influence the project with information about how to prevent problems. The Deliberator may want to do the deciding himself. Don't push a decision, ask for another meeting. You'll need to do your homework to get a vote. And stay with it. Perseverance is the strength of this brainstyle. They respect it in others.

- If you get stuck on a project, go to the Deliberator for a reassessment of the problem. Offer new goals. Don't argue on methods. Don't get hung up on what may sound "negative." Deliberators are best at determining the *gap* between where we are and where we should be. Being helpful and informative is what the Deliberator does well. Often this comes out as critique. Use the input to strengthen your execution of the plan.

- The Deliberator who works hard to get things right will expect you to do the same if you don't discuss strengths. Conceptors and Conciliators must set up realistic expectations with a Deliberator when working in their non-strengths of structure, sequence, and order. Explain what you *can* bring more clearly, otherwise Deliberators can write you off as unreliable or "flaky." When this is a clash between parent and child, maturity comes for both as they look past the differences and look to the other for love, not agreement.

- Deliberator companies thrive on analysis before action—the strength of the brainstyle—and last the longest when they do it well. Steady as she goes. There are many systems, rules and procedures to keep the even keel.

Note: When moving to a new job, a quick assessment of the dominant brainstyle in the culture can tell you whether you'll fit and what issues will come up as a result of your strengths.

THE CREATIVE MIX FOR BUSINESS AND PLEASURE
Each BrainStyle Needs to:

KNOWER	CONCILIATOR	CONCEPTOR	DELIBERATOR
KEEP:	**KEEP:**	**KEEP:**	**KEEP:**
• Cutting through the chaos, making it simple	• Being spontaneous, aware of people • Bring meaning	• Being "blue-sky," future-oriented, creative	• Bringing a neutral, balanced perspective • Assessing systems for gaps; stating standards
START:	**START:**	**START:**	**START:**
• Using the other three BrainStyles to round out your plan	• Asking for time before deciding or committing— then *do* it	• Acknowledging others' ideas • Keeping agreements, following through	• Using others' input for decisions • Managing your time and goals
STOP:	**STOP:**	**STOP:**	**STOP:**
• Judging others as incompetent if they lack quick logic	• Judging yourself as less because you're slow to logic • Competing with others for recognition	• Getting impatient with others' timing, especially Deliberators'	• Trying to do it all, be it all • Judging others by their "details"

TIME IS THE PROBLEM.   TIMING IS THE SOLUTION.

CHAPTER 9

The Changeless Path

No one at peace within himself can be troubled
by conflict without.

GETTING ON THE PATH: STAGES ONE, TWO AND THREE:

RECOGNIZING STRENGTHS, SEEING POSSIBILITIES, GETTING TO NEUTRAL.
As you begin applying brainstyle principles in your daily life, you may
go through learning stages similar to those that others have experienced. For example, one young woman who had just been introduced
to the brainstyles material was between full-time jobs working as a
temporary secretary. On her first morning at a new assignment her
boss took her to the copy machine and began a *very* elementary and
detailed step-by-specific-step description of how she should use the
machine.

"At first I couldn't believe what I was hearing," she reported. "He
was telling me how to put in the paper, showing me the marks that
any idiot could read, when suddenly I realized *he's not talking down to
me and trying to drive me crazy, he's a Deliberator—he's being thorough!*
Never before would I not have reacted to him, you know, been in-
sulted and just walked away, screaming inside." (Stage One, she recog-

STAGES TO MASTERY

Stage One: Getting on the Path: Recognizing Strengths

Interest: I wonder how brainstyles fits with what I already think of myself?

Resistance: I hate labels. I am not that simple.

Control: I can figure out everyone I know . . . and be one up on them.

Questioning: What are my real strengths? What does it mean that I am
  only one brainstyle?

Stage Two: Seeing Possibilities

Recognizing close friends or family members in the brainstyle descriptions.

Seeing possibilities for greater understanding of yourself and others.

Becoming aware of the differences between natural strengths and
  learned behavior.

Stage Three: Getting to Neutral (the power position)

Noticing timing differences between new and learned behavior.

Defining collaboration as a brainstyle and brainspeed mix.

Noticing a change in the why and how of arguments.

Feeling more comfortable with non-strengths.

Decreasing personal judgments and comparisons.

Appreciating the strengths behind a behavior.

Stage Four: Releasing

Becoming neutral.

Feeling more sure of yourself, less competitive with others.

Achieving greater clarity.

Letting go of the need to please, be perfect, and control others.

Informing others how to use your strengths to mutual advantage.

Reevaluating long-term relationships and letting go of old hurts.

Stage Five: Mastery, Reaching the Seamless Life

You use timing with others, rather than control, avoidance, or threats.

You support others as they do it their way.

You define the situation, job, or event and are not defined by it.

You stop reacting to others with the judgments of the past.

You learn from everyone; you are a victim of no one.

You see life as an opportunity to use your strengths everywhere,
  effortlessly and naturally, at work, at home, at play.

nized that his behavior was a result of his strengths, then, Stage Two, she saw the possibilities in their differences.) She continued, "I know now that he was trying to be helpful, and so I was able to just relax and listen. This has always been hard for me. Knowing that I'm a Conciliator and how I react has helped me a lot. (Stage Three, she didn't take it personally, she was able to detach from the situation.)

As she continued to work with him during the day she found herself "more relaxed" with someone "I never could have gotten along with in the past as well."

Her plan for the future (to realize Stages Four and Five) is to explain her strengths and limitations in a new way, "I'm telling him about how I'm quick to react. I can make the phone calls in a flash but sometimes I'm slow to think things over. I think he can help me organize the work if I ask—which I've never thought to do before—so I can get work out faster than he ever thought it could be done. I'm also asking for assignments where there are opportunities to deal with people."

She had hated her temporary assignments before. "Now I see I can learn a lot from them, and can finally appreciate what I always saw as just annoying behavior."

That same Deliberator boss called her temporary agency and specifically requested her for a new assignment.

UNCOVERING STRENGTHS IN THE FAMILY

Her eighteen-year-old son was in his room doing "nothing." Well of *course* he wasn't doing anything. With his whole life in ruins, what could she expect? He had just flunked out of his freshman year at the state college and was really bummed out. He'd joined a fraternity and made some great friends, brought them home on weekends, breezed through the social life away from home, but he just couldn't make the grades. He had failed. Flunked out. He knew it was coming, but he could not work hard enough to pass the computer classes he took. The other classes were hard too. They all seemed to need more time and effort than he could put in. It was all crash-and-burn. Now, he didn't even have a life. He'd let his parents down. He had no friends whom he would see. *Major* problem.

His mom and dad were really upset. Nothing they said seemed to help. They steered him to a summer job to keep him busy.

How had he gotten in this mess? His mother did a good deal of thinking since her son had come home depressed and defeated. He had never been a great student. Bs and Cs were his speed. He wasn't terrific at sports either. Oh, he'd play and keep up, and he had the normal amount of friends, she thought, but he was just an average kid. How do you figure out how to guide and support your child when he seems to be just fine? No genius, but happy enough. You just let things take their course and support where you can, don't you? Well, obviously, that hadn't been enough, and now the biggest frustration was not knowing what to do.

She thought about how he had chosen a major in college. Essentially, since he hadn't excelled in any one subject in high school, the guidance counselor had asked him how he spent his time and what he liked to do. Video games were the rage. He spent hours at them. So the answer for college came up COMPUTERS. Of course! The wave of the future. And what a career! Of course he would have to buckle down and study, that was college. That was being an adult. So he went to college and couldn't do the adult thing. Maybe he wasn't ready. Maybe he just needed time. Maybe he should just work for a year. But the question more than nagged, it was in capital letters all over his dull eyes and face, it hung from his slumped shoulders: What *can* I succeed at doing?

His mother thought about her son's life. Since the time he was very little, starting with his Lego blocks, he had loved making models. When the other kids were out playing ball, he would just as soon stay in his room and build models. They had to put in shelves and more shelves. The shelves were loaded with planes, dinosaurs, trains, spooky animals. The walls were covered with his drawings. But no one in the family ever took his "hobbies" seriously. He never took an art class at school. *Maybe we've overlooked the obvious. Maybe the answer is the thing he's always loved to do,* she thought.

Their first conversations about his going to a local junior college to try some art classes were not fun. He was so discouraged, so full of the pain of his failure, that he was defensive and sullen, and very reluctant to try again. He also seemed to have some judgment about art as a major. When she asked him about this, he said that some other kids had said he was "weird' when he was younger and that's why he'd kept his models and drawings to himself and only shared them with one or two closest friends.

He agreed to take a part-time job, go to the local junior college and take two art classes in the fall "just to see."

Two As. Magic. The work was effortless for him. He went from skeptical to mildly interested to outright thrilled by the end of the first semester. His college career as a graphic designer and illustrator was fun, easy, and a lot of work that he thoroughly enjoyed, and he got no lower than a 3.4 grade average (about a B+). Today, as a Conciliator who found his niche, he is one of the best graphic artists at a high-dollar design firm in Manhattan.

UNCOVERING STRENGTHS AT WORK

Robert discovered *his* strengths by running into his own brick wall. Unlike the graphic artist, Robert had always had goals, had *always* worked hard, and had *always* done well. Then, in his first job, the beginning of his career in business and the very place he knew he'd been meant to succeed, things weren't going well. He was a recent college graduate with a business major working for a manufacturing company in Michigan. He was an excellent athlete in college and continued to work hard in his job as a logistics supervisor. When Robert's new general manager routinely inquired about each department's performance, the word on the logistics department was "average to mediocre." Robert came in to meet with the new boss. He knew there were problems and proposed that the company sponsor him in returning to college for a master's degree in logistics and business because he "had a lot to learn" and knew he could improve the department's performance *if only he had more training.*

In talking with him, the boss was impressed with Robert and couldn't understand the "mediocre performance" reports. As they met, the boss became aware that Robert, with no effort at all, was quite fun, charming, imaginative, and a great storyteller as he discussed his problems in logistics. Robert told him he "had a great team" backing him up. The boss proposed that Robert might have a natural gift for a sales position and did not really need more schooling. At this suggestion, Robert got very quiet. "Is there a problem with sales?" the boss asked. Robert said he wanted to think it over.

After another conversation, Robert admitted that he had reservations about sales. "I never knew anyone in sales, couldn't imagine if I'd like it. It just *wasn't in my plans.*" So, reluctantly, Robert attempted a trial period in sales.

Robert not only quickly picked up the ideas and skills needed for the job, he really enjoyed himself. By the end of the first year, logistics was history and key accounts were Robert's pride and responsibility.

In twenty months, Robert's gifts saved the major accounts with the angriest of customers; Robert's sales literally saved the company when shipments were late, or formulas failed. Customers stayed with the company who had the salesman who would be there in his jeans, any time of the day or night, and who knew and was liked by everyone in their operation.

Robert's strengths were invisible to him as he struggled to learn in areas using his *non-strengths—only to produce average results.*

Robert was not just a star as a salesman, he became "the best in Detroit," according to the head of the company. In discovering his brainstyle strengths he produced more, achieved outstanding results, loved what he did, made lots of money, and defined a career that he could master.

Moral: When natural strengths are invisible, we work to be who we are not.

TRANSFORMING PERCEPTIONS

"In the holy relationship, we don't seek to change someone,
but rather to see how beautiful they already are. . . .
It is our failure to accept people exactly as they are
that gives us pain in a relationship."

—MARIANNE WILLIAMSON, *A Return to Love*
(HarperCollins, 1992)

"WEAKNESSES" VERSUS *NON-STRENGTHS* VERSUS SELF-CRITICISM

Most of us do not know how to communicate in the language of strengths.

When you are acting fully in your strength, you are most *unlike* anybody else in any other *brainstyle.* You *are full of yourself,* and others may find that fullness unlike the way *they* do things. Conventional wisdom says, "Strengths taken to extremes are weaknesses. Modify your behavior. Pull back." This is imposing a limitation in exactly the wrong area. Keep focusing on your strengths. The discipline needed to apply your strengths where you bring the most value will occur naturally. You will not be competing or acting inappropriately when you focus on things you love to do. You will find a way to use your abilities to serve others sooner rather than later.

Your "non-strength" is another brainstyle's strength. Trying to improve in a non-strength is something you should do only on an as-needed basis. Ultimately you will have to work much harder and longer than others to achieve less.

A *non-strength* is different from a quality that is misnamed "a weakness." For example, if you are a Conciliator, you are excellent at "personalizing" or making the job and issues personally meaningful. Your weakness is *not* the fact that you "take things personally." This is your *strength,* adding feelings to data. It may be that you don't like this aspect of your strength. Others may get uncomfortable with your emotions or think you are using your emotions in a "manipulative way." These are all judgments we add to our strengths. So if acting with feeling is your strength, what's your non-strength? Your *non-strength as a Conciliator is the strength of the Deliberator brainstyle: collecting and receiving data in an objective, neutral way.*

When someone describes something about you as a "weakness," they do so because of their own expectations. They undoubtedly want you to do something well that they do well and you do not. When you try to live up to *others'* expectations rather than negotiate relationships based on your *natural* gifts, you lose—in self esteem, and effectiveness—and so do they.

When you are most yourself and appreciate your own gifts, you create your own self-esteem and contribute more clearly. Otherwise, you will believe others when they tell you to change so they in turn will feel more comfortable. This is a neat way to make you responsible for their personal comfort.

Look in the "self-help" section of the bookstore. There you will find books, each teaching you how to act like its author, to improve by changing into someone else.

Be your best by being yourself. You're the only one we've got.

The following worksheets are exercises to get you on the path to transforming your self-perceptions. First try a translation exercise, that is, break down a weakness into a strength and non-strength. Then, using your new perspective, try filling out your Personal Strengths Summary Sheet.

As you get familiar with your strengths and non-strengths, a very natural process unfolds in your acceptance of others. New and exciting possibilities begin to emerge in your relationships to reinforce your own growth and confidence. You feel more neutral, and less frustration, as old regrets and resentments fall away.

IMPROVE YOURSELF BY BEING *MORE* OF YOURSELF

- Make a list in the "weakness" column of all your personal criticisms of yourself.
- Use the BrainStyles Chart on the following page to name the strengths underlying your criticisms.
- Then go to the description of the brainstyles you may be comparing yourself to, and write in *their* strength.

Translating "Weaknesses" or Self-Criticisms Into Strengths and Non-Strengths

	"Weakness" judgment about myself	Strength natural ability	Non-Strength the strength of another brainstyle
Example:	too slow	methodical, thorough	responsive, spontaneous

The above example was given by a Deliberator.

His first example of a "weakness," "too slow," is translated into his real gifts of being methodical and thorough. He was comparing himself to a friend who is "exciting and quick."

	Weakness judgment about myself	Strength natural ability	Non-Strength the strength of another brainstyle
1.	_____	_____	_____
	_____	_____	_____
	_____	_____	_____
2.	_____	_____	_____
	_____	_____	_____
	_____	_____	_____

A SUMMARY OF THE FOUR BRAINSTYLES AT TIME ZERO

The KNOWER At Time Zero	The CONCILIATOR At Time Zero	The CONCEPTOR At Time Zero	The DELIBERATOR At Time Zero
• Rapid left-brain response • Logical, clear answer	• Rapid right-brain response • Rapid reactions or answers	• Rapid right-left-right-brain response • Generalized or vague answer	• Rapid memory search • Thinks before reacting

Often the brainstyle response appears as:

• Conclusive • Unemotional decision-maker • Confrontational • Black-or-white thinker • Simplifier • Deductive	• Spontaneous • A rapid, changeable decision-maker who acts quickly • More imaginative than strategic • Informative, friendly, talkative • Inductive	• Assuming broadly without facts, a stereotyper • Possibility explorer • Inventive, yet strategic • Aloof • Deductive	• A questioner, a challenger • Knowledgeable • Indifferent or thoughtful at first • Analytical • Complex • Inductive

Over time, core strengths are:

• Someone who clarifies things first without emotion • A person who gets to the cause and poses simple solutions • A person who fixes things • A problem-solver • A logical person	• Someone who rapidly imagines possibilities • An emotional, intuitive person • A changeable decision-maker • A caring, even charismatic influencer • A social person • An inspiring person	• Someone who poses solutions and then tests them out • An inventive person who is hard to understand at first • A risk-taker • A pathfinder • A visionary	• Someone who assesses things first and then learns widely • Steadiness in important things • Uses step-by-step analysis to reach the overview • A planner • A multifaceted person

See Chapter Three	See Chapter Four	See Chapter Five	See Chapter Six

Personal Strengths Summary Sheet

My brainstyle: _____
I make the best decisions when:

_____
_____

My specialties (expertise, knowledge, experience):

_____
_____

I need an opportunity to do more:

_____
_____

I bring value to new things by:

_____
_____

I bring value to my family by:

_____
_____

I am best with _____ and have most difficulty with _____
           (brainstyle)   (brainstyle)
I need support from others with *timing* in the following *non-strength areas:*
(For example: *new decisions, delaying action, listening with empathy, listening for content, meeting deadlines, staying on schedule, inventing multiple solutions, creating harmony, facilitating agreements, attending to the rules.*)
1. _____
2. _____
I will start: _____
_____
I will stop: _____
_____

THE PURPOSE OF RELATIONSHIPS

The larger purpose for all relationships is to learn forgiveness. Forgiveness relieves the guilt, resentments, or regrets that exist between you and another, and leaves only love or respect behind. Forgiveness is complete when you understand that others are perfect just the way they are, right now, warts and all.

Miraculously, seeing another with this perspective heals your own misperceptions of *yourself* based on guilt, regrets, or feelings of inadequacy. As we realize that another, especially someone we've disliked, is fine just as he is, we become powerful, purposeful, and peaceful ourselves.

APPLYING BRAINSTYLES TO RELATIONSHIPS

The power of *brainstyles* becomes apparent when you use your strengths to make relationships more satisfying. The steps to releasing this power are:

1. Define and appreciate your own strengths,
2. Define and appreciate the other's strengths,
3. Use timing to create a rhythm with the other, then
4. Make the relationship a kind of dance using the synergy of both your strengths.

CRITICISM AND COMPARISONS

When we admire "role models," we often base our admiration on our own lack of strengths, in something they do well and we do not. We compete with them. Competition provides a goal and a focus. The focus, however, is *out there.* Stay focused on others too long, and you lose sight of your own gifts. You get excited by a whole world of accomplishment that is based on a shaky foundation: *another's* natural strengths. When you admire someone with strengths similar to your own, it's a different process. The envy is gone, along with the effort. That path to achievement stays solidly your own and you are an apprentice to a master.

Our perception of *the right way to do things* is governed by our brainstyle. Our lens sees the world with a shutter speed governed by our personal strengths. Until we understand the strengths of those different from ourselves, we see them as *wrong* and think they should *change* to be more like us.

How much easier it would be to redefine our expectations for their strengths. The following exercises will help you remove some obstacles that commonly arise when you start the process of redefining relationships with others, especially those you don't like very much.

ALLOWING OTHERS TO BE WHO THEY REALLY ARE
EVEN WHEN YOU DON'T LIKE THEM VERY MUCH

Write some descriptions of others. Redefine your description with strengths.

What People Say About Another	Underlying Strength	Underlying Non-Strength
Example:		
hysterical	*responds with*	*neutrality, dealing*
reactive	*feeling first*	*first from facts*

Put in your own descriptions of someone you dislike, or something about someone you dislike. Ask yourself: What is the strength behind their behaviors?

What People Say About Another	Underlying Strength	Underlying Non-Strength
1. _____	_____	_____
_____	_____	_____
_____	_____	_____
2. _____	_____	_____
_____	_____	_____
_____	_____	_____

This process of looking beyond "what people say" is nothing new for you. You do it with your close friends all the time. You look past how they act because at times you know *who they really are.*

Next Steps

I will start:_____

_____

I will stop:_____

_____

I will keep:_____

_____

HOW TO DEAL WITH PEOPLE I DON'T LIKE

An Overview

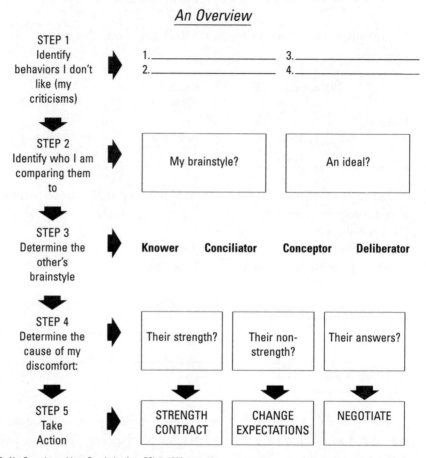

STEP 1
Identify
behaviors I don't
like (my
criticisms)

1._____ 3._____
2._____ 4._____

STEP 2
Identify who I am
comparing them
to

My brainstyle?   An ideal?

STEP 3
Determine the
other's
brainstyle

Knower   Conciliator   Conceptor   Deliberator

STEP 4
Determine the
cause of my
discomfort:

Their strength?   Their non-strength?   Their answers?

STEP 5
Take
Action

STRENGTH CONTRACT   CHANGE EXPECTATIONS   NEGOTIATE

Do Not Reproduce without Permission from BSI © 1993.

A REAL EXAMPLE OF DEALING WITH PEOPLE I DON'T LIKE USING THE BRAINSTYLES SYSTEM

Terry, an administrator for a small company, solicited bids for a proposal. The salesman for the vendor who got the bid, Roy, was the most helpful and thorough in the bidding process. Terry was glad that Roy's company won the contract because she thought Roy would be easy to work with. In just two weeks, however, Terry told her boss, "I was wrong. Roy is a pain in the neck. He's driving me *nuts. And* he's a sexist and talks down to me." When asked why Roy was such a problem, Terry came up with the following list.

(STEP 1) Identify Behaviors I Don't Like (My Criticisms)

- He winks at me in meetings and calls me "little lady."
- He *says* he's going to deliver something, but is late or has a problem getting here when he said he would.
- He asks all the time if I'm happy, or how I feel, or if everything is okay.
- He tries to be friendly, when all I care about is the contract and the deadlines.

(STEP 2) Identify Who I Am Comparing Them To

"What do you *wish* he would do?" asked Terry's boss.

"I wish he'd be organized, more formal, keep his promises, and stop trying to be so familiar," Terry responded.

"Who is like that?" her boss followed with.

"Well, I guess I am," Terry admitted. (Terry's boss knew Terry was a Deliberator.)

"So one of the main reasons you're uncomfortable with Roy is that he has a different approach to business than you do. And you don't like him for it," her boss concluded.

"Yes. He's a pain in the neck."

(STEP 3) Determine the Other's BrainStyle

"Take a look at these *brainstyle* descriptions and think about where Roy fits. Which is he best at, *assessment, being decisive, inventing new solutions,* or *building relationships* and *having quick responses?*" her boss offered.

"Oh, he's the relationship guy all right," Terry said.

"What strengths does he bring to his job, if you step back a bit and assess it?"

"Well, like the brainstyle description says, I guess he's quite good at being friendly, coordinating, responding quickly, making things personal. He either overdoes it or I just don't like the way he does things," Terry finished.

"Which is it?" her boss asked.

(STEP 4) Determine the Cause of My Discomfort

This is a turning point for Terry. In order for Terry to take another point of view or look for any alternatives, she needs to choose between two perceptions: 1) Roy is to blame or 2) her own discomfort is the problem and, therefore, might be changed. In the first instance Terry is *out* of control of the situation, in the second she's not.

Terry may need time to think over her answer, or she may need to talk it over further. She is ready to move on when she acknowledges that she *can't* change Roy, but she *can* change her point of view. The boss needs to emphasize that *neither* needs to change their strengths in order to solve the problem.

"So, if his strengths are those of a Conciliator, which *brainstyle* do you *wish* he'd be like?"

Terry said that she wished Roy were a Deliberator like herself, thinking and approaching the job as she does. But for Roy, she listed Deliberator strengths under non-strengths. They agreed Roy couldn't change the way he was, and neither could she.

"Now the question is: How can you, Terry, use your strengths as a Deliberator in scheduling, organizing, being accurate and thorough for this project *and* take advantage of Roy's being a Conciliator to coordinate, make contacts, act quickly, and try to make the customer like him?" the boss asked as he passed the written worksheet on "How to Deal with People I Don't Like" across the table to Terry. (See Appendix E.)

(STEP 5) Take Action

Here is the solution Terry and her boss arrived at:

1. Terry would present the idea to Roy that she was an "expert" in her job at scheduling. She would suggest that Roy seemed to be an "expert" at customer service, and that they might complement each other.

2. Terry would set up due dates for the project that Roy would agree to in advance. Terry would call Roy ahead of schedule and not count on him to call her, to be consistent, or to be organized.

3. Terry would ask Roy to solve a current problem by using his contacts.

4. As the project went ahead, Roy's "sexist behavior" was no longer an issue. Terry forgot to notice it. Roy got more comfortable, more genuine, dropped the forced attempts at making friends (winking, "little lady"), and they talked "business" more easily. They ended up on friendly terms.

NEGOTIATING A STRENGTHS CONTRACT

Overview

The meeting that Terry will hold next with Roy can be called a *Strengths Contract* because she will meet to see how each of them can contribute to a larger goal (getting the project finished) *using each of their strengths to get there.*

Preparation

In this real situation, Roy knew nothing about *brainstyles.* It was not necessary for things to work out between him and Terry. *Only one dedicated person is required* to make a relationship work. Terry had to prepare by sorting out her comfort-based judgments and comparisons from her larger goal. Her willingness to take personal responsibility for her own feelings and judgments, to use her knowledge of *brainstyle* strengths, and to speak honestly in everyday terms are what was essential.

The following pages outline how she ran the meeting and proposed a schedule that *both* of them were able to deliver.

Negotiating

This is what happened between Terry and Roy when she conducted a Strengths Contract meeting:

ME (Terry)	YOU (Roy)

Terry prepared a list of *brainstyle* strengths each brought to this project.

GOAL

Terry presented the project goal to Roy with a question: "I think we both want this project completed as quickly as possible, do you agree?" Roy added how *he* wouldn't be satisfied unless Terry was satisfied with the project's quality. Terry agreed.

| WORK |

The real focus of the discussion was on the specific part of the project where the two of them needed to collaborate, rather than on distracting personal issues. Terry proposed that the part of the project they needed to work on together was *scheduling*. She emphasized they needed to set up and keep deadlines in order to deliver the goals.

Terry offered, "We've worked together for a short while now, and I think we bring different strengths to getting this project completed. I'd like to use some teamwork here to get the best out of both of us."

| ME | YOU | PLAN |

Terry then made the following points based on her brainstyle analysis:

- I've (Terry) met with my boss and we're proposing this schedule. I'd like you to think it over. If you can meet it as is, fine. If not, let's make it so we can *both* keep all the dates.
- You (Roy) are excellent with people and making contacts. Can you coordinate with your supplier for us?
- I (Terry) have real concerns about the quality. I need time to look over rough drafts. I want to schedule them ahead.
- You (Roy) have so many obligations, I want to call you for progress checks, and to make sure we're on schedule.
- I will time my requests of you (Roy) so that you have time to think about them and consult someone else, if possible. I *don't need* the fastest answer every time to be happy—I need an answer you can really follow through on.
- When you (Roy) ask me for a change, I need lead time. The changes are complicated here. I will try my best to meet your quick changes if I can, but I'm slower and more methodical on some things than you are. I may need to get some approvals.
- I (Terry) don't want to ask you for something you may not be able to deliver. Even if you think it'll make me happy to tell me yes, don't do it if you aren't sure. I'd rather have a date I can count on."

Their discussion was simple and honest. Terry admitted that she couldn't have approached any of these subjects before without being irritated. *She assumed he should know how to conduct business this way if he were a professional.* She also realized that her idea of "professional" was really someone who acted according to *her own brainstyle* expectations.

There is a blank *Strengths Contract* for you to use with someone else in Appendix E. There is no special order for the topics or specific format to use. Your intention must be to have a *win-win* outcome. The format and principles apply to friends and family alike; however, you may need to prepare more thoroughly for someone you don't like.

HOW TO DEAL WITH PEOPLE I DON'T LIKE

Now that you've seen how Terry handled her difficult situation, you can have a turn.

There are some conditions that must exist before this exercise has any value. If you have a difficult relationship now that you'd like to be happier and without difficulties, you must answer YES to the following question: Am I really willing to have this relationship work? You must have a real commitment to want things to work for both of you. You must be willing to hang in there when you don't feel like it.

Step 1: Identify behaviors I don't like (my criticisms)

List your criticisms. What are the things that irritate you, or seem to make it difficult for you to work with this person?

Step 2: Identify who I am comparing them to

Write who you wish this person would be more like. It might help to use the sentence: "If only she/he would be more like_____."
What kinds of things are you expecting from this person that she/he doesn't deliver?
1._____
2._____
3._____

Step 3: Determine the other's brainstyle

Now for some analysis. You need to determine this person's real gifts by looking for either or both of two things:
1. How does she/he react in NEW situations? What is the overall pattern of strengths?
2. Where does she/he consistently fall short? (*Either* can indicate brainstyle.)
_____
_____
_____

Step 4: Determine the cause of my discomfort

Look back at Step 1. If you were to translate the behavior you don't like into underlying brainstyle strengths, what is it that is bothering you?

1. *Their natural strength?*

    This person *can't* change their strengths and you'll do them a disservice to ask them to do so. Not changing does not mean this person does not care about you.

2. *Their non-strength?*

    If you expect this person to perform in a non-strength area as well as someone who is gifted in that area (like yourself, perhaps), forget it. He or she can *learn to improve* in this area—but only with a personal desire to improve. Otherwise, the learning will be temporary.

3. *Their opinions or solutions?*

    The best chance you have to influence another and negotiate an alternative solution is to establish a relationship in which the other person has a chance of winning too. Use as reference the table "Each BrainStyle Looks for Opportunities to Apply Strengths" from Chapter Eight.

    How can you make room for the contribution the other needs to make?

Remember: *You can influence more easily when* you *can be influenced.*

Step 5: Take Action

Use the Strength Contract to guide your conversation. There are worksheets to write on in Appendix E.

TEAMWORK: USING DIFFERENCES TO GET SOMEWHERE TOGETHER

Teams Who Apply BrainStyles

UH OH. THERE'S A NEW BOSS. It was a pretty typical story: When Mel, the Knower you met at the end of Chapter Three, was evaluated negatively for "poor people skills," as well as "dropping the ball" on a project by the new director, his hopes of promotion were put on hold. In fact, he was spending most of his time trying to recover his reputation for decisive action on a couple of major accounts when the news was announced: a woman was being brought in to head up his team. Not only was Mel passed over, his new boss was younger and less experienced than he was. "Affirmative action" was mentioned only in private, and then it was said in code: "corporate commitments" had to be met. The bottom line was that Mel was not pleased with the new arrangement. Mel confided to his good friend and fellow team member, a quietly effective Deliberator, that he was probably more worried about his *own* future than he was about having a new boss, but even so, "this was not going to make things any easier."

Meetings took "forever," from Mel's point of view. The new boss, a Conciliator, had to "include everyone," was alternatively defensive, then apologetic, quick to make decisions, make the phone calls, and then, on a number of occasions, the team had to "mop up." The inevitable "glitches" occurred as a result of her too-rapid action and desire to cover all the bases.

A breakthrough came for the team when they outlined their individual strengths. For a start, Mel became aware of what he could add in a way that didn't make everyone else wrong for being too slow. With his future in mind, he came to appreciate what others were adding and just naturally paced himself to interact with them.

"In the last six or seven months it's been really helpful for me when I go into meetings or work with the team to think about how I come across to them. I wasn't aware of this before. And I see that each of us adds something different. The Conciliator makes sure no one is offended, The Deliberator gets us on the plan and looks at the accuracy of it, and I help us keep decision-focused."

He adds, "The team is not expecting people to be different. We're expecting more of the right things from each other. At first we were awkward, stumbling over the [brainstyle] names, assigning things according to the 'rules,' you know, the Conciliator only facilitated the meeting, the Deliberator checked the numbers, the Conceptor talked about the future. It was real stilted. Then we figured out that we just needed to loosen up. Then we all talked about everything until we got into a problem. That's when brainstyles was real helpful. The boss and I had a disagreement. So I suggested a break. She said it helped. We got stuck about how to structure a presentation and I said I'd like a crack at organizing it. It was easy—took me ten minutes. The Deliberator said he *wanted* to review our presentation after the meeting to check the details. The last several meetings have actually been *fun* for us. We're getting real efficient. And I'm seeing new positives in how the boss handles things. And she's backing off more as she relaxes. She still feels a little more comfortable with the Deliberator, there's no threat from him (he's never wanted her job), but I think she respects what I can do. And, come to think of it, she's already gone to bat for me once." He concludes, "We're doing good things *together*."

OH BOY. A NATIONAL TASK FORCE.   A team of customer service managers was gathered by their Conceptor director from all over the country to formulate, for the first time, a set of national policies rather than the regional ones they had previously been using.

Meetings were strained. There was a lot of "going along with what the boss wants." The team was unable to make decisions at the pace of the Conceptor boss. Resentments were building and follow-through lagging. After a brainstyles workshop, the group decided that the rea-

---

BrainStyle Clues:

How BrainStyles try to control a meeting:

- *The* Knower *comes in with a clear agenda and takes control, clarifying issues with priorities, deciding conflicts, and moving to a quick conclusion. At meeting's end, he will have formulated a clear plan of action.*

- *A* Conciliator's *natural strength is to promote harmony by building on common interests or drawing them out of others. Summaries are easy. A Conciliator leader can be very imaginative, pose exciting possibilities, and, unlike the Conceptor, want personal support for a favorite idea or agenda. When the agenda is the whole team's, it works. Otherwise "politics" of the worst kind begin.*

- *The* Conceptor *sends a burst of personally exciting ideas ricocheting around the room, doodles, draws, and thinks out loud, talks about the future, often heating up the discussion and raising the energy level of all assembled. Controlling the pace, he may ask those attending to come back with plans to support the big picture generated in the meeting.*

- *The* Deliberator *arrives with a list of items. The most natural product of a brainstyle that processes information so readily is to consider discussions and information-sharing the most important activity to be engaged in. All items have importance. Priority is difficult to determine. New projects are updated and milestones measured in what seems to other brainstyles endless dialogue in search of the perfect decision. Urgency is continually balanced by a need for thoroughness and accuracy. Decisions are on small items. The* Deliberator *can measure success by the quantity of tasks handled.*

Meetings and BrainStyles

Use Them First To:

KNOWER	CONCILIATOR	CONCEPTOR	DELIBERATOR
Focus agenda and the meeting process	Get the people Sell it Facilitate	Broaden the agenda Name future issues	Plan it Get it complete. Compare to a standard or model Build consensus; meet one on one

Their Maximal Contribution:

KNOWER	CONCILIATOR	CONCEPTOR	DELIBERATOR
State goals, results, and pitfalls Be practical Expedite Confront Advocate	Facilitate group, include others Brainstorm Summarize Visualize possibilities and how to sell them Give support	Name the issues Strategize Start the project Open possibilities Initiate Negotiate	Assess the plan Make it workable, doable Ask the tough questions Look for what's next Compromise, refine

When Stuck on Own Goals:

KNOWER	CONCILIATOR	CONCEPTOR	DELIBERATOR
"No" "It won't work" "That's wrong"	"I must be heard" "No" "It's personal"	"My idea" "My world"	"I'm right" Silent stone who works alone

When at Time Zero:

KNOWER	CONCILIATOR	CONCEPTOR	DELIBERATOR
The Knower structures data	The Conciliator responds to data	The Conceptor reframes data	The Deliberator assesses data and accesses memory

son they weren't making much progress had to do with *timing*. As a Deliberator reported afterward, "The Deliberators and Conciliators needed more time to discuss, to talk things through—and 'think out loud.'" They decided that subgrouping would work best for the Deliberator/Conciliator group. They would meet the night before their meeting with "the Chief" to discuss and post ideas all over a hotel room until they reached agreement. With that premeeting preparation, the formal decision-making meetings began taking one third the time and covered more topics. Folks were prepared. The Conceptor boss was able to use his strengths to strategize and to provide overviews and even challenges that the team felt comfortable with because they were not at Time Zero. The brainstyle strengths helped "sort out assignments, neutralize conflicts, and move us forward." "And we still have our problems," the director emphasizes. I understand *why* quicker now, so we can get untangled faster. The timing ideas help . . . a lot."

STAGE FOUR: RELEASING

How do you include those who have no real motivation to be team players? What do you do to impact their self-esteem when they don't relate to the concept in the first place? How can you move past hurt feelings and old prejudices?

A KNOWER'S INCLUSION.   Gabriel's understanding friend (and boss) told me a lot of personal information that she would probably be embarrassed for me to know. Gabriel (not her real name) is intense and private, dark-haired and dark-eyed. She dresses in rather snug-fitting business suits, with a style that might be called Provocative Professional. As with most Knower women, she has a very individual personal style. I imagine that how she dresses is something she doesn't discuss with another woman (she doesn't seem to have many women buddies), and that she would rather look to men for the results of her clothing choices. She does not like to discuss anything personal, interpersonal, social, or anything to do with the "touchy-feely" stuff. She is not a team player.

When asked what she is interested in, "making money" is her reply.

"But she doesn't spend any of it," her boss confides. "It's much more the game of making it, counting it, and stacking up the wins that she seems to enjoy." He shakes his head in disbelief. "I say this because I'm one of the few men who understand her and have gotten inside her head. She is one of the most interesting people I've ever known. She's tough outside, but there's a very sensitive girl inside. I think we get along because I understand this about her. And also because I can challenge her on what she does as a professional. She can tell me anything—I don't flinch. When she tries to tell *me* what she's going to do, I listen and tell her very clearly what she can and cannot do. We know where we stand. She wouldn't respect me if I didn't do this." He's a patient and sensitive man. He knows his business. He has to, to deal with Gabriel.

She is an extremely effective salesperson in a field where quick contacts, sure decisions, and follow-through on promises count for sales, where you don't take no for an answer, and you just keep on coming back. And her bottom line is more than *triple* what the average producers pull in. Problems? "Sometimes she gives away the store [by charging too little] and justifies it with volume. She *hates* to lose an account." She *hates to lose* might be just as accurate. It becomes clear that she stays in this job when there are higher paying offers from competitors because of her relationship with her boss. She doesn't *talk* about her relationship with him directly, though, the way another brainstyle might. Gabriel doesn't quit. She made a decision to stay, so she's here. She gets on with the job, which is, in her case, racking up the numbers.

The rest of the staff stay at arm's length from her. "She can say the most cutting things," one says. Another volunteers, "She's a snob, in my opinion." As Gabriel sits in the team meeting, she is quiet most of the time. When she speaks the tone seems somewhat defensive, which doesn't make sense, given that she's being asked to tell about her results for the month and all she has to tell is good news. But her conquests come out like dares. Her sales dollars are bullets sprayed up on the board, zinging past the heads of her sales sisters and brothers. Her attitude as she gives the winning numbers seems to be *like it or lump it.*

But, then, to interpret her attitude as some kind of confrontation is to misunderstand her real strengths and misinterpret her non-strengths.

After learning about brainstyles, it is clear to the sales team that Gabriel is the only Knower and everyone else has a different brainstyle. One woman blurts, "Gabriel, I never thought you liked us or wanted to work with any of us." Gabriel looks neutral at first, then stunned. Hurt. She says something to the effect that that is not how she feels at all. She says very matter-of-factly that she never saw that anyone else really wanted her advice or input. She says she would really like to help anyone who asks. Is this the reason for the strange tone when she presented her numbers?

Everyone in the room is aware—just for a flicker—of the intensity of Gabriel's feelings. The expression is so rare. Her vulnerability is enormous. It's an illuminating moment. Gabriel looks terribly uncomfortable. She's *human,* you can practically hear everyone thinking.

At the end of the seminar everyone else is very effusive with their appreciation and excitement about what they learned. They have canceled lunch appointments (!) they tell me, in order to stay for the session. And then they all dash to the phones in their offices. Only Gabriel stays. She says very quietly, "I never knew they felt that way." It's an important moment for her and I try to stay out of the way of her realizations, to underscore how valuable she is to the whole team. She looks blown away with the idea that people saw her as unfriendly and uncaring. *She had only seen things her way.*

Later, her boss has a heart-to-heart talk with her about how she is perceived by her co-workers. He was able to tell her that she seems to put all her charm, all her diplomacy to work with customers. "She is Miss Personality when she wants to be—when something tangible is on the line and she's decided that it's worth going after," he says. "And it does seem to be easier for her to get along with men. Men she respects," he adds. She evidently hasn't decided that there is anything on the line with her peers. Gabriel brushes off his feedback about her teamwork with a one-liner: "There's nothing in it for me." Relationships are not her strength. She's not going to play where she can't win.

Gabriel's boss offers an analysis (he's a Deliberator) that seems to help him work through her tempers, demands, and brusque way of doing things. His gift is assessment and a deep and thorough appreciation of history. He tells of Gabriel's history of abusive relationships with former bosses—screaming matches, firings. He says this is a result of her traumatic childhood. Previously he had only two solutions for her: therapy ("She'd never try it"), or sympathy, which admittedly doesn't help her own abilities, tends to imply someone else is to blame, and adds to her resentments. He is excited for Gabriel by the new possibilities raised by brainstyles, to build on her strengths *now,* without analysis, without expecting her to change, which allows everyone to feel powerful. He also, he grins, "has a new way to appreciate her strengths, *and* my own."

Six months later, Gabriel's boss tells me that staff relations are better all around, and sales are "through the roof." "Everyone is more comfortable with one another. The rest of the staff is more openly respectful of Gabriel. And even though Gabriel won't say so, she's more friendly and relaxed. We're *learning* from one another. The rest of the staff understand her now, so they don't take her so seriously. They can also tell her how she's coming across when she's off-base. Everyone's numbers are up significantly and so is teamwork."

The pressure has eased up for Gabriel. She is still not willing to fake team play in a game based on her non-strengths. She gives advice and answers when asked; she talks one-on-one. But there are no team discussions or interpersonal pattycakes for her. She does look more comfortable in the staff meeting, though. She even laughs. The focus is off her social skills and her past and onto her success now and into the future.

Gabriel's Deliberator boss respects her for what she has to offer. He is direct, straightforward, and willing to tell her no. Her colleagues, as losing competitors and spurned friends, demanded that Gabriel make friendships in the same way they did, and rejected her when she couldn't deliver. Everyone on the team lost in *that* game. In the new game, *everyone* gets to contribute.

Because each brainstyle evaluates the world, the performance of others, including their value and promotability, by measuring against their own strengths, building teams that use the strengths of all brainstyles sometimes requires releasing old prejudices before each one can contribute most powerfully.

The following is a chart that summarizes the most natural approach and response of each brainstyle at work.

Each BrainStyle Approaches Projects Differently

KNOWER	CONCILIATOR	CONCEPTOR	DELIBERATOR
INITIALLY	**INITIALLY**	**INITIALLY**	**INITIALLY**
Determines the issues, lines up facts to support initial conclusions	Assesses all the feelings (dynamics) regarding an issue	Generalizes all facts and feelings into a few broad concepts; picks facts to support them	Collects and assesses first, sorts issues later
Limits information collected	Lines up facts to support the feelings	Delays start until clear on whole project	Organizes in steps
Prefers clear measures	Organizes for initial action	Prefers overview	Prefers a clear plan
	Wants involvement		
DURING	**DURING**	**DURING**	**DURING**
Sorts information for efficiency	Continues adding information	Uses new information selectively	Continues collecting details
Drives the system, not the people	Takes action immediately	Flexible to change	Most comfortable when an expert
Follows the plan; impatient with other issues	Can start and drive many projects at once	Broad definition of entire strategy	Often expands the project with new information
	Often unclear on completion	Tends to drive the project, not do it	Left-sided Deliberators follow the plan exactly
	May expand project	Not detail-oriented	
COMPLETION	**COMPLETION**	**COMPLETION**	**COMPLETION**
When task goals are met, the job is done	Feels complete when all people/feelings are satisfied	Measures broadly for success	Completes a project thoroughly
To right brainstyles, job is incomplete (no people issues handled; little negotiation)	To left brainstyles, their work appears incomplete (task is not handled, only feelings)	Others see them only as starters, with no follow-up	To other brainstyles it seems they never finish or are too slow
		Must have systems in place for follow-through	

STAGE FIVE: MASTERY, REACHING THE SEAMLESS LIFE

> This is your life and nobody is going to teach you. No book, no guru.
> You have to learn from yourself, not from books. It is an endless
> thing, a fascinating thing. And when you learn about yourself, from
> yourself, out of that learning wisdom comes. Then you can live a
> most extraordinary, happy, beautiful life.
>
> —KRISHNAMURTI[1]

How do you find your own path to satisfaction, growth and, ultimately, mastery? What happens when you find what you do best? For most, it's a discovery of the obvious rather than an invention of the new. This is how a young man found first a niche, then a path to mastery of his own gifts.

A DELIBERATOR'S MATURING.   Robert was in his twenties, working not very happily as a laboratory technician in a medium-sized company. He was just out of college, working at a temporary assignment he took while looking for a "real job." Typically, those who are not gifted in foresight (vision) for the future recognize opportunity only when it's in front of them. He was often frustrated with the job, his co-workers, and was having trouble staying in any dating relationship longer than a few months. "I took myself too seriously then. What I was working on was very serious too," he says, looking back on those years. Robert was hired full-time to test chemical formulas for consistency. He enjoyed learning about testing the new formulations just because there was a lot of variety in the work, even though his background was in general business. His boss at the time described how he saw Robert's strengths: "Robert was *competent* technically—he did a fairly good job. What he would do that was really valuable was to thoroughly research things that no one else had answers for. He really enjoyed learning and finding out things that no one else knew. He was always going to seminars. He would look around and see what wasn't getting done and he would ask about it. That was what was unique about him. He had a terrific attitude about taking on challenges that would make things better for everyone. *That* was remarkable."

Robert, a right-sided Deliberator, was promoted into Quality Control after a few years. The worst part of the job was when, after finding all the mistakes everyone else made, he had to go confront them about all the problems, over and over again. He was quite uncomfortable doing this. He would complain regularly to his boss about the lack of management direction in Quality; how without Quality the company would never get anywhere. He spent a great deal of time explaining how much was lost because of the lack of management attention. At the height of his frustration, he talked with his boss several times about leaving the company and going back to school.

Outside of work, however, Robert was getting excited about his life for the first time. He was discovering a personal spirituality through reading, seminars, and church. His gift for exploration and learning began to pay off. He stayed on the job and went back to school for an MBA on his own time. He also attended a seminar on Quality. Sometime during this process, he made the boldest move yet —right out of his frustration with the problems he couldn't seem to solve. Using his natural gift for defining a problem, relentlessly tracking down the answer, then thoroughly and steadily working toward his solution, Robert took the next logical step and unwittingly defined the most satisfying and lucrative path for his future.

On a Sunday morning, his boss recalls, he was startled to get a call from Robert asking if he could drop off a proposal that was "too exciting to wait until the following morning." The boss was certainly interested.

Robert arrived about noon and "appeared agitated."

"What's up?" asked the boss.

Robert stood up and started to pace. He looked very serious. Intense, in fact. When he spoke, it was to make a pronouncement, which was most unlike his usual laid-back, thoughtful style. He handed his boss a fairly thick report and said, "Consider this proposal as my first step in taking personal responsibility for Quality in this company. I've realized that I've been sitting around complaining, waiting for you to fix it. I can see that now. I've been to a seminar on what it'll take for everyone in the company to learn the basic skills of making and producing quality products." The boss remembers that Robert, his eyes shining, paused before his next statement, caught his breath, then said, "I want to teach them." The boss's eyes fill with tears as he recounts the story. "He changed the entire company, all by himself," his boss said.

Within a year, Robert had trained all 150 employees in the company.

He *loved* teaching. He was patient, gentle, thorough. He persevered.

He let no one—especially the top management—out of any of the seven A.M. sessions. Within two years, the company was recognized as the top supplier in the entire industry by Ford Motors based on their superior quality. It was a tremendous victory for everyone in the entire firm.

Robert left the company to embark on a new career as a Quality consultant, using all his natural strengths, loving his work so much he "loses track of time" because he's "having so much fun." He laughs a lot; he is a real-life example of "flow." He made several *times* his former salary the first year out. He is now happily married with a new son.

Robert describes what he does today:

I learn constantly. I'm in an ongoing university. When I began, education was a way to get knowledge, and knowledge was valuable. Now I know that knowledge has little value; learning how to think in different ways and from different perspectives is what is really worthwhile.

My real expertise is in facilitation—helping others to grow and develop and work together. In Quality, I assist people in learning about the quality of their *lives*. Clients tell me they ask me in to learn about how to produce better products, and they end up getting something else, something more. I use the surface level, the details, to teach a more profound lesson in moral principles or ethics.

I know now that the smartest people will always maneuver themselves into situations where they don't know the answers. Before, I always wanted to have, and was frustrated by people who wouldn't listen to, *my* answers. My life vision today is to assist others in creating their *own* miracles.

A CONCEPTOR'S TRIAL BY FIRE. David, the young maverick you met earlier (in Chapter Five), went on to become a general manager of several businesses right at the time of our marriage in 1980. One of these was a small plastics manufacturing subsidiary of Ciba Geigy.

Soon after he took the job as a general manager, consultants were hired to assess the potential of the plastics operation and predicted that the business "would never be more than mediocre." The corporation decided to divest it.

Meanwhile, David had been told that, after building a successful product line into a highly profitable business for the corporation, he did not "fit in with senior management." According to his immediate supervisor he wanted to move too far too fast, did not fit in well with this Deliberator-run company, and would not be promoted regardless of his business success.

David, then, had many reasons for wanting to leave his corporate job and purchase the small ailing plastics firm that was on the block. "It was more exciting than anything I had ever done in my life. Everything I had done to date was in preparation for this task." He put together an investor group and, along with bank support, bought the company. The move put everything he had on the line, including his life's savings. But he was confident. He was finally in charge. He had envisioned everything that could go right. And, as only a wife knows, he was scared out of his wits.

Within six months all the equipment in the plant had broken down, idling the production operation. It was 1981. Interest rates on the cash that was keeping the company afloat soon soared to 24 percent. Product was shipped and returned. While I worked in New York during the week, he threw himself into building his company on three to four hours' sleep a night and high tension for the other twenty. David's foresight and ability to boil things down were the gifts that carried him through an increasingly difficult situation. He worked on the few things he could fix, the ones that would bring the biggest payoff, and let the rest go.

While the company was shut down for equipment repairs, David focused on negotiating prices for raw materials, making sure those costs were low enough to give the company its only edge. He turned his love of inventing to formulating only those products that would resolve field problems. Priorities were always clear.

On the human level, he built the future of his company by leaving behind corporate procedures and formality and turning his considerable personal energy into active support for the employees' ability to get the job done. He had learned through his corporate experience the value of gathering support and creating loyalties. "I tried to be a cheerleader for my people who were skeptical about keeping their jobs in what looked to be a very shaky company. I let a million things go and concentrated everything here."

David often showed up in the plant at four or five A.M., too worried to sleep, too concerned to stay at home. Working alongside maintenance workers to unclog pipes, he lived a philosophy of teamwork— a hard-won personal lesson taken from his maverick days.

In the middle of what eventually consumed three years of incredible personal intensity, David spent extra time with the managers on teamwork, confronting tensions, teaching principles, doodling on white boards for hours with indecipherable arrows and boxes. Meetings were large affairs, with anyone who could contribute an idea able to get a say written onto the board. Everyone could be challenged, especially him. "Mistakes weren't punished; everyone screws up. But if you weren't willing to own up if you screwed up, *then* there was a *big* problem. I would fire my howitzers at anyone, especially the managers, if they were reluctant to take responsibility for what they messed up."

He talked of the long term and attended to the short term— keeping afloat, attending to people, getting the product right. The creditors said it was "a very risky venture" but, with the plans working, continued the funding. There were so *many* problems. "All it seems I was doing was repeating over and over those few simple priorities. I saw myself as a teacher. I probably drove people up the wall repeating how I was there to teach them 'how to fish.' "

He strategized to get to daylight just over the horizon. One month he had only enough cash to make it another thirty days. And then the first Big Order came in, and "we were golden." They'd carried the day. Those who knew finally got to exhale.

The company built and maintained market dominance, while winning the industry award for Quality. His leadership drove home the idea of learning from mistakes. All strengths were valued for what they could deliver. David was the driving force. He continued to generate a vision of success beyond the breakdowns.

After five years, the mediocre plastics company boasted nearly two hundred employees, two plants, and plans for a Canadian operation. David had claimed two patents for technology in the same area several mega chemical firms had worked on for fifteen to twenty years to no avail. The company was profitable at over $40 million in sales. The competition at home and with Japan was ferocious.

After being approached by four major corporate suitors, David personally negotiated the sale of the company. His attorney remarked that after having been involved in some eighty or so business acquisitions, he'd "never seen anyone negotiate so well or think so strategically."

David was an entrepreneur who had made good. He was wealthy. He bought a big new home, his first new car in five years, and talked of Hawaii.

He got restless after five weeks. Within seven months he'd moved into new offices, and started a company to buy and invest in start-up companies. He got into the stock market. He became majority owner of a retail firm, expanding it from one to five stores.

In the same time frame he started another high-tech plastics company where he has proceeded to develop another whole new line of products. Now in his sixties, he still spends hours at the erasable white boards with a team of highly talented experts who have been hired for their diverse (brainstyle) strengths. It's been another long hill to climb over the last five years to launch the second business in a whole new area.

Yes, he's had setbacks. Lawsuits. Personal disappointments. Even a few betrayals by those he's trusted. Harder still, he's had to overcome the "arrogance of his success" to realize he's "not better than anyone else," he just has "different gifts."

"I have less need to be in control now," he says. "I've learned about my limits. I'm more content with life, but I know that I'll never be happy just playing golf all the time." He is most fulfilled, he says, with a place to do what he loves best: "work with people, and make use of my creativity." He still scribbles his magic formulas on his white boards in the wee hours of the morning.

He is a seasoned Conceptor.

A CONCILIATOR'S STORY: MY OWN. The Swiss, statesmanlike Otto Sturzenegger, chief executive officer and chairman of the board of Ciba-Geigy, was standing in front of the assembled senior managers of the company—all of them. All eleven Management Committee rulers of the entire thirteen-thousand-employee empire, and all sixty-plus senior vice presidents, were in the audience. And Dr. Sturzenegger was intoning, "And when I think of excellence, I think of"—*and right here he said my name.* I stopped breathing. The whole audience turned and faced me, where I was seated in the back of the huge conference room, as he continued, ". . . We all owe her our gratitude, for without her efforts we would never have been here today, accomplishing what we have accomplished." The audience, a forest of gray and blue suits, applauded loudly. They were smiling. My eyes filled and ran over.

It was an incredible moment for someone who had lived nearly all her life craving attention, always seeking some sort of spotlight. It was an enlightening moment, a revelatory experience. It was a total surprise for me. As I stood there and received their acknowledgment— without doubt, it was the peak of my career—I realized it wasn't nearly as important as the moment this same group had created just about ten minutes earlier. That was the real story.

In an unprecedented, dare I say *historic,* moment, that very same chairman of the board and chief executive officer of Ciba-Geigy corporation had announced to the assembled senior VPs that he and the executive board would, "as of Monday morning," raise the amount of money that those in the audience could personally approve by more than *three times!* From $125,000 to *$500,000.* There was a gasp, a pause of amazement in that room at the measure of trust being placed in their leadership. It was a tremendous step for everyone in the room. They had to work very hard together to reach that conclusion.

That announcement marked the conclusion of three years of cajoling, influencing, networking my head off, standing up to gossip and even an open confrontation with a volatile division president. But this pushy broad had gotten all these men in a room for a six-day executive seminar for the first time ever. The closest they'd ever gotten before was a twenty-four-hour, dry-as-dust financial report day. You know the kind: presentations of hours of black and white overhead slides with columns of teensy, illegible numbers with the chief financial officer droning over them like a high priest at an endless mass. The company had had terrible results in the last two years, and senior management had a reason to listen to my arguments that they needed to work together to turn it around. Though certainly not at first, and certainly not for the reasons *I* thought they should, they moved on this project. After all, if the Swiss at corporate headquarters had an executive seminar, it wouldn't seem too radical if we did it in the United States too.

Now here they were, actually making a real, honest-to-God change in the way they did their daily bottom-line business. It mattered deeply to me; but the big shocker was, in that very moment of applause, that I cared more for what *they* had done than what I had done for the personal recognition.

I had come a long way since high school when my mother thought I should be a lawyer and I wanted to be a choral conductor. I majored in history and English in college and started out teaching both subjects in high school—which is still the hardest job I ever had.

I was never satisfied with whatever I was doing as I started my career. When teaching, I wanted to influence the parents; when I next became a trainer, I wanted to change the system. I was always working my way up the ladder. I was ambitious. I put together my own personal graduate degree program of seminars and graduate courses. The city of New York provided additional training in organizational development and humanistic education from some of the best resources in the country with funding for the pioneer program in drug prevention I became a director of in the early 1970s in New York City.

I got a job in private industry in 1976. Divorced and scared, I was, I guess you could say, defensively independent. I was the only woman manager for miles. I was teaching now about something right out of my own experience: personal change and leadership. I was a corporate trainer. My job was to develop and teach management seminars. I pushed to consult out of the classroom to business teams in order to "make a difference."

In 1979, the managers I taught at Ciba-Geigy and the teams I consulted all whined a single refrain: *you should teach this stuff to my boss,* he's *the one who needs it.* They were probably right. But although I was good at hamming it up in front of a room with a flip chart, I didn't know how to write a good formal proposal. So when I got my boss to agree that it was time to try to teach those bosses who really needed all the help, I presented my proposal not in writing but in an unheard-of videotaped interview. My boss asked me questions and I presented my assessment of senior-level training needs. The chairman and chief operating officer agreed to let me into the deep pile of the sanctum santorum boardroom to see it; I still remember keeping my hands in my lap so they couldn't tell I was shaking.

Even though I was doing something that was, by company standards, outrageous, I had no sense that what I did reflected my innate strengths. I knew I'd worked hard training hundreds of people and consulting all over the country for the two-hundred-year-old, conservative chemical firm, introducing new companywide programs, and developing and teaching a seven-day management training course. My feet hurt just thinking about it. (I always wore high heels.)

I know now that this company was led primarily by Deliberators who wanted proof ahead of time that something would work. Their idea of "executive education" was to send executives one by one to Harvard for six weeks so they could make business contacts. Well, that technique wasn't working. In 1980, the entire U.S. operation made a 1 percent return on sales. The consultants were called in and changes were being made. The time was ripe to shape up those guys at the top. So I marched in with my video proposal, the gist of which was to bring all those brilliant senior executives together and get them singing off the same page.

I finally had a single mission, a true focus for my life that I was passionate about.

The victory with the top executives didn't come cheap for me. As I sat in the back of that conference room, I was assailing myself with doubts and self-criticism. Why, I wondered, if I was so smart, was *I* not in front of the room instead of the Harvard professors? Why couldn't I have developed the whole program without using consultants? Why was I so mentally defective that I wasn't getting my MBA like a colleague of mine? Why was I so unsure and inept as a parent? My answer was optimistic and consistent: I could work harder, try more, learn more, and maybe someday I would get "there." I didn't know I was already "there."

Meanwhile, I was a goal-setting, focused, learning machine who hated being told when she made a mistake, and who opened her own doors, thank you. If you have read Chapter Four, dear reader, you know much more about me than I knew about myself in those days.

The hardest time was yet to come. Not only was I commuting from Dallas to New York for this job, I was now a stepmother. The job at Ciba-Geigy was easier than the new role as a parent. It was a stressful time, which lasted almost five years. But the seminar concept was a great success. After providing seven such executive seminars for all four hundred senior executives—living and eating with each group, playing poker and ordering their meals and arranging their limos and trying ever-so-respectfully to modify their presentations—I helped coach my replacement and stopped traveling. I was going to try to build a practice out of an office in my home, a marriage, and a family in Texas. All alone. What a fate for a Conciliator!

Those first two years were horrible. My worst fear was that I'd find myself in front of the TV watching soap operas all day. I had to figure out what to do with my life.

My husband, David, had developed the concepts that were to become brainstyles by this time. His company was flourishing. I started reading a spiritual self-study program called *A Course in Miracles*[2] as a spiritual foundation for my life. As I settled into a happy marriage and built a new practice, I also affirmed the best answers were the simplest: be who you are and do what you love and the rest falls into place, easily and naturally. I am still learning how to live this way. As David asserted, you really can't change yourself or others.

I had never appreciated my own strengths, even when my gifts for teaching and influencing others had been so obvious in the work I did for corporations. I couldn't acknowledge my own accomplishments, I was trying too hard to get somewhere.

But my brainstyle was always there from the beginning. The early happiness teaching human relations in high school, the impulses to personally influence the parents and students, to change the system when a trainer, and to "make a difference" consulting to teams were all expressions of a natural drive to realize my strengths to solve people problems. During my twenties and thirties I was developing the skills and discipline I needed to be successful in those strengths, and that have eventually led me to the work I do currently.

For the Conciliator, life seems mysterious, accidental, unplanned. It takes time and trust to understand that our gift is to live from that spontaneous, fresh place within and to dedicate that gift to something bigger than stamping out others' criticisms.

Recently, a woman in her twenties, a Conciliator and younger version of me at that age, asked me, "How can I accept myself when I'm not always the best that I can be? When I have so many shortcomings? When I'm so petty about little things people tell me? How can I grow up to be what my mother always told me I could be?"

It seems I wrote this book to tell her the answer.

WHEN I TALK TO MYSELF NOW, HERE'S WHAT I SAY:

What am I here for?
  To be myself.
What must I learn to do this?
  Stop trying to be perfect.
  Go beyond pleasing others to perfecting ideas.
How will I become a success?
  Find what I love to do; know that I am on my path.
  Discipline, excellence, and mastery will follow.
How can I accomplish this?
  Learn from everyone. Be a victim of no one.
How shall I relate to others?
  Honor the best in others, *not* their appearance.
What happens when I stumble in my belief in myself?
  Reach for a purpose larger than my own needs, with goals larger than I alone can reach.
What will I gain?
  Joy. Satisfaction. Freedom.

Appendix A:
Brain-Based Aptitudes

CAREER counseling and testing has reached such a level of specificity and predictability that if you are willing to invest from eight to sixteen hours and about $500, you can identify, from a list of fourteen to eighteen *aptitudes,*[1] very precisely what your abilities are. Aptitudes are defined as "natural talents, special abilities for doing, or learning to do, certain kinds of things easily and quickly. Manual dexterity, musical ability, spatial visualization, and memory for numbers are examples of such aptitudes."[2] Vocabulary, however, is not, because it can be learned and improved with study.

Aptitudes are measured after the age of thirteen or fourteen. They have been found to mature by about twenty years and level off in their impact on performance. They do not change. As the Johnson O'Connor Research Foundation points out, "Aptitudes are not based upon knowledge or educational background."

A brainstyle, then, describes a combination of aptitudes.

Since many people do not have access to, or cannot afford, this extensive and expensive testing, the four brainstyle descriptions are offered as a way to help you identify several central aptitudes. Additionally, findings are included in the chapters describing each of the brainstyles from testing *The BrainStyles Inventory* along with a battery of standard psychological tests (see Appendix B) to broaden the implications of what it means to describe yourself as a certain brainstyle. The database for validating *The BrainStyles Inventory* is well over one thousand people at school and work in a variety of occupations.[3]

Five aptitudes particularly important for brainstyles are grouped under "conceptualizing aptitudes," which "determine how you pro-

322 / APPENDIX A

duce ideas, organize them, and perceive relationships among them. They establish the way you evaluate problems and generate solutions to them. Imaginative or critical thinking indicate your strength in these aptitudes."[4] These five are central to the list of some seventeen aptitudes measured by the AIMS research group, and explain the central abilities of each of the four brainstyles:[5]

The IDEAPHORIA aptitude: the ability to generate ideas, to be naturally imaginative in a random way rather than in a "straight line" or logical fashion. Brainstorming is a breeze, as is daydreaming, and talking, chatting, or making conversation. When this is a strength, there are limitations: routine, repetition, or consistency is boring and can be intolerable. Attention span is limited, and variety is essential. Conciliators and Conceptors are most likely to be strong in this aptitude.

The ANALYTICAL aptitude: the ability to bring mental order to chaos; organizing, coordinating, and planning are easy, as is balancing complicated daily schedules. This is the central aptitude of the Deliberator.

The DIAGNOSTIC aptitude: the ability to draw conclusions from assorted bits of information, to see the common denominator in seemingly unrelated things; to detect the cause. Strength in this aptitude gives an ability to question situations and events, look for the downside, and be strong in critical or judgmental thinking. When applying this strength to people the person is able to figure out underlying motives, and when they choose to, to handle the situation diplomatically by responding to the unstated feelings or needs. Often impatient or judgmental, the aptitude does not promote tolerance for differences or strong relationship skills. Knowers and left-sided Deliberators are strongest in this aptitude. The presence of this aptitude separates a Conceptor from a Conciliator.

The FORESIGHT aptitude: the ability to envision long-term possibilities and implications for the future. The person is generally motivated by long-term rewards, and finds it easy to minimize current obstacles in favor of a longer view; they do not need as much feedback or frequent indicators of how they are doing to keep from getting discouraged as long as they have long-range goals to shoot for. This is the dominant strength of the Conceptor, and most often present for Knowers. Deliberators and Conciliators, less gifted here, resist being told what to do often because they are slower to see future implications; the future scenario described by the other brainstyles seems preposterous because it is not a part of the abilities of the listener.

The STRUCTURAL VISUALIZATION aptitude: the ability to envision objects in your mind in three dimensions. People with this ability are best in jobs like construction, medical technology, computer hardware design, architecture, or manufacturing fabrication. Interpreting a contour map or a blueprint requires this aptitude. It is the opposite of ABSTRACT VISUALIZATION, or the ability to mentally work with ideas and concepts. To be good at abstract visualization means you are better selling services than products, or relate better to an *idea* and its meaning than tangible *things*. Statistically, more men than women exhibit this aptitude. Genetically based, any brainstyle can have this strength.

Additionally, a big part of how we relate to others depends on our SENSORY PROCESSING ABILITIES. You may be aware of any of the following: shades of colors and how they go together, when music is slightly off-key, when food starts to go "off," or where precisely in your body a pain is located. If you have sensitivity in one, you most likely have equal sensitivity in all five senses, and are probably good at "fine motor skills," like playing a musical instrument or typing, golf, tennis, or doing something with your hands. Not everyone has these abilities. Others may be best at smooth muscle control, sports like football, basketball, or soccer, and be able to withstand pain better, but they may not be very musical or visually sensitive. These abilities show the difference in how strongly you access your senses. Conciliators, Conceptors, and right-sided Deliberators generally have stronger sensory abilities.

If you have the sensory abilities, there are many avenues open to you for work and play. If someone close to you does not have them, it does not mean they are stronger and you are a hypochondriac because you feel more pain. It does not mean that the other is "an insensitive clod who has no appreciation of culture." They have an ability to focus and achieve differently than you—they don't have all the distractions of sensory input constantly bombarding their brain that you have. These differences can enrich a collaboration in the home especially: one wife tells of how her husband enriches their dining with his fine taste for wine and food; she appreciates how he plays the piano and cooks. Another wife says her husband is marvelous at machine repair. She counts on him for his ability to stay with anything he "sets his mind to." But when he slammed his little finger in a car door, he didn't even notice until he saw blood on a piece of paper he'd handled! He is able to focus intensely on a job, without distraction, something his sensorily able wife has much more difficulty doing.

Appendix B:
The BrainStyle Inventory®
Scoring Interpretation
and Discussion

HIGHEST SCORE INTERPRETATION FOR
THE BRAINSTYLES INVENTORY

Column 1	Column 2	Column 3	Column 4
The DELIBERATOR At Time Zero	The KNOWER At Time Zero	The CONCEPTOR At Time Zero	The CONCILIATOR At Time Zero
• Rapid memory search	• Rapid left-brain response	• Rapid right-left-right-brain response	• Rapid right-brain response
• Thinks before reacting	• Logical, clear answer	• Generalized or vague answer	• Rapid reactions or answers

Often the brainstyle response appears as:

• A questioner, a challenger	• Conclusive	• Assuming broadly without facts, a stereotype	• Spontaneous
• Knowledgeable	• Unemotional decision-maker		• A rapid, changeable decision-maker who acts quickly
• Indifferent or thoughtful at first	• Confrontational	• Possibility explorer	
• Analytical	• Black-or-white thinker	• Inventive yet strategic	• More imaginative than strategic
• Complex	• Simplifier	• Deductive	• Informative, friendly, talkative
• Inductive	• Deductive		• Inductive

Over time, core strengths are:

• Someone who assesses things first and then learns widely	• Someone who clarifies things first without emotion	• Someone who poses solutions and then tests them out	• Someone who rapidly imagines possibilities
• Steadiness in important things	• A person who gets to the cause and poses simple solutions	• An inventive person who is hard to understand at first	• An emotional, intuitive person
• Uses step-by-step analysis to reach the overview	• A person who fixes things	• A risk-taker	• A changeable decision-maker
• A planner	• A problem-solver	• A pathfinder	• A caring, even charismatic influencer
• A multifaceted person	• A logical person	• An initiator	• A social person
		• A visionary	• An inspiring person

See Chapter Six	See Chapter Three	See Chapter Five	See Chapter Four

BrainStyles Percentages

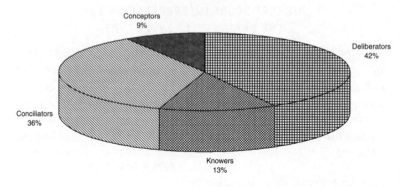

The chart above reflects *The BrainStyle Inventory*® database, as of January 1996. The sample tested was 1,235. Of that total, 685 were male and 550 were female.

The data were drawn from a wide variety of white-collar occupations, primarily those who work outside the home, although the self-employed, students, homemakers, and retired persons were represented. Major groups responding were those who worked in manufacturing (approximately 25 percent), those who work in a staff position such as Quality, engineering, logistics, or planning (approximately 15 percent), and marketing/sales (approximately 13 percent). College students made up another 25 percent. Entrepreneurs were about 4 percent of the total.

Executives, supervisors, managers, and nonmanaging professionals made up approximately 60 percent of the database across a variety of occupations, including human resources, real estate, technical research, customer service, and public relations, serving industries as varied as health, interior design, computing, and electronics.

Some preliminary findings:

Deliberators made up 60 percent of those surveyed in staff functions, 50 percent of those working in finance, 52 percent of those in manufacturing or distribution, 35 percent of those in customer service and only 30 percent of those in marketing/sales. This brainstyle was about half of all managers and professionals surveyed.

Conciliators were slightly more numerous in the customer service and marketing/sales functions surveyed.

Data are still being collected and analyzed.

The BrainStyle Inventory Database:
Male/Female Comparisons for Each BrainStyle

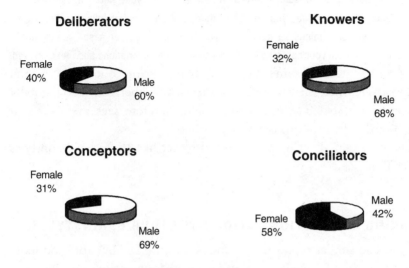

Total Population 1235*

Male Population = 685 Female Population = 550

*BrainStyles Inventory data as of January 1996.

AFTER TAKING *THE BRAINSTYLE INVENTORY**

Questions or Concerns

If you had two or more scores that were within one point or are still unsure of a match between the summary description of the brainstyle in which you scored highest and your strengths, read this section and then go to the appropriate chapter. Talk over your strengths with someone who has known you over a period of years, if possible, and who has some objectivity about you (usually a friend or a friendly relative).

There are three potential barriers to identifying your brainstyle:

1. You are in a situation right now, especially at work, where the requirements are for a brainstyle different from your own; or

---

* *The BrainStyle Inventory*® is available in quantity as a complete self-scoring package from BSI at 1–800–374–9878.

2. The situation is very undefined, you do a variety of things continually—like working in the home and raising a family; and/or

3. You have decided, somewhere along the way, that your sister or dad or friend does things in a way you admire or detest, and you either follow or resist their way of doing things so much that you have put together a self-image that is different from your natural gifts. Then you read the descriptions and feel confused.

Another reason some have trouble figuring out their natural strengths is when their brainstyle is that of a Deliberator, who naturally looks at the specifics in situations, and therefore sees themselves in each of the descriptions (see Chapter Six).

Remember, all of us have learned to act like the other brainstyles *after* Time Zero.

MAKING DISTINCTIONS AMONG THE FOUR BRAINSTYLES

If you had similar scores in Column One (the Deliberator) and Column Four (the Conciliator), think about these questions:

- Overall, do people count on you for a more steady, thoughtful approach to life in spite of your feelings? One where you are more even than emotional, more reliable than changeable?
- Do you bring self-control, organization, or structure over the long term? Do you take charge by thinking and using rational arguments? Do you like having proof? Keeping things consistent? Do you look for the factual, *then* the imaginative? *(See Chapter Six, pp. 205–9)*

—or—

- Overall, do people count on you to be more unpredictable, personal, imaginative, or open with your feelings than methodical or objective?
- Are you a great starter of things?
- Are you warm, insightful, and informal in relationships? Are you openly spontaneous?
- Do you take charge by offering creative ideas, drawing from intuition, or selling your ideas while having difficulty being consistent? *(See Chapter Four)*

Are you unsure whether you fit the Deliberator or Knower description? (Your scores are similar between Column One and Column Two.) Think about these questions:

- Do you value information for its own sake?
- Do people comment on your witty or clever remarks?
- Do you like learning about new or unrelated topics just out of curiosity?

- Are you someone who tends to think about new things before deciding rather than just "shoot from the hip"?
- Do you avoid conflict if at all possible?
- Are you decisive in subjects you know well but not as decisive when you're in a new situation?
- When you're in charge, do you tend to get all the facts first and distrust incomplete or quick answers? *(See Chapter Six, pp. 209–12)*

—or—

- Do you come up with clear answers, no matter the subject?
- Do you focus most of the time on the future and not care very much about what was done before or what is "the proper way" to do things?
- Do clear ends tend to establish methods?
- Are you best in a crisis? Do you consistently simplify?
- Do people count on you to see things pretty much in black or white? To give answers more than explanations?
- Do you take charge most naturally by giving decisions and providing direction first, and getting people involved later? *(See Chapter Three)*

If you are unsure whether your real strengths are those of a Knower (Column Two) or a Conciliator (Column Four), start with Chapter Four.

If you are unsure whether you get the big picture early or later (and are unsure whether you fit the Deliberator [Column One] or the Conceptor brainstyle [Column Three] best):

- Do the novel ideas you come up with make sense, make something better, or more efficient? Can you explain the ideas or talk them through almost as soon as you get them?
- Are you good at "politics" in any group, knowing how to impress others?
- Do you evaluate problems pretty carefully in order to come up with ideas?
- Are you better at spotting problems, taking longer to solve them?
- Does your intuition—your *ah ha!*—come *after* getting the facts?
- Are you good at managing the impression you make on others when talking to them?
- Can you work on a variety of projects all at once? Do you have a problem limiting yourself to one or two? *(See Chapter Six)*

—or—

- Do you have to work harder at communicating and socializing than you do at coming up with new ideas?
- Do you set the direction that others follow, especially in new areas?

- Do you lead by describing the future and selling the possibilities?
- Do you use facts as only one element of an equation? Do conclusions or generalizations come to you *first* before you get to the facts, steps, or the particulars?
- Do you tend to focus your attention, curiosity, and projects on only one or two at a time?
- Would you rather be the inventor or the originator than the expert who has all the answers?
- If you don't mind tooting your own horn about the risks you take, you may need to read Chapter Five first.

If you are confused about whether your *first* response is more or less "conceptual" (Conceptor or Conciliator), think about:

- Are you a good storyteller?
- Do you often make random and spontaneous associations between ideas as you talk?
- Are you more aware of people's feelings than you are correct with an analysis of their facts?
- Is it harder for you to set a career direction or personal goals and stay with them over a long period of time than it is to explore new avenues and start new projects?
- Do you take charge best by making close relationships over periods of time?
- Do you use personal introspection and empathy as the main tool to predict what'll come next? *(See Chapter Four)*

—or—

- Do you make up random and spontaneous images and ideas in your head and have a hard time putting them into words for a while?
- Can you see patterns or outlines more easily than you see the details or fine points of an image? Can you generate overviews, solutions, and strategies that invent whole new projects immediately rather than build on and synthesize what is offered?
- Are you more at home with ideas than people? *(See Chapter Five)*

Appendix C:
TECHNICAL REPORT
Construct Validation
of a New Measure
of BrainStyles

Lawrence H. Peters, Ph.D., Neeley School of Business, Texas Christian University,
Fort Worth, Texas
Marlane Miller, Miller Consulting Services, Dallas, Texas
Linda Hoopes, Ph.D., ODR, Atlanta, Georgia
May 1995

ABSTRACT

A study was conducted to examine the reliability and construct valid-ity* of a developmental measure of a new construct, called brainstyles.

* It is one thing to find the inventory capable of putting persons into a single category. It is quite another to conclude that these persons were placed in the "proper" category. That is the issue of construct validity. As described above, one can generate support for the construct validity of a measure to the extent that persons respond in other ways that are consistent with underlying theory. That is, if persons designated as Deliberators, Knowers, Conceptors, and Conciliators are properly categorized, then we should find those persons to a) differ in their reactions to other variables in ways that b) reflect expectations derived from the theory of brainstyles.

The brainstyles construct, derived by extending theory on brain-behavior linkages, defines four distinct ways that people take in, process, and express information. These are termed Deliberator, Knower, Conceptor, and Conciliator. A 24-item, forced-choice scale was developed to help people identify their unique brainstyle. This developmental measure was administered, along with a battery of 25 other psychological tests, to a group of 225 persons. Based on item analysis procedures, the 24-item scale was reduced to 18 items that demonstrated exceptionally strong evidence of reliability and construct validity. In all, 23 specific predictions were made, of which 18 were statistically significant. As important, the pattern of means for these significant results supported the validity of this measure. The large number of significant findings not only supported the validity of the new measure of brainstyles, but the theory underlying that new measure as well.

In this study, a number of predictions were made regarding how persons in different brainstyles should respond on a series of measures of other psychological constructs. In total, 23 separate predictions (involving 11 different psychological constructs) were made. Results from this investigation indicated significant, supportive findings for 18 of those 23 predictions! (See Table 1 for a summary of findings.) Given the large number of rather diverse psychological measures used in this study, these results provide a level of support seldom found in the measurement literature. Such support is not only rare in measurement literature, but rare as well in support of any theory in psychology.

CONSTRUCT VALIDATION OF A NEW MEASURE OF BRAINSTYLES

This report summarizes a research investigation into the reliability and construct validity of a paper-and-pencil measure of a new construct, called brainstyles. The original version of the brainstyles instrument, examined in this study, was studied for its ability to classify persons into distinct brainstyle categories and for its construct validity. Data were collected from a large sample of persons who completed Version 1.1 of *The BrainStyles Inventory* (Peters & Miller, 1992) along with a battery of other psychological tests. This report will briefly review brainstyles theory, summarize how the original version of the instrument was developed, overview the procedures used in the present study, report pertinent results, and finally, draw a conclusion regarding the reliability and validity of this new measure.

BrainStyles

The conceptual foundation for brainstyles theory can be traced to basic research in the area of brain-behavior linkages (see, for example, the work by Ornstein, 1986, or Gazzaniga, 1992). That research has shown that hemisphere dominance (left-brain versus right-brain people) tends to be systematically associated with how persons take in, process, and express information. Persons with left-brain dominance, for example, tend to rely more on data and treat those data in linear, logical, and rational ways when making decisions and judgments. On the other hand, persons with right-brain dominance tend to be more comfortable with using their intuition and feelings, and, as a result, are more conceptual, holistic, and spiritual when making decisions and judgments.

David Cherry and Marlane Miller (1992) have taken the left-brain/right-brain distinction to a next step by asking how quickly the two brain hemispheres communicate with each other. From this starting place, they derived a series of implications that describes how persons who differ in their ability to quickly engage both hemispheres would react and respond to life problems. In particular, Cherry and Miller argue that both brain hemisphere dominance and the capability of quickly moving back and forth across hemispheres differ across people, and these differences define four distinct brainstyles.

Each brainstyle is said to be associated with very specific ways that people interact with the world—ways that come naturally, especially the first time a problem is encountered, and with which people feel most comfortable. These are said to be brainstyle strengths. When dealing with problems in ways that are consistent with one's brainstyle, persons should not only be more effective, but should enjoy a more positive experience than if they had attempted to use competencies that are associated with one of the other three brainstyles. (Brief descriptions of each brainstyle are given below.)

Importantly, Cherry and Miller point out that the connection between the left hemisphere and right hemisphere, through a tissue bridge called the corpus callosum, defines a *structural* difference among people. This assertion is important because it clarifies how posited differences among people are created. Because the hemisphere linkage is said to be structural in nature, Cherry and Miller conclude that differences across people are fixed. By implication, this means that one brainstyle's strengths are another brainstyle's weaknesses, and these weaknesses cannot be compensated for through learning. Thus, they argue that all persons have a set of strengths that, if used, not only make them more effective, but make their experience more positive as well. If persons attempt to operate "out" of their own brainstyle (i.e., attempting to deal with life problems in ways that reflect the strengths of one of the other three brainstyles), both their effectiveness and their experience are expected to suffer.

Brainstyles theory, then, posits that there are four distinctive groupings of people who can be expected to take in, process, and express information in distinctly different ways. Further, because these differences are said to reflect differences in underlying brain architecture, people will have strengths in one area *and* also will have weaknesses in other areas. Further, because of this structural determinant, no amount of effort aimed at learning will make up for deficiencies that are structural in their origin. Thus, brainstyles theory posits that persons' brainstyle strengths need to be identified, nurtured, and used.

Types of BrainStyles

DELIBERATORS. Deliberators have a stronger left-brain dominance, but often make a delayed, balanced response. New stimuli prompt an immediate search of memory where facts, details, and feelings are stored. These people first look inward to their experience, and are good at remembering how information was originally presented. Deliberators can appear neutral, detached, factual, and objective. They tend to sort information in terms of existing mental models and established standards. A decision comes quickly *if* it has been made previously or *if* it evokes the reapplication of a known process. Otherwise, Deliberators delay making decisions. They first apply logic, reason, facts, and details; only later do they add intuition and feelings to their conclusions.

KNOWERS. Knowers have a rapid left-brain response and come across to others as persons who are quick, clear, and certain when presented with a new problem to handle. They are practical thinkers who can evaluate a great deal of information, sift through complexity quickly, and identify high-leverage solutions to problems. Knowers tend to be very decisive and are gifted in making unemotional responses. Thus, emotions or relationships do not deter them from logical, factual approaches to solving problems. Their strong left-brain response is followed by a delayed right-brain response. Thus, from hours to days later, they may become aware of the emotional impact that their decisions and interactions have had on others.

CONCEPTORS.   Conceptors process information quickly with both left-brain and right-brain input, and produce very creative responses as a result. This left-brain/right-brain exchange happens instantaneously and makes it possible for fact and feeling to come together in unusual ways. Because they move rapidly back and forth from fact and logic to emotion and intuition, Conceptors are capable of forming sweeping hypotheses and envisioning possibilities to big, unusual, and complex problems. Thus, Conceptors, more so than any of the other brainstyles, think in nonlinear ways (which can appear illogical to others) and, as a result, are able to make conceptual leaps, rather than incremental extensions, in their thinking. It is often hard for others, however, to follow or understand the logical flow of ideas, since Conceptors create their own personal cognitive "shorthand" for how ideas go together.

CONCILIATORS.   Conciliators have strong right-brain dominance. They look first to the emotional and intuitive side of their experience when evaluating new issues. In so doing, Conciliators tend to be somewhat spontaneous and nonlinear in their thinking, and as a result can be very creative in their suggested solutions and decisions. They will eventually, however, reconsider their initial reactions using available factual information in a more logical way. This delayed left-brain response will come from just a few minutes to several days later. As a result, Conciliators may get excited about early insights that, when eventually evaluated against relevant information and criteria in a more logical way, will cause them to change their minds. Conciliators are especially good at "reading people" and in sensing unspoken group dynamics. As a result, they are comfortable working with people and in encouraging others to work together collaboratively.

Validation Study: Overview

The validity of any new measure of a psychological construct can only be established by basic research into its reliability as a measure and the extent to which persons with different score patterns behave in ways that are consistent with the underlying theory of the construct. To the extent that brainstyles theory is correct, one should expect persons with different brainstyles to respond to life's experiences in very predictable ways, corresponding to the way they take in, process, and express information.

In the present study, a large sample of persons completed a battery of tests designed to measure a wide variety of psychological variables.* These variables represent a diverse set of psychological states, styles, and reactions. Thus, the data set provides a strong backdrop against which the newly developed brainstyles measure could be examined. The battery of tests included several variables for which specific predictions could be derived regarding how persons with different brainstyles should respond. Support for the validity of the brainstyles measure would be reflected in empirical results that supported the existence of these expected relationships. In addition, other variables were included in this battery for which no a priori predictions could be made. Analyses of these variables were, therefore, exploratory in nature, and significant results involving them will help to further clarify the psychological meaning of the brainstyles construct.

Hypotheses describing the expected relationship between each of these variables and brainstyle scores are given in the Results Section.

METHODS SECTION

Subjects and Procedure

A total of 225 undergraduate psychology students at Georgia Institute of Technology completed a battery of tests designed to measure a wide range of individual difference factors. Students completed this test battery as part of a requirement to participate in basic research. Extra credit toward course grades was offered as an inducement to sign up for this study. Due to incomplete responses on several items, some scale scores could not be calculated.† The resulting missing data reduced the sample sizes for some analyses reported below.

---

* The present study was conducted in conjunction with another validation effort (by Hoopes) designed to provide evidence regarding the validity of a new measure of "personal resilience." The test battery used in this study was chosen specifically to support that validation effort. However, since many variables chosen for that purpose were also appropriate for the present validation study, data from all available scales were used.

† In particular, two persons did not complete all items on the brainstyles instrument, reducing the effective sample size for this measure to 223.

The test battery was administered in a single session lasting approximately two hours. Individual scales within the test battery were grouped into four sets. These sets of scales were distributed to respondents in different random sequences. As a result, any given scale was completed at different points in the total test battery. This was done to control for order effects and potential effects due to fatigue.

Scale Development

The BrainStyles Inventory was developed over a one-year period by writing items based on the conceptual definition of each of the four brainstyles. Items were developed using a forced-choice scaling format. Each item contained two statements that conceptually distinguished between two of the brainstyles. Respondents were asked to choose the single alternative within each pair that best described them. A response alternative also was provided for respondents who could not choose one of these two statements, but instructions discouraged respondents from choosing this alternative often.

Scores were computed by counting the frequency with which each brainstyle category was chosen. Since brainstyles theory states that persons have a single brainstyle, the category with the greatest frequency was then identified as the respondent's specific brainstyle. All analyses reported below are based on these specific category assignments.

The original item set (Version 1.0) included 36 pairs of statements, six for each possible direct comparison of the four brainstyles. This original set of items was, iteratively, rewritten based on a series of interviews and results from item analyses from two preliminary data collections. The result was a developmental questionnaire measure (Version 1.1) containing a series of 24 paired items. This version (see Cherry & Miller, 1992) was administered in the present study.

Measures

With the exception of the developmental version of the Personal Resilience Questionnaire, all scales used in this study are standardized instruments that have been previously found to possess adequate reliability and construct validity. Brief descriptions of each variable, as well as the predictions made regarding the relationship of each to the new brainstyles measure, are given in the Results Section.

RESULTS SECTION

Results are reported in two sections. First, the issue of *reliability* of measurement is addressed. This is followed by an examination of evidence regarding the *construct validity* of this version of the brainstyles measure.

Reliability

Reliability was assessed relative to the measurement purpose of identifying a single, unique brainstyle for each respondent. A second goal was to produce a scale with as few a number of items as necessary to make this classification—to reduce the item set from 24 items down to 18 items. Both goals were pursued simultaneously.

Specifically, a series of item analyses was conducted to identify items that did not seem to produce internally consistent results. At each iteration, the number of "tied category scores" was monitored, and items were removed to see their impact on this index. The final set of 18 items were those for which the greatest percentage of persons could be classified into a single, unique brainstyle category—that is, the chosen items minimized the number of tied category scores and, therefore, maximized the reliability of measurement. In this instance, the final set of 18 items resulted in 193 (or 87 percent) of the 223 respondents being classified into a single brainstyle category. Of these 193 respondents, 61 were Deliberators (32 percent), 25 were Knowers (13 percent), 27 were Conceptors (14 percent), and 80 were Conciliators (42 percent).

Further evidence that the measure was able to classify people reliably was based on comparing total scores for each brainstyle, across all four brainstyle groups. Evidence supporting the internal consistency reliability of the measure would be reflected in results that indicated that Deliberators had the highest total Deliberator score, Knowers had the highest total Knower score, and so on. In order to conduct this analysis, we calculated, for each respondent, a total score for each brainstyle category. These summated scores (minimum $= 0$; maximum $= 9$) were used, in separate analyses, to examine differences across brainstyle groups. Results, based on One-Way Analysis of Variance procedures, indicated statistically significant differences across the brainstyle groupings, and in every instance, persons in the appropriate brainstyle category reported significantly higher self-ratings compared to persons in other brainstyle groups. These findings, reported below, are very supportive of the reliability of the measure.

Results:

DELIBERATORS: For Deliberator items, Deliberators (M = 6.84) rated themselves significantly higher than Knowers (M = 3.76), Conciliators (M = 3.60), and Conceptors (M = 3.48). Means for the other three groups were statistically equivalent.

KNOWERS: For Knower items, Knowers (M = 6.44) rated themselves significantly higher than all other groups (Deliberators, M = 3.69; Conceptors, M = 2.89; Conciliators, M = 2.85). Also, Deliberators rated themselves significantly higher on Knower items than both Conciliators and Conceptors.

CONCEPTORS: For Conceptor items, Conceptors (M = 6.70) rated themselves significantly higher than all other groups (Knowers, M = 2.24; Deliberators, M = 2.20; Conciliators, M = 2.18). Means for the other three groups were statistically equivalent.

CONCILIATORS: For Conciliator items, Conciliators (M = 7.10) rated themselves significantly higher than all other groups (Deliberators, M = 3.46; Conceptors, M = 3.15; Knowers, M = 3.00). Means for the other three groups were statistically equivalent.

Construct Validity

As indicated earlier, the construct validity of the new measure of brainstyles would be supported to the extent that persons with different brainstyles responded to different psychological measures in ways that are predicted by the theory that underlies brainstyles. In the present study, 11 variables were assessed for which specific predictions could be made. In addition, 14 other variables were included in this data set for which no differences, across the four brainstyles, were anticipated. Analyses of these variables were, therefore, exploratory in nature, and results involving them help to further clarify the psychological meaning of the brainstyles construct.

This section is divided into two parts, focusing first on variables for which specific predictions could be made; then, on those additional variables for which no such predictions were made.

I. VARIABLES EXPECTED TO RELATE TO BRAINSTYLES

Eleven variables (plus related subscales) were identified in this data set for which specific predictions could be made. That is, for each of the variables in this section, one, or more, brainstyle groups could be expected to differ from others in ways that follow from brainstyles theory. The variables were: Self-Monitoring, Tolerance for Ambiguity, Need for Achievement, Sensation Seeking, Creativity, Higher Order Need Strength, Coping Style, Personal Resilience, Social Support, Need for Cognition, and Action Orientation. Descriptions, predictions and results are presented for each variable.

1. Self-Monitoring.

This refers to the extent to which a person is sensitive to situational cues and is attuned to how they come across to other people. High scores reflect greater self-monitoring.

Prediction: Conciliators, because of their sensitivity to and ability to "read" others, should be most concerned about self-monitoring. Knowers, because of their delayed right-brain response, should be least concerned with self-monitoring. Deliberators and Conceptors should fall in between these two groups.

Results: A significant effect was observed for Self-Monitoring. As predicted, Conciliators (M = 11.43) rated themselves highest on this measure. Knowers (M = 9.56), along with Deliberators (M = 9.30), had the lowest scores, and Conceptors fell in between (M = 10.04). These findings tend to support the prediction.

2. Tolerance for Ambiguity.

This refers to the extent to which persons can tolerate ambiguity in their life versus being uncomfortable in ambiguous situations. High scores reflect persons with greater tolerance for ambiguity.

Prediction: Conceptors, because they quickly go back and forth between, and bring together, logic and intuition, should have the greatest tolerance for ambiguity. Knowers and Deliberators, because they focus on logic and rational processes, should have the lowest tolerance for ambiguity. Conciliators should fall between these extremes.

Results: A significant effect was observed for Tolerance for Ambiguity. As predicted, Conceptors (M = 9.74) rated themselves significantly higher on tolerance for ambiguity than did Deliberators (M = 7.13) and Knowers (M = 7.08). Conciliators fell in between (M = 8.49). These findings strongly support the prediction.

3. Need for Achievement.

This refers to the extent to which persons strive toward being successful against defined standards of success. High scores reflect a higher need to achieve.

Prediction: Conceptors, because they naturally envision unique, far-reaching, and dramatic possibilities to big, unusual, and complex problems, should be expected to have significantly higher need for achievement than persons in the other groups. No specific prediction about how the other three brainstyle groups should respond can be made.

Results: A significant effect was observed for Need for Achievement. As predicted, Conceptors (M = 11.81) rated themselves as having a stronger need for achievement than did persons in all other brainstyle groups (Knowers, M = 11.08; Deliberators, M = 9.98; Conciliators, M = 8.66), who did not differ from one another. These findings strongly support the prediction.

4. Sensation Seeking.

This refers to the extent that persons seek out mental and physical stimulation from their environment. There are several different types of sensation seeking:

SSTAS—Dangerous Thrill/Adventure Seeking
SSES —New Experience Seeking
SSDIS—Disinhibition/Behaving Contrary to Social Norms
SSBS —Boredom Susceptibility

All four aspects of Sensation Seeking, in addition to a total score, were analyzed. In all cases, high scores reflect greater need to seek additional stimulation from the environment.

Prediction: Conceptors and Conciliators, because they are more open to the emotional side of experience, should have the greatest need for additional stimulation from their environment. Deliberators and Knowers, because they focus on the left brain, should have less need for added stimulation from their environment.

Results: Significant effects were observed for three of the four types of sensation-seeking dimensions, as well as for the overall score. These findings, overall, provide considerable support for the predictions.

SSTAS (Dangerous Thrill/Adventure Seeking): Conceptors (M = 8.56) rated themselves higher on SSTAS than did persons in any other brainstyle group (Conciliators, M = 7.29; Deliberators, M = 7.11; Knowers, M = 6.72).

SSES (New Experience Seeking): Conceptors (M = 8.85) rated themselves higher on SSES than did persons in any other group (Conciliators, M = 4.75; Deliberators, M = 4.33; Knowers, M = 4.08).

SSDIS (Disinhibition/Behaving Contrary to Social Norms): Conceptors (M = 6.04) and Conciliators (M = 5.81) both rated themselves statistically similar and both rated themselves significantly higher on SSDIS than did persons in the other two brainstyle groups (Knowers, M = 5.56; Deliberators, M = 4.36), who, in turn, did not differ from each other.

SSBS (Boredom Susceptibility): No significant differences were observed for this variable.

Overall Sensation Seeking: Conceptors (M = 24.92) rated themselves higher on the overall sensation seeking variable than did persons in any other brainstyle group (Conciliators, M = 21.34; Knowers, M = 20.04; Deliberators, M = 19.25).

5. Creativity.

This refers to the extent that persons organize inputs in new, novel and more creative ways. High scores reflect greater creativity.

Prediction: Conceptors, because they quickly go back and forth between, and bring together, logic and intuition, should be the most creative of the four brainstyles. Because Conciliators make right-brain, intuitive responses, they should also display a high degree of creativity. Deliberators and Knowers, on the other hand, because of their focus on experience, logic, and rational thinking, should be the least creative of the four groups.

Results: A significant effect was observed for Creativity. As predicted, Conceptors (M = 23.81) rated themselves as most creative. Also, as predicted, Conciliators (M = 20.70) had the second highest score. But, while higher, they did not see themselves as significantly more creative than Knowers (M = 18.65) or Deliberators (M = 17.98). These results, then, only partially support the prediction.

6. Higher Order Need Strength.

This refers to the extent that persons have active growth needs, as reflected by the higher levels of Maslow's need hierarchy. High scores reflect more active growth needs.

Prediction: Conceptors, because they a) can envision future possibilities, both personal and professional, and b) understand that they can have dramatic, sweeping impact where others cannot do so, should be expected to have significantly greater higher order need strength than persons in the other groups. No specific prediction about how the other three brainstyle groups should respond can be made.

Results: A significant effect was observed for Higher Order Need Strength. As predicted, Conceptors (M = 39.92) rated themselves as having the strongest higher order need strength. Persons in the other three brainstyle groups (Deliberators, M = 37.48; Conciliators, M = 34.95; Knowers, M = 34.71) did not differ from one another. These findings strongly support the prediction.

7. Coping Style.

This refers to *how* persons cope with life's stressors. It has four component factors:

COPEORG —Cope by organizing and planning better
COPESOC —Cope by interacting with others for social support
COPESELF —Cope by using more self-focusing activities
COPEPERS—Cope by lowering one's standards, thus creating fewer stressors
     for which coping is necessary

Prediction: Specific predictions can be made for three of the coping styles. Deliberators, because they bring order to things, would be more likely to employ coping styles that reflected organization and planning (Copeorg). Conciliators, because they deal with the emotional side of life and because they are comfortable being with others, would be more likely to employ a coping style that reflected social support (Copesoc). Both Conceptors and Conciliators, because they have more immediate access to their right brain, will be more introspective and, therefore, engage in more self-focusing activities (Copeself). No prediction can be made regarding use of lowering standards (Copepers) as a coping mechanism.

Results: Significant results were observed on all Coping Styles for which significant findings were predicted (Copeorg, Copesoc, and Copeself). These findings provide strong support for the prediction.

COPEORG (Cope by organizing and planning better): As predicted, Deliberators (M = 29.41) rated themselves statistically higher on Copeorg than did Conciliators (M = 26.81), Conceptors (M = 26.27), and Knowers (M = 25.92), who, in turn, did not differ from one another.

COPESOC (Cope by interacting with others for social support): As predicted, Conciliators (M = 36.24) rated themselves having a significantly higher Copesoc than did persons in any other brainstyle group (Conceptors, M = 32.31; Deliberators, M = 32.25; Knowers, M = 31.04), who, in turn, did not differ from one another.

COPESELF (Cope by using more self-focusing activities): As predicted, the data indicated that Conceptors (M = 36.15) and Conciliators (M = 35.82) both rated themselves statistically similar and both rated themselves significantly higher on Copeself than did Deliberators (M = 33.51) and Knowers (M = 32.04), who, in turn, were not different from one another.

COPEPERS (Cope by lowering one's standards): A significant difference was neither predicted nor observed for this variable.

8. Personal Resilience.

This refers to the degree to which persons can rebound from, bring new energy to, and continue to cope with life's stressors. The Personal Resilience Questionnaire is comprised of seven separate scales:

POSITIVE: THE WORLD—Sees life as challenging and filled with opportunity

POSITIVE: YOURSELF —Sees oneself as a capable and effective person

FLEXIBLE: SOCIAL —Draws on resources from outside of oneself

FLEXIBLE: THOUGHTS —Is pliable when responding to uncertainty

FOCUSED —Has a clear understanding of what is to be achieved

ORGANIZED —Applies structure to help manage ambiguity

PROACTIVE —Pushes for change instead of evading it

All subscales in this battery are in the developmental stage, and in all cases, high scores reflect the more positive end of each continuum.

Prediction: Specific predictions can be made for each of the Resilience subscales: a) Conciliators would have the most positive outlook on life (Positive: The World) and draw most on their social network (Flexible: Social); b) Knowers would have the highest belief in their capabilities (Positive: Yourself); c) Deliberators should have the strongest desire for details and structure (Organized) and the greatest clarity regarding what needs to be achieved (Focused); and d) Conceptors would have the greatest flexibility in responding to ambiguity (Flexible: Thoughts) and the strongest need to push for change (Proactive).

Results: Significant results were observed on four of the seven Personal Resilience factors. In this instance, Flexible: Thoughts; Flexible: Social; Organized; and Proactive all were found to be significant, and all means fell in the predicted pattern. Thus, results involving resilience were only partially supported. Specific results are reported below.

Positive: The World (Positive outlook on life): Results were nonsignificant, meaning that all brainstyle groups responded similarly.

Positive: Yourself (Belief in one's capability as a person): Results were nonsignificant, meaning that all brainstyle groups responded similarly.

Flexible: Social (Draws on one's social network): As predicted, Conciliators (M = 70.10) rated themselves as having a significantly higher degree of social interconnectedness than did persons in any other brainstyle group (Conceptors, M = 61.93; Deliberators, M = 61.57; Knowers, M = 57.42), who did not differ from one another.

Flexible: Thoughts (Flexible when responding to uncertainty): As predicted, Conceptors (M = 62.15) rated themselves as having a stronger tolerance for ambiguity than did persons in any other brainstyle group (Conciliators, M = 53.90; Deliberators, M = 53.28; Knowers, M = 51.92), who, in turn, did not differ from one another.

Focused (A clear understanding of what is to be achieved): Results were nonsignificant, meaning that all brainstyle groups responded similarly.

Organized (Applies structure to help manage ambiguity): As predicted, Deliberators (M = 65.70) rated themselves as having significantly more concern for organization and detail than did persons in any other brainstyle group (Conciliators, M = 58.78; Knowers, M = 56.24; Conceptors, M = 56.22), who did not differ from one another.

Proactive (Pushes for change): As predicted, Conceptors (M =

65.23) rated themselves as having the strongest desire to push for change. Conciliators (M = 58.40) and Deliberators (M = 57.37) were not statistically different from each other, but all three of these brainstyle groups rated themselves as being more change-oriented than Knowers (M = 50.40).

9. Social Support.

This refers to the extent that persons have a need to receive social support from others. High scores reflect a greater expressed need for social support.

Prediction: Conciliators, because of their sensitivity to others and lack of left-brain dominance in analyzing and deciding, should be most concerned about social support.

Results: As predicted, Conciliators (M = 67.92) rated themselves as needing significantly more social support than did either Knowers (M = 63.42) or Deliberators (M = 63.35). Deliberators, Knowers, and Conceptors (M = 64.15) did not differ significantly from one another. These findings support the prediction.

10. Need for Cognition.

This refers to the extent to which persons have a need to think about things a great deal. High scores reflect a greater need to consider/think things through.

Prediction: Conceptors and Deliberators would be expected to have the greatest need to cognitively consider/think about things, while Conciliators and Knowers would have the least expressed need in this area.

Results: As predicted, Conceptors (M = 171.32) and Deliberators (M = 162.00) both rated themselves statistically similar and both rated themselves as having a significantly higher need to think things through than did Knowers (M = 149.33) and Conciliators (M = 149.24), who, in turn, were not different from each other. These findings support the prediction.

11. Action Orientation.

This refers to the extent to which persons prefer to act versus think, plan, and consider a particular course of action. High scores would reflect persons who prefer taking action to delaying action for more information and consideration.

Prediction: Knowers, because of the quickness of their thinking, were expected to be the most action-oriented group, and Deliberators, because of their need to look inward before making decisions (particularly where no existing model existed), were expected to be the least action-oriented group. Conceptors and Conciliators were expected to fall between these extremes.

Results: No significant differences, across brainstyle groups, were observed.

II. VARIABLES FOR WHICH NO PREDICTIONS WERE MADE

The rest of the variables included in the test battery were grouped into three general classes for purposes of presentation. For each of these variables, no specific predictions regarding differences across brainstyle groups were made.

Each of these classes of variables is described below. Only significant results are reported.

1. Self-Focus Class of Variables.

Persons who have a strong self-focus spend time thinking about themselves and are concerned with what others think about them.

The broad category of self-focus was reflected in six specific variables in this data set:

SELF-PREOCCUPATION—the extent to which persons spend a great deal of time thinking about and being preoccupied by thoughts of themselves.

SELF-DECEPTION—the extent to which persons deceive themselves about the impression others have about them.

IMPRESSION MANAGEMENT—the extent to which persons actively work to make a positive impression on others.

SOCIAL DESIRABILITY—the extent to which persons respond in ways thought to make them look positive, normal, and natural to others.

VALUE FOR SELF-CONTROL—the extent to which persons express a positive value for self-control in one's affairs.

INTERNAL/EXTERNAL LOCUS OF CONTROL—the extent to which persons believe that they are causal agents in their lives versus believe that their fate is in the hands of others or the result of happenstance.

Results: Results indicated no differences between brainstyle groups on four of the six Self-Focus variables. These variables were Self-

Preoccupation, Self-Deception, Social Desirability, and Internal/External Locus of Control. The other two variables differed significantly across brainstyle groups, as described below.

VALUE FOR SELF-CONTROL

Results: Although no specific prediction was made, a significant effect was observed. In this instance, Deliberators (M = 13.03) rated themselves higher on valuing self-control than did either Conciliators (M = 12.15) or Conceptors (M = 12.04). Conceptors, Conciliators, and Knowers (M = 12.28) did not differ significantly from one another.

IMPRESSION MANAGEMENT.

Results: Although no specific prediction was made, a significant result was observed. In this instance, Deliberators (M = 5.39) rated themselves significantly higher on impression management than did persons in the other three groups, who, in turn, did not differ significantly from one another (Conceptors, M = 4.85; Conciliators, M = 3.86; Knowers, M = 3.44).

2. Positive Self-Regard Class of Variables.

Positive Self-Regard refers to a class of variables that express a person's self-evaluation of their personal worth—in this instance, all specific variables reflected self-evaluations of a more generalized nature.

This broad category includes three specific variables in this data set:

EXPECTANCY OF SUCCESS—a generalized belief that one will be successful in life.

SELF-EFFICACY—a generalized belief that one can be successful in task settings.

SELF-ESTEEM—a self-appraisal of one's worth as a person.

Results: Results indicated no differences among brainstyle groups on two of the three Positive Self-Regard variables. These variables were Self-Efficacy and Self-Esteem. The third variable, Expectancy of Success, differed significantly across brainstyle groups, as described below.

EXPECTANCY OF SUCCESS

Results: Conciliators (M = 122.53) rated themselves as having a significantly higher expectancy for being successful in life than did persons in any other brainstyle group (Conceptors, M = 119.04; Deliberators, M = 117.98; Knowers, M = 112.33), who, in turn, did not differ from one another.

3. Generalized Affect Class of Variables.

Generalized Affect refers to a class of variables that reflect the affective, or emotional, experience or appraisal of persons. However, persons who tend to experience emotional reactions more strongly are not necessarily more positive or negative in their reactions; they are simply more extreme in their emotional reactions. The broad category includes five specific affective variables, as described below:

Affective Tone—the extent to which people tend to feel generally positive or negative in their affective makeup. Two separate measures of affective tone were used.

LIFE SATISFACTION—satisfaction with one's life and life circumstances.

ATTRIBUTIONAL STYLE: HOPEFUL—inferences about the causes of positive life events.

ATTRIBUTIONAL STYLE: HOPELESS—inferences about the causes of negative life events.

ALIENATION—dissociative reaction that is marked by negative emotional undertones.

Results. In no instance was a significant difference across brainstyle groups observed.

DISCUSSION SECTION

Results from this study provide strong evidence regarding the reliability and validity of the new brainstyles instrument. Each will be discussed in turn.

Reliability

In the present sample, 87 percent of the respondents were classified into a single brainstyle category. While ideally 100 percent of all respondents should obtain a unique category placement, the fact that nearly nine out of ten did so is regarded as encouraging for two related reasons.

First, the conceptual model underlying brainstyles suggests that one can only expect to reliably observe the effects due to brainstyles when faced with a Time Zero event. Time Zero refers to the first occurrence of a problem that requires a decision or an action. Time Zero must reflect persons' "hardwiring," because they cannot draw from their memories or from their past experiences. At Time Zero, then, one's brainstyle is the only source from which one can take in, process, and express information. Few adults will experience enough recent Time Zero events to help unambiguously reveal their brainstyle. Rather, they will tend to rely on how they behave each and every day when attempting to answer survey questions. Importantly, everyday behavior is influenced by a host of factors, to include persons' unique experiences and learning from throughout their lives. This, then, is the second issue.

Over time, how people respond to recurrences of the same or similar circumstances can reflect more than one's brainstyle—it can also reflect prior learning, practice, and other factors that reflect experience. Persons who work in a setting that regularly rewards deliberate, thoughtful, and careful planning, for example, may be influenced to try to behave in those ways, despite brainstyles that make such acts unnatural and uncomfortable. Persons in such situations, however, may come to believe that these learned, rewarded behaviors are natural, because that is how they try to act. But those same persons cannot be fully natural or comfortable acting in ways that are inconsistent with their brainstyle. This "confusion" between what is natural and comfortable versus what is "learned" (i.e., taught, expected, and rewarded) clearly can cause persons some degree of confusion when attempting to choose between statements describing different brainstyles. In these circumstances, one would expect some degree of inconsistency in their pattern of responses. Psychometrically, this would reflect "noise" that masks the underlying "signal," and, as a result, lower scale reliability. From this perspective, then, the present results are very encouraging because so many persons were able to screen out so much noise and attend to the underlying signal—as reflected by the ability of the instrument to classify nearly nine in ten persons into a single brainstyle category.

This conclusion is strengthened by counting the number of times persons in each brainstyle group chose the alternative in each paired-comparison statement that reflected their own brainstyle. These results indicated that persons in each brainstyle group "saw themselves" in about seven of the nine opportunities they were given to pick a statement describing their own brainstyle compared to one of the other three brainstyles. In particular, Conciliators chose Conciliator alternatives 7.10 times, Deliberators chose Deliberator alternatives 6.84 times, Conceptors chose Conceptor alternatives 6.70 times, and Knowers chose Knower alternatives 6.44 times.

Taken together, these data provide strong support for the internal consistency reliability of the new measure of brainstyles. Its use suggests that people can be classified into a single category because they can see themselves consistently in the nine paired-comparison items.

Construct Validity

It is one thing to find the inventory capable of putting persons into a single category. It is quite another to conclude that these persons were placed in the "proper" category. That is the issue of construct validity. As described above, one can generate support for the construct validity of a measure to the extent that persons respond in other ways that are consistent with underlying theory. That is, if persons designated as Deliberators, Knowers, Conceptors, and Conciliators are properly categorized, then we should find those persons to a) differ in their reactions to other variables in ways that b) reflect expectations derived from the theory of brainstyles.

In this study, a number of predictions were made regarding how persons in different brainstyles should respond on a series of measures of other psychological constructs. In total, 23 separate predictions (involving 11 different psychological constructs) were made. Results from this investigation indicated significant, supportive findings for 18 of those 23 predictions! (See the table on the next page for a summary of findings.) Given the large number of rather diverse psychological measures used in this study, these results provide a level of support seldom found in the measurement literature. Such support is not only rare in measurement literature, but rare as well in support of any theory in psychology.

The picture that emerges about each brainstyle, based on these empirical findings, was:

1. Conceptors were most likely to be creative, tolerate ambiguity, have stronger higher-order needs, in general, and need for achievement and need to think, in particular, to seek out mental stimulation, cope by using self-focusing activities, and push for change compared to persons

in the other three brainstyle categories. Appropriately, Conceptors described themselves as having low scores on coping through organization or by interacting with others. They said that they disliked details and structure, and expressed disinterest in social support from others.

2. Conciliators were most likely to engage in self-focusing activities and be sensitive to how others viewed them, and said they draw on others, in general, and looked to their social network, in particular, as a coping style.

3. Deliberators were most likely to value structure and organization to manage ambiguity, use coping mechanisms that reflected organizing and planning, and be thoughtful. Appropriately, Deliberators rated themselves low on variables such as tolerance for ambiguity, desire for more stimulation from their environment, and creativity.

4. While no statistical means were significantly higher for Knowers when compared to the means of the other three groups' scores, Knowers were predicted and found to have low scores on factors such as self-monitoring, need for cognition, social support, tolerance for ambiguity, sensation seeking, and coping by social support.

Summary of Predicted Results

Variable	Number of Predictions	Significant in the Predicted Direction
Self-Monitoring	1	1
Tolerance for Ambiguity	1	1
Need for Achievement	1	1
Sensation Seeking (4 types/ overall)	5	4
Creativity	1	1
Higher Order Need Strength	1	1
Coping Style (four types)	3	3
Personal Resilience (seven types)	7	4
Social Support	1	1
Need for Cognition	1	1
Action Orientation	1	0
TOTALS	23	18

Additional Findings

Three additional classes of variables (Self-Focus, Positive Self-Regard, and Generalized Affect) were also examined for their relationships to brainstyles. Conceptually, no specific predictions regarding the relationship between these variables and brainstyles could be made. Their examination, therefore, was for exploratory purposes. It should be underscored that failure to find significant associations with brainstyles for these variables does not speak to the validity of the instrument since no predictions were made. These findings, however, help extend, empirically, the meaning of brainstyles by suggesting additional ways the brainstyle groups do, and do not, differ.

In this instance, results indicated few significant associations with brainstyles. In total, only three of the 14 statistical tests were found to be significant. These results indicated that Deliberators had the highest desire for self-control and the strongest need to make a positive impression on others. Conciliators, on the other hand, expressed the highest belief that they would be successful in life.

Construct Validity: Conclusion

The present findings strongly support the construct validity of the new measure of brainstyles. The fact that so many predictions derived from brainstyles theory were supported helps to underscore that this measure is capable of appropriately placing persons into their proper brainstyle category. Given the abstractness of the brainstyle construct, along with the difficulty that respondents might have in separating "natural" from learned ways of responding, one can only conclude that the evidence in support of this new measure is impressive. It should be noted that these findings not only support the construct validity of the new measure, but, because they so closely parallel the predictions regarding the meaning of each brainstyle, they support the theory underlying brainstyles as well. Together, they suggest that brainstyles is a meaningful way to both conceptualize differences among people and to predict their behavior and reactions, and that *The Brainstyle Inventory* (Peters & Miller, 1992)* examined in this

* Copies and information regarding the use of *The Brainstyle Inventory* can be obtained by contacting Marlane Miller at BrainStyles, Inc., 15851 Dallas Parkway, LB 140, Dallas, Texas 75248/1-800-374-9878 (phone/fax).

research is a meaningful way to categorize people into their appropriate brainstyle categories.

References

Cherry, D., & Miller, M. (1992). *BrainStyles: Be who you really are.* Dallas: BrainStyles, Inc.

Gazzaniga, M.S. (1992). *Nature's mind: The biological roots of thinking, emotions, sexuality, language and intelligence.* New York: Basic Books.

Ornstein, R. (1986). *Multimind.* New York: Doubleday.

References to Measures Used in This Study

1. BrainStyles
Peters, L.H., & Miller, M. (1992). *The BrainStyle Inventory (Version 1.1).* Dallas: BrainStyles, Inc.

2. Self-Monitoring
Gangestad, S., & Snyder, M. (1985). "To carve nature at its joints": On the existence of discrete classes in personality. *Psychological Review, 92(3),* 317–49.

3. Tolerance for Ambiguity
MacDonald, A.P., Jr. (1970). Revised scale for ambiguity tolerance: Reliability and validity. *Psychological Reports, 26,* 791–98.

4. Need for Achievement
Fineman, S. (1975). The Work Preference Questionnaire: A measure of managerial need for achievement. *Journal of Occupational Psychology, 48,* 11–32.

5. Sensation Seeking
Zuckerman, M., Kolin, E.A., Price, L., & Zoob, I. (1964). Development of a sensation-seeking scale. *Journal of Consulting Psychology, 28(6),* 477–82.

6. Creativity
Holland, J.L., & Baird, L.L. (1968). The preconscious activity scale: The development and validation of an originality measure. *The Journal of Creative Behavior, 2(3),* 217–25.

7. Higher Order Need Strength
Hackman, J.R., & Oldham, G.R. (1975). Development of the Job Diagnostic Survey. *Journal of Applied Psychology, 60,* 159–70.

8. Coping Style
Leader, D.S. (1987). The well-being of working family women: Demands, rewards, social support and coping with interrole stress. Unpublished Doctoral Dissertation, University of Tennessee, Knoxville, TN.

9. Personal Resilience

ODR. (1993). Personal Resilience Questionnaire. Atlanta: ODR, Inc.

10. Social Support

Pollack, L., & Harris, R. (1983). Measurement of social support. *Psychological Reports, 53,* 466.

11. Need for Cognition

Petty, J.T. (1982). The need for cognition. *Journal of Personality and Social Psychology, 42,* 116–31.

12. Action Orientation

Kuhl, J. (1985). Self-regulatory processes and action versus state orientation. In J. Kuhl & J. Beckmann (Eds.), *Action control from cognition to behavior* (pp. 105–28), New York: Springer-Verlag.

13. Self-Preoccupation

Fenigstein, A., Scheier, M.F., & Buss, A.H. (1975). Public and private self-consciousness: Assessment and theory. *Journal of Consulting and Clinical Psychology, 43(5),* 924–31.

14. Self-Deception

Paulhus, D.L. (1988). *Assessing self-deception and impression management in self-reports: The Balanced Inventory of Desirable Responding.* (Manual available from the author, Department of Psychology, University of British Columbia, Vancouver, B.C., Canada V6T 1Y7.)

15. Impression Management

Paulhus, D.L. (1988). *Assessing self-deception and impression management in self-reports: The Balanced Inventory of Desirable Responding.* (Manual available from the author, Department of Psychology, University of British Columbia, Vancouver, B.C., Canada V6T 1Y7.)

16. Social Desirability

Crowne, D.P., & Marlowe, D. (1960). A new scale of social desirability independent of psychopathology. *Journal of Consulting Psychology, 24,* 349–54.

17. Value for Self-Control

Scott, W.A. (1965). *Values and Organizations: A study of fraternities and sororities.* Chicago: Rand McNally.

18. Internal-External Locus of Control

Nowicki, S., & Duke, M.P. (1983). The Nowicki-Strickland life span locus of control scales: Construct validation. In H.M. Lefcourt (Ed.), *Research with the locus of control construct.* New York: Academic Press, *2,* 9–43.

19. Expectancy of Success
Fibel, B., & Hale, W.D. (1978). The generalized expectancy for success scale—A new measure. *Journal of Consulting and Clinical Psychology, 46(5),* 924–31.

20. Self-Efficacy
Paulhus, D. (1983). Sphere-specific measures of perceived control. *Journal of Personality and Social Psychology, 44,* 1253–65.

21. Self-Esteem
Rosenberg, M. (1965). *Society and the adolescent self-image.* Princeton: Princeton University Press.

22. Affective Tone. There were two separate measures of affective tone.
Watson, D., Clark, L.A., & Tellegen, A. (1988). Development and validation of brief measures of positive and negative affect: The PANAS scales. *Journal of Personality and Social Psychology, 54(6),* 1063–70.

Kammann, R., & Flertt, R. (1983). Affectometer 2: A scale to measure current level of general happiness. *Australian Journal of Psychology, 35,* 259–65.

23. Life Satisfaction
Neugarten, B., Havighurst, R.J., & Tobin, S. (1961). The measurement of life satisfaction. *Journal of Gerontology, 16,* 134–43.

24. Attributional Style: Hopeful
Peterson, C., Semmel, A., von Baeyer, C., Abramson, L.Y., Metalsky, G.L., & Seligman, M.E.P. (1982). The Attributional Style Questionnaire. *Cognitive Therapy and Research, 6,* 287–300.

25. Attributional Style: Hopeless
Peterson, C., Semmel, A., von Baeyer, C., Abramson, L.Y., Metalsky, G.L., & Seligman, M.E.P. (1982). The Attributional Style Questionnaire. *Cognitive Therapy and Research, 6,* 287–300.

26. Alienation
Jessor, R., & Jessor, S. (1977). *Problem behavior and psychosocial development.* New York: Academic Press.

Appendix D:
BrainStyles—
Myers-Briggs Relationships
Research Report
January 1995

Prepared by Lawrence H. Peters

OVERVIEW

This report summarizes results of an analysis of how BrainStyle and MBTI category scores relate to each other. Data for both the Brain-Styles and MBTI inventories were collected from three samples of people. Two samples were drawn from among MBA students at Texas Christian University (TCU), and the third was a sample of graduate students from the University of North Texas (UNT). In total, data were available from 133 respondents. However, due to missing data and/or tied category scores, the effective sample was 118 persons.

One TCU respondent group took Version 1.0 of the BrainStyle Inventory; the other TCU group took Version 1.3. The UNT sample took Version 1.3. Standard scoring procedures were used to identify the single BrainStyle category that was most frequently endorsed. Results indicated that the combined sample had 44 Deliberators, 10 Knowers, 15 Conceptors, and 49 Conciliators.

With regard to the MBTI, data were available to group respondents from all three samples into meaningful categories on only two MBTI dimensions: 1) Sensing (S) versus Intuiting (N) and 2) Thinking (T) versus Feeling (F). These data were used to place respondents into one of four possible MBTI category prototypes that combine these two dimensions: ST, SF, NT, and NF. Results indicated that the combined sample had 62 STs, 17 SFs, 23 NTs, and 16 NFs.

Brief descriptions of each dimension and each prototype are provided below.

MBTI DIMENSIONS

The complete MBTI categorizes respondents along four dimensions:

1. Extroversion-Introversion
2. Perceiving versus Judging
3. Sensing versus Intuiting
4. Thinking versus Feeling

However, because data were unavailable for all four of these dimensions for some respondents, data from only two of the MBTI dimensions were used. Thus, only the Sensing-Intuiting and Thinking-Feeling dimensions, and the four MBTI prototypes created by these dimensions, were considered. Had all four MBTI dimensions been available and considered simultaneously, the sample size within each of the resulting 16 cells would be too small to meaningfully analyze. Each dimension, and then each of the resultant four MBTI prototype combinations, is briefly described below.

SENSING TYPE (S): A person who has a high Sensing score is one who likes established routines and established ways of doing things, likes details, data, and facts, wants to work through problems step by step, tends to be good at work that requires precision, and seldom makes errors of fact.

INTUITING TYPE (N): A person who has a high Intuiting score is one who likes new tasks and problems, likes learning new skills more than using them, works in bursts of energy powered by enthusiasm, frequently jumps to conclusions before the facts are all available, becomes impatient with routine, and, as a result, doesn't take time for precision and tends to make errors of fact.

THINKING TYPE (T): A person who has a high Thinking score is one who likes analysis and putting things in order, is relatively unemotional, who makes decisions somewhat impersonally and, as a result, may hurt others' feelings without knowing it, who needs to be treated fairly, can easily reprimand others when necessary and, as a result, may seem hardhearted.

FEELING TYPE (F): A person who has a high Feeling score is one who tends to be aware of other people's feelings and enjoys pleasing them, who likes harmony, who lets decisions be influenced by feelings and other people's likes and dislikes, who needs occasional praise, who doesn't like telling unpleasant things to others, and who tends to relate well to most people.

MBTI STYLES

When using the MBTI, one is supposed to consider several dimensions together. These combinations are referred to as prototypes, or Myers-Briggs styles. In this instance, dimension scores were combined to form four MBTI styles: ST, SF, NT, and NF. Each is briefly described below.

ST: An ST is a person who wants the organization to be run in an orderly manner. STs are decisive persons who make decisions that reflect the facts. STs admire common sense and tend to look at the logical consequences of decisions before making them. She/he can be realistic about what can be accomplished and works steadily and with great effort to accomplish goals. STs can absorb, remember, manipulate, and manage a great deal of detail, are steady and hard workers, and they know, respect, and implement the rules in the work setting. STs will be on time and on schedule, are best when planning work and following through on those plans. STs like to get things "clear," and others know where they stand on issues. This person will establish a formal, impersonal style of relating to others.

SF: An SF is a pragmatist. He/she can deal with concrete problems in a methodical fashion, first analyzing, then identifying where the problems are, and finally determining solutions that solve those problems. They tend to live in the immediate moment, view philosophy statements as academic exercises with little relevance, and would rather deal with today's problems rather than focus on past commitments. They have acute powers of observation, and as a result seem to know what's going on in their organization. These people are very matter-of-fact about reality and deal with what is; not what was or what might yet be. As a result, they work well within "the system" in which they find themselves, adapt easily to new situations, and often welcome change.

NT: An NT is a person who asks why events occur, who sees the big picture and the connections between seemingly unrelated things, and who dreams big dreams. While NTs love to define the possibilities, they are more than willing to allow others to develop the detail and do the "legwork" to implement their ideas. They tend to expect a great deal of competence from others, and they often react impersonally, favoring ideas over sentiments. As a result, NTs may encounter difficulties in interpersonal transactions.

NF: An NF is an intuitive person who can communicate caring and enthusiasm. NFs hunger for contact with others. They are sociable, seek good interpersonal relationships with colleagues, are empathetic, and often try to "rescue" others who have problems. NFs seem to focus on the strengths of others intuitively. They excel in working with and through others. They are happy working in unstructured settings and are usually "in touch" with the climate of the organization. Because they are very sensitive to others' feelings, they want to please them and often need others' approval. As a result, they sometimes make decisions on the basis of these considerations rather than on the basis of "hard criteria." This vulnerability to the approval of others can get the NF in trouble when hard decisions need to be made.

RESULTS AND DISCUSSION

A cross-classification table was constructed by identifying the Myers-Briggs style associated with each brainstyle for each person in the sample. That table appears below. Results from a Chi-square goodness-of-fit test indicated a significant association between BrainStyles and MBTI styles ($p<.001$). This means that the relationship between these instruments is beyond that which can be expected by chance alone. An examination of the rows and columns of this table clarify the nature of the relationship between MBTI styles and BrainStyles.

Myers-Briggs and **BrainStyles**

BrainStyle:	Deliberator ↓	Knower ↓	Conceptor ↓	Conciliator ↓	Row Total
Myers-Briggs ST→	27	7	5	23	62
SF→	11	1	0	5	17
NT→	5	1	8	9	23
NF→	1	1	2	12	16
Column Total	44	10	15	49	118

Examination of this table clarifies how BrainStyles and MBTI categories are related. Results will be examined in detail below, by discussing how respondents with different MBTI styles fall into the four Brain-Style categories.

The data clearly suggest a strong correspondence between Brain-Styles and MBTI styles, in ways that are predictable from theory. For example, one would expect that Deliberators would describe themselves, in general, in terms of a left-brain MBTI style, meaning that they would have a high score on the Sensation dimension. Deliberators should also see themselves more in terms of the Thinking than the Feeling dimension, thus suggesting that the most common MBTI style among Deliberators would be an ST. The data strongly support this prediction (i.e., 27 of the Deliberators are STs and 11 are SFs). Thus, within the sample of 44 Deliberators, over 60 percent of them are STs and approximately 86 percent of them characterized themselves as either an ST or SF.

The same should be true for the 10 Knowers in this sample. One would expect Knowers to describe themselves as left-brain persons as well, and again do, with more Knowers choosing the ST over the SF category. Here, 70 percent of the Knower sample chose the ST style and 80 percent of them chose a left-brain MBTI category. Taken together, the MBTI and BrainStyles show strong convergence on the left-brain side and suggest that either the MBTI or BrainStyles theories could be used somewhat interchangeably.

Conceptors would be expected to rely on both left- and right-brain functions, but in more global and intuitive ways. As a result, one would expect a higher degree of correspondence between Conceptors and persons who have high scores on the Intuition dimension of the MBTI. Further, of the two Intuition-related styles, NT is the category that seems to best correspond conceptually with Conceptors. The data bear out these expectations. In this sample, 10 of the 15 Conceptors had high Intuition MBTI scores, and eight of these 10 persons were NTs. Again, these findings support the correspondence between two fundamentally different ways of characterizing people.

This conclusion does not hold, however, for the Conciliator Brain-Style/MBTI style categories. It is among the Conciliators that correspondence between these two theories of human behavior diverge. Theoretically, one would expect Conciliators to describe themselves in terms of both the Intuition and Feeling dimensions of the MBTI, thus choosing a right-brain MBTI style, especially an NF style. However, less than 30 percent of the Conciliators chose an MBTI style with a high Feeling dimension score, and only 43 percent chose an MBTI style with a high Intuition score. These results were unexpected. Further, the single highest category chosen by Conciliators was not NF (chosen by 12 of the 49 Conciliators), but ST (chosen by 23 of the 49 Conciliators)! Finally, approximately 65 percent of the Conciliators chose a Thinking, rather than a Feeling, MBTI style.

Taken together, these later data do not fully conform to theoretical expectations. They do, however, point to where MBTI theory and BrainStyle theory are not fully redundant. Since these two theories are not expected to be redundant, this degree of divergence should not be regarded as either unexpected or problematic. It suggests that both theories may have something useful to offer to persons who are attempting to identify their unique strengths and make judgments about how to respond to that information.

Of particular note, the MBTI seems to lump together both Deliberators and Knowers into the ST category. Given that many of the STs were also found to be Conciliators, these results suggest that the MBTI is not capable of making differential explanations about people who are clearly different in fundamental ways according to BrainStyles theory. Likewise, BrainStyles theory makes a single description of people with high Conciliator scores that would require different, and contradictory, conclusions based on MBTI theory. While we have no way of currently explaining the nonconforming results, both theories do have considerable support for their separate predictions and, until competing hypotheses can be devised and tested, there is no reason to discount either theory.

The upside of these results is that many people who differ in predictable ways according to one theory correspond to those expectations from another theory. These convergent findings lend considerable credibility to the validity of both theories.

Finally, the divergence suggests that further research might help explain why Conciliators might have such varying MBTI scores. For example, other MBTI dimensions, especially the P-J dimension, might help explain the spread of MBTI scores among Conciliators. Unfortunately, such data are not available in this data set, and thus such conjectures are not testable at this time.

Myers-Briggs and **BrainStyles**

	Deliberator	Knower	Conceptor	Conciliator	*Row Total*
ST (# participants)	(27)	(7)	(5)	(23)	(62)
Myers-Briggs %	*43.5*	*11.3*	*8.1*	*37.1*	*52.5*
BrainStyle %	**61.4**	**70.0**	**33.3**	**46.9**	
SF (# participants)	(11)	(1)		(5)	(17)
Myers-Briggs %	*64.7*	*5.9*		*29.4*	*14.4*
BrainStyle %	**25.0**	**10.0**		**10.2**	
NT (# participants)	(5)	(1)	(8)	(9)	(23)
Myers-Briggs %	*21.7*	*4.3*	*34.8*	*39.1*	*19.5*
BrainStyle %	**11.4**	**10.0**	**53.3**	**18.4**	
NF (# participants)	(1)	(1)	(2)	(12)	(16)
Myers-Briggs %	*6.3*	*6.3*	*12.5*	*75.0*	*13.6*
BrainStyle %	**2.3**	**10.0**	**13.3**	**24.5**	
Column Total	**(44)**	**(10)**	**(15)**	**(49)**	**118**
	37.3	**8.5**	**12.7**	**41.5**	**100.0**

Number of missing observations: 15

Appendix E: Additional Worksheets

HOW TO DEAL WITH PEOPLE I DON'T LIKE:

STEP ONE: Identify behaviors I *don't* like (my criticisms)

_____

_____

_____

STEP TWO: Identify who I am comparing them to (my preferences)

_____

_____

_____

*What brainstyle do I prefer?*_____

STEP THREE: Determine the other's BrainStyle.
Consider the behaviors you don't like as clues to underlying strengths. Look for a pattern. Especially look for responses in new situations that give a clue to a main strength in decision-making.

Their Strengths:	Their Non–Strengths:
1._____	1._____
2._____	2._____
3._____	3._____

STEP FOUR: Determine the cause of my discomfort
Strengths?   *Non-Strengths?*   *Their Values, Solutions?*

STEP FIVE: Take action (my strategy)

1._____

2._____

3._____

A BRAINSTYLES STRENGTHS CONTRACT

| WORK |

We need to collaborate on:_____
_____

| ME |

My brainstyle strengths to apply here are:_____
_____

| YOU |

Your brainstyle strengths to apply here are:_____
_____

| GOALS |

To deliver excellence, we both agree to:
1._____
2._____
3._____

| PLAN |

Our brainstyles strengths + Our timing needs + Specific agreements

_____
_____
_____
_____

Other brainstyle strengths we need:

_____
_____

Notes

Chapter One: Change Your Life Without Changing Yourself
1. Richard Restak, *The Brain Has a Mind of Its Own* (Harmony Books, 1991).
2. Mihaly Csikszentmihalyi, *Flow: The Psychology of Optimal Experience* (Harper & Row, 1990), p. 49.

Chapter Two: Why You Don't Have to Change
1. Michael Rutter and Marjorie Rutter, *Developing Minds* (Basic Books, 1993), particularly Chapter Two, "Why Are People So Different from One Another?"
2. The Rutters estimate 30 to 60 percent, David Lykken documents 70 to 80 percent. David T. Lykken, University of Minnesota, Presidential Address to the Society of Psychophysiological Research, 1981, "Research with Twins: The Concept of Emergenesis," p. 371.
3. Emmy E. Werner, "High Risk Children in Young Adulthood: A Longitudinal Study from Birth to 32 Years," *American Journal of Orthopsychiatry*, 59 (1), January 1989.
4. Rutter and Rutter, *Developing Minds*, pp. 24–26.
5. R. Plomin, *Development, Genetics and Psychology* (Hillsdale, N.J.: Erlbaum, 1986), as cited in ibid.
6. See the work of Oliver Sacks, especially the article "Prodigies" in *The New Yorker*, January 9, 1995.
7. "The Infinite Voyage: Fires of the Mind," television documentary produced by QED Communications, Pittsburgh, PA, 1991.
8. In 1981, Lykken reported a "surprisingly strong (70–80%) influence of genetic variation on abilities measured by I.Q. *speed* of processing information, aptitudes (skills), psychophysiological characteristics like brain activity, personality traits and even dimensions of attitude and interest (including hobbies, having traditional values, being outgoing, liking to lead others, and skin response, among others)."
9. Michael Gazzaniga, *Nature's Mind* (Basic Books, 1992), p. 110.
10. Robert Plomin and Judy Dunn, in *Health*, a magazine section of *People*, October 1991.
11. Robert Plomin and Judy Dunn, *Separate Lives: Why Siblings Are So Different* (Basic Books, 1990), p. 166.

12. Ibid., p. 167.

13. Russell Mitchell, "Seeing the World Through a Different Lens," *Business Week,* December 19, 1994, p. 44.

14. Gene Bylinsky, "The Inside Story of the Brain," *Fortune,* December 3, 1990, pp. 87–100.

15. V. Vernon Woolf, *Holodynamics: How to Develop and Manage Your Personal Power* (Harbinger House, 1990), pp. 23–24: "All your senses have this dualistic nature. Take your sense of hearing, for another example. In each of your ears you have a coiled inner organ called the cochlea, filled with fluid and lined with tiny hairs of different lengths, called cilia. Each hair, or cilium, is tuned to a different note or frequency and each picks up a different sound "particle" and sends this information to your left brain to be processed. Not far from the cochlea is the eardrum. Which takes in the whole sound "wave," the "beat" of the sound, and sends this information to your right brain to be processed."

16. Robert Ornstein, *Multimind* (Doubleday, 1986), p. 73.

17. Howard Gardner, *Frames of Mind: The Theory of Multiple Intelligences* (Basic Books, 1983).

18. As interviewed in ibid.

19. Hans J. Eysenck, a British neurological researcher, has proven that the genetically determined speed and efficiency of brain processing correlates directly with "intelligence" measured on intelligence tests. Eysenck, followed by those studying artificial intelligence with computers, has explored the beginning of what brainstyle theory proposes: genetics (with a factor of 80 to 90 percent) determines brain makeup and speed (the hardware), and brainspeed is responsible for communication between parts of the brain itself, and is the critical factor in determining strengths. This communication between parts of the brain is the natural way of processing information we call a brainstyle. It also defines the kind of memories you store.

Chapter Three: The Knower

1. James Hörger conducted the original work that became "The Profile of the Successful Entrepreneur" described in detail by John A. Welsh and Jerry F. White in *The Entrepreneur's Master Planning Guide* (Prentice Hall, 1983).

2. Philip Goldberg, *The Intuitive Edge: Understanding and Developing Intuition* (J.P. Tarcher, 1983), p. 57.

3. Ibid., p. 45.

Chapter Four: The Conciliator

1. According to neurologist Antonio Damasio of the University of Iowa as interviewed by science editor Tom Siegfried of the *Dallas Morning News,* January 16, 1995, now the topic of Daniel Goleman's best-selling *Emotional Intelligence* (New York: Bantam, 1995).

2. "Researchers Link Personality Trait to Gene Variation," *Dallas Morning News,* January 2, 1996, p. 1.

3. Natalie Angier, "Variant Gene Tied to a Love of New Thrills," *New York Times,* January 2, 1996, p. A1.

4. Material quoted from the script for the video "The Role of Intuition in Decision Making," directed and produced by Weston H. Agor (University of Texas at El Paso, P.O. Box 614, El Paso, Texas 79968 [915-747-5227]).

5. Ornstein, *Multimind,* p. 53.

6. The conference, "Intuition at Work: From Insight to Application," was held in Denver, Colorado, in November 1995. It was sponsored by the Intuition Network of the Institute of Noetic Sciences, 475 Gate Five Road, #300, Sausalito, CA 94965.

7. An excellent resource to expand this ability is by Marcia Emery, *The Intuition Workbook: An Expert's Guide to Unlocking the Wisdom of Your Subconscious Mind* (New York: Prentice Hall, 1994).

8. Goldberg, *Intuitive Edge,* p. 58.

9. Further references: Douglas Dean and John Mihalasky, *Executive ESP* (Prentice Hall, 1975), tells how predictive intuition goes to the bottom line. Tony Buzan, *Use Both Sides of Your Brain* (Dutton, 1974, 1983), gives techniques for right-brain "mind-mapping" and memory techniques.

Chapter Five: The Conceptor

1. Goldberg, *Intuitive Edge,* pp. 47–48.

2. Ibid., p. 53.

3. As described by Woolf, *Holodynamics,* p. 43.

4. Joshua Hyatt, "Reconcilable Differences," *Inc.,* April 1991, pp. 78–87.

Chapter Six: The Deliberator

1. Rutter and Rutter, *Developing Minds,* p. 85, who also cite R. Plomin, *Development, Genetics and Psychology* (Erlbaum, 1986).

Chapter Seven: Test Yourself

1. Michael Meyer, *The Alexander Complex: The Dreams That Drive the Great Businessmen* (Times Books, 1989), p. 29.

2. Steve Bostic as quoted in *Inc.,* "Thriving on Order," December 1989, pp. 47–54 in an article by Bo Burlingham and George Gendron.

3. Peter Nulty, "America's Toughest Bosses," *Fortune,* February 27, 1989, p. 40.

4. Ibid.

Chapter Eight: Getting Along When Nobody Changes

1. Mark Bowden, "You Might Call It a Real No-Brainer: Men and Women Truly Don't Think Alike," *Philadelphia Inquirer,* January 25, 1995.

2. John Gray, *Men Are from Mars, Women Are from Venus* (HarperCollins, 1992), p. 124.

3. Deborah Tannen, *You Just Don't Understand: Women and Men in Conversation* (Ballantine, 1990).

4. Gazzaniga, *Nature's Mind,* p. 134.

5. A story related in Rick Fields et al., *Chop Wood Carry Water,* Audio Renaissance Cassette Tapes, 1988.

6. Studies conducted by Granovetter, 1974; Helgensen, 1985; Smith, 1983; Stark, 1985, as cited in the *1990 Annual: Developing Human Resources,* "Networking Skills Inventory" (University Associates Press); pp. 153–56.

Chapter Nine: The Changeless Path

1. A story related in Fields et al., *Chop Wood Carry Water.*

2. *A Course in Miracles* (Foundation for Inner Peace, 1975).

Appendix A: Brain-Based Aptitudes

1. This material is drawn from two nonprofit research and testing organizations. The Aptitude Inventory Measuring Service (AIMS) of Dallas, begun in 1975, has a database of over 10,000 tested; the Johnson O'Connor Research Foundation, with offices in major cities across the nation and a database of many times that of AIMS, has tested people's aptitudes since its founding in 1922. AIMS's founder and current corporate officer, Brenda Smith, published *How to Strengthen Your Winning Business Personality* (Career Press, 1990) in which aptitudes, their definitions, and applications in business are explained. The AIMS work was originally published in Brenda Smith, John Gaston, and Irvin Shambaugh's *You and Your Aptitude* (Aptitude Inventory Measurement Service, 1983).

2. This definition was taken from the Johnson O'Connor brochure, 1994, which substantially agrees with the AIMS definitions.

3. The recently revised and shortened version of 18 questions has a face validity for those tested of 90 percent. It is available for testing purposes for a nominal fee at 1-800-374-9878.

4. Smith, p. 17.

5. Smith, *How to Strengthen Your Winning Business Personality,* pp. 18–24.

Index

communication skills of, 140, 141, 142, 143, 144, 149–51, 171, 172–173

in conflict situations, 157–59, 198

confrontation by, 112, 147

creativity of, 142–45, 152, 171

decision-making of, 140, 154–56

deductive reasoning of, 141, 143

delegation by, 145, 152

emotional expression of, 167, 169

examples of, 145, 146–48, 149–50, 157–59, 160–61, 162–63, 167–71

feelings of difference in, 141, 146, 149–50

flexibility of, 152, 155–56, 162

"flow" for, 139

follow-through of, 152–53, 175

foresight of, 139, 146, 180, 314, 322

holistic approach of, 143, 146, 148, 154, 165, 173, 175

idea files kept by, 172

ideaphoria in, 140, 146, 322

impatience of, 160, 172

information processing by, 139, 143, 149, 150, 202

insight of, 151, 171

intuition of, 141, 144–45, 154, 166

invention by, 139, 141, 146, 163, 180, 314

Janusian thinking of, 144

lateral thinking of, 144

learning by, 127, 164–66

in management, 268–71, 313–16

mature vs. immature, 160–64, 170, 175

needed by other brainstyles, 75, 113, 201

non-strengths of, 149–54, 175

optimism of, 85

other brainstyles needed by, 154, 174–175

others' impressions of, 81, 141, 142, 145, 150

others inspired by, 145

planning and, 151

predictive abilities of, 167

problem solving by, 149, 150, 155, 156, 157, 166–67, 170

random associations used by, 142, 149

relationships of, 147, 153, 172; see also brainstyles, relationships among

risk-taking by, 142, 166–67

stability and, 152

strengths of, 139, 141–49, 218

structural visualization by, 146, 147

structure and, 160–62, 174

teamwork of, 145, 148, 150–51, 162, 314–15

at Time Zero, 139, 141–42, 149, 155, 291

timing of, 152, 153, 157, 160, 171

as visionary, 79, 139, 140, 166–67

at work, 145, 147–48, 149–50, 157–164, 268–73, 303, 304–6, 310, 313–16

conceptualizing aptitudes, 321–22

Conciliator, 69, 76, 88, 93–138, 140, 142, 152, 162, 169, 173, 174, 183, 184, 206, 233, 323

ADD in, 126

appearance important to, 136, 147

applied understanding of, 130–38

appreciation needed by, 106–7

boys, 97

brainspeed of, 126, 132, 137

brainstorming by, 120, 163–64

career choices of, 94, 97, 126

celebrity, 218, 224

change resisted by, 127–28

characteristics of, 93–94, 99

charisma of, 94, 95, 137

as children, 96–97, 107

comfort sought by, 94, 96

communication skills of, 99, 134–35

in conflict situations, 93, 99, 111–12, 119, 120–21, 122, 133–34, 157–59, 198

confrontation by, 111–12, 128–29, 133

as consensus-builder, 97, 111–12, 120

decision-making of, 113–18, 134, 155

defensiveness of, 129–30

delegation by, 123–25, 133

Deliberator vs., 206–9

emotional expression of, 94, 95, 99, 111–12, 120–21, 128–30, 131

empathy of, 97, 110, 112, 131–32

examples of, 100–102, 104–6, 108–111, 114, 116–17, 128, 284–88, 296–301

feeling in control needed by, 110, 129–130

"flow" for, 93, 125, 138

harmony sought by, 93, 94, 95, 96, 99, 112

ideaphoria of, 107, 322

imagination of, 93, 98, 101, 115

impatience of, 74, 134

inconsistency of, 118

information processing by, 83, 125–26, 202

About the Author

Marlane Miller, President of BrainStyles, Inc./Miller Consulting Services, has been a professional in the human development field since 1965. A graduate of UCLA, most of her career has been spent evaluating and teaching leading-edge concepts that positively impact people's productivity and self-esteem. Working in the public sector as a training director, organization consultant, and teacher, she entered private industry in 1976. In a multinational corporate setting, she created and taught management development seminars, leading to a corporate-wide cultural change effort for hundreds of senior executives.

Entrepreneur and former CIBA-Geigy top executive David J. Cherry made the initial breakthroughs that resulted in The BrainStyles System.®* David and Marlane are a husband-wife team who have put their brainstyles concept to good use in the corporate arena, as well as in their marriage since 1980. Corporate consultant Marlane Miller researched, tested, applied, and eventually wrote their first book over a period of four years, entitled BrainStyles: Be Who You *Really* Are *(1992).*

David Cherry, a chemical engineer by training, built and recently sold a turnaround company that became a multimillion-dollar business, having applied The BrainStyles System to determine the best combination of people to build a winning corporate team. He is now president and CEO of several companies and uses brainstyles to staff and operate them.

Leaving CIBA-Geigy in 1985, Marlane started her own consulting firm in Dallas, Texas, specializing in team building as a strategy to improve productivity. She has built a broad corporate client base throughout the United States, from PepsiCo, Northern Telecom, and Kodak, to Rockwell, Monsanto, and Procter & Gamble, and major restaurant chains, law firms, and manufacturing

---

* The BrainStyles System is registered in the U.S. Patent and Trademark Office, Number 1,898,347.

operations. She has also served as a human resources consultant for such nonprofit organizations as the United Way, Junior Achievement, and the Dallas Women's Foundation. Currently a frequent speaker on radio and at conferences nationwide, she has been teaching The BrainStyles System to enthusiastic audiences for several years.

Marlane and David created BrainStyles to help people discover and master who they are when they are at their best.